TEXTBOOK

Jurisprudence:
THE PHILOSOPHY OF LAW

SECOND EDITION

EDITOR: MICHAEL DOHERTY
BA Law, MA Criminology, Senior Lecturer in Law,
University of Glamorgan

OLD BAILEY PRESS

OLD BAILEY PRESS
200 Greyhound Road, London W14 9RY

First published 1997
Second edition 2001

© The HLT Group Ltd 2001

ISBN 1 85836 409 4

British Library Cataloguing-in-Publication.
A CIP Catalogue record for this book is available from the British Library.

Acknowledgement
The publishers and author would like to thank the Incorporated Council of Law Reporting for England and Wales for kind permission to reproduce extracts from the Weekly Law Reports, and Butterworths for their kind permission to reproduce extracts from the All England Law Reports.

Printed and bound in Great Britain

Contents

10 Modern Positivism *110*

The concept of law – The rule of recognition – Hart's and Kelsen's theories of validity – Judicial positivism – Morality and law – The internal and external points of view – Raz's theory – The demarcation of law – The 'uniqueness' of law – Raz's formulation of validity – The position of rules – Raz and Dworkin – Evaluation of Raz – The idea of a 'hard case' – The implications for judicial reasoning – The doctrine of the separation of powers – The way lawyers and judges talk – Retrospective legislation – Conclusion on Dworkin – Hart's posthumous postscript to the second edition of *The Concept of Law* – Hart and post-modernism

11 Natural Law *143*

Introduction – What is natural law? – Natural law and legal validity – The origins of natural law – Hume's attack on natural law – Some conclusions – Positivism as a reaction to the naturalistic fallacy – The attributes of being a human being – The Nazi informer case – Hartian positivism as a moral theory – Introduction to Fuller – Procedural morality – Finnis – The basic goods of human nature – Evaluation of Finnis – Dworkin's 'grounds' and 'force' of law

Legal and Social Theory

12 Sociological Jurisprudence *179*

Introduction – Sociological jurisprudence (idealist) – Sociological jurisprudence (evaluative) – Socio-legal studies – Sociology of law

13 American Realism *199*

Introduction – The realist approach – Karl Llewellyn's rule scepticism – Frank and the experimentalist approach – Jurimetrics and judicial behaviouralism – Contributions and evaluations – Patterns of American jurisprudence

14 Scandinavian Realism *212*

Introduction – General approach – Hagerstrom – Olivecrona – Evaluation of Olivecrona – Ross – Evaluation of Ross – Comparison with American realism

15 Historical Jurisprudence *226*

Introduction – Maine – Evaluation of Maine – Von Savigny – Evaluation of von Savigny

16 Anthropological Jurisprudence *236*

Introduction – The anthropological school – Evaluation

17 The Origins of Marxism and Its Application in Real Societies *245*

Introduction – The Hegelian dialectic – Law as superstructure – Law as ideology – The tension between material forces and ideology – The state – The withering away of the state – The emergence of dichotomy – Lenin's theoretical contribution – Pashukanis – The post-Stalinist era up to the break-up of the Soviet Union – Alternative schools of Marxism

18 Contemporary Marxism *253*

The failure of applied Marxism – The implications for law of Marxist-Leninist contradictions – The failure of the revolution to materialise in capitalist countries – Modernised Marxist conceptions of law – A critical evaluation of main Marxist conceptions – Evaluation

Preface

This work is generally designed for use by undergraduates who have Jurisprudence as part of their syllabus. It has been written by a number of teachers involved in the teaching of the subject for the University of London. For this reason, since the contents of different syllabuses in this subject vary to a degree and some emphasis is unavoidable, the emphasis in this text has been weighted more particularly towards that of the syllabus of the external LLB degree of the University of London. It should be stressed, however, that this book covers not just all that is covered by that syllabus but a considerable amount of extra material. It should therefore be of equal interest to any student of jurisprudence, wherever taught or examined and, indeed, to any student of politics, and political philosophy and sociology.

Due to the nature of the subject, the student is encouraged always to challenge the views of jurists. Any jurisprudence textbook should be regarded as essays on the *merits* of the views of the various jurists – what the force of their ideas is – not as just providing an account of *what they said*. This edition emphasises this point, in line with a general trend in modern jurisprudence courses away from learning 'schools' of jurists, to studying the general philosophical, sociological and other problems of law, state and morality. It is written in the firm belief that *ideas* have the greatest premium in the subject.

It includes a large section on methodology, particularly in relation to the presently much-discussed idea of interpretation of law; a discussion of the increasingly influential views of Ronald Dworkin, including both his account of 'law as integrity' and his work on abortion and euthanasia, *Life's Dominion*; an account of the economic analysis of law as espoused by Posner and the Chicago school, a revised account of the growing school of feminist jurisprudence and, importantly, a discussion of Hart's important posthumous Postscript to the recent second edition of his *The Concept of Law*.

In line with the critical approach, the topics have been arranged to reflect the relatively few but grand themes of the subject. So, for example, unlike a number of other textbooks, questions of whether moral judgments are part of the law, which includes the question of the justification of legal positivism, are distinguished from the different questions of what constitutes a just society, and whether society has a right to enforce its generally accepted moral standards through the use of punishment.

In this latest edition, the attacks upon and the defences offered of the major theoretical propositions by Dworkin and Rawls are presented and commented upon. An account is given of the attempts to push Jurisprudence in a more practical direction as seen in the work of Posner and Sunstein. The advantages of the economic analysis of law are presented and new approaches to both judicial reasoning and statutory intention are included.

Table of Cases

The Method and Point
of Jurisprudence

1

The Nature of Jurisprudence

1.1 What is studying jurisprudence all about?

1.2 The scope of jurisprudence

1.1 What is studying jurisprudence all about?

The idea behind this textbook is to help students through the examination on jurisprudence and legal theory. It cannot be a substitute for either the primary sources or, indeed, other textbooks and students will go badly astray if they attempt to use it in this way. It is, however, intended to give students an overview of the main areas.

Jurisprudence is a different sort of subject to study from most aspects of the law which largely deal with case law and statutory materials. This is mainly because ideas, and not facts, are at a premium. Jurisprudence has facts, true, and case law subjects are not, of course, completely devoid of intellectual content. But it is clear that there is a greater proportion of abstract, theoretical material in jurisprudence, and students often fail to come to terms with it.

As we all know with a case law subject, it is possible to be very lucky in preparation the evening before an examination and to hit upon a topic that will be fresh to mind the following day and which is in the examination paper. That sort of possibility does not exist for jurisprudence. Instead, you have to show the examiners that you have developed a speculative cast of mind in your reading and study. You should, however, be aware of the following:

The relevance of legal practice

There is in the English tradition a scepticism for anything theoretical in connection with the law. This is in marked contrast to the position in Europe where theoretical perspectives are welcomed. In English law schools many of the lecturers are also practitioners in the law and have little time for what they often perceive to be abstract waffle. Despite this, lawyers often display in practice an approach to the subject of law that would legitimately be the scope of inquiry of a jurisprudence course. If law students were to avoid the study of jurisprudence they would fall into the trap of accepting without question the correctness of *other* people's views on the issues within the jurisprudence course without necessarily knowing why or how.

Jurisprudence will help you formulate what questions need to be asked and gives guidance on how others have sought to answer these questions. In the UK, most people accept as valid a theory of law known as legal positivism. That theory was the invention of only a few legal philosophers, the most notable of whom was Jeremy Bentham. Those who say that jurisprudence has no effect on the real practical world should contemplate what sorts of people influenced their beliefs. It is certainly true that Bentham (and Austin and, in turn, Hart) have had an enormous effect on the way we think about law in the UK today. Ronald Dworkin, too, is having an increasing effect on the way we think about law, particularly since the publication of his book *Law's Empire* in 1986. Note, for example, the following remark made by Sir Leonard Hoffman, a distinguished judge of the Chancery Division of the High Court, in an article in the *Law Quarterly Review* in 1989: 'Dworkin is one of the few writers on general jurisprudence who accepts and engages with the reality of what judges have to do'. (Hoffman ends by saying that 'Readers who want to know what judges are supposed to be doing [should] buy *Law's Empire.*')

Jurisprudence has relevance to the real world. It will not convey houses for you, or help you make a case for a company insolvency. But those are not the only matters of practical interest in the world. It will help you develop a sense of what law is about. To give examples: Austin and Bentham thought it was about power. Hart and Kelsen think it is, instead, imbued with 'authority' but not 'moral authority' as do Dworkin and Fuller. Austin thought judges were deputy legislators. Dworkin thinks that judges only 'create' law from what is already there. Marxists think that law only serves the interests of the powerful and the rich. Those in the American critical legal studies movement think law schools serve the insidious purpose of placing a veneer of respectability over what is essentially chaos and conflict. Some jurists believe that courts enforce moral rights, others, such as Bentham, think that idea is 'nonsense upon stilts'!

All these ideas are relevant in varying ways to the practice of law. Lenin once wrote that theory without practice is pointless and practice without theory is mindless. He was espousing a Marxist notion that the point was not so much to interpret the world as to change it. Without necessarily adopting a Marxist analysis in the context of jurisprudence, we can argue that legal practice outside of a theoretical context would be mindless, while acknowledging at the same time that a legal theory that did not refer to practice would be pointless. With this in mind, and in spite of the heavy emphasis upon practical training in English law schools and of the practitioners' scepticism about the subject, we shall emphasise the practical aspects of jurisprudence.

In any case, it is 'practical' to develop your intellectual skills. Try pitting your wits against any of the jurists mentioned in this textbook. Try, for example, to see whether you agree with what Hart says about the law. Then see whether you agree with what Dworkin says. You may find you agree with both of them. But you cannot, for they give fundamentally contrary theories. You must try to develop a habit of analysing what it is you accept and, more importantly, why. It is extremely difficult, especially when you are first faced with these theories, to develop such a habit. It is just very difficult to say something new in jurisprudence. That is why we need to study the 'greats' of the subject, to get some clues as to what position we ourselves should hold.

The hope is that by orienting you towards the subject and encouraging you to approach the various materials in a sensible way, you will develop your own critical awareness of the issues, of what jurisprudence is about. This should place you in the best position to answer the examination questions and help you to organise your work and time efficiently.

How to read a jurisprudence text

You should therefore examine the criticisms that have been made of the theory, reflect on these and evaluate their validity in the light of your own legal knowledge. In this way you will (really!) develop your own understanding of law and the legal system. Essentially, you should enter into a dialogue with the texts being read. Imagine the person who wrote the text is beside you. One does not try to learn what the other person in a conversation is saying. Rather one engages them in conversation and either agrees or disagrees with what they are saying.

Professor Twining has identified three levels on which to read a jurisprudence text:

1. The *historical* level, where the reader places the text in its historical perspective and asks questions such as: what were the issues of the day on which the text was written? Today many of those issues may just be irrelevant. In examining a text on its historical level it should be borne in mind what was available to that author. To whom was he replying? What was the problem at that time? Whose work was available at that time?
2. The *analytical* level, where it would be appropriate to examine the questions raised, scrutinise the answers given and then evaluate the reasons provided for those answers. On this level it is important that the student clarifies the nature of the question before accepting the author's answer. Some questions do contain false assumptions and it would be necessary to identify these.
3. On the *applied* level, where the reader examines the implications of accepting the position outlined by the author. It is on this level that one can decide why the author wrote what he did when he did, particularly with regard to the political implications of the text.

This is what will be required from you. The technique for the study of jurisprudence is to engage in such a critical and evaluative discussion. This requires the student to develop his own understanding and to recognise that there may be a number of ways in which a text can be read, each one aspect as illuminating as any other.

1.2 The scope of jurisprudence

By its very nature this is a topic whose province has been redetermined from time to time. Why not start with what the nineteenth century legal philosopher John Austin, who made legal positivism famous, thought constituted the study of jurisprudence? You might be surprised to learn that John Austin, Bentham's distinguished pupil (see Chapter 8), was one of the first two professors appointed in the Faculty of Law of the University of London. This university was the first in England to open its doors to people from all walks of life. It was also the first in England to teach common law in a systematic way. It is fitting, especially since Austin and Bentham (largely through Austin's writings) had such a profound effect on the way lawyers in England even now reason and decide, to see what Austin himself said about the nature of jurisprudence.

In 1832 Austin published the first six lectures of the total of 57 he gave when first appointed professor. The best copy of these, published in 1954 under the title *The Province of Jurisprudence Determined*, is edited by H L A Hart. At the end of this edition, there is a short piece entitled 'On the Uses of the Study of Jurisprudence' with which Austin originally began his lectures. In it he sets out a number of reasons why jurisprudence should be regarded as an integral part of law teaching. He says that there are two ways of studying the subject. There is 'particular jurisprudence', which is the study of the positive law of a particular legal system, and there is 'general jurisprudence', which is the study of 'the principles, notions, and distinctions which are common to systems of law'. He says that he means by 'systems of law':

'... the ampler and maturer systems which, by reason of their amplitude and maturity, are pre-eminently pregnant with instruction.'

As a comparative lawyer, Austin was well versed in the European legal systems. He thought it was blind of lawyers to be concerned only with their own particular systems. What was needed was a general overall view of the structure and content of law, a view of the *nature* of law. Only then, he thought, could lawyers fully appreciate in practice what they were doing. To give you a flavour of his views, note the following (you would benefit from reading the whole paper, but for present purposes you will find a suitable extract in Lloyd and Freeman at pp23–5):

'... a previous well-grounded knowledge of the principles of English jurisprudence, can scarcely incapacitate the student for the acquisition of practical knowledge in the chambers of a conveyancer, pleader, or draughtsman. Armed with that previous knowledge, he seizes the *rationale* of the practice which he there witnesses and partakes in, with comparative ease and rapidity; and his acquisition of practical knowledge, and practical dexterity and readiness, is much less irksome than it would be in case it were merely empirical. Insomuch, that the study of the general principles of jurisprudence, instead of having any of the tendency which the opinion in question imputes to it, has a tendency (by ultimate consequence) to qualify for practice, and to lessen the natural repugnance with which it is regarded by beginners.'

What does Austin mean in this passage by 'rationale' and 'empirical'? He means that a full education in the law requires more than just empirically pocketing bits of statutes, or bits and pieces of the common law. By studying the nature of law, a knowledge of how it is coherent becomes more apparent. If you do not agree with this view of Austin, you should consider why you disagree. You also might consider reasons why jurisprudence is taught as part of a *university* degree. You might consider what a university is for and what ought to encompassed by the idea of a university education.

The different classifications of jurisprudence

There are different classifications of jurisprudence. General jurisprudence is concerned with speculations about law as distinct from speculations about a specific law. There are many ways to arrange the questions that are posed in general jurisprudence. One will not find any agreed list from the literature. Questions such as the following seem to be common to most.

1. What is law?
2. What is *a* law?
3. What is a legal system?
4. Should law enforce morality?
5. How does the nature of society affect law?
6. What role does law play in society?
7. What is the purpose of law?
8. Is law necessarily just?
9. What are the appropriate criteria for assessing a legal *theory*? (This is a very difficult, but very important question.)

These are a few of the questions that are the concern of general jurisprudence. They demonstrate that general jurisprudence is the area where the work of the legal scientist overlaps with other disciplines such as the study of morality, anthropology, politics and economics. These questions make up a substantial portion of the course covered in this textbook. The student ought to be thinking about some of these questions throughout the course. Experience shows that the student's answers will undergo a substantial change towards the latter part of the course, when the questions may be asked again.

You might note that Harris' view, expressed in his book *Legal Philosophies*, is that general jurisprudence is of little value in instilling the technical skills of legal reasoning and argumentation. He believes that these skills come, as he puts it, from 'immersing oneself in substantive legal studies'. On the other hand, he sees some value in *particular* jurisprudence which involves speculations about particular legal concepts such as rights and duties.

We study the various theorists because they throw light on these rather difficult topics. The perception, of course, should remain that of the reader. In a study by

King entitled *The Concept, the Idea and the Morality of Law* (1966) the author asks whether it is possible to define the object of inquiry without anticipating the result. Take the work of John Rawls (see Chapter 21). His theory of justice arrives at the conclusion that might be expected from a democratic liberal, viewing justice as fairness yet subjecting economic inequality to political equality. Did he arrive at that view only after writing his book or did he have in mind his conclusion before he set pen to paper? The argument that King makes is that our assumptions will find their way into our account of law, having a considerable influence on subsequent exposition. By reflecting on this point at an early stage the student will equip herself to deal with the plethora of literature. An easy way to test this concept is to check what assumptions an author makes in the Preface or Foreword to a work. Great insights into Hart's and Kelsen's work, for examples, can be made in this way.

2

Language and the Law: the Problem of Definition

2.1 The point of a definition

There are, of course, problems about what is meant by defining law. It is not as if you can just look the matter up in a dictionary. Try it and see for yourself what an unhelpful endeavour that is. More importantly, why bother to define it? Well, the examples of the Romanian regime and the Nuremberg trials show that such questions can be of very great importance. In a very important sense, for example, the theories of law of the jurists are themselves definitions of law. Get into the problem of definition by examining continuously the question of what the jurists are trying to do. Hart, for example, in Chapter 2 of *The Concept of Law*, sets out three major reasons why he wishes to define law: he wants to be able to answer the problems of the relationship between law and coercive orders, the difference between legal and moral obligation and the definition of what it means to say that a social rule exists. What are Hart's answers to these questions? What are different ways of defining things? Can we define ideas? What does a theory try to do? What is the relationship between theory and practice? What is the use of a model? Is there *anything* that is real? What is morality? Do important moral issues hinge on how we define law? Is it possible to choose one legal theory rather than another on moral grounds?

2.2 Jurisprudence, the law and words

What is the problem? What are we doing when we try to work out what law is? We can imagine all sorts of motivation. We have been asked to provide an hour-long talk to a women's institute entitled 'What law is'. Or we might have been asked to address a group of Marxist students on the same subject. We may just want to satisfy ourselves, from a purely self-interested point of view, on what we are permitted or required to do by law. Or we may want to know what law is with a view to considering how it fits in with, or could contribute to a more just society. There are all sorts of reason. Even just unanalysed 'interest' is enough.

We can, of course, make ourselves and other people *more* aware of the way we understand language which expresses the law. We could, therefore, use a dictionary as a start in this direction. We might follow up all the words that relate to law, like 'obligation' and 'police' and 'courts' and 'rule'. Then we could test all the possible uses of these words, trying them in different sentences and different contexts. We could also contrast law-related words such as 'morals', or 'custom' with other kinds of words that appear in the same sorts of contexts. In this project, we will be refining our sense of what amounts to correct and incorrect use of language.

However, take the Marxist. He appreciates the difference in our linguistic practices but he is unwilling to say that law is fundamentally different from naked coercion. He is not keen to affirm that it has any connection with the idea of obligation. He will produce the argument that law only *appears* to have legitimacy because a dominant class of people has encouraged such a view to further its own economic interest.

This sort of argument cannot be met by merely citing dictionary definitions. It makes a point beyond that of showing our agreement in linguistic practice. It is *most* significant that Hart, whose theory is central to some of the debates examined in this book, has recognised the serious limitations of this form of approach in an admission in the Preface to his book *Essays in Jurisprudence and Philosophy* (1983):

> 'The methods of linguistic philosophy which are neutral between moral and political principles and silent about different points of view which might endow one feature rather than another of legal phenomena with significance ... are not suitable for resolving or clarifying those controversies which arise, as many of the central problems of legal philosophy do, from the divergence between partly overlapping concepts reflecting a divergence of basic point of view or values or background theory, or which arise from conflict or incompleteness of legal rules. For such cases what is needed is first, the identification of the latent conflicting points of view which led to the choice of formation of divergent concepts, and secondly, reasoned argument directed to establishing the merits of conflicting theories, divergent concepts or rules, or to showing how these could be made compatible by some suitable restriction of their scope.'

The tools of the lawyers' trade are words. These tools are not expressible in terms of mathematical precision, yet they are the only tools available with which the lawyer will perform his function. This can be seen as the cause of many of the problems of the law. The majority of appellate court cases concern the construction of words and phrases used in statutes. As Oliver Wendell Holmes observed, words are not crystals, they are not clear. They are capable of different meanings. Jurisprudence, according to Holmes, should be concerned with the reality of the legal experience. To that extent definitions are useful if they correspond to the way in which lawyers actually behave and think. Otherwise a definition is of no value.

Much in jurisprudence is concerned with definitions. Indeed one of the earlier writers on this subject, John Austin, in his *The Province of Jurisprudence Determined*, sought by definition to determine the limits of the course of study. The problems with definitions are that they may be derived from inadequate prior knowledge and involve misconceptions formed at the outset which further burden the definition, and thirdly that they impose artificial limits on the area of study. Professor Hart has attacked the practice of building a theory on the back of definition and shown that it is preferable to engage in an essay in descriptive sociology – descriptive at least of concepts.

Hart has identified in words a core of settled meanings around which there will be no dispute and a penumbral area of doubt in which disputes will arise. Say a hypothetical law provided that all vehicles were to be taxed at £100 per annum. Within that core meaning would come cars and lorries, but what about a skateboard? Or a spaceship? Or a chariot? The issue would become important when a person in control of a chariot was charged with failing to tax his vehicle. He would not argue that the law was unjust, rather he would argue that it did not apply to chariots. The whole issue will be determined on the basis of the interpretation given to the words.

The same difficulty is faced in jurisprudence where many problems can be reduced to questions of semantics. For example, Hohfeld (see Chapter 26) attempted to clarify some of the linguistic problems surrounding the use of the word right. Wittgenstein observed that the meaning of a word depends on the context in which it is used; the meaning of a word is its use in the language. The context will require an explanation for the whole sentence or phrase. Hence the phrase that X owns Y will require an explanation of the concept of ownership. Would it include the control over Y exercised by a thief? Would it include the right of a tenant to enjoy for the present exclusive possession of the property? In many instances this approach will be satisfactory; however, even then, it will not be sufficient in all cases.

Since language is dynamic the meaning of words can change. An example would be the use of the word gay which has changed in time to have a meaning not that which it originally held.

2.3 Refuting essentialism

Essentialism is a term employed to denote two ideas that are related, but distinct. On the one hand there is the view that behind every noun there is an actual reality that it denotes on a physical or metaphysical level. Thus, when we say box we can find a reality that is some sort of receptacle, so too behind the word right there is a real metaphysical entity, floating around on a metaphysical level. Obviously, if this is so, then it might be possible, by reason and philosophy, to gain an understanding of what this reality is. There is a strong relationship between this notion and some early natural law theories (see Chapter 11) which saw an ideal legal system residing in some metaphysical supermarket.

A second strand of essentialism is less troublesome, and may be found reflected in some positivist thinkers, particularly Kelsen. This sees a word as denoting a common factor or essence intrinsic to a class of objects, things or practices. By a process of logic, this essence might be distilled out from other factors in order to express the real nature of the word. A commitment to the search for such logical unity need not entail a belief that concepts have a reality lurking in obscurity, but does commit one to the view that there is one right answer to the question: What is law? or: What is a legal system? This is a commitment to the view that one central idea can be and is shared by all people who use the word law. This idea might be expressed in the form of a definition.

We can, with relative ease, describe a material object such as my dog Frankie. When, though, does a description become a prescription? For example, if I seek to define what weeds are, at what point do I stop merely describing the features which are commonly regarded as characterising weeds, such as a tendency to stifle other plants and infest lawns? That it is a 'weed' means that it is a plant I do not wish to cultivate; in other words, a weed is a plant I should not grow. Similarly, by defining what law is, do I not tend to end up deciding what ought to be regarded as law? (See section 2.7.)

Hart prefers to concentrate on the focal usages. He does not posit a definition of what law is, which requires a linguistic recommendation, that is, suggesting what it is appropriate to call law. Hart engages in a description of legal discourse seeking to ask what certain key concepts are being used for. He describes his concept of law as an essay in descriptive sociology since he is attempting to view law as a form of linguistic behaviour from which we can infer certain attitudes (see Chapter 10 for an account of the critical reflexive attitude, which Hart regards as the focal area of law). Thus, for Hart, the nature of the jurisprudential enquiry is a search for the revelations of language use.

2.4 Hart's approach

In *Problems of the Philosophy of Law*, Hart says: 'Descriptions of methods [of deciding cases] actually used by courts must be distinguished from prescriptions of alternative methods and must be separately assessed.' The linguistic philosophy of Wittgenstein and of J L Austin seems to offer a method of determining meanings of concepts and words, rather than prescriptions of what that word should mean in the Marxist sense noted above. For example, why is the dictionary's meaning of the word law not a sufficient definition to work from? The answer is that the dictionary tries to provide us with a descriptive account of how people actually use the word.

For this reason, definitions in the dictionary are changed when they cease to be descriptively accurate statements of how people use the words.

Hart sees actual legal acts of speech as being properly legal in the context of their use. When one says, 'I have a right to silence' it presupposes rules, currently regarded as expressing a reason for action. Thus, isolated concepts are not essentially legal, but legal because they refer to other things that are legal. The distinctive feature of legal discourse is that it employs concepts that are not properly explicable in terms of everyday definitions. Therefore one should not seek to understand the word contract when used in legal discourse, in any other way than by reference to the rules that require performance of obligations embodied in the totality of legal discourse. Thus, for Hart, legal concepts are legal because they belong to legal discourse. Law concepts belong to a language game called law, rather in the same way as the meaning of 'Park Lane' on a Monopoly board is only explicable by reference to the rules of that game. While both contract and Park Lane have counterparts in ordinary discourse, they are separated by their usage in a different form of life. The relationship between a legal word and its ordinary counterpart might thus be merely that of analogy. If we look at the concept of reasonableness under the Wednesbury rules, we find that the analogy with the everyday usage of reasonableness is very slim. Similarly, if I have a piece of paper that I think is a contract, that says contract on it and looks like other contracts I have seen, it may still not be a contract, legally speaking. Ordinary reality is thus only the same as legal reality when ordinary reality accords with the rules of the game of law.

2.5 An evaluation of linguistic analysis

Hart's linguistic analysis does not explain the meaning of the legal game and its constituent concepts, but merely describes how to find out how the game is played. Hart is fond, as was Wittgenstein, of the games motif, yet games are often described in terms of their particular purpose. Even subtle games such as cricket can be described in terms other than their rules either by their purpose (a combination of athletic skill, tactical ability and chance pursued by competing groups of individuals for pleasure and/or profit) or analogy (the Englishman's version of baseball). These purposes are more elucidating than what Hart would postulate: primary rules interacting with secondary power conferring rules (if there is an umpire) in more developed contests, where there may be consideration of human vulnerability (such as is found in the bad light rule and others in cricket).

Hart's linguistic approach loses something of the spirit of the legal enterprise. Much criticism of Hart's linguistic approach comes from those with an orientation towards critical legal studies. However, others, such as MacCormick and Dworkin, who are not averse to a linguistic analysis of some kind, see Hart's views as descriptively inaccurate. Each critic of Hart has, however, his own agenda. The critical legal studies movement seeks to develop new ways of reading law so as to evaluate it in the light of reforming goals. So too does Dworkin, who emphasises that judges search for political morality and principles in their decisions with the aim that judges continue law in a democratic and rights orientated genre, likening the process to literary analysis of a chain novel. MacCormick searches for narrative coherence to explain how laws interact, in pursuit of the key to legal reasoning.

2.6 Interpretation and 'interpretive' concepts

Dworkin developed the theory that the correct way to understand law, and law-related concepts, is through the idea of interpretation. The essential principle is that interpretation attempts to make 'the best' of something, and this very abstract principle is to be applied to the idea of law. A number of ways can be used to describe the idea of 'making the best' of something. One may consider the idea of a thing 'having point', for example, or the idea of 'placing a thing in its best light', whereby we assume that 'the thing' has some point and we examine it as thoroughly as we can to see what is the most sensible way of viewing it.

How does interpretation become an aspect of law? Dworkin says that we may understand a social practice in three analytical attitudes: the pre-interpretive, the interpretive and the post-interpretive. These important ideas can be described by the use of a simple example. Take the pre-interpretive attitude first. Imagine a society in which there is a social practice requiring that men doff their hats to women. In this society, no opinion is held about the value of the rule. No point is ascribed to it. Members of the society just accept it in an unquestioned way.

There will be two parts to the introduction of the 'interpretive' phase, one where there is an attitude of questioning, and giving of 'meaning', to the social rule of courtesy, and a second where the idea of what this meaning of the rule requires in *particular* cases is considered. We can test these distinctions by reference to games, such as cricket, in which a description of a rule is distinguishable from a discussion of its point (is it fun? does it test skill? is it competitive?), which in turn is distinguishable from the way particular rules are to be interpreted (does 'bowling' include throwing? or underarm bowling? and so on).

We now imagine that after a while people begin to ask questions about the practice of courtesy, about what the reasons are for conforming to it. It is easy to imagine, too, that people will differ about their understanding of it and will argue amongst themselves about what precisely the practice of hat-doffing entails. For example, some people might take the view that hat-doffing to women shows respect for the 'weaker' sex, while others believe that it shows a more genuine respect for the ability of women to bear children.

The second interpretive stage occurs when people extend their understandings of the meaning of the rule to unclear cases. Those who think that the rule embodies respect for the 'weaker' sex, may not think that hat-doffing by men is necessary when a woman is doing a 'man's job', or to lesbians, for example. Someone who thinks that hat-doffing is a mark of respect for people who have the capacity to bear children may not think the rule extends to an elderly spinster or the wife of a childless couple.

Dworkin posits the existence of a third, a 'post-interpretive' phase. This will be where, as he says, interpretation 'folds back into itself' and has the effect of changing the original rule. So, in our example, some people, perhaps through argument and discussion, will come to have an altered perception of the original rule and this altered perception will lead them to modify it. Those who saw the rule as marking a respect for the 'weaker' sex, may now see it in terms of respect for those who have served society in some deferential but faithful way. They may now want to see a change to the rule so that it includes a smaller class of women (exclusion of lesbians, say), but a wider class of people (including old servants, say). Those who saw the rule as marking a respect for child-bearing ability, may now see it as one that should recognise certain other abilities, such as the ability to contribute to society in other ways, say, through leadership. These people might take the view that the rule requires hat-doffing not only to women who have actually borne children but that it should also extend to the more important political leaders, for example.

Making sense out of nonsense

The idea of interpretation put forward by Dworkin is that, in interpreting legal practices, judges (and lawyers, and so on, who advise, cajole and criticise judges) should 'make the best *moral* sense' of the practice. Dworkin says that that is what we are in fact doing whenever we make some judgment about the law (eg 'the defence of duress extends – or doesn't extend – to first degree murder'). But this idea has been fundamentally attacked by Howarth in his article 'Making Sense out of Nonsense' in *Jurisprudence: Cambridge Essays*, ed Gross and Harrison (1993) Oxford. Howarth's article relies heavily on a well-known study by an American social psychologist, Garfinkel, in which the following experiment was conducted. In an experiment to which they consented it was falsely represented to ten students that they were being given counselling for their problems. The counselling given was scrambled and the actual verbal counselling each student received was utterly unrelated to the personal psychological profile and personal problems of each student involved. That is to say, student A would receive the counselling (via a confidential telecommunication system) designed for student B, and so on. What happened was that the students 'made sense' of the counselling and thus, according to Howarth, made sense out of what was actually 'nonsense' counselling for the student concerned.

Howarth maintains that judges are in the same position as these students; they have to make sense out of a mass of conflicting and contradictory – ie nonsensical – principles. At first sight, Howarth concludes, there is a real problem for anybody, like Dworkin, who supposes that we live in a community of interlocking, coherent principles and that judicial interpretation is a matter of applying legal principles to situations of fact in well-ordered decisions. If it is possible to 'make sense out of nonsense' then the argument that judges appear to base their decisions on an assumption that we live in a community of principle is no argument at all for showing that we do, in fact, live in such a community. There are serious costs in supposing that the judges are right, says Howarth:

> 'The first cost is that we give a false, and inflated, impression of the wisdom of judges. We imply that they are architects of some great cathedral of law, when in fact they may be throwing bricks in the dark. Secondly, by ignoring the possibility of randomness in previous decisions, we eventually force ourselves to elevate *ad hoc* distinctions into the status of principles, and thus to boost principles which, on any reasonable view of the subject, ought not to be boosted at all. And thirdly, to the extent that we believe that we are "seeing" sense in the material to be interpreted, rather than acknowledging that we may be creating sense out of nonsense, we are deceiving ourselves.'

The initial force of the argument is thought-provoking and important but there are some difficulties. First, a correct interpretation of the experiment requires understanding that the students have made a mistake, and thus a full interpretation can be given of the experiment which shows simply that the students did not have all knowledge to hand. Since that interpretation is always open to a judge, there is nothing particularly sinister in the idea – which is Howarth's main thrust – that a judge could be *fundamentally and irretrievably* mistaken. Actually, judges do make judgments which are novel and creative and which recognise conflicting lines of interest, authority, logic, moral judgement and so on. This is not to say Howarth is wrong but that his argument does not fully support the depth of the conclusion he wishes to reach.

Second, in any case, what, in the real world, would anybody want judges otherwise to do? It requires a larger argument than Howarth supplies to say that judges are wrong to act on the assumption that the law should be regarded as if it treats all people as equal human beings, entitled to the same 'payout' of justice before the law. The idea that law should 'work itself pure' makes sense and, indeed, is a noble enterprise (see Hart, *Essays in Jurisprudence and Philosophy*, Essay 4). Think of the alternatives: that we scrap having judges, or that judges only express to hapless litigants the 'true' conflicts and give up trying to come to a decision?

Raz and Dworkin on definition

Raz (1998) focuses on Dworkin's criticism that Hart and Hartian type theories, because they rely on picking out the exact meanings of law-related words, succumbed to the 'semantic sting', namely, that such theories could never settle genuine (as opposed to linguistic) disagreements between lawyers. Although many philosophers have thought that this account of linguistic philosophy was facile, they did not think that it touched Dworkin's general project of producing a full normative theory of law. Raz argues, on the contrary, that the semantic sting argument is crucial to Dworkin so that he can deny that there is a possible alternative to his conception of the tasks of legal philosophy, which is to provide moral justifications.

Criticising Dworkin's account of linguistic philosophy because he does not show that linguistic philosophy cannot account for what Dworkin calls 'theoretical' disagreement (and what Raz calls 'criterial' disagreement), Raz says that Dworkin should have paid more attention to explicating 'the concept' of law. He would then have noticed that the concept of law had general application to legal systems even of Nazi persuasion, and so Dworkin's theory cannot be about the nature of law and therefore not about law's 'empire', but only about law's 'provinces'. Raz notes, for example, the relevance of Dworkin's theory to legal systems of the Anglo-American type. And so Raz concludes:

> '(Law's Empire) is not so much an explanation of the law as a sustained argument about how courts, especially American and British courts, should decide cases. It contains a theory of adjudication rather than a theory of (the nature of) law. Dworkin's failure to allow that the two are not the same is one reason for the failure of his conception of the tasks and method of jurisprudence.' (at p282)

This conclusion by Raz is sweeping as it would be a very stern a critic who would say that Dworkin's account of the moral justification of judicial decisions so completely misconceived the nature of law. Dworkin can say, certainly without contradiction and with at least the glimmerings of sound sense, that his theory of law is not restricted to Anglo-American type systems. Rather, he would say that his theory supplies full justification for (some) such systems, and provides good critical force for systems that are thoroughly evil, like the Nazi system.

This is not a strange thing to say. His theory is fundamentally normative, after all. Raz's comment is like saying of an economic theory, which justified a particular account of the perfect – the ideal – market that 'such a market hardly exists in the world'. The point of Dworkin's theory is to show why Nazi type legal systems, and all systems that do not respect people's rights, are not properly termed 'legal systems'. Of course, there has to be some relationship to the way that people actually speak because Dworkin is talking about law, not fish, nor bicycles and all those things that are uncontroversially not law. But the hold onto language does not have to be so precious that Dworkin is debarred from denying that what is important about law exists in the Nazi legal system.

It is as if the theorist of the perfect market really had to take into account the selfish conception of the free market employed by the property speculator, or the morally confused conception of the free market that Margaret Thatcher and her followers were claimed to have had. Dworkin's idea is to give such conceptions short shrift. Why should he be bound by some duty to find 'the nature' of 'the concept' of law?

Marmor's Interpretation and Legal Theory

This work was published in Oxford in 1992 and its importance is gradually being recognised since it contains a lengthy criticism of Dworkin's theory of interpretation and a reaffirmation of the doctrines of legal positivism. Marmor argues that a proper theory of interpretation does not undermine positivism. He bases his own view of interpretation on a positivistic type model of communication, and his argument throughout the work puts forward the thesis that interpretation is an exception to the standard understanding of language and communication, as it relates only to those aspects of understanding which are not clearly defined by rules or conventions of understanding. Chapter 3 is entitled 'Dworkin's Theory of Interpretation' and, while difficult, is a useful – deep – critical examination of Dworkin.

Stavropoulos's defence of Dworkin

Nicos Stavropoulos's book *Objectivity in Law* (1996) is an excellent but difficult book which exhaustively examines the arguments for and against objectivity ('one right answer': see Chapter 25) in the law. It is very technical and beyond the requirements for an undergraduate law degree. Nevertheless, he usefully and clearly discusses, in a short passage, what Dworkin means by 'the thing to be interpreted'. The relevant section is entitled 'Dworkin's pre-interpretive agreement: some misunderstandings' at (pp137–143), which consists of a defence of Dworkin against attacks on the idea of interpretation made by Raz (see Chapter 10, section 10.12). Raz's major mistake was to have ignored the fact that the pre-interpretive judgment is itself an interpretive judgment. It was highly unfortunate that Dworkin used the pre-prefix, since that suggests that there is a *thing* there to be interpreted:

> 'Calling those judgments "pre-interpretive", therefore, is to some extent misleading, for it suggests that they are essentially unrevisable ... but this is to mistake their role – their not being doubted, in the context of some dispute – for their being indubitable.' (at p139)

In the light of this, Stavropoulos (who was a doctoral student of Dworkin) then goes on to discuss what he calls 'extravagant' cases, which are cases of the sort where a seemingly ridiculous interpretation is argued before the court, as where, for example, a lawyer might argue that under the US Constitution the provision for minimum age for presidential candidacy should read '50' rather than '35' as appears in the text of the Constitution. Here he says that there is no 'flat contradiction'. There is no semantic rule that, independently of context, says that '35' does not mean '50'. Rather, it is that the absurdity of the proposed interpretation arises from the proposed variation from what best carries conviction. All students have come across this sort of interpretation before. A good example is *Fisher* v *Bell* (1961) (see Chapter 3) which is the famous flick-knife case. It is absurd, but not semantically so in the sense that there is a 'flat contradiction', to say that a man who places an article in a shop window with a price tag on it is not 'offering it for sale'. Context, argument or otherwise, denies that, but not the logic of contradiction.

Stavropoulos also discusses, in contrast, the 'easy cases', repeating the point made so often by Dworkin, that the clarity of the easy cases arises by virtue of an interpretation. The mere fact that many, if not most, lawyers agree on a single interpretation makes the interpretation no more or less correct:

> 'That there are cases on whose resolution we are confident is beyond dispute; the point is to explain the source and nature of our confidence ... Once substantive theories about what the law requires are admitted, there is no way back to positivist simplicity. For this reason it is a serious error to believe that Dworkinian theories are innocuous complements to positivist accounts of settled law. Yet that is exactly what is being claimed by many critics.' (at pp140–141)

2.7 Jackson's *Law, Fact and Narrative Coherence*

While Wittgenstein concluded that philosophical discourse should best take place in poetry (leading to suggestions that he was mad) and Iain Stewart and Peter Rush see Kafka's novel *The Trial* as a significant contribution to jurisprudence, John Jackson sees a humble but significant role for analysis of legal discourse. He sees social sciences and social psychology as a means of describing the way in which lawyers seem to reason, but he does not see them as explaining how lawyers actually make decisions. This combination of linguistic and other enquiries into signs and narrative meanings of behaviour is termed semiotics.

Jackson sees legal discourse as a form of story telling. Law students, when they learn to think like lawyers, are actually being encouraged to 'internalise a set of frameworks of understanding which represent the conventions of that particular profession or semiotic group ... a set of narrative frameworks regarding the legal recognition of typical behaviour patterns'. He adds that these stories are related with accompanying judgments of institutional approval or disapproval. Thus, the student who has a vast resource of legal stories with happy endings in terms of a judgment in favour, as well as horror stories, may learn to expect in analogous stories, analogous endings. Amongst other things, Jackson concludes that legal statements are encoded messages that call upon the listener to bring into play his prior knowledge of other legal stories. Furthermore they have a purpose relating to practical action. He also sees legal adjudication as a series of interlocking narratives. The book is primarily an attempt to reconstruct the common law trial process, although it concentrates on the adjudication process, which is the point at which a judge seeks to justify his position logically.

Semiotics claims to be a multi-disciplinary approach to legal analysis, but one which concentrates on the language element of law, simply because language is so great a part of the law. It does not exclude other disciplines such as history and social psychology. However, it does not sacrifice reasons given in legal statements for valuations from those disciplines. This is probably why the critical legal theorists are disapproving of Jackson, even though there is a shared resource of information for both lines of enquiry. The analogy with stories is a strong one, especially considering the common law orientation towards case law. Stories are constructed on the basis of credible (or incredible) events that seem coherent if they conform to the genre. Furthermore, this approach advances our understanding of the quality of law that refers to previous cases (stories) and statutes (new story lines) in a way that is natural and elucidating. The semiotic approach or, more broadly, the literary approach, seems to be an interesting direction for jurisprudence to take, since law is the result of human creativity. Certainly, this approach has certain similarities to Dworkin's idea of 'making the best sense' of law: make the best sense of all the legal materials so far as they inculcate a story-telling approach.

2.8 Descriptive and normative statements

Description

There are a number of important distinctions that run right through all jurisprudence courses. Let us first contrast the ideas of description and 'normativity'. The question is whether we can *describe* things. It is clear that we can. The description of occurrences that are known by observation – 'empirically' known – is the most obvious sort. We can describe the chairs or blackboards in the lecture theatre or the style and colour of the lawyer's gown, or the latest model Ford car, or the weather, or the shape and colour of a person's face.

Normative statements have a different purpose, which is to ask us to do something. They tell us what we should have done, or what we ought to do. A normative statement may, for example, tell us about a possible utopia, not existing in present society, but one which we should, perhaps, attempt to bring about. Or it may be a statement of law or morality, expressed as a conclusion about our own, or others', acts. Normative statements would include exhortations to universal vegetarianism, or the abolition of personal property and so on.

But descriptive statements do not apply only to the present and past, or only include empirical concepts, and normative statements do not apply only to the future or the past. We can describe things that will exist or that do not exist, such as cars that run by nuclear fusion, or colonies on Mars, without exhortation or approval or disapproval. And, of course, we can make normative statements about existing things, for example, when we condemn or support the current arrangements for private health care, or the political system of apartheid.

Normativity and interpretation

We should now turn to the question of the relationship between *interpretation* and normativity. They are alike in the following way. If we interpret something, we recommend or endorse a particular understanding of that thing. We do not merely record some observation we have made. We are 'offering an interpretation', one that we are prepared to encourage others to accept. On the other hand, a 'purely' normative statement may be made which does not refer to an understanding of a 'thing'.

The best example may be drawn from law. It is possible to make an interpretation of the law but at the same time say that the law is not as it should be. An anti-abortionist may interpret the law so as to agree that it provides for legal abortions in a certain category of case and, at the same time, urge that the law 'ought to be changed'. Or a judge may decide that the best interpretation of the common law he can produce is one which does not produce the 'best' result. He may reluctantly conclude that nevertheless this is what the law is, but that the law ought to be changed.

It is the idea of a 'thing' or activity to be interpreted that is important. Consider, for example, Hart's theory of law. It is sometimes taken as providing both a description of a modern municipal legal system ('an essay in descriptive sociology') as well as a *normative* account of how law should be. It is thought to provide, in other words, a justification of the way things actually are, by way of an endorsement of its description of law as centrally the union of primary and secondary rules.

According to this theory, the primary rules are rules of obligation and the secondary rules are those rules concerned with the primary rules, chiefly through their conferring various kinds of *powers*. What Hart really gives, in *Law's Empire*'s terms, is an exhaustive account of the pre-interpretive model for law. He *then* considers whether it is preferable to restrict that model to cases of morally acceptable rules (what he calls the 'narrow conception' of law, in *The Concept of Law*, Chapter 9) and he concludes, on normative grounds, that it is not.

Note that one of the aims of Hart's theory is to preserve the distinction between a person's moral conscience and the demands made on him in the name of law. It is wrong to suppose that Hart's aim here is normative and not interpretive. Let us imagine that his theory of law in which, in his words, the 'key to jurisprudence' lay in the 'union of primary and secondary rules', is a special set of measures, a package, invented to enable men to live in a civilised way in society. Perhaps we could think of this package of measures, as we might regard the creation of an inventor who makes something entirely new which makes life easier or more pleasant. It would then make sense to encourage members of other societies, say, societies composed of extreme religious fundamentalists, to adopt the social device, for the supposed civilising reasons contained in the device (in Hart's case, the preservation of individual moral judgment against the incursions of the state).

But the inventor and the jurist are different. The inventor is not selling a version, as it were, of something. The 'thing' is new. But Hart recommends a version of *law*. He does this by investing that idea with a particular point, located in the generic ideas of clarity and objectivity. His endorsement of this version has a strongly moral quality, but this is the result of his *interpretation* of law.

3

Law as an Argumentative Attitude

3.1 Introduction

One way of looking at law, recently given added impetus by Ronald Dworkin, is not to think of it as a set of rules to be 'learned', but to think of it as an 'argumentative attitude'. Think of law as an attitude of mind. In the final Chapter of his important work on legal philosophy, *Law's Empire* (1986), Dworkin says:

> 'Law is not exhausted by any catalogue of rules or principles, each with its own dominion over some discrete theater of behaviour. Nor by any roster of officials and their powers each over part of our lives. Law's empire is defined by attitude, not territory or power or process.'

This idea, that law is primarily about an argumentative attitude towards our legal institutions, understood in the broadest sense, is particularly well understood by lawyers used to court practice. Observe some lawyers at work. Arguments are what make or break their day. The invention of a new argument that 'makes sense', that works, is what an advocate thrives on, what a judge understands and, very importantly, what a law student studies.

3.2 Legal education

The idea has significance for understanding the point of legal education. It is interesting to note that English lawyers are more suspicious of 'theory' than lawyers in the United States. Although in England there has been an increase in the theoretical content of some academic law courses over the past decade, much of this has been marked by a lack of rigour in thinking about what 'theory' means. To some it means economics and to others just a critical attitude. Some law teachers think, quite wrongly, that our knowledge of theoretical issues is so far developed that we need now *only* have separate 'theories' of, for example, contract, tort, labour law and so on.

In law, landmark judgments have been provided with later and widely accepted theoretical explanations. Examples are the 'High Trees' principle, now understood as reasonable reliance, and Lord Denning's famous dissenting judgment in *Candler v Crane, Christmas & Co*, now seen as an important early statement of the principles of liability for negligently induced economic loss. And, in the United States, not only are judges more generally aware of the different theories of constitutional interpretation but theoretical issues actually enter the domain of public discussion.

One reason is clearly the role of legal education. The differences here between the United States and the United Kingdom are famous. Teaching law students legal argument beyond the citing of relevant statutes and precedents is impossible without some sort of theoretical structure within which, or against which, arguments can be compared, weighed, criticised, adopted or dropped.

An important and recent work on the present state of legal education takes this point up. William Twining, in his set of Hamlyn Lectures for 1995 published as a book, *Blackstone's Tower: the English Law School* (1994), is strongly opposed to the idea that law should be seen centrally as an argumentative attitude since that is to 'privilege' only the barrister's point of view (or the judge, or the intending practical lawyer). In fact, he prefers to link jurists like Hart and Dworkin together claiming they both place too much emphasis on viewing law as only a practising lawyer does, when there are many other profitable ways in which it may be viewed. Twining's views arise primarily out of a discussion of the contemporary state of legal education in England and Wales in which, in his view, there is an unhealthy fixation with the vocational element.

This book contains many helpful and clear analyses of the role of critical legal studies, feminist jurisprudence, legal philosophy, sociological and psychological studies of the law, and the status of law reform, and its general theme is that between Blackstone's time (mid-eighteenth century) and the present there has been a dominance of rule-centred, narrow vocation-mindedness in the law schools. His analogy (borrowing from the post-modernist Roland Barthes) is that of the Eiffel Tower: a pointless but arresting monument which has had a great effect on the view people take of Paris. The narrow but towering vocational orientation of the modern law school is similarly pointless, although Twining is optimistically of the view that legal scholarship is on the road to becoming reinstated as part of 'our general intellectual culture', as it was in Blackstone's time.

This general line of attack on traditional forms of legal scholarship is becoming increasingly common. Part of the popularity of the view arises from the fact that legal argument is just so narrow. Why, for example, should the psychology of judges (the judge's 'state of indigestion' – see later on in Chapter 13 'American Realism') not be part of legal study? Or the study of the jury (see also in Chapter 13 the discussion of 'Jurimetrics'), or the study of the economic forces behind decision-making (see Chapter 7 'The Economic Analysis of Law' and Chapters 17 and 18 on

Marxism)? It is interesting that Twining runs both Hart and Dworkin together on this point since one popular way of distinguishing the two jurists (as it is done, for example, by John Finnis) was to say that Dworkin was interested in the *justification* of judicial decision-making, and was thus open to the charge that he was too 'judge (or practising lawyer)-centred', and that Hart was, rather, concerned with providing a universal *description* of law. So Dworkin's model (Hercules) was a judge; Hart's model was, in the union of primary and secondary rules, that of a modern municipal legal system in its entirety.

But it is not so clear that this general line of argument can be maintained. There are two main points to bear in mind. First, it is very reasonable to suppose that a universal theory of law should, in order to achieve universality, be able to account for how it is that judges reason and so a simple distinction between 'justification' and 'description' is insufficient to perform that task. It *is* reasonable, surely, to suppose that a theory of law can account in some way for why we think that lawyers deal in legal argument involving the justification of court decisions. Secondly, it is also reasonable to say that the focus of even psychological studies on judicial behaviour (the famous example is on the state of the judge's indigestion) are parasitic on the idea of what it is a judge is supposed to do. Why is it that we are, or should be, interested in the psychology of judges? Simply because judges play a unique role in our legal system; the uniqueness of that role has, therefore, to be made clear, through a legal theory which focuses upon the judicial role.

Another way of putting the point is to ask whether it would be possible to give a full account of mathematics (a theory of mathematics) without having to refer at all to any ability at numeracy. We could describe the social antics of mathematicians, or their typical states of digestion, or the size of the books they write, or the average salary they earn. We could, in the style of the critical theorists and post-modernists, say that mathematicians strive to place unity and consistency upon the world when there is in 'reality' no unity and consistency 'out there'. But all this endeavour would seem peripheral – odd, even – without any account at all of what mathematicians conceive of themselves to be doing.

3.3 The logic of legal reasoning

If adjudication is something more than the telling of stories, we would expect that legal reasoning has a foundation in deductive logic. Thus, we might ask the question: Is legal reasoning logical?

In Professor Griffith's view, as expressed in *The Politics of the Judiciary*, legal reasoning is nothing more than a smokescreen for a political decision. However, most writers concentrate on examining the form rather than the content of the reasoning and it is here that consideration can be given to the question as to whether legal reasoning is logical. As to form then, legal reasoning can take either a deductive or an inductive form. By deductive is meant that a logical necessary conclusion is drawn from major and minor premises. By inductive is meant that propositions are arrived at after collection and sorting of data. The former, deductive reasoning, may well be valid when dealing with factual propositions but is not available in normative terms. This was demonstrated by David Hume in his *A Treatise of Human Nature* in which he denied to the natural lawyer the use of the deductive syllogism. As for the inductive form, this would closely resemble the type of reasoning used in the common law with reference to the reliance and emphasis placed on precedent as authority.

The observation that legal reasoning is not logical stems from the premise that as the tools of the law are words and that as these words are not instruments of mathematical precision, then it would not be useful to apply logical reasoning to the resolution of legal problems. Words possess an open texture. There is, as Hart has said, a penumbral area of doubt as to their meaning. It is in these penumbral areas that legal problems arise, for if the matter fell within the core of meaning of the word(s) then there would hardly be more than a trivial dispute involved. Where the matter falls within the penumbral meaning, then it is said that logical reasoning is less useful than the employment of legal rules which act as a means for deciding disputes.

This is not to say that the method of resolving disputes on the basis of legal rules is arbitrary. Lloyd and Freeman see legal reasoning as essentially a justification for a value judgment. Rules of law are not linguistic or logical rules. They point out that the choice of which rule to apply is not logical in the sense of being deductively inferred from given premises, but it has a kind of logic of its own, being based on rational considerations which differentiate it sharply from mere arbitrary assertion. Hence the logic is that these considerations are not arbitrary, but rather that in law reasoning is done by analogy and that there is a certain logic to that process.

MacCormick in *Legal Reasoning and Legal Theory* takes the view that in the litigation of a question of law deductive reasoning is not possible. An example would be the case of *Donoghue* v *Stevenson* (1932). Here no amount of logical reasoning would have produced Lord Atkin's formulation of the neighbour principle. Lord Atkin gave the game away when he said:

> 'I do not think so ill of our jurisprudence as to suppose that its principles are so remote from the ordinary needs of civilised society and the ordinary claims it makes upon its members as to deny a legal remedy where there is so obviously a social wrong.'

The essence of his technique, now widely used in duty of care cases, is to use previous cases as examples rather than as authorities. This allows the court to find new duty of care situations in circumstances where these are not contradicted by previous authority. The speech of Lord Buckmaster, dissenting, adopts an alternative view, being one of incremental legal reasoning by which any new proposition must find support in an already existing authority. This can be illustrated in the passage where he said:

> 'The law applicable is the common law, and though its principles are capable of application to meet new conditions not contemplated when the law was laid down, these

principles cannot be changed nor can additions be made to them because any particular meritorious case seems outside their ambit.'

The attack on the proposition that legal reasoning can be logical in any but trivial cases finds further support in the area of statutory interpretation. The golden rule of statutory interpretation (see, for example, *R* v *Allen* (1872)) illustrates the way the application of a literal meaning of a word can lead to absurdity. The circumstances under which the court would consider the consequence to be absurd are not found in any logic. A comparison of the case of *R* v *Allen* and *Fisher* v *Bell* (1961) illustrates this point. In the former case the court was concerned that the legislature might have enacted an absurdity in that according to the literal meaning of the words the offence of bigamy could not have been committed and so they applied a varied meaning to give effect to the intention of Parliament as they perceived it. Yet in *Fisher* v *Bell* the court did not concern itself that the offence of offering for sale of a certain type of knife could not be committed as the statute was worded. That merely led to the amendment of the law by a further Act of Parliament. The point being made here is that the circumstances where the courts will follow one meaning in preference to another cannot be logically determined.

MacCormick sees legal reasoning as consequentialist. In this way he seeks to explain the difficulty identified above. Nonetheless, even within the consequentialist school no matter how desirable the consequences may be, no reasoning is legally permissible unless it is either authorised by a legal principle or is analogous to an existing legal rule.

Harris in *Law and Legal Science* suggested that legal science constructs the law according to four logical principles. These he identifies as (1) exclusion, by which he means that the law is identified by a finite set of sources; (2) subsumption, meaning that rules originating in an inferior source must be subsumed under rules originating in a superior source; (3) derogation, which stipulates a priority amongst rules depending on a ranking of sources; and (4) non-contradiction, which insists that any contradiction must be eliminated.

We can therefore see that both Harris and MacCormick argue that it is part of legal reasoning to eliminate logical conflicts between legal rules. Nonetheless, it has been argued that logical reasoning need not be coherent. Even so, the system of precedent is intended to be coherent in that it attributes a rational purpose to the law. What is clear is that these coherence and consequentialist arguments are not dictated by logic. As Holmes J said: '[Because] the life of the law has been not logic but experience, we can conclude that if a matter has come to litigation, it would tend to indicate that it could not be resolved by logical reasoning.'

Legal reasoning and political conflict

Sunstein (1996) examined the nature of legal reasoning in his book *Legal Reasoning and Political Conflict*. It was published in the United States and it has just arrived in the United Kingdom. He asks what the whole business of legal philosophising and theorising is actually for. In effect, he says that in real practical life it is not necessary to be too closely bothered with the precise justifications for arguing for any particular decision in the law. Like a number of other American writers, he thinks that one of the important aims of jurisprudence is to adopt a pragmatic approach. In this he is very much in line with the whole tenor of the American legal realist movement, which has adopted the line that formalist and deductive methods of legal reasoning are unsuited to explain precisely what goes on in the courts. In general tenor, too, the approach is that of Ronald Dworkin who has consistently and strongly advocated a merger of practice and theory.

Sunstein's basic theory is that it is unnecessary to find a justification that 'goes all the way up' to be seen as consistent with the highest order abstract principle of law. Why not? He says that if the other side is willing to accept a 'lower-level' justification, then that is all that is required, in a pragmatic sense, to justify the result. Thus, the attraction in the idea is that a result is reached without the heat of the battle at the level of high principle. Such features are seen in Alternative Dispute Resolution, with negotiation and practicality at the forefront and principle left in the background. The main problem with these ideas is that it does not follow that because two parties to a dispute, and the judge, are willing to accept a particular solution, that that solution is the correct one. All parties can get something wrong, and that not infrequently occurs in the context of the law and, in fact, is one of the reasons we have an appeals system. Hutchinson (1988) in a critique of Sunstein suggests an alternative approach to legal reasoning:

'While most lawyers and judges continue to insist that legal reasoning has a logic of its own whose structure fits it to give meaning to ambiguity, I maintain that such a formalistic position is both untenable and unnecessary. Shorn of its legal nomenclature and doctrinal dressing, legal reasoning is simply a general and non-specific style of reasoning which lawyers have colonised and at which judges have become particularly adept; the claim that legal reasoning is special not only in its formal attributes, but also in its ability to arrive at substantively better and worse answers cannot be sustained. As a normative exercise, it is not an empirical matter of truth or falsity: legal reasoning is less a demonstration of logical necessity and more a practice of human justification. More particularly, legal reasoning is a mode of playful and rhetorical activity. This insight has been latched upon as the basis of a neo-pragmatic revival in jurisprudence. However, as exemplified in the esteemed work of Sunstein, these efforts to construe law and adjudication as a practical activity flatter, but only to disappoint: the new non-formalist packaging belies the old formalist commitment. In contrast, I will offer a different understanding of legal reasoning that is thoroughly pragmatic in ambition and elaboration. I insist that adjudication, like much of life itself, is best understood as a playful attempt by judges to engage in a language game that seeks to regulate social life. By depicting adjudication as a non-formalist game of infinite proportions my account seeks to explain and evaluate adjudication in such a way that it captures its sense as a peculiar professional practice (in which it stands as something of its own thing) and as a profoundly political undertaking (in which it is organically related to the larger context of society). In this way it might be possible to realise that law is not so much a site that is located aside or away from ordinary life and that adjudication is not so much an activity that can be appreciated as separate from ordinary living: law is a part of, not apart from, life and adjudication represents one site and way of playing the game of life.' (at pp263–264)

The pragmatic nature of law

Richard Posner's (1995) book *Overcoming Law* has the fundamental thesis that law and legal reasoning should be seen to be concerned always with solving problems in a pragmatic way. His basic idea may be well grasped in his Introduction, where he considers two major influences on both the development of legal education and judicial reasoning in the United States, those of 'formalism' and 'realism', and then says that neither of these divide up the 'jurisprudential universe'. There is, instead, he says the 'middle way' of pragmatism. He sees this as having two main components. These are: being concerned with the 'forward-looking' (so you can see his impatience with deciding cases in a formalistic way, which is essentially backward-looking) and the 'consequential'; and being concerned with questions of empirical fact. These are the twin ideas, which he couples with two attitudes of mind that should accompany the 'pragmatic' approach, those of being 'anti-dogmatic' and socially concerned. In this way, he hopes to 'nudge the judicial game a little closer to the science game'.

You can see practical sense in all of this, of course, but it is not so clear that he is fair to the modes of legal reasoning which he sets up in opposition to it. For example, he comes down very heavily on what he understands to be the project of the 'analytic philosophers' (amongst whom, one assumes, he would position Hart, Fuller, Dworkin, Finnis, Raz, etc). The analytic philosopher who engages in thinking about legal reasoning is, he says:

> '... too prone to equate disagreement with error by exaggerating the domain of logic and thus prematurely dismissing opposing views, and, what is related, insufficiently interested in the empirical support for those views. The pragmatist is especially dubious that the methods of analytic philosophy and its twin, legal reasoning, can be used to establish moral duties or legal rights.'

In some ways, Posner's more abstract account of law can be seen to be a logical extension of his views about the relationship between economic reasoning and legal reasoning. He regards his view that judges should decide on economic grounds – which, despite the odd comment in some previous writing in which he appeared to recant, he still clearly holds – as pragmatic in approach. Economics is both forward-looking and empirical, although one might wonder whether his personal view of economics, embracing as it does the idea of wealth-maximisation as a virtue, is really so anti-dogmatic and social in outlook. Nevertheless, he thinks that his pragmatism 'epitomises the operation in law of the ethic of scientific inquiry, pragmatically understood'.

Posner not only says something about pragmatics and economics but claims that pragmatism offers the best account of liberalism, which he thinks is the mode of reasoning best suited for placing constraints on majoritarian excesses of democracy (where a democratically-elected majority starts hounding an unpopular minority). Posner is genuinely trying to solve the problem of irreconcilable differences of opinion. Pragmatism in his view is not in the business of supplying foundations – so it is not necessary to look to anything other than the reconciliation of difference. Liberalism is best for achieving this, he claims, since liberalism, too, is best suited for societies in which people do not agree on foundations. Therefore, he says, the pragmatic way is the best way to constrain democracy.

This could all be challenged. There are, for example, well-known and distinguished attempts to found liberalism in terms of fundamental principles (Mill and Raz are two obvious candidates), and equally well-known and distinguished attempts to combine representative government with liberalism (Mill, again, as an obvious candidate). But Posner – as so often – has a point: we must pay great attention to the actual practices of people, to their disagreements, and to the real, not imaginary, possibilities for them to live in harmony.

3.4 The case of the Speluncean Explorers

As a way of seeing how, if 'argumentative attitude' is the correct focus for law, we should judge which arguments are good, and which are bad, it is extremely useful to examine Professor Lon Fuller's famous article in which he compared some radically different ways judges might argue.

As an introduction to jurisprudence and the idea of legal argument, Fuller used among others the hypothetical example of a case involving a situation very similar to the facts of the case of *R* v *Dudley and Stephens* (1884) in which survivors have to cannibalise one of their number in order to survive. One should notice how the judgments are a product of their own time. They are influenced by the theories of Marxism and feminism and so there are limits to the value of this as an introductory text. Students can find an extract in Lloyd and Freeman's *Introduction to Jurisprudence* and are strongly recommended to read this in detail.

Fuller was attempting to examine the relationship between law and morality and the use of moral and legal excuses and justifications in a particularly hard case. He also examines the role of the judge in a hard case, the technique of legal reasoning and the perennial question of the fidelity to law: under what circumstances if any may the citizen disobey the law? Professor Twining thinks that the introduction is fair as far as it goes but it does not tackle enough questions and he has cited as an example the failure to take account of Marxism.

In the judgments Fuller focuses on certain divergent philosophies of law and government. Handy J examines the question in terms of practical wisdom. He wants to know what should be done with the defendants and expresses concern that the judiciary will lose touch with reality. He seems less concerned with the letter of the law and more concerned with public perception. He states that public opinion is relevant in the criminal law. The judges may take account of public opinion in the sentencing of offenders, yet in this case the sentence is mandatory. Given that the sentence is mandatory, Handy J seeks to take account of the personality of the chief executive, the elected official in whose hands the question of clemency would constitutionally rest. This approach appears to be an abdication of the role of the judge although it does look at factors that might well influence a real-life judge. Handy J states that he is becoming more perplexed at the refusal of the judiciary to apply a common sense approach to problems. Quite what the connection between common sense and the letter of the law is remains the unanswered question in this judgment.

Staying true to the literal interpretation tradition that was prevalent in the common law, Truepenny CJ approaches the problem from the point of the strict letter application of the law, regardless of the potential injustice of the outcome. He demarcates the role of the judge in the application of the law as separate from the role of the legislature in the making of law. According to the constitutional arrangements in this hypothetical country the executive branch have the power to grant clemency. Truepenny CJ says that it is no part of the role of the judge in the case and indeed in doing so the judge would be usurping the role of the executive branch if he granted what would in effect be clemency.

Foster J outlines two alternative approaches to the answer to the problem. It is not difficult to detect that Fuller himself identifies with and supports the second of these approaches. Foster firstly postulates that the premise on which the positive law is based is that of the possibility of men's coexistence. He maintains that where that coexistence is impossible then the condition that underlies all positive law ceases to exist. Therefore what the defendants did was not a crime because the law which said it was a crime did not exist. Foster J then continued that if that line of reasoning was not acceptable then he suggested the line favoured by Fuller himself, namely that positive law should be interpreted reasonably in the light of its evident purpose, and gives as an example the law on self defence. He states that the correction of obvious error is not to supplant the legislative will, but to make that will effective. This is the purposive approach to the role of the judges in the interpretation of statutes.

We now turn to a rather unusual judge. Tatting J approaches the case and becomes confused. He is worried about the implications of his decision but is also mindful of the strict letter of the law. He asks by what authority do we resolve ourselves into a court of nature? He is unable to resolve the doubts that so trouble his mind about this case and therefore seeks to withdraw from the decision. Tatting is not fulfilling his duty by withdrawing. He seeks to shift blame on to the prosecuting authority who he suggests ought to have exercised their discretion and not prosecuted these defendants. Had they done so that would have absolved the court, including Tatting, from having to reach a decision. Tatting insists on withdrawal even when it is made clear to him that his failure to participate will lead in the end to the death penalty being imposed on the defendants. He seems simply to wash his hands of the whole affair. Can a judge actually do this?

Finally, Keen J states that it is not the proper role of the court to instruct the executive on the exercise of clemency. He maintains that the court is not in session in order to apply conceptions of morality, rather it should apply the law. He cannot take the speech of Foster seriously since in his opinion Foster J has failed to distinguish the legal from the moral aspects of the case. As to the purpose of the argument, Keen maintains that due to the supremacy of the legislature it is not always possible to know what purpose it had in mind and it would not therefore be possible to fill the gaps. He would affirm the convictions of the defendants on the grounds that judicial dispensation does more harm in the long run than hard decisions. Nonetheless he seems to go on to say how the matter should be approached from the point of view of an ordinary citizen. The case of the Speluncean Explorers was reconsidered by Kozinski, J *et al* (1999).

Are Moral Judgments
Part of the Law?

4

The Nature of Morality

4.1 Introduction

There has been a long association between morality and law. Traditionally, law has been associated with religions, customs and divinity. In the West, the revealed laws of God in the form of the Bible have dominated legal concepts. Similar relationships with other religions have attributed the origin of law to the spiritual rather than the rational.

Most legal systems appropriate to themselves the enforcement of contemporary moral and ethical values. The purpose of law can therefore sometimes be confused with morality. Olivecrona suggests that morality is the product of law and certainly developed social morality would probably be impossible if it were not for legal enforcement. However, there are moral elements which appear primarily to stem from human nature such as love and consideration. On the other hand, there are certain legal rules that are morally indifferent such as those concerning which side of the road to drive on. To this extent there is quite evidently a difference in content between law and morality. Morality may inform the legislator but the question must be raised as to whether law has to be morally valid in order to be legally valid.

4.2 What is morality?

Before we try to address some of the issues raised here it might be helpful to define some closely related concepts of morality. If we say something is moral or immoral, we might mean a variety of things, but issues of morality are normally decided by conscience or instinct. It is not our place at this moment to ask whether conscience and instinct are learned responses or pre-programmed. It suffices to say that there is no requirement to look to outside information or reason in order to find an answer to some moral dilemmas. Often moral feelings run against the grain of other people's views and even our own reasoning. As such, morals defined in this way are capable of producing infinite disagreement, since different people's consciences dictate different things.

Positive and critical morality

A useful distinction to be drawn is that between 'positive' and 'critical' morality. The distinction and terminology is present in Bentham and Austin and surfaces in contemporary times in Hart's work attacking Lord Devlin, *Law, Liberty and Morality*. In Austin, the distinction arose in connection with the distinction between the 'Divine law', which was the law of God, as laid down in the Ten Commandments, for example, or, for the utilitarians, as revealed in the index of utility.

The difference between these two possible bases for morality is important. That people in general agree that something should morally be done or is morally permissible, cannot be a sufficient justification for doing that thing, otherwise slavery would have been right once. What people believe, namely, what is a *positive* set of beliefs, is not a ground for saying that what they believe is true, and so constitutes morality. Or, another way of putting exactly the same point, is to say that morality is not explained merely by reference to conventional morality.

Of course, the existence of certain conventions may provide a reason for behaving in a particular way as, for example, the convention that you take your hat off in church should be followed in order to avoid offending people. But that is not the same as saying that the convention creates the moral rule, except in the misleading and unimportant sense in which we might say 'theirs was a morality of slavery'. The unimportance (and danger) of the use of the word 'morality' in that phrase becomes crystal clear when we use phrases such as 'the morality of the Nazi party was an *immoral* morality'. The relevant distinction here was drawn neatly by Bentham and Austin, who talked of the distinction between 'positive' and 'critical' morality, positive morality being those social conventions created by man, and critical morality being the standards *by which those social conventions could be judged*.

Where, however, a society shares certain moral values on such matters as adultery, prostitution or abortion, we might say that these are social mores. This could also be termed morality. But social mores are to a certain extent a matter of faith. Even in the age of opinion polls we cannot be sure whether contemporary people actually feel prostitution is morally wrong, since they might have been persuaded by arguments rather than conscience or conviction. Propaganda and indoctrination have a powerful effect on so-called shared morality. Not just in Nazi Germany, but in thirties America and many other societies, public morality has been manipulated by subtle propaganda about racial hygiene. In Germany the desire for healthy beautiful babies led rapidly to the sterilisation of the disabled and the eradication of undesirable populations.

Thus, relying on what people's 'revealed preferences' are may succeed in producing moral norms that offend against many people's consciences. This problem has plagued moralists and lawyers for centuries. The obvious response was to find a way in which moral imperatives could be translated into practical imperatives, without perverting the original moral intentions. This is the task that ethics has set itself.

Ethics and practical reason

The language of ethics and the language of law are similar and centre upon questions of obligation, duty and so forth. Much jurisprudence such as that of Finnis is inspired by ethical studies; however the differences between these disciplines are wide. If an ethical scholar says I should follow a certain code, I may ask why, and I will obey only if I am convinced by his reasoning. But I cannot avoid the binding effect of a law simply because I do not agree with the reasoning behind it. Ethics change according to improvements in practical reasoning. But although jurists, such as Raz, concede that practical reasoning is not entirely excluded from the law, they also insist that part of the process of law becoming law is the exclusion of further debate.

This may be illustrated by simple analogy. Parliament may debate a Bill on the basis of practical reasoning, ethics, social mores or individual consciences. However, once the Bill is made into law such debate is largely excluded. Cases such as *Cheney* v *Conn* illustrate the finality of debate, even when norms of international morality are invoked. The law to this extent differs from ethics. This closed-minded system of legal reasoning often leads people to say that law is formalistic, pedantic or simply unjust.

We have seen, however, that social mores are difficult to ascertain and not necessarily related to personal morality. Law is shy of taking account of personal conscience simply because one cannot necessarily look into a person's mind to tell whether it is a genuinely held conviction and because of the vast differences between people's attitudes.

4.3 Morality and objectivity

The objectivity of morality does not depend on an external world of moral reality or on the existence of conventions. It is not, on the other hand, 'totally subjective' because its coherence must be testable in the public domain. It must, too, as we shall see, be subject to the stringent requirements of rationality.

The idea of the public accountability of the moral assertions one makes is apparent in the famous Hart-Devlin debate. Lord Devlin propounded this thesis in his famous lecture delivered in 1958. He argued with the case in mind of the legalisation of homosexual acts between consenting adult males proposed by the

Wolfenden Committee of the United Kingdom which had produced a report in the previous year. Devlin's position was that we have to understand that a society like the United Kingdom is made up of various ties and traditions such as, for example, a common morality based upon the Christian religion. Appealing to our conviction that the state has the right to protect itself by using the criminal law to punish treasonable acts, Devlin argued that the state could, in principle, outlaw acts that threatened to undermine the state's moral existence (although he did not himself regard the prohibition of private homosexuality as falling within this ambit). Those acts would be those determined by a jurybox 'litmus paper' test of what the public opinion was at the particular time.

There are famous problems with these ideas. One is that many object to the idea that the state somehow has a right to protect itself from moral change. But the strongest one is that 'the public morality' is vastly more complex than a description of what the public 'feels' at a particular time, and allows for the holding of sincerely held views of a different and contrary nature. Since this is what 'public morality' means, and not what the man in the 'Clapham omnibus' feels a real sense of 'intolerance, indignation and disgust' about, the idea of the state enforcing 'public morality' is not so simple as to allow the crude expression of public feeling.

We may come to this conclusion by way of analysis of the idea of a 'moral position'. It is initially an argument about the way we in fact speak in moral discourse, but it is intended, too, to make moral sense. The idea of a consensus in which public morality allows for a variation of moral views is one that lies squarely on the idea of a democratic community in which each individual enjoys an equality of respect. That idea itself is the engine for Dworkin's criticism and it is an idea that is not easily to be extricated from Devlin's position that it is society or community that is important. Implicit at least in the Clapham man's vision is an egalitarian premise that the ordinary man's view, about the kind of moral environment in which he wishes to live, be given voice.

We can examine more closely the place of reason in morality. Are *prejudiced* views permitted as genuinely moral views? Clearly not. The admission of prejudice by someone disqualifies him in our eyes from speaking sensibly on the matter. The man who says, 'I just hate queers' is not someone who we feel is expressing a genuinely moral view.

Let us now consider the place of the following reason: 'That action just makes me sick'. Is it sufficient to offer a mere emotional reaction to something to establish one's moral position? We often criticise some forms of moral argument as being 'emotive', meaning that the appeal they make bypasses reason. If it is a legitimate way of criticising a person's moral stance, then it supports the view that reasons, rather than emotions, are an essential ingredient of having a moral view.

But that way of putting it can be misleading, for having a particular emotion may be a way of stating at least part of a reason, as when we say we feel angry about something. And having emotional reactions to some sorts of thing – say, seeing a cat being tortured – is, we feel, right and proper. Nevertheless, a statement of 'feeling' alone is not enough because we always want to know the reason for the feeling or the anger or whatever. In other words, it is the reason that comes first.

If someone claimed that he morally disapproved of blacks and, in response to the question why, said: 'They just make me angry, that's all,' we would not think that this was sufficient. In fact, the absence of a proffered reason, or any reason at all that we can think makes sense of the remark, would in all probability make us conclude that this person had a phobia, or an obsession.

What about mistakes of fact? What if a person says that he morally disapproves of the Clinton administration because it started the First World War? Rationality requires that some minimum standard of evidence be complied with in any view put forward based on a proposition of fact. What sort of view would it be if it did not need to pass through that sieve of rationality? The Emperor Justinian was said to have disapproved of homosexuality because it caused earthquakes (presumably, an act springing from the wrath of the Gods).

Just repeating what another says, too, is insufficient. Imagine someone says that he disapproves of abortion and, when asked for a reason, replies, 'because my mother disapproves'. We expect a person's views to be his or her *own*.

These are four sorts of reasons that have the result of disqualifying a person's expressed attitudes from counting as a moral position. But there are others we can imagine once we get the idea. We cannot have moral views about inanimate objects, say, earthquakes ('earthquakes are irresponsible, or frivolous') for example, and our moral conclusions must follow logically from the premises we claim to hold.

4.4 The method of 'reflective equilibrium'

'Reflective equilibrium' is the name that the contemporary political philosopher John Rawls gives, in his *A Theory of Justice* (1970), to what he regards as the correct method of moral reasoning. It envisages an equilibrium being attained between moral intuitions, or convictions, and abstract positions on general questions of morality (moral theories) that we hold. The 'equilibrium' between the two should be reached by our comparing our intuitions with our structured moral beliefs.

Sometimes our intuitions embarrass our theories, as when our intuition that just wars are morally permissible embarrasses our theory that innocent life must never be taken. The process of reflective equilibrium justifies the moral psychology whereby either the theory is modified or developed in a way that can explain the intuition (say, innocent life must not intentionally be taken, with some attendant theories about what constitutes innocent life and what intention means), or the intuition begins to lose its impact and finally disappears given the coherence of the theory.

Of course, the abstract positions on general moral questions that we hold will make sense of the particular intuitions we have. So the process is ongoing. We modify, or even eventually abandon, intuitions in the light of our generalisations and acquire new intuitions both in the light of theory and new experiences. Arguments we have with others about moral issues should develop in the same way. We test intuitions we hold against general positions we hold. We embarrass others by pointing to inconsistencies between their intuitions and their general positions.

4.5 Cultural relativity

One of the most common arguments used to establish that morality is 'subjective' only is the argument from cultural relativity. Other cultures have different values so, crudely, it follows that there is no one 'essential' morality and all values are 'relative'. Advocates of this kind of thinking are fond of saying such things as that slavery in the southern states of the United States in the nineteenth century was 'morally permissible' *for them*, or cannibalism in certain primitive tribes was 'moral' *for them*, and so on.

Someone who holds the sceptical view that values are 'subjective' because of cultural relativity, must hold the view that values *can* be objective because, in order to be so, they *must* be cross-cultural. Why else would he argue that values are subjective *because* they are intra-cultural only? One kind of argument for cultural relativity can be dismissed here, although it is very common indeed. This is the 'who are we to judge?' sort and it may be useful to label it the 'cultural arrogance' argument. It says that cultural differences are just so great that it is simply arrogant to suppose that anyone can transplant the values of one culture to another. This kind of argument relies on the strength of our dislike, for example, of Victorian missionaries being shocked by African tribal morality and the insensitivity with which judgments were made and carried out, often with appalling consequences. But does it make a difference that slavery occurs, or occurred, in another culture? Usually where arrogance is not a factor, people are willing to accept that 'trans-cultural' moral judgments can be made.

4.6 Law and morality in history

It is difficult for the law student to gain an objective perspective of the debate on law and morality since issues of morality are largely excluded from the study of substantive English law. This may be as a direct result of the tradition of classical English positivism in legal studies. Duncan Kennedy in *The Ideological Content of Legal Education* (cited Chapter 8, Lloyd and Freeman) posits an interesting insight into this situation. Discussing the education techniques employed in law schools, which he views as liberal in their ideological approach, rather than being pluralistic, he states:

> 'If one thinks about law in this way, one is inescapably dependent on the very techniques of legal reasoning that are being marshalled in defense of the status quo.'

To begin with, let us consider the understanding of the nature of law in times past when such a view was perhaps less prevalent. The case of John Lilburne, though it might be taken as exceptional, illustrates the wide gulf between the law's own definition of itself in the mid-seventeenth century and the modern view. During the English Commonwealth, Lilburne was subject to an Act of Parliament banishing him on pain of death. Lilburne fought the case on the authority of Coke's *Institutes* which stated:

> 'Where reason ceaseth, the law ceaseth … All customs and prescriptions (Acts of Parliament, laws and judgments) that be against reason are void and null in themselves.'

The court was persuaded by this argument even to the extent of deciding that the jury was the judge of law as well as fact. That such arguments were entertained and indeed prevailed was no mere anomaly of the Commonwealth. Coke's laws and cases are taken to be accurate statements of the law to the present day, even though it has been shown persuasively that at least in *Slade's* case Coke's reports contain more of his opinions than those of the judges.

This seems strange to the modern English eye, but very much in keeping with the legacy of early English jurisprudence. Perhaps the most positivist and modern of sixteenth century juristic writings was Smith's *De Republica Anglorum*, in which, while conceding the absolute power of the king in Parliament, Smith takes a very non-committal position on the question of immoral laws. To Smith the question of whether a law's validity is linked to morality depends, in hindsight, on whether civil disobedience results in political success.

If, on the one hand, there was an assertion that reason and common sense governed the application of new law, there was also a deep-seated belief that law was a heritage stronger than governments or kings, a guarantee of rights in itself. The Elizabethan lawyer, Maynard, contends that the king is subject to law because the law doth make him king. Therefore, if he sought to change the law to something immoral or irrational he could not.

The view that law was immutable and fixed was implicit in the common usage of the word law itself and adherence to law was partly due to the wisdom of antiquity which had been tried and tested over the ages. Moreover, in the early sixteenth century, law enforcement was scarcely in the hands of the government, being more dependent on the practice and teachings of the Church.

The Church contributed two great factors to the law and morality issue.

Firstly, until the English Reformation, it represented a supra-national entity with real political and theological sanctions at its disposal, in an age when, although its power was on the decline, the fear of excommunication could still keep an unruly prince in check. In theory the Church was itself accountable, not politically, but morally to God.

Secondly, it had a monopoly on the truth of moral determinations. If the Church said something was wrong, it was wrong! There was therefore no problem in the law determining what moral standards it must conform to. In essence England was a place where there was the Church's law, the people's law and the king's law in Parliament.

The Enlightenment

Across Europe similar situations prevailed, but also the same problems arose. Kings and Parliaments became wealthier and consequently more efficient at government. Science was eroding superstition and religion. The moral and religious authority of the Church was being challenged, because of the growing feeling that the Church was a mere number cipher for national powers and riddled with moral corruption.

With apologies to historians, these factors may be seen as accounting for some of the jurisprudential developments that urged law and morality to part company in the minds of lawyers, legislators and jurists alike.

Absolutism

With the increasing strength of national kings and the declining fortune of the Church, James I, Richelieu and Louis XIV among others denied any legal or religious fetters on monarchic authority. Law became simply what the sovereign willed law to be and matters such as morality or religion were solely in their keeping. England had an edge on the rest of Europe, since the English Reformation had unified Church and state in the person of the monarch.

Not surprisingly, since the absolute monarch was no longer necessarily king by virtue of the law and custom of the land, another reason was needed. Conveniently, therefore, the monarch became the monarch by Divine Right, requiring moral and religious obedience, and the link with morality was thereby maintained. In this also the seeds of the imperative theory are to be found, law is the will of the sovereign, irrespective of subjective moral or other considerations.

Europe was rapidly realising that the rest of the world had moralities of a different kind: every nation has its own type of wisdom – Mahomet symbolises the wisdom of the Arabs, for example. Moral truths did not seem to be so certainly the exclusive monopoly of any particular Church, wrote one Elizabethan jurist.

Secular morality

The secularisation of morality and its application to law at the hands of Grotius and others is largely relevant to the natural law issues of the next chapter. Instead of relying on religion, the secular natural lawyers sought to superimpose moral standards on law by the application of reason. Bayle philosophically separated religion from morality, but in doing so contributed to the theoretical separation of the law from morality, which was quite opposite to his desire.

The eighteenth century saw scientific development, which engendered an absolute faith in observation and reasoning to solve all problems. If Newton could make a law true for all falling objects, then Locke could find the key to law that would explain the science of legislation. His *Essay Concerning Human Understanding* was widely read and influential, especially his emphasis on observable facts and inductive knowledge as the preferred methodology for jurisprudence. As to the question of morality, that was simply a matter of human sensations of pleasure and pain, backed by the power of desire. Others of his conclusions, although influential, are manifestly contradictory to his espoused methodology, being more the result of his political opinions rather than empirical observation. However, his influence is very evident in the writing of Hume and others, in the American Constitution, the Glorious Revolution, while his account of morality is to be found in the writings of Bentham, among others.

If we combine Locke's psychology with Hobbes' pessimism, for the latter thought that men's desires were naturally brutish, we not only come to Hobbes' conclusion that all power should reside in an absolute sovereign, but may also come to feel that popular morality is not necessarily a good thing. Thus Voltaire, although advocating a humane legal system, dismissed ordinary people as the rabble, following Lockean logic.

Locke's infectious ideas reached even the priesthood in the shape of Condillac. He viewed man as being born morally neutral with the capacity to develop morally only by learning. It was, for Condillac, the environment and education that made man good or bad and he rejected determinism altogether. Thus, by improving the environment, man could become perfect. Following in this mould, Helvetius concluded that man was simply sensitive matter to be motivated simply by pleasure and pain. On this account, morality was simply what is good, that is, pleasure, so that the object of morality could simply be seen to be obtaining the greatest pleasure for the greatest amount of sensitive matter.

It is following this, admittedly short, history that the stage is set for understanding the philosophical developments that lead to the contemporary debates, which are set in the context of utilitarian theories of morality (see Chapter 6). And it is utilitarianism which is at the foundation of legal positivism. First, however, we need to turn to the important moral question of when citizens have a duty, if they have, to obey the law.

5

The Obligation to Obey the Law

5.1 A claim to moral authority

5.2 The positivist view

5.3 Social contractarian theories

5.4 Finnis

5.5 Conclusion

5.1 A claim to moral authority

If law is distinct from morality, we need to establish whether the obligation to obey the law is to any extent a moral one. It is a manifest fact of legal systems that they claim moral authority for themselves. Even the most reprehensible of laws made by the most reprehensible regimes are couched in moral terms. In South Africa the illegality of inter-racial marriages was based on the premise that it would be immoral for a white to be in union with a lesser species. Even where there is obvious brutality that cannot itself be justified, the moral rectitude of the political order may be invoked. If a government in England were to pass a law that was regarded as immoral, it could still point to the moral legitimation of being electorally accountable.

The tradition of moral marketing in England is well illustrated in Douglas Hay's account of the ideology of force, justice and mercy in *Albion's Fatal Tree*. It is hard to understand the genuine paternalism of generations past that enshrined the belief that the ruling classes had a moral duty to rule. Still harder to understand is the widespread acceptance, by the ruled, of the repressive legal system as being not only naturally but morally right.

Speaking of the arbitrary nature of eighteenth century criminal law, Hay says:

'Englishmen ... tended to think of justice in personal terms, and were more struck by understanding of individual cases than by the delights of abstract schemes. Where authority is embodied in direct personal relationships, men will often accept power, even enormous despotic power, when it comes to the good King, the father of his people, who tempers justice with mercy. A form of this powerful psychic configuration was the law's greatest strength as an ideological system, especially amongst the poor, and in the countryside.'

Certainly, in the static and personal world of the eighteenth century, patterns of authority and obligation had more in common with the feudal morality of loyalty to one's lord than to an allegiance to a social idea such as law. However, the same cannot be said of the modern situation in England, leading to a particular mystique about the nature of legal obligation.

The fact that law is still thought of as being in the interest of society can be seen in the judgments of most criminal cases. To this extent, Detmold in *The Unity of Morality and Law* claims that all legal judgments seek to refer themselves to corresponding moral norms. This may well be an insincere attempt on the part of the law giver to gain moral approval.

Even if it seems that a law does not accord with the consensus on individual morality, it does not mean that there is no appeal to morality. In dramatic terms, the judge who regrets having to apply a law, because it seems to be unfair, but stresses that it is nonetheless his duty to do so, reinforces the feeling that there is a higher moral duty binding the judge.

There is considerable evidence to suggest that moral reasoning is learned, rather than innate (see Kohlberg's *Moral Development and Behaviour*). It may be that our response to legal obligations is learned in a related way. When we are children we are told that certain things are wrong because they are not 'nice' and others are wrong because they are against the law. The difference between the obligation to obey the law and the obligation to obey moral laws is obscure, but the difference is defined by the differences between practical and legal solutions to moral problems. If faced with the choice of breaking the law and betraying moral principles, the language of legal marketing often encourages us to see it as a moral dilemma. When a judge criticises a person for seeking to set himself above the law, this implies a moral argument: everyone else surrenders their problems to the law because it is socially right and prevents anarchy, so why should the individual be the exception?

To suggest that there is no moral element to legal obligation would be to contradict this marketing approach, but then who believes packaging? However, this brings us no nearer to understanding the nature of legal obligation. Asserting that law is to be obeyed because it is binding is a tautology. It is simply to repeat that it should be obeyed. We might take the Kelsenite view that law should be obeyed because it is validated by an unwritten rule or *Grundnorm*. This is an ultimate rule or norm that requires the legal system to be obeyed. Such a norm in Kelsen's eyes is a presupposition of juristic thinking which amounts to a lawyerly assumption.

Morally, this is the least satisfactory solution. It amounts to a suggestion that the obligation to obey law stems from lawyers saying that it should be obeyed. This appears unsatisfactory, because it provides us with no firm rationale. It is rather like a child asking his parent why he must go to bed at bedtime and being answered 'because I say so'.

However, there is still truth contained in the idea. In modern civilisation, few aspects of life are not impinged upon or dependent on the legal system. So the citizen might feel he has little alternative but to play along with the rules of the game. However, this passive attitude would not seem completely to explain what ethical scholars would term the pro-attitude towards law that is manifest among the ordinary population.

Harris, in *Legal Philosophies*, notes that although most people will participate in law-breaking activities themselves, they are still critical of others' illegal activities. This can be explained. Certainly, some legal prohibitions accord with the common view of what is morally unacceptable, while other minor laws seem simply an administrative nuisance. Thus, one could easily envisage even a petty thief criticising a rapist. This is not necessarily a moral endorsement of the obligation to obey law, but an endorsement of the obligation to obey what are subjectively felt to be morally correct laws.

5.2 The positivist view

That one need not obey an immoral law has always been conceded by positivists, although their tones are resonant of Anglicanism. One need not obey an immoral law, but one cannot evade the legal consequences of so doing. For this reason, it is the consequences of disobedience to the law to which its binding effect is largely credited. For many positivists law should be obeyed, to a certain extent, because some benefit may be accrued from doing so, and to a greater extent because of the apprehension that a sanction might be imposed.

However, the nature of benefits anticipated by the upright citizen is viewed by writers such as Bentham as being more in the nature of a bribe. If part of the recognition of an obligation to obey is the acceptance that a law might be of benefit to oneself or to others, then this might explain some of the moral element of legal obligation. This explanation is not difficult to accept when we consider that living in society requires a submission of freedom as well as a corresponding acceptance of obligations. This explanation remains conditional on a law being *seen* to be morally justified by the common good. The law in question need not actually be advanced for moral reasons by the legislator, but it needs only to have the appearance of being morally right. Thus, social security reforms in the 1980s which made life significantly harder for many people at the poorer end of society, were seen by many as being morally right because such people were often represented as less worthwhile, or lazy.

5.3 Social contractarian theories

A particular version of the theory that law is obligatory because it satisfies social needs is to be found in the so-called social contract theories. We have already noted that Hobbes viewed humans, in their natural state, as nasty and brutish. To Hobbes the legal system is the instrument by which order is achieved and, in fact, he considered it the only means of maintaining social cohesion. Law should therefore be obeyed in return for the maintenance of order.

In contrast, Locke considered that although humans had certain inalienable rights, they surrendered their freedom for the purpose of channelling their efforts in the collective enterprise of society. As such, the law-maker holds their interests on trust, directing society through the agency of the law. However, if this trust is betrayed, then the law-maker cannot command obedience.

These theories are dubbed social contract theories because they see the relationship between legal authority and civil obedience resting on unspoken mutual promises. To Hobbes, the brutes obey, but in return the law-maker must maintain order. Locke's premise is that the partial surrender of freedom is in return for good order. It is thus as if the parties had entered into a contract. The major difficulty with these theories is that they fail adequately to explain how such promises were obtained. Do I, by being born into a society, automatically consent to be ruled? It may be argued that by my presence within the territory I have given my consent, but there is hardly an inch of the world now where law does not claim to exist. Alternatively, it might be said that by being born, I have already taken the benefit of society and as such have accepted my obligation to obey. This would seem very unsatisfactory as an explanation.

The broad, political morality of the social contract theory is, thus, not very convincing. When we consider justice we will consider Rawls, who postulates a theory not dissimilar to the social contract theory, which proposes a calculus of fairness suggesting what laws should be obeyed and when there is no longer an obligation to do so.

5.4 Finnis

In response, Finnis postulates a view of legal obligation based upon natural and self-evident principles of what is good and principles of what he calls, borrowing from Aristotle, 'practical reasonableness'. While law is whatever is legally valid, the obligation that accrues to law is obviously greater, the more respect a legal system has for these principles. Legal systems are seen as carrying with them a general moral obligation if they carry with them moral approval. Without such approval Finnis would not dispute that a law is a law, but would assert that there is no obligation to obey it. Such a conclusion has great attractions and, it should be noted, the strength of Finnis' argument is based on his derivation of objective moral values.

5.5 Conclusion

That there is the possibility and even likelihood of a link between the strength of the obligation to obey the law and general moral obligations cannot be denied. Raz's views are useful here. He offers a marriage of practical and moral reasoning with positivism in a way that has gained him widespread respect. When addressing the question as to whether law is value-free, he identifies the process of law creation as being a process of gradual purification. The debates that precede the creation of statutes are ultimately based on practical and political reasoning, including moral consideration. Once a Bill becomes law, part of the broader debate is excluded. However, there may remain executive decisions. It may be necessary for executive action to be taken in the form of delegated legislation. Even when a court is faced with a complete statute, there are clearly still issues to be addressed in the form of the correct principles to apply. Court decisions are influenced by the participants, and to this extent even those subject to the law can affect legal values by pursuing legal arguments. However, law is for Raz a matter concerned with the executive stage of institutional decisions and, as such, what has been decided by Parliament or a Ministry or a court excludes further discussion. However, the deliberative stages that continue until the final decision of the final court of appeal of a particular case reflect our moral and intellectual interests and concerns.

6

Utilitarianism

6.1 Introduction

The utilitarian ethic is based on the promotion of the greatest happiness for the greatest number. Not surprisingly, the utilitarians' belief is that the obligation to obey the law is based on the promotion of the collective good. Certain actions might be prohibited by the law, such as the sale of liquor in 1920s America. The evil that the law seeks to prevent might not be viewed in itself as being important. However, the consequences of disobedience might be wider than the perpetration of the offence. The infectious effects of lawbreaking are well illustrated by the effect of breaking prohibition. or of the narcotic trade, with the associated gangland activities. In the felicific calculus of the utilitarians, the benefit of the few who gain their happiness or make money from the sale and consumption of drugs and alcohol would be outweighed by the harm to the collective good.

However, such examples are perhaps *sui generis*. Moreover, to judge the obligation to obey the law in terms of potential consequences is difficult. Such a view seems to be a complex way of expressing the dictum: what would happen if everyone were to do that? Furthermore, there is an assumption implicit in this principle of act-utilitarianism that the individual believes that if he breaks the law others will too. There is little evidence of the imitative nature of lawbreaking, except where collective lawbreaking is used as a weapon against an unpopular law.

A subtly different utilitarian principle is based upon the consequences of observing a rule. Act-utilitarianism asks whether a particular person's disobedience or the hanging of one man is in the interests of the collective good. Rule-utilitarianism asks whether a particular practice required by a rule is, on the whole, more beneficial than harmful to the collective good. For example, if the law required the top 15 per cent of wage earners to be compelled to give half their salary to hospitals, more people would benefit than would lose.

However, as a representation of reasons why people obey the law the utilitarian point of view seems unconvincing. Popular notions of the collective good are tempered by our feelings that certain things such as human rights are of fundamental importance. The utilitarian view has often been criticised on the basis that the greatest happiness for the greatest number could mean the greatest misery for the few. Not surprisingly, this brings us back to the problem of moral safeguards against the binding effect of an immoral law.

6.2 Utility as the sole criterion

Bentham insisted that the principle of utility be the sole valid criterion for the evaluation of a just measure. He also stated that to prove the rightness of the principle of utility is both unnecessary and impossible. There is much appeal in the idea that the sole valid criterion for the ascertainment of what is just is the application of the principle of utility. This principle that sees a measure as just if it has a tendency to increase happiness or to reduce pain is one that we apply in our daily lives. We undergo dental treatment in which pain is inflicted in order to alleviate a long-term toothache. That we therefore apply a utility calculus to the decision whether to undergo that dental treatment explains why the idea is attractive on the social level. A further advantage to utility is that it is secular and does not require any understanding of abstract principles. It is a simple way of telling the difference between what is right and what is wrong.

The concept of the principle of utility was developed out of a distaste for the use to which natural rights were put as the criterion for the evaluation of justice. In spite of certain clear appealing aspects whenever the principle of utility is put into practice, there are serious defects in the idea.

One difficulty is that there are two types of utility. The total utility looks at the total level of happiness and says nothing about the distribution of happiness among the population. As such it could allow for slavery in that it has the potential of increasing the total of happiness in the world. On the other hand, what is known as 'average utility' fares little better. With the same example of slavery, average utility would hold that slavery is just so long as on average happiness is increased. But this, too, could be achieved if the slave owners had greater happiness than the slaves had misery.

Mill made it clear that, regardless of the various pleasures and pains that would enter the equation, the only thing that the utilitarian would be interested in calculating would be the consequences. Thus the means always justifies the end so long as the end has the tendency to increase total or average happiness. From a deontological point of view this is unpalatable. As Lumb has observed, it can be used to justify the arbitrary deprivation of human rights. Indeed, Bentham regarded natural rights as nonsense on stilts. The criticism against the application of the utility principle is that it can lead to the most horrendous outcomes. Torture would be regarded as just so long as the victim divulged information that led to a greater happiness. With regard to terrorism, a suspected terrorist could justly be tortured if that torture actually led to his disclosing the location of a bomb, providing he disclosed it in time for the location to be evacuated with no loss of life. Why? Because it is the actual consequence that matters and not the intention behind it. Thus it would not avail a utilitarian to plead that the terrorist died during interrogation but that the torturer had intended to get the relevant information from him. Good intentions do not count.

To take an example. Imagine my being in a position of being able through torture to attempt to extract information from a terrorist that related to, say, the fate of someone close to me. We might then torture in order to obtain the information. It would not follow that utilitarianism was right, because we might not regard what we were doing as just or right but as something like an 'unjust necessity'. Utilitarianism would require that the act be fully justified.

The problem arises because of the attention paid to the consequences. These consequences can only be ascertained as they happen. They will only happen if we do the act. If the consequences turn out to have a negative effect on the felicific calculus then what we have already done is unjust. The utility principle thus provides no guide to action but a mere *ex post facto* criterion for the evaluation of past events. This is a severe limitation on its applicability and appears most unsatisfactory. If we are to seek to do justice we must have a means of finding out what would be just before we do the act, and not only afterwards.

A deontological approach holds that there are criteria for the evaluation of what is just that have no connection to the consequences. An appeal to absolute values would be one such approach that would, from the point of view of the sanctity of the human being, probably hold that torture is unjust no matter what the circumstances. It would *degrade* not only the victim but the torturer and the entire society through guilt by omission to prevent. However, this is exactly the very notion that the utilitarians rejected. Bentham thought that the two sovereign masters of man were pain and pleasure and therefore designed his felicific calculus around his fourteen pleasures and twelve pains. Why should we be limited to these?

Other criticisms of the use of the felicific calculus in this way would address the issue of the impracticability of its application. In order to assess whether a measure is just or not, a mammoth task of calculation would be involved, taking into account everyone affected and the impact on their pain and pleasure. If this were actually adopted then there would be little to do other than continuously to ask everyone what are the effects etc. It would rather be like the painting of the Forth Bridge which, once completed, has to start all over again.

Note that all the arguments so far rest on the assumption that pains and pleasures are measurable. They clearly are not. How can one person's stomach pain be measured against another's pleasure gained from playing the violin? Even though Mill developed certain rules of thumb to guide the calculation, these are not real substitutes for the actual ascertainment of the result.

As Rawls has observed, utilitarianism fails to account for the separateness of persons. It regards persons as mere receptacles for the pain-pleasure calculation.

Thus Rawls writes in *A Theory of Justice* that the utilitarians assume just that as rationality requires the making of small sacrifices for longer term gains so it also requires a trade-off of the welfare of some against the welfare of others. This idea of trading off the welfare of some against the welfare of others conflicts with our moral intuition.

Rawls' second objection to utilitarianism is that it seeks to define the right in terms of the good. Utilitarianism begins with an account of good and defines as right that which brings about the good. Rawls here draws attention to the fact that utilitarianism takes account of unjustly obtained happiness. According to Rawls:

> 'Justice is the first virtue of a social institution in the same way as truth is the first virtue of thought. And like truth, justice is uncompromising.'

What is good must therefore be defined in terms of what is right hence utilitarianism is unable to satisfy this requirement of justice. I would therefore reject the application of the principle of utility as the sole valid criterion for the evaluation of justice.

6.3 Criticisms of utilitarianism

We have considered several of the criticisms that have been made of utilitarianism within the context of its use as the sole evaluative method for assessing justice. These are not the only criticisms that have been made of this very influential theory and it is proposed to discuss a few of the other criticisms in this section.

1. As has been demonstrated, the modern theories, particularly Rawls', can be seen as attacks on utilitarianism and attempts to remove it from its pre-eminent position.
2. The criticism mostly made of total utility is that it ignores the lot of the average person. If, by increasing the total population by a large number the total utility can be slightly increased, society should follow a programme of encouraging production of children, even though on average everyone's lot will be less happy. For this reason average utility is preferable, but this, too, appears unpalatable. For a start, how does one measure utility or happiness or welfare? Is it psychological, is it based on want, satisfaction or what? How does an unemotional man's quiet happiness measure against the super-sensitive person's ecstasy? How does our enjoyment of a plate of fish and chips relate to the satisfaction of a country walk, or a symphony, or solving a chess puzzle?

    Another way of putting this is to consider the following example. Someone offers a man £1000 with a request that the man hand over his wife for sex. The man refuses. £100,000 is then offered. And then £1,000,000 (the offerer is exceedingly rich and desires the man's wife very greatly). The point is that it is not the *amount* that is at stake. The values just simply are not interchangeable, or commensurable.

3. But let us assume 'commensurability' is possible. Three problems still remain.
   a) Some preferences or wants must be disregarded for reasons of consistency: for example, preferences for anti-utilitarian arrangements, such as a ban on alcohol for religious reasons, or, more fundamentally, desires for a state run according to the rules of a religion, even if that did not match happiness or want maximisation.
   b) Utility would offend our intuitions of justice, because it would countenance unacceptable inequality. We should test all possible conceptions of justice against our own convictions of what is right in particular situations (see paragraph 4.4). When we apply utility to one or two factual situations, we can see that it runs counter to these convictions. To take the simple case of a slave-owning society. Should we keep slavery? Assume that we are measuring utility in terms of satisfaction of wants or preferences. If 20 per cent of the population are slaves, they would have to feel four times as strongly about becoming free as the 80 per cent slave owners feel about life without slaves. It is not implausible to assume that slavery will be kept. Thus, utility will frequently accept situations where the majority benefit from the poverty or oppression of a minority.
   c) A more complex example can lead us to a further point. Should discrimination against blacks be illegal? A decision on this question, on any utility scale, will take into account the views (wants, happiness, preferences) of those who see blacks as unequal, and therefore less deserving of respect. The very decision will therefore be based on an unequal view of blacks. And yet, utilitarians would claim to be egalitarian in that each person is counted as the same weight. The discrimination decision clearly does not give them that weight.
4. Hart's criticisms to the extent that they are not already mentioned can be stated briefly as follows.
   a) Hart believes that while justice is an aspect of morality it is yet different from other aspects of morality such as right and wrong, good and bad. He gives the example of a father who maltreats his child and states that it would not be correct to describe this as unjust. It is bad or wrong but not unjust. Hart therefore observes a distinction between a bad law and an unjust law. This is a distinction which utilitarianism cannot recognise.
   b) Hart further observes that there can often be a conflict between justice and other values such as freedom. The unfettered freedom to compete, if not regulated by law, is bound to lead to injustice because all persons are not competing on equal terms. Hart observes that law resolves this conflict by means of anti-monopoly laws, so restoring some semblance of justice at the expense of freedom.
5. Julius Stone argues that even if it is accepted that each person deserves their happiness so that their happiness is a good to them, how does it follow that the general happiness is a good to the aggregate of all? He also argues that hedonism

assumes that pleasure is found by being sought, but pleasure comes as an incidental to the seeking of other things rather than as the intended result of the search. He says that pain and pleasure are nothing but the names for an infinitely perishing series of feelings, hence hedonistic morality seeks to realise an idea which can in itself never be realised. It is striving towards an impossible future.

6. Rozen (1998) examined the most common criticism of the utilitarian principle as enunciated by Bentham. This is that it appears to advocate the sacrificing of a few for the sake of the many. Rozen starts by examining Bentham's view that his theory of the greatest good for the greatest number was necessary to overcome the 'subjective' element in all hitherto existing theories of morality. Rozen argues that this 'subjectivity' was more likely to lead to 'sacrifices' and that the objectivity of utilitarianism, being dependent on the actually existing motives, feelings, pains and pleasures of living creatures, was less likely to give rise to it. Rozen stated:

'Bentham did not dictate which pleasures and pains the legislator should employ to maximize happiness. He wanted to link his account of pleasure and pain more closely to what humans actually experienced ...' (at p135)

Rozen claims it was because of a misunderstanding of what Bentham meant by 'maximise' that his principle is so frequently misunderstood. The legislator did not detach herself from individual experiences and then engage in 'doing sums' with a totality of happiness – which idea might lead to the 'sacrifice of the few'. Instead:

'The task of the legislator is not to impose policies and laws on the community simply because he or she approves of or prefers them, but to determine principles and policies in which most members of society find happiness. The test of the selection is that they contribute to happiness, as a means to an end. Here the legislator presents reasons so that the selection might be questioned and debated.' (at p135)

7. Utilitarianism views the community as a mere aggregate of the individual members. This is seen in the discussions on the separateness of persons. It therefore places little emphasis, if any, on the relationship of community over the individual. Bentham's extreme individualism is thus open to objection. Maybe it is only in the context of his/her community that an individual is recognisable as such. Certainly, it seems to be only in this context that he/she can be spoken of as a moral being. Further, a person's identity is closely associated with his/her status as a member of the community so that his/her nationality, family background, education, career and so on, describe him/her as a person and must involve a reference to the context of the community in which he/she lives.

This is an important point because the idea of a community implies a high degree of co-operation and mutual trust among its members who share certain common standards. This means that justice is based not on an individual utilitarianism but on the existence of a community where the machinery of distributive justice is dependent upon the degree of mutual co-operation among its members.

8. By way of an evaluation, we can see why utilitarianism was attractive as a secular philosophy in that it was not tied to any religion. Further, in interpreting a pluralistic society it demonstrated the possibility of taking account of different views. It represents a common currency we can all agree on, that is, that we use it with reference to our own decision-making process with regard to our own lives. That is to say that there is much that is intuitively attractive about utilitarianism. The theory looks good but on analysis proves defective. There are too few ideas in utility to meet the demands of our more complex intuitions. It must therefore be treated with care. It is now necessary, however, to look at a modern, fairly widely accepted version of utilitarianism, that of Richard Posner's justification of the economic analysis of legal decision-making.

7

The Economic Analysis of Law

7.1 Introduction

Economics and the law is an excellent topic, particularly for those students who have studied economics before. The position is that economic thinking is coming more and more into the law. There is a very large group of followers of the 'Chicago school'. This line of thinking might loosely be termed the 'cost-benefit' analysis of legal decisions. It is a good topic to ponder when considering the arguments for and against utilitarianism, since it seems that this analysis is fundamentally a version of utilitarianism, whereby money is substituted for utility. The theory of Ronald Dworkin is presented here, since it runs counter to Posner's utilitarianism, but still regards the resources, an idea that includes but is wider than money, as the fundamental agent of distribution. Students should take each theory in turn and compare them.

We first need some definitions. In many ways, it is best to start with the idea of the market. One reason is that, for many liberal philosophers, the abstract principle of equality finds its best expression in justifying questions of distribution. And for the Chicago school, and economists of many other hues, the market constitutes the central concept of their discipline.

To understand the idea of market we have to appreciate the directly practical aim of much of the thinking in economics. Economics is thought of as a practical subject, directed to decision-making and in this respect is like law. As a result, and to a greater degree than law, it must take short cuts. It does this by making certain psychological assumptions about people which are, in many respects, patently false, but which are nevertheless sufficiently appealing to be workable.

An important assumption, for example, is that people are 'rational self-maximisers', that is, they always act so as to maximise the satisfaction of their preferences. We could call this the assumption of rationality. We can link this idea to that of the ideal market and say that people, ideally, will make decisions in the market place with the intention of satisfying the maximum number of their preferences.

Many of the working propositions of economics depend upon assumptions that exist in a strange category which is partly to do with ethical attractiveness (the autonomy of the market and its workability) and partly to do with untested empirical propositions (such as rational maximisation or the declining marginal utility of wealth). Models of economic activity, because they are models, cannot be directly tested against empirical data. On the other hand, economic models are intended to be workable, and so the major assumptions about human psychology and motivation have to have some empirical link with what is actually true.

We can trace the development of one or two of the ideas from preference utilitarianism. Economists can bypass, with relative ease, the problem of the measurement of what is of value in a person's life, by talking of the 'satisfaction of preferences'. People state what it is they want and are assumed to be the best judge of their own interests.

Using the idea of what people are prepared to give up, measured in currency, for what they want, interpersonal comparisons become possible. Further, making people the final judges about what is good for them, or what constitutes the best life for them, is a pleasantly liberal assumption which many people are inclined to accept.

The market place uses these two ideas. If a person is willing to forgo the satisfaction of one kind of preference in order to have another preference satisfied, we can measure what the value of the satisfaction he wants in a quantifiable way, namely, by the measure of what economists call 'lost opportunity'. Someone who trades his teddy bear for a book of poetry values the book of poetry more than the teddy bear. He has, in other words, increased his wealth. It does *not* follow, note, that he has increased his welfare.

Currency makes measurement of wealth easier. A and B swap a typewriter and a book. A would be willing to hand over the book and accept the typewriter, but B uses the typewriter and he feels that just having the book is not sufficient. He says that he will only trade for the book and £10. He calculates that he will have the book plus enough money to put a deposit down on a new typewriter. A accepts this, because he is willing to give up this sum of money as well as the book, because he wants the typewriter and he is willing to forgo both the book and the opportunity costs (say, a restaurant meal) in order to get it.

We achieve the commensurability of values here by just comparing the choices people are prepared to make. We see what they are prepared to give up in order to get something they value. Since generally people are willing to give up things for currency, and currency for things, the numerical count of the currency provides a guide to what is valued and by whom.

This is not to say we are free from difficulties but it is a start. Obvious difficulties must arise from the separation of value, what people actually want and believe is worthwhile in their lives, and the idea of having the means to acquire it, known by economists as 'wealth'. Speaking loosely, a person's wealth is his stock of possessions which have a market value.

There is a useful chapter in Fletcher's *Basic Concepts of Legal Thought* (1996) on the economic analysis of law. It is entitled 'Efficiency' and in it Fletcher traces the development of the 'law-and-economic' movement describing in a clear but sufficiently detailed form the ideas of the voluntary market, Pareto-efficiency, the Kaldor-Hicks criterion, Pigouvian-efficiency and the Coase theorem. Fletcher is particularly strong on the idea that any theoretical intervention by economics in legal argument cannot make sense except by explicitly adopting a stance on 'controversial moral and political principles of individual rights and group interests'.

7.2 Paretonism

The idea of the market is best expressed, in many writers' view, through the economists' concept of 'paretonism', named after the Italian economist Vilfredo Pareto. Paretonism has great ethical appeal because it derives its force from the importance of both personal well-being and personal autonomy. It provides a criterion, combining these two aspects, for measuring increases in welfare or utility. Situation B is 'pareto-superior' to situation A if in situation B at least one of the parties is better off and neither of the parties is worse off. A 'pareto-*optimal*' situation envisages the end of a possible chain of pareto-superior changes whereby there is no further situation where one party would be better off without the other being worse off.

Paretonism provides a measure for marginal increases in utility or welfare. No one is worse off and at least one is better off. According to the theory that the greatest number should be better off, the criterion must measure some increases in utility. It does that at the same time as nodding in the direction of personal autonomy. Two people enter the market and leave with at least one of them better off and neither of them worse off. The appeal of paretonism is that the market appears to achieve a nice balance between overall utility and personal autonomy.

Of course, in the real world things are very different. But the ideal market does have a use. What, then, is the correct characterisation of that ideal? Generally, economists define a perfect market in the following way. A perfect market transaction is one where the parties bargain to mutual advantage, measured against the choices of the 'rational maximiser', or they bargain, at least, to the advantage of one and with no disadvantage to the other; the market is not 'distorted' by, for example, the existence of a monopoly; the parties have 'perfect knowledge'; and there are no 'transaction costs'.

Given this widely accepted definition, it is plain to see that the problem with paretonism is that in the real world, because of various market imperfections, pareto-superior situations occur with relative infrequency, the more usual situation being that one party is left worse off after a transaction. Because of this fact about real markets, there will be a large number of pareto-optimal situations in the real world, because mostly no further market move can be made without some party becoming worse off. In short, in the real world, there will often be some loser, maybe a third party, in any market transaction.

7.3 The Kaldor-Hicks criterion

But the idea of paretonism, with its inborn ethical attractions, is not used by the Chicago school economic lawyers. They use an alternative criterion of *wealth* maximisation, as opposed to welfare maximisation which attempts to overcome the practical difficulties in real markets. Such a criterion was first proposed by Kaldor and Hicks and states that a decision, or policy, is wealth-maximising if the amount of wealth created by the decision is enough to compensate those who are left with less wealth after the decision. However, there is no requirement that those who lose wealth in the process should be compensated.

The criterion is a formal description of what we understand as cost-benefit or cost-effective analysis. A factory moves to another town to avail itself of the cheaper labour and land prices. The town it moves from suffers financial loss but the factory and businesses in the new town gain enough financially from the move for it to be possible, in principle, to compensate those who lost out in the move. The move is a cost-effective move.

The idea is an important one because it places emphasis on efficiency. It directs our attention very precisely to the fact that more wealth can be created by certain sorts of decisions even although those decisions place some people at a disadvantage. It is an important idea also because it is workable. That must be an argument in its favour. If we accept that it is, at least, one factor in favour of a decision that it produces more wealth, the cost-effective criterion is helpful. It is not a criterion which says what, ultimately, should be done. It just tells us what the cost-effective move is.

The criterion appears to assume that increases in wealth overall will bring about increases in welfare. Wealth replaces welfare on the assumption that wealth has the potential for increasing welfare although, of course, not necessarily the welfare of those who lose out in the wealth created by the Kaldor-Hicks move.

7.4 The Coase theorem

We need one more definition to understand the Chicago school. This is the 'Coase theorem', very commonly used by lawyer economists, and named after an economist from Chicago. The idea is that whatever legal rights the parties have before entering a market they will bargain for the most economically efficient result. (In the perfect market, remember, they are 'rational maximisers'.) For example, A lives close to B's glue factory. Let us say that, according to the law of nuisance, B has the legal right to pollute the air. The theorem states that in the perfect market, independently of the initial assignment of legal rights, A and B will bargain to produce the most efficient result. A, if he is willing to forgo the lost opportunities, will pay B to reduce the pollution by the amount which will enable B to reduce the pollution and still make a profit. With a different assignment of initial rights, whereby B is entitled to pollute only to the extent to which he pays compensation to A, B will reduce his pollution to the extent to which his payment to A does not prevent him from making a profit. Either assignment of legal rights, in other words, does not affect the overall efficiency of the outcome.

This theorem has fundamental importance for decision-making in the real world where, of course, markets are imperfect. In particular, the lawyer economists focus on the imperfection of what they call 'transaction costs'. In the pollution case, for example, there will, in all probability, be many people in A's position and the costs of the negotiations leading to the separate bargains between these people and B and the costs of the creation of the contracts will be large. The initial assignment of the legal rights under the law of nuisance, in the real world of transaction costs, will affect the efficient outcome of bargaining because in many cases, as one can easily imagine, people in the same position as A will be deterred by such costs from even beginning to negotiate.

A famous judicial formulation of an economic test for working out liability, and one which has been seen by Posner and others as confirming the incidence of judicial decision-making in economic terms, was that by the United States judge Learned Hand. He devised a test of 'reasonableness' to govern the distribution of liability in tort cases. It is sometimes known as the 'least cost avoider' test. A litigant had acted 'unreasonably' when he had done something which caused loss to another and which would have cost less for him to avoid than it would have cost the victim to avoid. (See *United States* v *Carroll Towing Co*) Judge Learned Hand said that the defendant was negligent if the loss caused by the accident in question, multiplied by the probability of the accident's occurring, exceeded the burden of the precautions that the defendant might have taken to avert it.

What is striking about the concept is its application to judicial decisions. We do not find it particularly difficult to see the sense in market intervention by the legislature to reduce unnecessary expenses. But we may feel that courts should deal with altogether different sorts of decisions. We can attack it from the point of view that economic efficiency is one particular form of community goal and has nothing to do with litigants' rights to decisions based on the integrity of the law. The arguments are essentially those attacking what we could call 'undistributive' utilitarianism.

So, by using the idea of opportunity costs measured by units of currency the theory of wealth-maximisation purports to resolve, in a practical way, the problems of incommensurability of welfare. But since wealth itself can be merely instrumental to welfare, and that must be 'an empirical question', the maximisation of wealth by the courts must be a false target. It may be a justifiable way of aiming towards welfare in the real world, although it appears to assume that the legislature will then redistribute court-created wealth to produce welfare. But, in any case, if a court has the choice between the false target, wealth, and utility, what on earth could the reason be for choosing wealth over utility?

7.5 Dworkin's equality of resources

Dworkin agrees with the Chicago school to the extent of thinking that it is resources, in the form of wealth, among other things, which govern fair dealings between people. His theory is idealistic. He posits a 'principle of correction' by which he means that imperfect decisions may be 'corrected' so as to bring them closer to the ideal. That principle must never compromise a person's freedom, however. In the real world, the idea, that of people having a right to 'equality of resources', albeit in a highly qualified sense, surfaces in the application of the law of tort.

Resources and freedom

The first general insight is this: resources are a major source of freedom. They are not the only one, but certainly a major one. Generally speaking, we are more free the more resources we have. But note the following, at least for the real world. We have more resources if we are talented and fewer resources if we are handicapped. In other words, the more talented and the less handicapped you are the more freedom you have.

Let us refine the idea of freedom. Is it an important idea? Yes, because if you are free to develop and shape your life in accordance with your own convictions and ambitions you live a better life. In fact, it may be that it does not make much sense to say that you can live a life, properly called *your* life, that has been shaped for you by, as it were, external forces.

There seems to be, then, a distinction, in the real world between those aspects of you which are part of your capacity to form ideas and convictions about how you would like to live your life, and those aspects which are a help or hindrance to living that life. The aspects will include access to physical resources as well as talents and handicaps.

Let us now apply the principle, absolutely fundamental to Dworkin, that people are equal as human beings. We do not distinguish between people on any basis other than our concern for their humanity. Are talented or handicapped or rich or poor people any better or worse *as human beings*? Are people of different castes, or of different coloured skins, or of different sex or of different heights better or worse because of these attributes? If we endorse the principle that we must treat people as equals, clearly the answer is no.

Let us now turn to the twin ideas of equality and freedom. If the government must treat its citizens as equals, what should it do in the absolutely ideal world? Dworkin says that it should, crudely, make them equal in their freedoms, as far as that is possible. Treating a person as an equal means treating him in such a way as to give him maximum freedom to develop his life in accordance with his convictions. But it must follow that the freedom of each person is to be limited to the extent that that person's exercise of freedom reduces the amount of freedom of another. That *must* follow from Dworkin's initial abstract injunction that people be treated as equals (which you might, or might not, be inclined to accept).

Here we should connect freedom with the question of distribution of resources. No person or group of persons should be granted disproportionate freedom in the use of resources, says Dworkin, because the effect would be to *take away* freedom in the use of those same resources from other persons. At first sight, then, any justification for allowing unequal use of resources compromises equality.

Handicaps

But equality also requires us to make up for the potential freedoms lost by a handicapped person. Think about it. If he is as much a *person* as someone who has average potential, he loses out. Treating him equally as a person must mean distributing to him sufficient resources to bring him, as nearly as possible, to the level of potential freedom of the average person.

Talents

Further, someone who is talented has potentially more freedom. He can move through the real world more easily and will find it easier to acquire more resources, say, by the skilful use of the resources he already has. But if it is true that he is just as much a person as a handicapped or averagely competent person, then he gains, just by virtue of his talent, an unequal share of resources. That means that when he uses his talents (because, of course, he might choose not to) the freedoms gained which are attributable to talent alone (remember, we are in the absolutely ideal world) represent an unequal share of the total freedoms available.

Equality and freedom

Dworkin's key idea here is that equality demands that each person's freedoms, measured over his life, should be quantified against what their having that freedom costs other people in relation to *their* freedoms. How, though, can we make real sense of this measurement of relative freedoms? Dworkin suggests that the idea of the economic market provides an answer in the idea of relative cost. We distribute freedoms so that no person 'envies' (in the economic sense in which we assume that each person wishes to maximise the freedoms open to him) any other person's freedom. And we then allow bargaining to occur through the market place in order to reflect the different choices that people make over their lifetimes.

The presuppositions of the market

A problem arises in the setting up of the circumstances of bargaining. This is that the idea of the market presupposes the existence of a number of things, such as – the most obvious one – *people* to bargain. To get the idea of the cost of each person's life to other people, the concept of 'a market' is not in itself enough. We have to specify the conditions under which market transactions are properly conducted.

What does this mean? It means that the idea of a person is 'prior' to the market and the market does not allocate rights but is itself determined by them. What is important to the person must be specified in the conditions (the baseline) under which the market operates (remember that we are talking about the absolutely ideal world). What is important to the person? One thing is personal security. You cannot enter the market if you are prevented by physical coercion. Further, the market must consistently obey the injunction that people should be treated as equals. This means that market transactions that, for example, resulted in a *racially prejudiced* distribution, would be inconsistent with the baseline. And further, if the market cannot ensure bargaining that is consistent with that baseline because of technical reasons ('externalities' in economists' terms) then it must be corrected so as to produce a result consistent with equality that would have come about but for the technical difficulties (remember the Coase theorem).

The nature of 'resources'

These include wealth, namely, all those tangible and intangible assets with which a person may trade. But they also include talents, so, conversely, we must say that handicaps represent a lack of resources. This is not such a difficult or strange idea. Our talents are part of our potential freedoms, as much as are our bank balances. So, we make people equal in resources, with the appropriate adjustments in relation to handicaps (by giving handicapped people what they would have obtained had they not been handicapped) and talents (by taking from talented people all they acquired solely through talent). We then arrange the market so that it works in accordance with the principle of equality which includes the principle that the market transactions assume maximum freedom.

What are advantages of this – obviously ideal – way of looking at things? Dworkin intends there to be two main ones. First, the theory combines the insights of socialism, that men are inherently human beings, independent of their particular circumstances, with the insights of a popularly understood libertarianism, that men are best when they are free to make their own lives according to their own lights. It achieves this without falling into the obvious pitfalls of both socialism and libertarianism, namely, that socialism supports an unwarranted restriction of freedoms, a 'levelling downwards', and libertarianism supports the unjustifiable promotion of the liberty of a select few.

The second insight is that it provides an ethical basis for market mechanisms, and suggests ways in which the market should be corrected in accordance with that ethical basis.

The application to the law of tort

If we can assume rough equality of resources, in those areas of accident involving damage to property, equality of resources is the engine to providing the best resolution to hard cases in tort, by awarding damages to the party whose equilibrium of resources under a just distribution has been upset by his neighbour. Dworkin says that 'we do have sufficient general knowledge ... to make the principle of comparative financial harm workable enough in most cases'. The practical elaboration may require legislation (of the market-mimicking, Coasian sort) but Dworkin thinks that his thesis explains such ideas as reasonableness, contributory negligence and 'the other baggage of the law of tort'.

The intuitive idea is this. The torts of nuisance and negligence limit the impact of inequality when people's projects – their exercise of autonomy – intersect. Here we can see a more appealing interpretation of the Learned Hand formula. If you are required by the courts to pay damages on the least cost avoider test, it is not that you are being made to fulfil a utilitarian duty towards the whole community, but that you are, so to speak, being made to repair the cost to your neighbour's equality of resources. You are, in accordance with a sensible requirement to treat your neighbour as an equal, being made to restore his resource equilibrium.

7.6 In defence of the economic analysis of law

Bix (1999) provides a good account of both the objections to economic analysis and the defence that can be offered for them. He suggests that there is much of value in the economic analysis of law and notes for example the following advantages of such analysis:

> 'First, there are legal questions that turn (or should turn) on purely economic matters. For example, for the purposes of competition law, whether a particular kind of vertical or horizontal integration of companies in the long term, supports, hinders or has no effect upon competition. Secondly, economic analysis has often served to sharpen the existing somewhat fuzzy legal thinking in various areas. For some, economic analysis captures in quantitative terms what had only been vaguely described by long-standing common law

concepts like "reasonable care", "negligence" and "proximate cause". Also, economic analysis occasionally highlights concerns that had gotten lost when the questions were posed in traditional ways eg in terms of "fairness" and "justice". For example, in considering the rules of bankruptcy/insolvency law, the way legal rules are developed will affect not only the creditors' rights as against the debtor (the traditional focus for analysis), but also the extent to which individual creditors have incentives to act in ways which will shrink the total amount of assets available, thus working against the interests of the creditors as a group, and perhaps against the social interest as well.

Thirdly, even if one believes that efficiency/wealth maximization is at best one value among many (or an imperfect approximation of one such value), one would still want to know what effects a current legal rule or practice, or a proposed change to that rule or practice, has on efficiency/wealth maximization. At the least, there are occasions when an accurate (and subtle) delineation of the costs of the alternative rules or actions will influence the eventual (moral) choice between them. Fourthly, the method of analysis that law and economics promotes reminds us of long-term effects we might not otherwise have considered. A standard example is the landlord who wants to evict the poor, starving tenant for non-payment of rent. While our sympathies may go immediately to the tenant we should consider the long-term consequences of a rule where the landlord could not evict in such circumstances. What would likely ensue is that landlords would either become reluctant to lease apartments to those who are less well off, or that higher rents would be charged to everyone, to compensate for losses to non-paying tenants who can't be evicted.' (at pp199–200)

8

Early Legal Positivism: the Command Theory

8.1 What is positivism?

8.2 Bentham

8.3 John Austin

8.4 Evaluation of the command theory

8.1 What is positivism?

Legal positivism declares that morality is irrelevant to the identification of what is valid law. Hart provides a useful definition of legal positivism on p181 of his *The Concept of Law*:

> 'Here we shall take legal positivism to mean the simple contention that it is in no sense a necessary truth that laws reproduce or satisfy certain demands of morality, though in fact they have often done so.'

The most famous positivists are Bentham, Austin, Kelsen and Hart, although there are many others. It is important that you don't get misled by approaching just one of these theorists. Each theory has its own special insights. In particular, there is a problem with how to approach both Bentham and Austin. It is generally accepted that Bentham's theory is much more subtle than Austin's. On the other hand, Austin's is vastly more accessible. However, the important point is that Bentham and Austin are agreed on several things. They are both positivists and both thought that the key to law lay in the idea of the command of a sovereign. Readers should concentrate on the command theory, which is common to both authors' theories.

Long before legal positivism, Aristotle and Aquinas, to name only the most distinguished, asked practical questions and supplied answers about the way we should view law. But the legal positivists were unclear about the matter. There is a distinct ambiguity present in Bentham which continues through other thinkers to Hart. That ambiguity hovers between the following two strands of thought.

First, there is a sense in which some legal positivists intended simply to describe what law is. Law is simply a complex of social facts. That may have been the opinion of Jeremy Bentham. It certainly was that of John Austin, his disciple, and, albeit in a highly qualified sense, that of the German legal philosopher Hans Kelsen. Hart's brilliant work *The Concept of Law* certainly begins in that way, with its well-known affirmation in the Preface that, among other aims, he intends a 'descriptive sociology' of the law.

That is one strand of legal positivism. It is this idea of law that would lie behind, say, a comparative account of repressive legal systems. Such an account can, of course, serve practical purposes, such as those of historians, or dictators, or anthropologists in search of differences between legal systems.

The other strand is practical in a more obvious and appealing sense. It is the idea that positivism is a *liberal* doctrine. It is not a coincidence that the growth of positivism paralleled the growth of liberalism in the early nineteenth century. In what way was it liberal? The positivists emphasised the point in different ways. Essentially it is that the law must be identifiable by means of clearly identifiable and public criteria to enable the citizen to keep distinct the demands of his conscience and the demands of the state. Hart spoke for this strand of positivism when he said in *The Concept of Law*:

> 'What surely is most needed in order to make men clear sighted in confronting the official abuse of power, is that they should preserve the sense that the certification of something as legally valid is not conclusive of the question of obedience, and that, however great the aura of majesty or authority which the official system may have, its demands must in the end be submitted to a moral scrutiny.'

The idea is explicit in Bentham's distinction between 'expository' and 'censorial' jurisprudence, Austin's claim 'The existence of law is one thing; its merit or demerit is another', and Kelsen's promotion of law as 'science' to counteract tyranny.

Note, too, that the chief modern opponent of legal positivism, Ronald Dworkin, has a theory of law that is a liberal theory, too. This theory is imbued with the liberal idea that the state must protect personal autonomy. But the theory allows the idea of 'the right to be treated with equal concern and respect' to be debated, in the form of different and controversial conceptions of that idea, as a matter of *law*. It is at this point, obviously, that Dworkin's theory parts company with positivism. But notice that he nevertheless insists upon the requirement of what he calls the 'articulate consistency' of public officials (see his *Taking Rights Seriously* (1978) p162). This is in part what he means by decisions being made in accordance with principle. And to this extent, his theory shares the public criterion requirement of the positivists. (See Chapters 10 and 22.)

Whether legal positivism 'works' depends on the type of community in which it has sufficiently widespread acceptance. Its strong point is its declaration of the limits of state requirements. It tells us where the law 'stops' and 'ideology' starts. So, in a culture where there is little homogeneity of political opinion and where there are irreconcilable ideological or fundamentalist conflicts of view, legal positivism will be attractive because of its liberalism. According to positivism, since there can be little controversy about what the state requires, ideology cannot be covertly introduced under the guise of law (see the German idea of 'real' law embodying the idea of the will of the German peoples in von Savigny's legal theory in Chapter 15). In parts of continental Europe, and in Latin America, this feature of positivism is thought to be its virtue.

But, at least in the UK, in one straightforward and practical sense, legal positivism, as defined here, is valid. Even without the training of a lawyer, we can easily think of examples of laws where our ability to identify a rule as a rule of law does not, at first blush, require us to make a moral judgment.

Take as an example a homosexual act between two twenty-year-old consenting men in private. Such an act constitutes a criminal offence. There is no doubt that if it complies with the description of the prohibited act in the English Sexual Offences Act 1956, it is legally prohibited. No reason other than *being in accordance* with the statute is necessary in order for us to say that these acts are unlawful. Yet there are many (perhaps you are one) who think that the existence of those provisions is morally wrong because they legally prohibit what ought not to be prohibited. But these critics will nevertheless usually agree these rules have a status of law.

Another example. Before the Sexual Offences Act 1967 repealed the English statutory provision which made sexual acts between men punishable by 14 years in prison, there were those who, while affirming the validity of the law, thought also that the law was morally wrong. In fact, a little reflection should make us realize that it is because of this perceived distinction between law and morality that it makes sense to campaign to bring about *change* in the law. The idea of being able to change the law so as to make its provisions morally acceptable was, in the history of legal positivism, thought to be one of its major virtues.

8.2 Bentham

The definition of law

Reading the expository jurisprudence of Jeremy Bentham gives all the thrills of perusing a statutory instrument. Hart, in his understated style, says that he lacks the technical expertise to unravel much of Bentham's work. Yet it is the invented language ('international law' is his invention, but there are many others) and seemingly pedantic definitions in Bentham's work that make his writing so informative. It is fair to say that he anticipated many of the insights of later jurists. However, much of his expository work, aimed at defining the nature of law, was unpublished and is currently being sifted through for publication. The manuscripts were discovered at University College London, where Austin, the first purveyor of jurisprudence to law undergraduates, lectured. Austin's theory of law is a simplified version of Bentham's, perhaps because his lectures were directed at first year students. Thus, the teacher, Bentham, is often tarred with the same brush as the disciple, Austin.

Interestingly for law students, Austin's tradition has left a legacy that cannot be ignored. Much of our constitutional theory stems from Austinian perceptions. We will, however, need to examine Bentham first, since his insights are illuminating and more subtle than Austin's. Following the empirical tradition, he rejected the notion of natural law (see Chapter 11) and any idea of an 'internal' moral quality of law. When addressing the natural law fathers of the French Revolution, he described its written constitution as nonsense on stilts and bawling on paper. We shall analyse some of his definitions to give a little introduction into his expository theory as well as to arm the student with some knowledge that might help him cope with Bentham.

In his *Of Laws in General* Bentham seeks by demarcation to distinguish law from other activities. His method relies on the linguistic associations of the word law, while appreciating that language can be misleading. Bentham has a little in common with the natural law tradition of thinkers such as Aquinas. Aquinas' concept of law is any rule or measure of action in virtue of which one is led to perform certain actions and refrain from the performance of others. This is, of course, assuming that it accords with the eternal law, the will of God. Thus, laws are not only the prescriptions of those who are employed specifically for legal purposes, but any prescription that accords with God's sovereign will.

Bentham substitutes the will of the sovereign for the Divine will. The form that law is defined to take has the following elements.

Law is:

1. an assemblage of signs;
2. expressive of subjective will;
3. that which is directly or indirectly attributable to the sovereign in one of the following three ways;
   a) the author of the law is the sovereign himself;
   b) the sovereign has allowed a previous sovereign's law to continue in existence; and
   c) the law has been made by a person on behalf of the sovereign who is authorised to so do;
4. that which relates to conduct in a given situation;
5. that which is directed to persons who are supposed to be subject to the sovereign's power.

This sort of definition is typical of Bentham. The student should acquaint herself with Bentham's writing. In some ways it is amusing, because he seems to go to such pains to be exact. But shouldn't we all be exact? He attempts to bring the same precision to legal philosophy as a statutory draftsman attempts to bring to writing a statute. (And you will discover it is a quality of British philosophers, not shared to the same degree by their counterparts on the Continent.) It is absolutely impossible to accuse Bentham of waffle. You can accuse him of many other things, but not waffle!

It is important at this point to mention that Bentham's concept of a sovereign does not carry with it any 'natural law baggage'. It is simply the people or person to whom a political community are supposed to be in disposition to obey. This itself requires further elucidation!

Bentham talks of a political community as being one in which the members are supposed to be in the habit of obedience to a person or body of persons of known and certain description. A community is a fictitious body composed of individual persons who are considered to be its members.

Thus, to quote Bentham, we can use the word sovereignty in two different senses: 'at one time in its strict and proper sense; at another in its popular and improper sense ... Till men are sufficiently aware of the ambiguity of words, political discussions may be carried out without profit and without end'. To Bentham, therefore, the term does not carry with it any associations with concepts such as 'king by divine right' or even 'personal supremacy'. Nor is it a factual statement that the sovereign is the person who is habitually obeyed. It is the habit of obedience together with the feeling of collective identity that earmarks a political community. With Bentham's careful expression we should not ignore the words 'supposed' and 'disposition'.

The sovereign is the person whom, it is presumed, a society has the inclination to obey. The presumptive or suppositive element of the definition emphasises that sovereignty is not quite a matter of *fact*, you will notice (and this serves to distinguish Bentham from Austin). The sovereign is supposed to be the person to whom people have a disposition to obey, rather than who, in fact, is habitually obeyed. The distinction is a fine, but important one. If one is disposed to do something, it is not just the doing of the action, but the willing inclination to do it that must be appreciated. The supposition is that society, which Bentham says is a fictional body, is disposed to obey the sovereign. Or one might say that it is supposed that a fictive will deems that the ascertainable sovereign should be obeyed.

The eight different aspects of law

Bentham is useful to the student at least insofar as he points out several material focuses for enquiry into the nature of law.

1. *Source*. As has already been mentioned, the source of law, ultimately, is a sovereign. However, Bentham is aware that power is delegated in the name of the sovereign and exercised in the sovereign's name by subsidiary law-makers.
2. *Subjects*. Obviously, a law applies either to a person, or, in the case of, for example, English property law, to a thing.
3. *Objects*. The object of a law is the act, in the appropriate circumstances, which it seeks to regulate.
4. *Extent*. Obviously, a law must specify how widely it is to be applied, as well as to whom. The extent of the criminal law is its applicability to all but the legally immune, for example.

5. *Aspects.* Laws may take various forms such as commanding, permitting etc, in order to achieve a given purpose.

6. *Force.* Laws usually rely on motives, in the form of sanctions or rewards, to give force to them. Additional laws may be required to bring these motives into play, which Bentham terms 'corroborative appendages'.

7. *Expression.* There is a variety of ways in which laws can be expressed. We only need to think of the variety of English law forms.

8. *'Remedial appendages'.* If a principal law outlaws an act, a corroborative law directs someone to punish that act. But there still might need to be a requirement for another law to remedy the effect of that act. For example, the law says that an employee must be paid in accordance with his contract and it will enforce that contract if he is not so paid. This is the principal law and the motive for obeying it is the threat that payment will be forced by the law. However, someone has to judge whether the employer has not paid his employee and if so, that person must order payment. That person might be a judge, but he has to be empowered by law to perform this. Therefore, a corroborative law directs the judge to judge and enforce. However, imagine that payment has not been made for a period of time. In such a case, the value of the money owed under the contract to the employer might have decreased in real terms. There should then be the remedial effect of interest payments, ordered by a Supreme Court master. This would be an example of a remedial appendage.

The source of law

Bentham employs the concept of sovereign will to distinguish legal mandates from illegal ones such as those of a mafia boss. The unifying feature that lies behind all laws is, for him, that they accord with the will of the sovereign. However, not all laws emanate from the sovereign. Bentham accounts for this as follows. He regards all commands that accord with the will of the sovereign as legal mandates. Thus, a parent's order to a child, an employer's order to a servant, a magisterial, military or judicial order, are all legal mandates, providing they accord with the will of the sovereign. Bentham concedes that we are not accustomed to viewing such things as acts of legislation.

There is appeal in this idea. The fact that, by convention, lawyers look to limited sources and enforce and recognise only those sources does not mean that law does not have a force outside them. Bentham succeeds in emphasising that law is enforced and reiterated outside the purely formal context of legal practice.

The problem with such a wide definition is that the responsibility for making law is spread, while the authority for law stems from the sovereign. How, then, do we relate the source of a law to the authority that gives it its legal character? Bentham says that we have to consider how *any* person can have a mandate attributed to him. First, he says, a person decides, himself, that something is to be done, making the mandate his by conception. Secondly, someone else thinks something should be done and a person adopts that other person's thought, so that the mandate is his by adoption. This process is clearly more complex than the former one, and since the bulk of law-making in modern systems is not directly the conception of the sovereign, Bentham investigates it further.

If we imagine a simple idea of King Rex and his two advisers, his wife and his Prime Minister. Rex is not intelligent, but his wife suggests ideas for laws to him, which he subsequently declares to be his own. The mandate has already been conceived, but he endorses it and it becomes his, in Bentham's terms, by 'susception'. Rex is not greatly interested in the business of government, so he declares that everyone should do whatever the Prime Minister tells them to do until further notice. Thus, he *pre-adopts* the mandates that the Prime Minister is going to make in the future. He has thus invested in the Prime Minister a power to make law in his own right, and this is a power of 'imperation'.

Susception may equally apply to the adoption by a new monarch of the laws of his predecessor and pre-adoption to the mandates of all those who are authorised to issue mandates on behalf of the sovereign.

An interesting view of Bentham is that if a person issues a mandate and has no authority to do so, it is illegal and the issuing of it is an offence. Hart criticises Bentham for failing to take into account the concept of invalid, but not illegal, mandates. This appears a valid enough criticism, but note how it stems from the (reasonable and liberal) attitude that the Englishman is born free and may do anything that he is not prevented from doing. It is quite possible that Bentham, himself very conservative in many ways, did not conceive of things in this way. Bentham clearly envisages that the sovereign will is seamless: 'Take any mandate whatsoever, either it is of the number of those which he allows or it is not; there is no medium: if it is, it is his; by adoption at least, if not by original conception: if not, it is illegal, and the issuing of it is an offence.' Thus, an invalid command is one that is permitted to be made, but which the lawyer is not permitted to enforce or act upon. This quotation serves to emphasise the curious nature of Bentham's view, that the sovereign needs to know all mandates that are issued, and either permits them or prevents them.

The logic of the law

It is clear in Bentham's work that expressions of will can be imperative, such as commands or prohibitions which require adherence, or permissive, such as a non-command or non-prohibition, which allows action. Laws can therefore be expressed in any of these ways, but only as logical combinations of these expressions. Thus, expressions of legal will can have a variety of effects. But it is also clear that Bentham's is an imperative, a 'command', theory. How, then, can the law can be permissive?

We should remember that a legal permission is one that is guaranteed by the sovereign and, as such, may be equally expressed as a prohibition against people forcing someone to do what he does not legally need to do or a command to people to allow him to do what he legally can do. Thus, with respect to a court, if a person has a legal permission to act in a certain way this has the effect of prohibiting it from enforcing any previous law that would interfere with this action. With respect to other subjects of the law, if a person is given legal permission to graze his sheep on the common, it might equally be expressed as, let no man stop him!

The different parts of law

Although all law may be ultimately attributed to a sovereign, as we have seen, not all law-making is that of the sovereign. Bentham thus explains how such power is shared. A legislator may make a law requiring that an act be done or be abstained from. This element is the 'directive' element of law. Normally this will be accompanied by the motive for obeying. This is the 'predictive' part. However, it is unlikely that the legislator can verify that the law has been broken and order that the particular law-breaker be punished. This general law is the primary law. In order that breaches of law be verified and punished the legislator will have issued a law directing that someone such as a judge should do so. This is termed a 'subsidiary' law.

Equally, the judge might need to have the help of the police for verification, or the prison service for punishment, thereby requiring further subsidiary laws. These are 'remote laws' as distinct from more 'proximate' laws. In fact, these 'remote' laws are themselves backed with even more 'remote' subsidiary laws such as those regulating the call and conduct of witnesses, and so on, to contribute their part to the aim of the principal law.

With all these laws flying about it is not surprising that Bentham's view of laws is a complex one. However, he does have an idea of a 'complete' law. A complete law is the sum of all the subsidiary and principal laws needed to give complete meaning to a more general principle. Bentham's example is the general prohibition against meddling with another's property. This is characterised as follows: (1) a prohibition against occupying property, which is imperative; and (2) a permission for anyone who has good title to that property, allowing her to occupy it. However, this simple concept requires that there be procedures for the transfer of property, form for valid title and all the verifications, mandates and penalties in order to achieve the enforcement of this complete law. Bentham concedes that such laws are not written down in this complete form.

Bentham said that the title-holder of land in English law has two different types of power. He has the legal permission to use his land, which others may not without his permission. This power to do that which other people may not is, he said, a power of 'contrectation'. Such powers stem primarily from permissive laws. However, the title-holder may also rent his land to another, who, if he agrees, must accept duties and obligations. This power to confer on others duties and obligations is, as we have already mentioned, a power of 'imperation'.

The motives for compliance with law

Remember that Bentham is a legal positivist and thought morality irrelevant to the identification of law. Therefore, the reason people obey laws is that there are some motives provided *by the law* that encourage the subject to obey. In Bentham's psychology these are primarily the coercion of punishment and the allurement of reward. He admits that such motives may be provided by politics, religion or morality, although normally the legal system relies on rewards and punishments of its own creation.

'Praemary' or 'invitative' laws rely on the motive of reward, but as Bentham observes these are not often used. It is a lot easier and more economical for the legal system to inflict pain and more likely to have the desired effect, in his view. As such 'sanctional' or 'comminative' laws are far more popular.

The critical problem with this view of the force of law is that, as Summers remarks, there are other educative, supervisory and controlling factors that may be applied to law. We saw earlier that such motives are not necessarily attached to particular laws that permit or prohibit a particular act and thus there may be a mandate without an obvious sanction being attached. For example, an agent may have a power of imperation to impose obligations on another under a contract, but the power to sanction a breach of contract may lie with another body, such as a court. Power, including the power to sanction, is, in Bentham's model, frequently broken into shares. One reason for this is that frequently a law is directed at someone; for example, do not steal, but it can hardly be expected that the mandate should say also if you do steal, punish yourself. Likewise, with a contract, although the parties are permitted to mandate each other to do certain things, both are under the broader obligation of not breaking the legal obligations the other party has put on them, so that neither can be expected to punish himself at the mandate of the other, although there might be penalty clauses in the contract.

The idea of sovereignty

In Bentham's words: 'Now by a sovereign I mean any person or assemblage of persons to whose will a whole political community are (no matter on what account) supposed to be in disposition to pay obedience: and that in preference to the will of any other person.'

Bentham's concept of sovereignty is not one that is greatly elaborated by him. But it is important to give it some consideration here, since it is often dismissed as being the same as Austin's concept of sovereignty and as such dismissed as simplistic.

The sovereign is simply the ultimate authority in a legal jurisdiction. Bentham does not necessarily mean a single undivided and powerful entity. But he also does not employ the common usage that tends to view the concept of sovereignty as the body that exercises ultimate governmental power in a given jurisdiction. Bentham allows that powers may be separated infinitely and distributed through the law to numerous persons or bodies. Each would be sovereign in exercise of a given power, so long as they are the highest and only power in their particular branch of government.

If we look at the United Kingdom constitution, it seems reasonable to say that the Crown, Parliament, courts (in matters of common and European law), the European institutions and electorate all comprise the sovereign, for each in its own role in government has considerable legal powers. Parliament can no more create common law than the courts make a statute, nor can the government elect itself or the electorate make European law. Thus, with respect to Bentham's definition of sovereignty, the sovereign will is the will of this corporate venture, which involves much of the community. These bodies are sovereign because with respect to their particular branches of power it is *supposed* that society is in disposition to obey them.

Bentham does not require that the sovereign be determinate and does not stipulate that it cannot have a superior allegiance. His definition is not based on the empirical fact that people are in the habit of obedience to the sovereign, but on the supposition, for whatever reason, that society is disposed to obey one person or body of persons in preference to any other. Bentham's sovereign may bind himself in law and may be bound by predecessors.

Olivecrona says that Bentham ignores the fact that the concept of will is a fiction. Certainly, if Bentham allows for a divisible sovereign, how can two people have one will? Or indeed, does Parliament have a will? Parliament's will is seldom the will of all, but instead consists in the idea that a collection of people can speak as one. That Bentham would think this way is evident from the fact that he views a community as a fiction, a legal personality as a fiction. Therefore, how is a sovereign to be real, especially since it is merely something that is to be identified by its supposed authority? It may be, therefore, that Bentham is fully aware that the sovereign will is not an empirical fact in the same way as he is aware that a political community is a fiction. He can get around it by declaring that the sovereign will is only a fiction if we suppose there to be a mind and body possessed by the sovereign. There is no *nonsense*, no fiction, in the idea of Parliamentary intention, something to which lawyers refer every day of their working lives, just that it is a portmanteau word calling for a particular kind of argument.

Whether or not this is so, there is one considerable problem that Bentham avoids and which creates a trap for Austin. Austin's idea of legal obligation rests on the simple fact of power: there is a sovereign power *in fact*, that sovereign has commanded *in fact*, and that means that there is a likelihood of a sanction *in fact*. Therefore, the subject *ought* to obey the command. This looks like deriving an 'ought' from an 'is', as Kelsen was concerned to point out.

In contrast to Austin, Bentham does not say this. He defines the sovereign as the person whom 'the whole' of the political community are *supposed* to be in a disposition to obey. Now, the emphasis on 'the whole' would, in a factual test, mean that there would never be a sovereign, for a whole community would very seldom be disposed to obey the same person, but it is merely the 'supposition' of a disposition, an inclination or desire, to obey. Thus, he is saying that one supposes that everyone thinks they ought to or need to or must obey. A supposition is not a matter of fact, but an assumption. The validity of the law is based therefore on the existence of an assumption that everyone is either willing or feels they ought to or feels they must obey. Whose assumption this is, and on what basis this supposition is made, is not Bentham's concern. The power, as opposed to the authority, of a sovereign or a law is, however, based on the actual obedience to that law.

8.3 John Austin

The command

It is important to notice that Austin has a fairly sophisticated method of theorising about law. He tries to show what he thinks describes law centrally, in the same way as Hart goes about elucidating the 'concept' of law, although he is not so clear as Hart about this form of description or definition. Although Hart is too sophisticated to say, as Austin says, that international law is not law, it is clear that Austin is well aware of both the similarities and dissimilarities that international law has in relation to his central case of law, which is that of the command of the sovereign. Be careful of being critical of the abrupt way Austin begins his famous lectures entitled *The Province of Jurisprudence Determined* (1832): 'Laws proper, or properly so called, are commands; laws which are not commands, are laws improper or improperly so called.' This gives the impression that he is merely stipulating what the law is so that he cannot be contradicted, and Austin has been criticised for 'postulating' the nature of law and then deducing conclusions from his own 'postulates'. But Austin does not do this. The beginning of his work is not in the form of postulated 'axioms' about law; they are, instead, the results of his thoughts about law, which have been placed at the beginning of his work for the purpose of clarity of exposition.

Essentially, Austin's theory of law is simple and concise. The subject of jurisprudence is positive law and positive law is the command of the sovereign. According to him, the idea of a command is the 'key to the sciences of jurisprudence and morals'. You could perhaps note here that Hart also claims to have found the 'key to the science of jurisprudence' in the union of what he calls primary and secondary rules in *The Concept of Law*. Let us proceed by using Austin's own definitions: Law, he says, in its most general sense, is 'a rule laid down for the guidance of an intelligent being by an intelligent being having power over him'. A command comprehends the following three 'notions'.

1. 'A wish or desire conceived by a rational being, that another rational being shall do or forbear.'
2. 'An evil to proceed from the former, and to be incurred by the latter, in case the latter comply not with the wish.'
3. 'An expression or intimation of the wish by words or other signs.'

These three notions are, as Austin says, 'inseparably' bound up in the command. The first and third notions refer directly to the command because they express the wish of the person commanding. The second notion, he says, which *indirectly* refers to the command, has two aspects. When we refer to the evil that the commander will 'visit upon' the person he is commanding we either refer (1) to the evil itself, in which case we are referring to the sanction; or (2) to the likelihood or chance of that person having an evil visited upon him, in which case we are referring to the obligation.

Note that Austin's explanation of obligation amounts to saying that a person has an obligation to do X just when and because the person is threatened with some unpleasant consequence. Note, too, Austin's explanation of the sanction. This is the 'evil which will probably be incurred in case a command be disobeyed or … in case a duty be broken'. Austin says that the greater the chance of incurring an evil, and the greater the evil is, the greater is the obligation. Nevertheless, in order to establish whether there is an obligation, we have only to look at whether there is a chance of incurring evil. Even when there is the *smallest* chance of incurring the *smallest* evil, he says, the expression of the wish still amounts to a command and still, therefore, imposes a duty.

The sovereign

Thus far, we have untangled the various ideas involved in the idea of a command. The other part of Austin's theory of law as the command of the sovereign is the idea of sovereignty itself. This idea and that of the independent political society are fundamentally related notions, he says. He gives a definition:

> 'If a *determinate* human superior, *not* in a habit of obedience to a like superior, receive *habitual* obedience from the *bulk* of a given society, that determinate superior is sovereign in that society, and that society … is a society political and independent.'

Austin allows that the sovereign can be constituted by either a particular person or a particular body of persons. You should note what Austin calls the two 'marks' of sovereignty: first, the sovereign must be 'habitually obeyed' by the bulk of the society, this being the 'positive' mark of sovereignty and, second, the sovereign must not be in a state of habitually obeying another body. He says that two consequences flow from this definition. The first is that the sovereign is incapable of being legally limited. That is, the sovereign cannot, as a matter of logic, bind itself by law. This follows from the theory that law is the command of the sovereign. His argument takes the form of a *reductio ad absurdum*. If the sovereign were bound by law, it would follow that *that* law was the command of a sovereign. But who could this sovereign be? There are two possible sovereigns, either another sovereign or the original sovereign.

Let us take the possibility of another sovereign. Two things follow. Either the first sovereign is not in a state of habitual obedience to the second sovereign, in which case he has no duty to comply with the second sovereign's commands, or the first sovereign is in a state of habitual obedience to the second sovereign, in which case he (or it) is not a true sovereign because he does not exist in an independent political society. In other words, the negative mark is missing.

Let us consider the second possibility that the sovereign commands himself. Austin abruptly dismisses this. A sovereign cannot legally limit himself because, as he asserts, 'we cannot speak of a law set by a man to himself'.

Is this such an absurd idea? What is wrong with the idea of a person setting a rule for herself? If there is any absurdity in it, it is that we know that the follower of the rule and the author of the rule are one and the same person, so that if it does not suit her to follow the rule she can change it. But it is perfectly *possible* for a person to lay down a rule of conduct for herself and this happens frequently in our own lives. Many of us would regard our moral convictions as rules laid down, let us say, in accordance with our consciences, which we consider ourselves bound to follow. It is not clear that in order to think in this way we must presuppose a standard of behaviour laid down by someone else. Is there something odd about the idea of applying sanctions to yourself? People do apply sanctions to themselves. Dorothy, in George Orwell's *A Clergyman's Daughter*, carried a pin with her and jabbed it into her arm whenever she had what she thought were uncharitable thoughts. The 'absurdity' of the notion of complying with one's own rules, and with punishing oneself, is an absurdity that arises not from logic, but from some general assumption that the human will is weak. This is not a strong enough argument for asserting that a sovereign logically cannot limit himself legally. And, also, it seems perfectly possible in Austinian terms to command someone else not to obey your commands if they are of a certain type. Why can't a man say to his wife before they both go out to dinner, 'All of my commands for extra wine after I have had two glasses are to be ignored'? Why, in other words, cannot the sovereign command his subjects to disobey him when he transgresses certain areas of competence that he marks out for himself. Why, indeed, cannot he draw up a constitution restricting his power and then command his subjects not to obey him when he steps outside that constitution?

This analysis has been dealt with at relative length and it is designed to give the student a taste of the way Austin's theory may be approached. You should try to think of the command theory as a real 'live' theory of how things actually are. Be fair to the theory or you may be accused of missing its point, but do not accept it hook, line and sinker. By attending to the small print, as it were, you will obtain insights and be in a good position to comment critically upon it.

A second point which flows logically from Austin's theory of law is that, according to Austin, sovereignty is indivisible. Because the sovereign exists in an independent political society, it is logically impossible, he says, to divide the powers of sovereignty amongst different bodies. The idea of sovereignty means habitual obedience to a determinate person or body of persons, and if there are several independent and determinate persons or bodies of persons, then there must be different sovereigns existing in different independent political societies.

We can try some more analysis. Think about the following, for example. Can we imagine situations where it is not absurd to suppose that, within one independent political society, there are two different sovereigns, each enjoying habitual obedience from the bulk of that society *in respect of different subject-matter*? It is possible and is borne out by history. At one stage in Europe, people consistently obeyed the state on secular matters but the Church in Rome on religious matters. Does Austin have a defence to this example?

The province of jurisprudence: the different sorts of law

Having set up his basic theory of positive law, Austin proceeds to make observations about phenomena closely related to law. He says we must distinguish human law from divine laws issuing from God. Divine laws and human laws are both, to use his expression, laws that are 'properly so-called' because they are guiding rules laid down by intelligent beings for intelligent beings.

Divine law is revealed to us in different ways, says Austin, according to what our beliefs are. Thus, for some, it is revealed in the Bible and for others it is revealed in the form of inspiration or intuition. For others, and this includes Austin himself, the law of God is to be revealed through the principle of utility. This principle is that of utilitarianism which says, roughly, that the right act is the one which more than any other increases the total happiness or pleasure in the world. The command theory's separation of the Divine law from the human law is a significant step in legal theory. It is by use of this distinction that the distinction is drawn between our moral beliefs and what is moral law, and it lies at the heart of all positivist theories of law. Remember the definition of legal positivism at the beginning of this chapter. It is echoed in Kelsen's famous statement that 'Legal norms may have any kind of content. There is *no* kind of human behaviour that, because of its nature, could not be made into a legal duty corresponding to a legal right.' It is echoed in Bentham's famous distinction between 'censorial' and 'expositorial' jurisprudence, and Austin's famous claim that 'the existence of law is one thing; its merit or demerit is another'.

Austin now distinguishes between law 'properly so-called' and law 'improperly so-called'. Laws 'properly so-called' are commands, and they divide into God's commands (the Divine law) and human commands. But further subdivisions are possible. Austin distinguishes between two kinds of command that men give to one another. First, there are the commands of the sovereign to his subjects and he calls these laws those 'strictly so-called'. These commands form the *positive* law of an independent political society and it is these laws which form the subject-matter of jurisprudence.

Second, however, there are commands given by men to one another that are not from sovereigns to their subjects. These form three types:

1. those commands made in a state of anarchy and which are therefore not positive laws because there is no sovereign;
2. those commands made by sovereigns, not to their subjects but to other sovereigns (although not so frequently that the sovereign addressee now is in habitual obedience); and
3. those commands made within an independent political society which are not of these other sorts, such as the rules of clubs, rules made by parents to their children and so on.

At this point Austin begins to tighten up his definitions. He says that he prefers to call these types of law rules of 'positive morality' so as to distinguish them from the kind of law set by a sovereign to his subjects. He uses the term 'positive' to distinguish them from the law of God (that is, the law is *posited*), and the term 'morality' to distinguish them from the commands of the sovereign to his subjects. They are laws 'properly so-called' because they are commands, but they are better termed rules of positive morality.

The laws 'improperly so-called' are divided by Austin into two types: laws 'by analogy' and laws 'by metaphor'. They are 'improperly' called law because neither of these two types of law are commands. Laws by analogy may also be called rules of positive morality and they are the laws which are those of 'mere opinion'. These laws arise not in the form of a person, or body of persons, commanding other persons but from popular sentiment or convention. The examples he gives are of 'the code of honour amongst gentlemen, and the law governing fashion'.

You should note that he famously places both international law and constitutional law under this heading. International law, because it exists between sovereigns but does not arise in the form of direct commands from one sovereign to another, is a matter of 'mere opinion', he says. Likewise, because of his view that sovereignty is illimitable by law, constitutional law, which purports to limit the legal powers of sovereignty, is not law but rules of positive morality. Putting it in a modern way, the sovereign is accountable *politically* but not legally.

Austin here makes an advance in legal thinking. This is that in having the groupings of two kinds of rules, non-sovereign law and laws by analogy, under the heading of 'positive morality', he distinguishes between 'critical' morality and 'positive' morality. Note what Austin says about this distinction:

> 'If you say that an act or omission violates morality, you speak ambiguously. You may mean that it violates the law which I style "positive morality", or that it violates the Divine law which is the measure or test of the former.'

It would be a very useful exercise to try to use the distinction in real life. Are there social conventions which we call 'moral' which fail a *critically* moral test? Does it mean anything to say that a slave-owning morality is an *immoral* morality, thus using the two Austinian distinctions in the one phrase? This example shows how significant the distinction is and you might note that Hart employs the distinction, as well as the exact terminology of 'critical' and 'positive', in his attack on Lord Devlin's thesis that the society was justified in using the criminal law to enforce its positive morality as discerned from the reaction of a juror. One of Hart's major points was that 'just what people happen to believe or accept' is not to be equated with what were the correct standards from a critical point of view. After all, what people happen to believe or accept might be based on prejudice. (See Devlin, *The Enforcement of Morals*, Chapters 1, 5 and 7; Hart, *Law, Liberty and Morality*; Dworkin, *Taking Rights Seriously*, Chapter 10.)

The second category of laws 'improperly so-called' are called 'laws by metaphor', which are scientific laws. The important thing about these laws is that they cannot be obeyed or disobeyed and hence the idea of a command in relation to them is 'improper'. If something like an atom or molecule fails to conform to a scientific law purporting to govern its behaviour, we just say that the law must be wrong, not that it has been disobeyed. We therefore change or modify our law (or, better, our hypothesis) about how the particle or matter should behave. We are now accustomed to this distinction between laws governing inanimate objects and laws governing the willed behaviour of animate objects. However, you should realise that there was no such distinction drawn for a very long time and it was thinkers such as Austin and Bentham and others who first drew it so clearly.

To sum up so far, Austin has introduced three very important and useful distinctions. First, there is a distinction between the divine law and human law, that is, the *is* and the moral *ought*. This distinction shows that Austin is not a natural lawyer. Secondly, there is a distinction between *critical* and *positive* morality, that is, those rules of conduct made by human beings but not in the form of commands by a sovereign to his subjects. Thirdly, there is a distinction between laws governing animate objects and scientific laws.

International and constitutional law

International law is not law because it arises, not through the assertion of commands but through 'popular sentiment' and 'mere opinion' amongst nations and is thus positive morality. Constitutional law is not law because it is not possible for a sovereign to be under a legal duty. So constitutional law, which appears to place legal shackles around the sovereign, is not really law but positive morality too.

Students can find this sort of theorising unhelpful. It sounds as though Austin were playing around with meanings, or just talking 'semantics'. But this is not a fair interpretation. He is saying that although we think of international and constitutional law as law, we should no longer do so because it is a loose description. He is telling us to look more closely at the legal phenomena and appreciate that international law and constitutional law are not really like other forms of law at all. And what law student has *not* found appeal in the idea that constitutional law is 'politics', not law, or the idea that international law is not 'really' law? We are led by Austin to notice that international law does not arise by means of an international sovereign legislative body, and that constitutional law meets some paradox at least in the idea that supreme legislatures cannot be 'supreme' over themselves.

Rights and powers

Students should be careful not to suppose that the command theory says that there cannot be legal rights and powers. Indeed, it is common to suppose that Hart's division of laws into duty and power-conferring rules is better than Austin's idea of a command, because that division can account for more sorts of laws than the criminal law to which Austin's theory is often relegated. But this interpretation underrates Austin. The command theorists meant that the basic unit of law is the command. Hart meant that law is better understood as supposing that there were at least two basic units, the duty and the power-conferring rules. But legal rights and duties can be explained under the command theory. Austin's explanation is as follows:

> 'Every law, really conferring a right, imposes expressly or tacitly a *relative* duty, or a duty correlating with the right.'

His idea is that we must look upon laws that create rights, *really* as laws that impose duties upon people other than the right-holder. Note that he says that 'every law ... conferring a right imposes [either] expressly or tacitly' a relative duty. An express duty would be imposed where the law, or so-called law conferring a right, expressly provided for a remedy when that right was infringed. However, Austin says:

> 'If the remedy to be given be not specified, it refers *tacitly* to pre-existing law, and clothes the right which it purports to create with a remedy provided by that law.'

So Austin sees rights really only as correlatives of *duties*. His theory of law is a duty-based theory and, although in the legal phenomena we see things that we might prefer to call rights, these are in fact a different way of describing what are in essence duties or commands.

Austin explains delegated legislation in terms of rights. He says that such legislation is effected in pursuance of a right conferred upon the delegated legislator by the sovereign. In his own terms, when the delegated legislator, exercising that right, legislates by commanding, the duty to obey those commands comes directly from the sovereign, because the right has to read in the form of:

> 'I, the sovereign, command you to do what it is my delegated legislator commands within the area of competence I have determined for him.'

This approach has the advantage that it concentrates our attention on the fact that when we are obeying a delegated legislator, we are in fact obeying the sovereign. When we obey a local government decree, therefore, Austin's theory makes it crystal clear that we are obeying Crown in Parliament, because under that theory, the local government's right to legislate is properly described in legal terms as a command from the sovereign.

Sanctions

Note that Austin regard *punishment* as not synonymous with the evil which is possible or likely if the command is disobeyed. That is, Austin considers that punishments are only one kind of sanction. He says that the evil likely to be incurred by disobedience is frequently termed a 'punishment' but that is not strictly correct.

It seems reasonable to suppose from his broad view of sanction that Austin would claim that *nullity* is a sanction. There is some support for this view to be found, not in *The Province of Jurisprudence Determined*, but in his Lecture 23, where he says:

> 'Now, though physical compulsion or restraint is commonly the mean or instrument by which suffering is inflicted, suffering may be inflicted without it. For instance, certain obligations are sanctioned by nullities ...'

However, throughout his Lectures Austin barely develops this theme. Strongest emphasis is placed on the analysis of rights, or powers, as being protected by correlative commands, laying duties on *other* people. Therefore, it would seem that where a person transgresses a right, that is, steps outside his powers, or acts *ultra vires*, it is merely the case that other people do not have a duty to obey what he says.

Students should be prepared to dig deep at this sort of point. It is common for examination candidates simply to say that 'for Austin, nullity is a sanction' and that shows a misunderstanding of actually what that would mean for Austin's theory. Viewing nullity as a sanction would view a right, say, to pass delegated legislation, as a command backed by the sanction of nullity: thus a duty would be placed, not upon *other* people to do what the delegated legislator says, but upon the legislator *himself*. He must act in accordance with the right conferred upon him under the 'pain' of the possibility of a nullity being 'visited upon him'.

A more plausible interpretation of Austin (but you are allowed to disagree!) is:

1. A has a right (to legislate)   =   B has a duty to obey the sovereign when A exercises his right.

But, possibly, there is the alternative analysis of:

2. A has a right (to legislate)   =   A *has a duty* not to exceed his right by virtue of a sovereign command not to, backed by the sanction of nullity.

The argument for saying the second possibility is less plausible is that Austin does not discuss it much, or with his characteristic clarity.

Custom

The place of custom in the law has always bothered jurists. The difficulty with custom is that courts not infrequently declare to be law what are claimed to be customs, or customary ways of doing things, since 'time immemorial'. For example, ancient rights of fishermen to dry their nets in particular places, or the establishment of rights of way. And, further, widening the idea of custom, the common law seems in many parts to consist of the enforcement of practices which have just existed from an earlier time. Any theory, such as one of the most common forms of positivism, and one under discussion, that claims that law is to be identified only in terms of its origination from some definite, posited, source such as the sovereign, is faced with the difficulty of saying whether customary law is 'really' law.

Austin's answer is, simply, that when the judges make a decision that the custom is law, the custom becomes law *then*, although up to that point the custom is merely a rule of positive morality. So Austin says:

> 'Now when the judges transmute a custom into a legal rule ... the legal rule which they establish is established by the sovereign legislature.'

> 'Customary laws are positive laws fashioned by judicial legislation upon pre-existing customs. Now, till they become the grounds of judicial decisions upon cases ... the customs are merely rules set by opinions of the governed, and sanctioned or enforced morally ... '

Judge-made law

In Austin's view, we must think of the judge as a delegated legislator who, when he makes decisions, is commanding on behalf of the sovereign. Since the sovereign cannot know everything that is going on in his courts, Austin employs the idea of a tacit command here:

> 'Now when customs are turned into legal rules by decisions of subject judges, the legal rules which emerge from the customs are *tacit* commands of the sovereign legislature.'

Note that Austin is very much against the idea that judges merely 'find' the legal rules and do not legislate. Famously, he said that he 'cannot understand how any person who has considered the subject can suppose that society could possibly have gone on if judges had not legislated'. In his discussion of the place of custom, Austin clearly shows that judges are delegated legislators. He has often been taken to mean that judges should be creative innovators. Indeed, he thought that judge-made law was *better* than statute law (and differed sharply from Bentham in this respect). The passage just cited has been quoted many times in support of a claim that Austin is for great judicial activism.

You might consider whether you think that judicial activism is consistent with the rest of Austin's theory. Although he does not say so, Austinian judges are bound to create the law *within* the confines of what it is that the sovereign would have commanded had he known of the particular set of circumstances before the judge. That is, in saying that judges should openly legislate, we should not take Austin to mean that this is an unrestricted power. If the sovereign would not have tacitly commanded something that the judiciary declares, then presumably the judiciary has exceeded its powers. The idea of a 'tacit' command by which judges legislate, carries with it the modern idea of interpreting in accordance with the 'intentions' of the legislature. In the case of following precedents, presumably the judge is bound to make decisions that are as consistent as possible with the previous decisions of judges, since these, if not expressly overturned by legislation, are to be read as tacitly commanded by the sovereign.

Sovereignty in practice

How does Austin deal with the idea of legal illimitability? He does it simply by saying that the fetters that appear to bind the sovereign are in fact not *legal* fetters because constitutional law is not law. He sees the difficulties posed by the English sovereign but does not really face up to them. He admits that the Crown, the Lords and the Commons constitute the sovereign in terms of the language of writers on constitutional law. But then he says:

> 'But, speaking accurately, the members of the commons house are merely trustees for the body by which they are elected and appointed and, consequently, the sovereignty always resides in the king and the peers, with the *electoral* body of the commons.'

Austin seems to be saying here that everybody who votes ('the electoral body'), along with the House of Lords, and the Queen, form the sovereign, and that the House of Commons is merely a delegated legislator for the electors.

Note that this is a long way from his initially attractive, because simple, idea of identifying the sovereign by looking to habitual obedience. Now the position seems to be that the sovereign consists of the House of Lords, the Queen and all the electors.

Immediately after the passage just quoted, Austin appears to do a complete turn around. He says that the mistaken view that the House of Commons has an absolute power and not a delegated power from the electoral body, probably arises, first, because the trust or power vested in the House of Commons is 'tacit rather than express', and secondly, that the trust or power is 'enforced by moral sanctions'. The turn around is that if the body of electors cannot really command, and therefore enforce the trust or power by *legal* sanctions, then in Austin's terms they cannot 'speaking accurately' be called the sovereign. He is involved in a contradiction. He wants to say that sovereignty ultimately rests with the electors but he seems unconsciously to know that this would involve saying that the body of electors issues commands to themselves. That is why he backpedals and says the body of electors enforce the trust of power vested in the Commons, by *moral* sanction alone.

Austin will always get into these sorts of difficulties, as Hart has famously pointed out, if he does not use the idea of a rule in his definition of sovereignty. It is very difficult to describe the United Kingdom Crown-in-Parliament in terms of a 'body of persons'. Does the United Kingdom sovereign change every time a Member of Parliament dies, and every time a new MP or member of the House of Lords is either elected or appointed? Austin's theory cannot even explain why we can use the term 'Crown-in-Parliament' to refer to the changing mass of people that make legislation under the name of 'Crown-in-Parliament' because 'Crown-in-Parliament' just does not refer to anything concrete that we can point to. It is an institution defined in terms of complex constitutional rules and is as independent of persons as a company is an institution independent of persons.

It is the fact that sovereigns and companies are not composed solely of persons that means they cannot physically die, and it is only by virtue of these *non-physical* attributes of sovereigns and companies that we can say they 'continue' despite their changing membership. So, again it is because Austin's theory lacks the notion of a *rule* that it fails.

You might note the difficulties Austin gets into with the idea of continuity of sovereignty which flows from this point. Remember that his sovereign is a person or a body of persons. He affirms that this person or body of persons must be determinate and certain:

> 'If the sovereign one or number were not determinate or certain, it could not command expressly or tacitly, and could not be an object of obedience to the subject members of the community.'

It seems fairly clear, then, that he does not have in mind any 'corporate' idea of sovereignty. But then, on the following page, he says:

> 'The persons who take the sovereignty in the way of succession, must take or acquire by a given generic mode ... Or (changing the expression) they must take by reason of their answering to a given generic description ...'

Here he seems to be suggesting that sovereignty continues by virtue not of the subjects' or citizens' acquiring a new habit of obedience, but by virtue of their having a continuous habit of obedience to some 'generic description'. That is, Austin is hinting here at the idea of a corporate idea of sovereignty, the idea that sovereigns succeed each other by virtue of coming within some rule-defined description. This hints of persons being *entitled* to succeed to the position of sovereign by the very fact, not that they are habitually obeyed, but that they are to be described in a particular way. Later on, Austin actually uses the word 'title'. In discussing the Roman Empire (Austin's lectures are full of interesting observations, incidentally), he says that sometimes after the demise of an emperor, there would be a period of dissolution of central government, because there was no person to succeed the emperor by, in his term, 'generic title':

> 'Since no one could claim to succeed by a given generic title ... a contest for the prostrate sovereignty almost inevitably arose.'

Of course, Austin could claim that 'title' here was that as defined by constitutional law and therefore that of mere 'positive morality' and that positive morality determines who should succeed. But he is not clear on the matter and there are problems buried here which he does not bring out. After all, a hallmark of his theory and, indeed, a hallmark of the command theory, is the identification of the sovereign through the idea of brute power. There are many difficulties with the idea of identification of the sovereign in terms of entitlement by virtue of positive morality. (See Chapter 5.)

How does Austin deal with the idea of the indivisibility of sovereignty? There are great difficulties with applying the idea both to the United States and to the United Kingdom. For the US he says that all the states' governments, together with the common federal government are 'jointly sovereign' in each of the states and in the larger society of which the states form a part. He says this is so because if the federal government were the sovereign then there would not be a society composed of several *united* societies; and if any one of the united societies was sovereign, then it would not be a member of a *united* society. His conclusion for the US is that the federal government, consisting of the President, and the Congress, is a delegated legislator of the governments of the individual states. So he says:

> 'The sovereignty of each of the states, and also of the larger state arising from the federal union, resides in the state's governments *as forming one aggregate body*.'

This alone has the appearance of fiction, but he really gets into deep water in what he says next:

> '... meaning by a state's government, not its ordinary legislature, but the body of its citizens which appoints its ordinary legislature, and which the union apart, is *properly* sovereign therein.'

This use of 'properly' in the last sentence echoes his phrase 'speaking accurately', when he was talking about sovereignty residing in the body of electors in *England*.

That is, if it is 'proper and accurate' to describe the body of electors or the body of citizens as sovereign, then it must also, in consistency, be 'proper and accurate' to describe the body of electors or body of citizens as issuing commands, ultimately to themselves, and to describe them as habitually obeying themselves.

8.4 Evaluation of the command theory

Law as a command

The undeniable contribution of the command theory is the view that law is a result not just of a vague collective undertaking, but must be ascribed to a will. But the recognition of the normative and rule-creating aspects of law does not justify the requirement of a determinable author.

Bentham's appreciation that human laws are imperatives that are interwoven and broken into shares is a more realistic format than that of Austin. The complexities of deontic logic reveal that laws may be permissive as well as commanding.

The underlying view that law is based upon a will is less easy to justify. Certainly, Austin's sovereign is a real person or body. However, the legislative will is not something that is that easily understood. One may only determine what the law is, by reference to the interpretation that we put on expressions of will. These need not coincide with what the author actually intended us to understand. Thus, while the Magna Carta is regarded as the original authority for habeas corpus, there is palpable historical evidence that this was only intended to accord rights to a privileged feudal caste. On the other hand, the idea of a person's will being simply a mental state, a psychological event, is simple-minded, and we do not have to impute that idea of a 'will' to the sovereign.

Both Bentham and Austin fail, Austin more seriously than Bentham, to go far enough in their consideration of law as rules. A rule stands independently of the identity of its particular author, providing that it is in the acknowledged form that a legal system prescribes. Furthermore, at least Austin, if not Bentham as well, has no room to accommodate principles, which clearly are a necessary aspect of the legal enterprise (see Chapter 10, on Dworkin's criticism of positivism).

The notion of command also makes it logically difficult for rules to bind the sovereign. A man may lay down a rule by which he lives. Although Bentham accepts that a sovereign may bind himself, he still relies on the backing of a sanction or reward. However, the duty to obey a rule may not only be self-imposed, but that duty or responsibility may personally arise even though it cannot be properly framed or defined in an imperative.

Bentham supposes that the whole of the political community is disposed to obey it. Austin sees the will of the sovereign as a real feature. Both beg the question of how such a will may be attributable to mandates issued under it, which the sovereign cannot know. This emphasises that the concept of will presupposes knowledge on the part of a person doing the willing. Hence Raz finds it hard to understand how various responsibilities within a legal system are actually interlinked in the context of imperative theories.

A further problem must be noted in the limitation of which wills count as law. Austin requires that a law be an aggregate of commands formed to command the performance or forbearance of acts. This idea of generality, although convenient for a legal system, is not necessary for laws, since they may address a specific person and a specific act (for example, the Abdication Act). Moreover, the demarcation of laws on the basis of superior political wills, in Austin, limits the application of the term 'law'. This works in some respects, but we do not see the edicts of Conservative Central Office to the various constituutency associations as law. Bentham does not bother with demarcations, which has the advantage that his theory is not fettered by law-school conventions, but leads also to a lack of distinction between mandates with legal effect and mandates that are coincidental to the law.

Sovereignty

The fact that Austin requires an indivisible, determinate, unfettered sovereign that is continuous through time seems to be more a matter of convenience for the superimposition of a utilitarian system than fact. The criticisms of Austin are so numerous on this account that the student must be referred to another text, of which there are many, for a detailed evaluation. Suffice it to say that the United States has a divided, perhaps indeterminate sovereign that is bound by a constitution, where sovereignty has been succeeded from and extended over its history. The Austinian concept of sovereignty would certainly be unable clearly to account for the development and effect of the European community.

Both Bentham and Austin rely entirely on motives external to the subject of laws in order that laws may be enforced. Bentham does not limit himself to sanctions alone and it is evident in Austin's *Lectures* that he does accept that some laws do not in themselves require the direct backing of coercion. Both are agreed that, ultimately, all complete laws require some kind of external motivation.

However, education and persuasive argument, or indeed indoctrinated sympathy for a law, have similar, if not equal, effects. Milgram has sought to prove in some notorious experiments that people will go to extraordinary lengths to obey what they conceive to be authority commands. (See his *Obedience to Authority*.) In the complex modern society, the assumption that people in authority should be obeyed and indeed usually have good reasons for being obeyed, is a necessary one. We may well be employed in a complex undertaking, such as a production process, where the relevance of our actions as an employee is obscure. However, we perform to our function without necessarily having the fear of sanction.

The obscurity in Bentham's account of illegality and the insistence of coercion may partially be rescued if we substitute the question 'what is law?' with 'what is illegal behaviour?', as Foley suggests. Illegal behaviour might be termed behaviour that we are disposed to punish. This would lead to an easier recognition of rules, while giving a real understanding of what the law is seeking to do, which the rules alone do not reveal.

When Austin says, as he occasionally does, that the force of the power to enter into a contract is the threat of the nullity of the contract as a sanction, this is not only logically inadequate, but contradicts the whole purpose of encouraging people to engage in formal contractual relations.

Bentham may be criticised, too, for saying that there may be an exercise of legal powers by someone not explicitly authorised. That a law may be adopted by a sovereign without his knowing of it is only sustainable if that will is fictional. In such a case attribution of a law to a sovereign is merely an artificiality designed to add consistency to legal theory (Hart's 'theory on the back of definition'). Nevertheless, as it has been pointed out, law is often attributed with a will of its own in the courts and in common parlance. In this respect law becomes a system of independent imperatives, as Olivecrona terms them, which do not need to be ascribable to any mental state type will, fictional or not.

Anyone who listens to the outbursts of the Bruges group or notes the United Nations' reluctance to intervene in national issues will be well aware that the question of sovereignty has not left the legal or political arena. Rees and others have concerned themselves with the question of what sovereignty is and what the authority of sovereign laws might be.

In a very influential article, Rees identifies six possible ways in which to envisage sovereignty which are helpful in the context of the command theory.

1. Sovereignty in its *legal sense* is not concerned with the influence or power of the sovereign, other than in its legal sense. In a *political sense*, on the other hand, a body may be sovereign by conquest, resulting in the eradication of the previous sovereign. This aspect of political sovereignty is not the concern of the lawyer. Instead the lawyer is concerned to determine what the ultimate authority of the law is, rather than what power lies behind the ultimate authority of the law.

2. Early concepts of sovereignty, as well as the idealist concept of sovereignty, determine that the sovereign had supreme legal authority only insofar as it also had moral authority. This is sovereignty in its *moral sense* in that the requirement of sovereign authority can only be satisfied by moral authority.

3. A sovereign may instead be the person or body that holds the monopoly of coercive power in a state. The sovereign is the person who may guarantee or enforce any law, irrespective of whether it be made by the sovereign or some other body. Thus, in England the sovereign power would be that of the Crown in the form of the courts, police and military, among others. Rees terms this *sovereignty in the institutionally coercive sense.*

4. In strict contrast there may be envisaged the sovereignty of the majority or all of the people in the society, which could be viewed as the *sovereignty of social coercion.* Such a concept of sovereignty is obviously of limited application and must be viewed in terms that pre-date government. Such a sovereignty of collective coercion would be applicable to a tribal or primitive society where law is in the form of custom and is enforced communally. Alternatively, if sovereign power is based on a social contract theory, such a view of sovereignty may be applicable.

5. It seems clear that in a given society more than one of these criteria may apply, so that logically another definition of sovereignty is the body with the *strongest political influence.* Such a view creates a political rather than legal judgment.

6. A final category of sovereignty is that which differentiates between a body that has authority purely on the basis of force and the permanence of a sovereign that rules by authority. Sovereignty in the *permanent sense* differentiates between the ruler who is constantly mobilised in a quasi-military sense, and the sovereign who has stamped his authority on a society and can rule by law as opposed to force.

Rees employs these differing concepts of sovereign power in order to seek answers to four important questions. The first of these needs to be answered in the affirmative if the imperative theories considered here are to be considered as logically sustainable. The imperative theory is built on the assumption that law is the will of the sovereign. If it can be shown that there need be no sovereign in a state, then this definition is logically defective. Therefore the first question must be is sovereignty a necessary feature of a state? Rees analyses this question in some considerable depth, but for the present purposes a more simple analysis must suffice.

1. A sovereign in the legal sense is causally necessary in any given state, though not necessary by definition. In order to govern properly, laws are desirable, though perhaps not logically necessary. In order for laws to be of any effect there must be some ultimate authority: in the absence of such a final legal authority no legal issue could ever be certainly decided, and government would be impossible.

2. Equally, it is causally necessary that there should exist a sovereign in the coercive sense, though not logically necessary. Laws can only be enforced either by a supreme coercive power or by social solidarity which punishes transgressions. It would be unreasonable to assume that law can exist without social or institutional coercion.

3. It is not logically or causally necessary that (as in the fifth definition) there should be one body that can be said to be more supreme than any other body that could be described as sovereign. For example, the electorate is sovereign in the sense of its social coercion, Parliament is sovereign in the legal sense and the executive is sovereign in an ultimate coercive sense. They are, in England, mutually dependent and it would be impossible to ascribe to one more supreme power than the others, since they hold their power by virtue of the others.

Therefore, according to Rees, while it is not logically necessary for a state to have a sovereign, it seems causally necessary for a legal system to work well. What makes sovereignty of logical necessity is when there is a requirement to define ultimate legal authority. Without ultimate legal authority, there can be no ultimate determination of legal decisions, nor can rules be married to the coercive force that is necessary to enforce law. Rees concludes that the authority of law lies in the danger of sanction by a supreme coercive authority. However, if law is to be regarded as more than simply conventions of the exercise of power, then law must have some logical independence from power. Rules must in themselves be valid. Such a question is a question of validity.

Lawyers are ever concerned to differentiate law from other orders, such as that of the robber gang. Suppose a powerful gangster were to take over an island. Whatever the gangster says cannot be contradicted and there are standing rules, requiring the sort of things that a gangster might require. He is therefore the supreme coercive authority. Is he making law? The answer surely must be contingent on whether the rules that he makes have some features that differentiate them from any other mandate that he might give. It would surely be a perversion of the word law if it could apply equally to 'bring me another beer!' and 'only kill those people whom I say you can!' Both might be mandates of a gangster, but only the latter accords more naturally with the way *we ordinarily think about the law*.

Austin seems to escape from this problem by limiting the legal mandates of a sovereign to those that he makes by virtue of being a political superior. However, this is a mere disguise for the fact that Austin is seeking to limit the term law to things that have a specific purpose, termed as political, as opposed to domestic. It is this element that demarcates law from the dictates of a robber leader. However, as an exclusionary criterion, difficulties arise because of the ambiguity of the concept of political. The sovereign in Austin's theory provides the power and in the sense that he is the political superior, provides the exclusionary criterion. To this extent it is logically necessary to Austin's concept of law.

9

Continental Legal Positivism: Kelsen's Theory

9.1 The background to Kelsen

9.2 The Pure Theory

9.3 A comparison of Kelsen and Austin

9.4 An evaluation of Kelsen

9.1 The background to Kelsen

The 'pure' theory of law is more or less exclusively associated with the Austrian philosopher Hans Kelsen. Adherents of this theory are numerous, including Ebenstein, Merkl and, formerly, Radbruch, However, the strength of Kelsen's innovative approach has meant that little has been added by others and consequently most discussion and criticism has been aimed at Kelsen himself.

Misconceptions often arise from Kelsen's use of Kantian language and methodology. This should not concern the student too much. Kelsen's theory is marked by several propositions, some appropriate to Kant, but all appropriate to Hume.

1. There is a fundamental gap between 'is', which denotes *factual* statements, and 'ought', which concerns *normative* statements. *An understanding of the importance which Kelsen attached to this distinction is the clue to understanding the whole of Kelsen's work, in particular, the basic norm, and its misapplication in the early revolution cases.*
2. As a consequence the validity of normative statements can only derive from other normative statements.
3. Normative statements are made by human beings and thus are an aspect of subjective human will.
4. The only law is positive law, in other words that which is the product of the will of people. There are no natural laws therefore.
5. Objective facts may have an effect on each other in terms of causality. There is a law of gravity that causes apples to fall. Kelsen asserts there is an equivalent but

different relationship between norms. Thus, if X circumstance occurs, then you ought to do Y is a grammatical expression of what he calls 'imputation'.

6. The object of legal science is to understand the way in which law works, irrespective of content. The attempt is to explain law in terms of the laws of imputation and, as such, jurisprudence should be a *normative science*, as contrasted with the descriptive sciences that are used to explain facts, such as the disciplines of chemistry, biology and so on.

9.2 The Pure Theory

According to Kelsen:

> 'The Pure Theory of law is a theory of positive law. As a theory it is exclusively concerned with the accurate definition of its subject-matter. It endeavours to answer the question what is law? but not the question what ought it to be? It is a science ...'

It is crucial not to get too hung up on the idea that the theory is supposed to be 'pure'. It is mostly the same requirement for his theory as for any other theory of positivism, namely, that moral and other factors are irrelevant *as far as determining legal validity goes*. The objective of the theory is not to describe the way in which legal systems work, or what institutions normally are to be associated with law. Kelsen is not concerned with what considerations a judge takes into account when he decides a case, in determining questions of legal validity. He is solely concerned with legally valid reasons for action. Kelsen seeks to reconstruct rationally the way in which legal authority is transmitted in legal systems. In order to achieve an understanding of the way in which law itself works, Kelsen seeks to escape from any fallacies and judgments that might obscure the truth.

Kelsen's main works on legal theory are *The Pure Theory of Law* which was first published in German in 1934, and was published in English in 1960, and *General Theory of Law and State*, published in 1945. Kelsen's aim in producing what he called his 'pure' theory was to rid law of any kind of ideology. He had a motive for producing his theory of positivism, which was to distinguish questions of what the law is from ideological questions concerning what the law ought to be. This is clear from Kelsen's preface to his *General Theory*. Note that he is writing just after the experience of the Nazis:

> 'In social and especially in legal science, there is still no influence to counteract the overwhelming interest that those residing in power have in a theory pleasing to their wishes, that is, in a political ideology ...
>
> [I publish this] with the belief that in the Anglo-American word, where freedom of science continues to be respected and where political power is better stabilized than elsewhere, ideas are in greater esteem than power; and also with the hope that even on the European continent, after its liberation from political tyranny, the younger generation will be won over to *the ideal of an independent science of law*; for the fruits of such a science can never be lost.'

It is important for understanding Kelsen to draw the following two distinctions. First, separate the 'is' and the 'ought' of law. Since Kelsen is a positivist, the 'pure' theory of law is to be *descriptive* of law. But, second, it is important to note that the 'is' of law consists of the description of 'oughts', although not moral oughts. So when we describe the law we are describing a set of 'ought' propositions.

Kelsen is very careful about explaining this. He says the great mistake in Austin's theory was that Austin had tried to derive legal 'oughts' from 'is's', namely, the evidence of discovering the person, or body of persons, who was habitually obeyed and who habitually obeyed no one. The sovereign was identified as a matter of fact and the positive laws – 'oughts' – were supposed to exist simply by virtue of this. This was Austin's account of 'legal duty'. Kelsen is here saying much the same as Hart when Hart says that being obliged to do something is not the same as being under an obligation to do it.

Students should note that Kelsen says that the description of law, even although it is a set of ought-propositions, is something different from saying what the law *ought* to be, that is, is something different from *prescribing* the content of law. Most important, for his theory, saying that a description of the law is a description of ought-propositions is certainly not to say what the *moral* content of the law ought to be. Thus, Kelsen famously said:

> 'Legal norms may have any kind of content. There is *no* kind of human behaviour that, because of its nature, could not be made into a legal duty corresponding to a legal right.'

Before going on to describe what Kelsen means by a legal norm, you should note that he describes all ought-propositions as *norms*. This reference to the action-directing, or 'normative', character of rules governing behaviour is an advance on Austin's idea of rule-governed behaviour as acting according to habit. In a roundabout way, Kelsen has introduced a superior idea, that of rule-following, to Austin's (and Bentham's) idea of habitual obedience. Two points are important for understanding Kelsen here. First, for Kelsen, a norm is in essence *action*-directing, and should not by thought of only as imposing a duty, but also as including the idea of a *permission* or *power*. Secondly, Kelsen distinguishes between legal, moral and other norms. Moral norms are merely, in his view, propositions describing our subjective preferences for behaviour and he is critical of natural lawyers who think that morality is something objective. Kelsen in fact thinks that all moral judgments are essentially irrational because they are no more than expressions of our feelings or intuitions. Since all moral judgments are relative to the human being who makes them, he says that he is a moral relativist.

The legal norm

We should now look at the character of the legal norm and it is necessary first to look at how Kelsen views the legal phenomena that he sets out to describe. His views are clearly laid out in the first chapter of *General Theory*. His first sentence states: 'Law is an order of human behaviour' and, he says, that it 'designates a specific technique of social organisation'. Kelsen has views about the form this 'specific technique of social organization' takes. It is that the technique is essentially one of coercion, by the systematic use of sanctions, and is applied by 'agents' or officials authorised by the legal order to apply sanctions. He says that these two conditions mark out what is unique about law and is what is common to all uses of the word 'law', and 'enables', as he says, 'the word "law" to appear as the expression of a concept with a socially highly significant meaning'.

Kelsen develops the concept that law is essentially the idea of sanctions and officials. As a result he gives us a very specific description of the *legal* norm. This is that a legal norm is an 'ought-proposition' directed at the officials to apply a sanction in certain circumstances.

The key to the whole of Kelsen's theory is to understand that law consists of directions to officials to apply sanctions. An immediate objection to Kelsen's characterisation of a legal norm would be that we do not ordinarily think of laws as directed to the officials of a system. For example, we think of the criminal law as imposing duties upon *citizens* to do, or forbear from doing, certain kinds of things. Or we think of laws, say, governing the creation of wills, as conferring powers upon *citizens* to make wills. Kelsen's answer to this is simply that he is bringing to light something in the legal phenomena of which we are not normally aware, namely, that law is essentially a form of social control that proceeds by way of either imposing duties or conferring powers upon officials to apply sanctions.

The delict

In fact, a citizen, strictly speaking, according to Kelsen, does not have a norm directed at him at all. If a citizen does something which gives rise to the circumstances under which an official ought (or may) apply a sanction, then, according to Kelsen, that citizen has not done anything contrary to that norm, just because it is directed at the officials. The citizen has instead committed what Kelsen calls, borrowing from the Roman law, a 'delict'. Kelsen say that if we take a law such as 'one shall not steal' then everything contained in the meaning of that law is contained in the meaning of 'if somebody steals, he shall be punished'. It is thus not necessary to refer to the first norm 'one shall not steal' at all. However, Kelsen nevertheless says that it greatly facilitates matters if we allow ourselves to assume the existence of the first norm which, he emphasises, is not a genuine legal norm. He says that he prefers to express the first norm rather as the secondary norm, and the second norm, the genuine *legal* norm, as the primary norm. Thus, he says, only officials can genuinely break the law, because when we are speaking of the citizen we are only talking of his committing a delict, which is fulfilling the condition for the application of a sanction by an official. So, in one of the most famous statements of jurisprudence in the twentieth century, he says:

'Law is the primary norm, which stipulates the sanction, and this norm is not contradicted by the delict of the subject, which, on the contrary, is the specific condition of the sanction.'

If this does not look like law to you, be careful about criticising Kelsen here. He is, he claims, *describing* the law as it really is, in the same way as a scientist describes, or attempts to describe, the *reality* of matter. It would be useless to go about taking issue with a scientific theory that said that all matter was alike in consisting chiefly of certain basic substances by saying that it is not immediately apparent to us that all matter is alike. Kelsen is trying to find a uniform deep structure that underlies all law, and his claim is that law is a set of norms that take the form of directions to officials to apply sanctions in certain circumstances.

Rules of law in the 'descriptive' sense

It is for this reason he distinguishes between what he calls 'rules of law in the descriptive sense' such as, for example, the various sections of the Law of Property Act 1925, or the various rules that are obtained from case law. But these, he says, only partially describe what are the real laws, the legal norms which are ought-propositions directed at officials. In fact, he says that it is the task of 'legal science' to transcribe all the material produced by legal authorities into the form of statements describing what the legal norms are. In other words, a proper description of the law requires everything that we know of as law to be converted into statements of the form: 'if a person does X, then an official Y ought to apply a sanction Z'. Even then this is not the norm itself. Rather, it is a form of words that *describes* the norm. A prisoner, interpreting the orders of the commander of a prison camp, for example, when relaying the orders to his fellow inmates, only describes the norm that issues from the commander. This, of course, is the simplest way of describing the task of the legal scientist, because X, Y and Z will often require further complicated descriptions.

The idea of legal validity

Kelsen does not think that law is just a simple set of legal norms. He has a specific, and well-known, theory of legal validity. Students will find it useful to distinguish, not just for Kelsen but for jurisprudential thinking generally, the ways in which we use the terms 'legality' and 'validity'. Although we often use the terms together, there is a useful distinction. When we use the idea of 'lawfulness' or 'legality' we are referring to something as having the general character of law, for example, that it is a direction to officials, or that it imposes sanctions, or takes the form of a rule, and so on. But when we use the term 'validity' in relation to legal rules we are being more specific; in fact, we are most often being *professional*, because we are referring to the fact that the rule in question has come within the criteria of validity of a particular legal system.

Kelsen claims that he does not distinguish between the existence of norms and their validity:

'By "validity" we mean the specific existence of norms. To say that a norm is valid, is to say that we assume its existence.'

Thus a rule's having the character of law and its being *valid* are one and the same thing. He says at one point:

'The usual saying that an "unconstitutional statute" is invalid (void) is a meaningless statement, since an invalid statute is no statute at all. A non-valid norm is a non-existing norm, is legally a nonentity.'

This view of Kelsen is based on his theory that only norms can validate other norms. This is because as he says norms 'exist' in a different category of thought from that of propositions about the natural world.

How do norms validate other norms? What Kelsen has in mind is a 'root-of-title' theory of validity whereby one norm is validated by a more general norm which is validated by an even more general norm. Thus the validity of a norm is established by locating the norm within a hierarchy of norms. The ordinary way to think of this is to test, say, the legal validity of some official action such as imposing a fine. A person is fined a sum of money. We look into the decision and discover that he has been fined in accordance with a local bylaw that (say) requires him to park only in certain places. We examine the bylaw, but find that it has been made in accordance with a local government Act. We examine the local government Act, but find that it has been passed in accordance with the procedures that make it an Act of Crown-in-Parliament.

In each stage of this process, in searching for the root of title, we are looking for a more general norm that encompasses the more specific one. There is, therefore, a relationship of logical entailment between the more general norms and the more specific norms. All Acts of Parliament are valid; the Wills Act 1837 is an Act of Parliament; therefore, the Wills Act 1837 is valid. All instruments effected in accordance with the Wills Act 1837 are valid. Therefore, this instrument effected in accordance with the Wills Act 1837 is valid, and so on.

The basic norm

Going up the chain of validity, or hierarchy, of law in order to find its root of title, we must come to a finishing point, says Kelsen. If we were to continue the process, then we would never be able to establish the validity of any norm, because we would have to go to infinity. But, since we *can in fact* establish the validity of legal norms, then we must be able to get back to some ultimate norm that confers validity upon all other norms. This *norm*, for it *must* be a norm of course (because only norms can confer validity on norms), Kelsen calls the *Grundnorm*, or the 'basic norm'. How do we come across it in practice? We get to it, says Kelsen, when we cannot, in principle, trace our chain of validity back any further. Thus we find in tracing the root of title of the bylaw that we get back to the point beyond which we cannot go, namely, to the point where we find that the bylaw was ultimately validated by Crown-in-Parliament. When we ask ourselves what the reason is for the validity of the enactments of Crown-in-Parliament, the answer is that this is *just what we assume*.

Kelsen says that there is one such *Grundnorm* for every legal system. We might, in fact, for some legal orders have to go back to a constitution and find that it has been made in accordance with a previous constitution, and even there we might perhaps find *that* constitution has been made in accordance with a previous constitution. But ultimately, he says, we will get back to a point beyond which we cannot go:

> 'Ultimately we reach some constitution that is the first historically and that was laid down by an individual usurper or by some kind of assembly. The validity of this first constitution is the last presupposition, the final postulate, upon which the validity of all the norms of our legal order depends. It is postulated that one ought to behave as the individual, or the individuals, who laid down the first constitution have ordained.'

Now, students should note the following general principle as crucial to a proper understanding of Kelsen's theory of the basic norm. This general principle follows from the fact that only *norms* can validate other *norms*:

> 'The basic norm is that (coercive) acts ought to be done (by officials) in accordance with the historically first constitution and is not the *fact* of the first constitution.'

Thus, we should never say that the constitution itself is the basic norm, just because the constitution is a fact, not a norm. Rather, the basic norm is: 'acts ought to do in accordance with the constitution'.

To summarise so far: Kelsen's theory of validity is a hierarchical, or root-of-title type theory. Laws receive their validity from higher, more general laws, until a point is reached at which we stop. Here we come across the basic norm which imparts validity to the whole legal order. Now you will remember that the particular form of the *legal* norm, in order to capture Kelsen's perception of the legal phenomena, consists essentially of *first*, the systematic application of sanctions and, *second*, of officialdom, so that laws are in essence directions to officials to apply sanctions in certain circumstances. Thus, the hierarchy of norms should be thought of as a *hierarchy* of directions to officials to apply sanctions.

These sanctions range from, as Kelsen says, the 'concretised sanction' which take the form of a particular direction to a particular person to apply a particular sanction, such as a judge telling a bailiff to remove goods after a warrant of execution has been issued, through to the most general form, in the form of a basic norm, which says: 'coercive acts ought to be applied in accordance with the historically first constitution'.

Kelsen says that in legal systems where there is no written constitution, the constitution arises through custom. Therefore, the basic norm of such legal systems takes the following form:

> 'Coercive acts ought to be applied in accordance with the customary ways of making law in that particular country.'

Since the United Kingdom has no written constitution, we have to suppose that the basic norm of the United Kingdom is one of these. Now, one of the ultimate constitutional norms authorised or validated by *that* basic norm is:

> 'Coercive acts ought to be applied in accordance with what Crown in Parliament enacts.'

Another 'ultimate' constitutional norm would be:

> 'Coercive acts ought to be applied in accordance with what the common law courts decide.'

And so on. Students should read, for further elaboration, Harris, 'When and Why Does the *Grundnorm* Change?' [1971] *Cambridge Law Journal.*

The identification of the basic norm is the most difficult and obscure part of Kelsen's work. For this reason, this textbook will concentrate on getting that concept as clear as possible. Five important things must be noted about the basic norm.

1. If norms can only get their validity from other norms, how is it that the basic norm gets its validity? Kelsen says that it is simply assumed to be valid. In order to be able to talk about validity at all, he says, we must assume the system to be valid by reference to such a norm, even though we might not consciously think of it. The basic norm is not created by any legal procedure such as the enactment of a statute, so it is different from all other norms in that respect. It has, instead, the function of making sense of what we mean when we talk of legal acts as being valid. And since its function is to make clear *what we mean* when we talk of valid laws, it does not have the political, or ethical, or professional function of telling us *what* legal norms are valid or not. Since its function is only to make clear what we mean it has, to use a philosophical term, only a cognitive or an epistemological function. Thus, Kelsen says:

   > '[The basic norm] is not – as a positive legal norm is – valid because it is created in a certain way by a legal act, but ... is valid because it is presupposed to be valid because without this presupposition no human act could be interpreted as a legal ... act.'

   and in *The Pure Theory* he says:

   > 'Since the basic norm ... is only the transcendental-logical condition of this normative interpretation, it does not perform an ethical-political but an epistemological function.'

2. A second question that has to be asked about the basic norm is: *who* assumes it? Kelsen sometimes says that it is anybody at all who talks of certain laws being valid, because it is the basic norm that gives *meaning* to such statements. Thus he says:

   > 'The basic norm is only the necessary presupposition of any positivistic interpretation of the legal material.'

This statement follows from the quotations that I mentioned earlier about the basic norm not itself being a positive law, but a 'transcendental-logical condition'. But at times Kelsen talks of it being assumed by 'jurists':

'By formulating the basic norm … we merely make explicit what all jurists, usually unconsciously, assume when they consider positive law as a system of valid norms and not only as a complex of facts.'

At other times, he talks of it being assumed by what he calls the 'legal scientist'. And it is clear that it is the task of 'legal scientists' to describe the law. But two things are claimed: the first is that whoever interprets the laws as *valid*, and therefore, according to Kelsen, either consciously or unconsciously assumes a basic norm importing validity to all the laws, does not thereby accept that the laws are *morally valid*; and secondly, it is not *necessary* for anyone to assume the validity of a legal order: this is stated very clearly by Kelsen. (See Kelsen's 'Professor Stone and the Pure Theory of Law' (1965) 17 *Stanford Law Review*: 'An essential part of my theory of the basic norm is that it is not necessary to presuppose the basic norm.')

3. A third point about the basic norm is that it is a necessary condition of the presupposition or assumption of the basic norm that the system of norms to which it refers, and thereby validates, is *effective* over a particular territory or, as Kelsen says, is 'efficacious'.

Students should be very clear, especially when interpreting the so-called 'revolution cases', that this requirement is a *necessary* condition only and not a *sufficient* one. Thus Kelsen says:

'The efficacy of the entire legal order is a necessary condition for the validity of every single norm of the order, a *conditio sine qua non*, but not a *conditio per quam*. The efficacy of the total legal order is a condition, not a reason for the validity of its constituent norms.'

Two points should be noted about this.

a) The fact that there is an effective set of norms in a particular society which are in the form of directions to officials to apply sanctions in certain circumstances does not mean that there is a set of valid laws in that society (and therefore it does not mean, according to Kelsen, that there is a legal system operating in that territory). This follows, obviously, from his basic distinction between the 'is' and the 'ought'. That is, we cannot say that there are valid legal norms or a valid legal order *because of the facts of effectiveness* (or, putting it another way, the facts of cause/effect relationships between the application of sanctions by officials and non-delictual behaviour by the citizens). In other words, facts of effectiveness do not mean validity. *That* requires a *presupposition* that the norms of the system are valid.

b) But, secondly, since effectiveness is a *necessary* condition of the validity of a legal order, it means that we can *only* assume effective orders of norms as valid and it follows from this that as soon as a legal system loses its efficacy, then however much we want to assume that it is valid, we cannot.

What *practical* import does all this have? Let us say that I, personally, do not think of the laws of the Soviet Union as valid laws at all. This, it seems reasonably clear in Kelsen, I am able to do. I just do not presuppose any basic norm authorising the clearly effective sanction-applying acts of the Soviet officials. Now I might refuse to talk of the validity of the laws of the Soviet Union because I consider that the Communist revolution was illegitimate because it was not in accordance with the laws existing in Russia before 1917. If I take this view, says Kelsen, it is not open to me to consider the pre-1917 Russian laws as valid. This is simply because these laws are no longer effective. Thus I could not make a *legal* claim in the Soviet Union now to some property or title that would have been vested in me were the pre-1917 laws still valid. I am merely in the position of being able to say that, as far as I am concerned, there is no law in the Soviet Union; although, of course, I might say that *other* people assume a basic norm authorising the present legal acts of the Soviet authorities.

This is not, of course, to say that a single legal norm loses its validity because it is no longer effective; that is, that people are no longer acting in accordance with it. It is that in order for a legal norm to lose its validity, the whole legal order to which it belongs must lose its effectiveness. That is why, according to Kelsen, we can say that the pre-1917 laws in Russia, or the Roman legal system, are no longer *valid* law; we can only talk about them *as if* they were valid.

Summing up, you cannot have validity without efficacy, but you can have efficacy without validity. And to put this point of interpretation of Kelsen, which is so important for the understanding of the way his theory applies (or does not apply) to the 'revolution cases' as follows:

'Effectiveness is *not* a sufficient condition for the validity of a legal order, but it is a necessary condition.'

4. A fourth point about the basic norm is that it is axiomatic in Kelsen's system that there is only one, unique, basic norm for each legal system, and it is this basic norm that gives the system its *unity*:

'That a norm belongs to a certain system of norms, to a certain normative order, can be tested only by ascertaining that it derives its validity from *the* basic norm constituting the order.'

5. The fifth and final point about the basic norm is that Kelsen claims that it ensures, in some unclear sense, that all the norms that it validates do not *contradict* each other, and he talks of the basic norm unifying and giving 'meaning' to a set of non-contradictory norms. Thus, for example, he says:

'... the principle of non-contradiction must be posited in the idea of law, since without it the notion of legality would be destroyed. This presupposition alone, which is contained in the basic norm, allows legal cognition to supply a meaningful interpretation of the legal material.'

What happens, therefore, if two norms contradict each other? He explains this sort of case by saying that one of the norms *must* by invalid, and he states the principle that the *later* law in time is valid, as the first one loses in validity. This happens, he says, according to the principle of 'derogation' or the principle of *lex posterior derogat priori*. And it is through this principle that he explains the operation of repealing laws. Thus he says:

'When the norms whose contents contradict one another are separated by the time of their origin ... the principle of *lex posterior derogat priori* applies. This principle, while it is not ordinarily stated as a positive rule of law, is taken for granted whenever a constitution provides for the possibility of legislative change.'

In the case where there are contradictory legal norms referred to in the same statute, so they are not separated in time, he says that it is a matter of interpretation of the statute only: so that either one of them is valid, or perhaps *neither* of them are.

9.3 A comparison of Kelsen and Austin

It is useful to compare Kelsen and Austin. In general, Kelsen's theory fares much better than Austin's simply because the notion of a norm is much more like that of a rule than that of a command. Because of this, we might consider whether the following two advances are made on the command theory. First, the idea of a norm, imposing duties or conferring powers upon officials, replaces Austin's crude idea of a *predictable* sanction with the psychological element of fear, which cannot distinguish the social phenomenon of *being obliged* with that of *being under an obligation* (see Chapter 5). Secondly, the source of validity of the norm rests, for Kelsen, not on the fact of its issuance from a habitually obeyed and determinate person or group of persons, but upon *another norm*.

9.4 An evaluation of Kelsen

Kelsen seeks to explain not the reason why a judge gave a certain verdict in a case, but the reason why, in legal terms, he has the authority to do so. In legal terms, the reason why a judge may decide a murder case is because the law requires him to do so, irrespective of whether he does or does not actually so act.

In view of Kelsen's claim that he is only engaged in the normative science of jurisprudence, it is remarkable that he is criticised by people on descriptive sociological terms. Perhaps the greatest example of this is documented in Hart's essay 'Kelsen Visited' in *Essays in Jurisprudence and Philosophy* (1983). Hart observed that Kelsen agreed with everything that Hart was saying, yet Hart could not understand Kelsen. We only need to look at the aims of their two theories to see how this arises. Hart claims to be engaged in descriptive sociology following an analytical and linguistic train of thought. Hart asserts that one understands the meaning of legal statements only in the context of their use. This binds him to understanding legal theory in terms of the way people do behave and the reasons that they exhibit for their actions.

On the other hand, Kelsen is committed to understanding the conceptual meaning of legal reasons for action, divorced from the effect of those reasons on human behaviour. It is the difference between the computer programmer and the computer manufacturer. Both are essential to computer science, but are engaged in understanding how to make a computer work from different perspectives. One looks at the internal logic, presupposing that a machine exists that is capable of running the programme, the other looks at the problems of building the machine, supposing that someone has written a programme to run on it. However, that people are aware of the distinction allows them to work more effectively.

In the light of this proposition, it will be clear that those people who do not share Kelsen's philosophical point of view and who view legal norms as effects on behaviour as well as reasons for behaviour, are bound to get muddled over the theory. Hart points out that he fell off his chair when Kelsen vehemently reminded him norm is norm! However, as the rest of the essay illustrates, Hart still did not appreciate the distinction between a rule of law in the descriptive sense (the expression of a normative reason) and a rule of law in the descriptive sociological sense (the expression of a normative reason that has an effect).

Wilson described the criticisms of Kelsen as a log-jam. Ebenstein suggests that the Pure Theory has created a storm all over the world. That Kelsen is important is beyond dispute. However, there remains considerable dispute as to what Kelsen is actually saying. One of the problems with Kelsen is that he gradually refined and added to his theory so much so that criticism of Kelsen has been described as stamping on quicksilver. The issue has frequently been not, 'What is Kelsen saying that is wrong?' but 'What is Kelsen saying?'. As a result there is a considerable difference between criticising the Pure Theory and criticising what one thinks it is.

Sanctions

There is much criticism of Kelsen's view of law as resting on sanctions. Kelsen assumes that law is not a voluntary order. The purpose of law is to make all people behave in a way in which they do not already behave. However, it does not seek to achieve this by convincing people that the content of law is right and binding on the conscience, as moral systems do. Instead law indicates some objective reason why people should act, rather than a subjective reason, such as the dictates of conscience or an independent desire to act in accordance with the law. Kelsen is not saying that people do obey law for this reason, but that the reason law gives is the threat of coercion.

Thus, Lloyd is critical of Kelsen on the basis that he says that sanctions of some kind (or rewards) are a necessary feature of law. This seems wrong, since we do not consider that people obey law solely because of fear of sanctions. However, this is an evaluation of the effect of law, not the reasons that the law gives. Take, for example, a statute that says simply 'Thou shalt not kill'. Why should I obey it, unless I agree with it? The logic of the legislator is that persons should obey, even if they do not agree with it, so that some motive for obedience needs to be present. This is the result of the fact that people cannot be assumed to do what they ought to, which is the basic assumption of all law.

The delict

There is, however, a stronger criticism of Kelsen's concept of a delict as being any act that is the condition of the visitation of coercion. The question of the imposition of duties on the officials creates problems. Does a judge have a legal duty to apply a sanction? This thorny question is postulated by Woozley, who suggests that if the answer is yes then there must be a legal norm, accompanied by a sanction, which itself presupposes an official with a legal duty, stemming from a sanction–based norm. This would be a vicious regress back to an ultimate permissive norm with no sanction attached.

The question can only be answered if we address Kelsen's view of legal duty. Kelsen is only concerned with legal norms and not with the factual existence of people's beliefs. The mistake is to view the existence of sanction as creating a norm. According to Kelsen, the imposition of a sanction is a specific category of action that the law requires.

For Kelsen, an obligation cannot stem from a fact, but simply from a norm. The sanction does not create legal obligation, but is the intended effect of a norm. Woozley is surely viewing norms as predictive, that is, likely to be acted on. He is talking about the reason why people are psychologically likely to act in a certain way. If we ask, 'Does the judge have a legal duty to apply a sanction?', the answer in a normative sense is yes, since there is in existence a legal norm saying that he should. The difference between Kelsen and Woozley is the difference between someone saying that you have a duty, and you believing that you have the duty that a person says you have.

A further criticism of the concept of delict is that it does not differentiate between administrative acts of coercion, such as a compulsory purchase order, and a punishment. Lloyd finds it difficult to understand, however, why things such as the compulsory evacuation of a building in the case of fire are not regarded by Kelsen as delicts.

International law

One problem that has perplexed critics of Kelsen is his assertion in later writings that all legal systems could be seen to be subsumed under one basic norm. Kelsen suggests that in the modern world jurists must perhaps look at national law as being validated by international law. Take the following example. An English legal theorist may be asked, 'Why is the law in England valid?' His probable answer is that it is made in accordance with the procedural requirements of a valid constitution. He is here presupposing the basic norm of national law, that the authors of the constitution were vested with the authority from a fictive norm, to make a valid constitution.

If this is so he is presupposing that international law is valid. Why should he take the second course, to the exclusion of the first? Certainly, the modern jurist is aware of the validity of other legal systems. French law is valid in France and is recognised by the English legal system as being valid in France. How then can the English law recognise the validity of French law?

Kelsen offers two approaches. Firstly, we might see French law as being valid in France because the English legal system has recognised it as such. In this case the validity of French law is dependent on the validity of the English legal system as being empowered to recognise the validity of other legal systems. This is itself dependent on the validity of the English legal system generally, which stems from the basic norm. Thus, the English jurist would regard French law as being valid under the English basic norm.

Kelsen and morality

Hart is much perplexed by Kelsen's assertion that law and morality do not conflict as normative systems. Kelsen returns to the is/ought distinction to explain this. Norms and duties have a dual existence.

I might say, 'You must stand up!' That is a norm, whether or not it is heard or acted upon. Conceptually and grammatically, it is not a factual, but a normative statement. Equally, a law that says, 'Kill your brother!' is conceptually a norm and if made pursuant to the normative requirements of the legal system it is legally valid. However, most moral codes would say, 'Do not kill your brother!' If we ask what the law requires us to do, it is clear; I must kill my brother. In deciding what to do I am aware that the law says I have a duty to kill my brother. I am aware that morality also says I have a duty not to. I can know and accommodate both norms as reasons for acting. All this is on the normative level.

Whether I believe I have a duty to obey them is a question of my state of mind, a factual rather than normative issue. I can believe that I have a duty to the law and an opposite moral duty. A duty exists on two levels: as the meaning of a statement that says you have a duty, or alternatively as a belief in the mind of a person. The former is the content of a norm, the latter is the sociological/psychological effect of a norm. Kelsen is only concerned with the former kind. The law does not recognise that a moral duty is appropriate to deciding whether someone has a legal duty. For this reason Kelsen views the conflict between moral and legal duties as the coincidence of normative forces acting on the same person.

Other legal systems

Just as legal normative reasoning does not presuppose moral obligations, so an individual legal system does not take into account other foreign legal duties as a matter of legal consideration. For example, in the law of evidence, relevant foreign law is a question of fact, rather than law. What one ought to do legally in England is what English law says one should do.

The student will be aware that in England European law is treated as having primacy. This aspect relates to the change in the constitution that regards Europe as an authoritative law-making body and as such it is subsumed under the basic norm. It indicates, however, a tendency of jurists to see law as part of a worldwide phenomenon. Kelsen thus moves towards a juristic description of a legal world, where legal reasons are unified under the basic norm of international law. We will consider this further a little later.

Private and public law

Kelsen disputes that there is a natural legal distinction between private and public law obligations. He simply sees this as the law reflecting the political and social ideology of the distinction between law and state.

Public legal relationships tend to impose norms on citizens without the citizens having significant say in the content of those norms, for example, a tax demand. On the other hand private law obligations tend to have a mutuality, whereby both parties have a say in what their obligations will be. Kelsen is clearly thinking of contracts here.

Private and public law obligations consist of norm-creating acts. However, public law indicates an inequality in the status of parties, that is a reflection of the political order.

The basic norm

It is proposed only to deal in depth with one sophisticated criticism of Kelsen's idea of the basic norm, that of Raz. It is sophisticated because it focuses on the various obscurities surrounding the basic norm and makes suggestions. Students have already been warned against 'easy' criticisms of Kelsen. Use the following as a guide to how careful you must be.

Perhaps the idea of the basic norm is meant to explain for us, unlike the command theory, what it means to follow a rule. Remember that Kelsen thought that Austin's theory wrongly derived 'oughts' of law from the 'is's' of the facts of habitual obedience to a sovereign. His answer is to invent the concept of a norm and to say that, since norms only exist in the world of norms, they must therefore only be validated by norms. This, of course, led him to postulate a hierarchy of norms which led him, in turn, in order to avoid an infinite regression, to postulate a basic norm. Thus the whole idea of the *oughtness* or *normativity* of law is bound up in the idea of the basic norm.

Simply, does the basic norm help us to understand how following rules is more than a matter of habitual obedience? The major distinction between habitual behaviour and rule-governed behaviour is that, to borrow Hart's phrase, a rule has an 'internal aspect', that is, that some members of the group at least have a 'critical reflective attitude' (see Chapter 5) to the behaviour and this attitude justifies criticism of those who deviate from the standard pattern. That is, in addition to regularity, there has to be a *reason* justifying criticism of deviation.

How does the basic norm help us with this idea? Does it supply us with this idea of reasons for criticism for deviation from a pattern of behaviour? Well, the idea is contained in any case in the notion of a *norm*, so what help is the basic norm? Perhaps the basic norm is the *ultimate*, or somesuch, justification. Certainly, Kelsen is led towards this by the 'root-of-title' nature of his theory. That is, at the very end of any process of justifying criticism of someone's deviation from a norm, according to Kelsen, you can point to an ultimate or basic norm that says: 'You ought to do this (ie apply coercive acts) in accordance with ...'

There is a very useful (although very difficult) article by Raz on this point in his collected essays *The Authority of Law* (1979). Raz says that Kelsen's theory of the basic norm is a theory of 'justified' normativity, meaning that, according to it, any statement that any person makes about law must be in his own terms ultimately justified in accordance with an assumption made by him that, legally, this thing ought to be done.

However, Raz says that he sees no reason why we should accept this theory. Why cannot we say simply that laws are normative because they consist of rules and the existence of these rules does not have any *ultimate* justification but is merely identified by the fact that some people, say judges and lawyers, identify them as laws? Here we do not have to find an ultimate justification for the laws; rather, all we have to do in order to identify what the laws are is look to the 'social facts' of what judges and lawyers do to identify them. This bridges the gap between the 'is' and the 'ought' for Kelsen, so *he* could not accept it. On the other hand, what is so important about this gap?

Raz calls such a better theory one of 'social normativity' and he says that Hart has such a theory. What this means in simple terms is that we need not look beyond the social fact of acceptance of certain rules as defining what other rules are. Thus, in the United Kingdom, all we need do is look to see what judges and lawyers regard as constituting valid law-making. We find it is, for example, among other things, issuance of a rule in accordance with the procedures and rules that constitute Crown-in-Parliament. It is unnecessary to go further and, for example, say that we 'assume' that issuance from Crown-in-Parliament is a *valid* means of making law. We just simply say that *this* is valid law because Crown-in-Parliament has issued it and issuance by Crown-in-Parliament is one of the *tests* by which we tell whether certain laws are valid.

Hart makes the same point in *The Concept of Law* where he compares the basic norm with his rule of recognition. He says that no question of validity can arise about his rule of recognition because it is the *test* of what is valid. All that is necessary to do is to point to the fact that it exists. According to his theory, that means to point to the factual existence of a social rule among the officials of a system which identifies what the valid rules of the system are. As Hart says:

'To express this simple fact by saying darkly that its validity is "assumed but cannot be demonstrated", is like saying that we assume, but can never demonstrate, that the standard metre bar in Paris which is the ultimate test of the correctness of all measurement of metres, is itself correct.'

Too pure for its own good?

McCoubrey and White (1999) in the following extract offer a final comment on Kelsen's endeavours:

'Unfortunately, like many positivist, and other, analyses, but in extreme degree, the pure theory suffers from its own self-imposed limitations. It is acceptable for purposes of a particular discourse to focus upon some aspect of the working of law, indeed doing so is almost unavoidable. When, however, an "essence" of law is sought such limitations become problematic. Law, as an aspect of political society, may be argued to be inseparably linked, not only in its working but in its nature, with all the moral, ethical, political and sociological factors which Kelsen dismissed as "impure". If that is accepted, the pure theory gives only a very formalistic and partial description of the working of law. Kelsen did not deny the existence of these factors, but in excluding them from his jurisprudence he may be argued to have excluded much of the reality of law. On this basis the pure theory may be considered both interesting and useful within in its own appointed context, but that context is severely constrained.' (at p156)

10

Modern Positivism

10.1 The concept of law

A very important statement about how Hart intends going about things is contained in the Preface to his classic work *The Concept of Law* (1961). In his own words, he intends to produce 'an essay of descriptive sociology' of the law. He is going to pay attention to the language of the law although only to find out more about the social phenomenon itself. He places great importance on the idea of the distinction between the internal and external points of view. In *Utilities* (1993) an article on Hart, who died in 1992, by Raz gives an excellent nutshell view of Hart. It places special emphasis on Hart's views about definition and the purpose of the study of legal language.

Hart begins by identifying three questions of great importance, namely, what the difference is between law and coercion, what the relationship is between legal and moral obligation, and the question of what a rule is. He also gives a clue to his method: to set up a 'central case' of law by looking, linguistically, at the way we use law-related terms, and regard phenomena such as primitive and international law as 'fringe' or 'penumbral' to the central case (which turns out to be a modern municipal legal system'.

In Chapters 2, 3 and 4, Hart considers linguistically differences between orders and laws and it is in this chapter that it becomes clear that he is not attacking Austin's theory of law but a stronger variant purged of the inbuilt idea in Austin's (and Bentham's) theory of the command. That idea, says Hart, begs the question of the authority of law.

Taking the 'orders backed by threats' model 'writ large' he points out the difficulties with it in terms of its inability to distinguish duty-imposing from power-conferring rules, its inability to accommodate laws that apply to lawmakers, and its inability to identify laws that do not issue from a central source.

Hart criticises the idea of legal sovereignty as being identifiable only by factual identification of a source of power. Such an idea, he says, cannot cope with the problems of the continuity of sovereignty because it overlooks the part played by *rules* in this context. A 'habit of obedience' is fundamentally different from the important concept of 'rule following' which includes the idea of standards against which conduct may be appraised. Further, law both persists and can apply to the sovereign who made it. Indeed, he says that the sovereign itself is constituted by the rules. In sum, the 'orders backed by threats' model where those orders issue from a determinate body of people must fail because it ignores the corporate nature of the legal sovereign.

The crux of the whole book comes in Chapter 5. Here Hart sets up his own model of law. Law includes the idea of obligation and that idea implies the existence of strongly supported social rules. But law also includes the idea of permissions, or power-conferring rules, and Hart thinks that a society which had obligations, or duty-imposing rules alone (what he calls the 'primary rules'), would be 'pre-legal'. Why? Because such a society would be 'defective' because it would be uncertain, inefficient and static. To 'cure these defects' he proposes for his concept the introduction of three power-conferring type rules, which he calls the 'secondary rules'. The rule of recognition *identifies* the law for certain, and thus cures the defect of uncertainty. Now people know what is and what is not law. The rules of adjudication cure the defect of inefficiency by introducing the courts. Now administration of law is efficient. The rules of change introduce private and public powers of legislation and repeal and cure the defect of lack of progress. In this union of primary and secondary rules, Hart claims to have found the 'key to the science of jurisprudence'.

Hart's main thesis is thus that the central set of elements constituting law is the 'union of primary and secondary rules'. So, he says:

> '... we shall make the general claim that in the combination of these two types of rule there lies what Austin wrongly claimed to have found in the notion of coercive orders, namely, 'the key to the science of jurisprudence.'

and, a little further on the same page:

> 'We accord this union of elements a central place because of their explanatory power in elucidating the concepts that constitute the framework of legal thought.'

In general, the primary rules are rules of obligation, or *duty*-imposing rules, and the secondary rules are *power*-conferring rules.

Now it is important to see the method by which Hart analyses the law into this union of primary and secondary rules. He does so by imagining, for analytical purposes, a society that lives by primary rules alone. This would be a society where the rules would restrict acts of violence, acts against property, and so on. Hart says that such a society would suffer certain sorts of 'defects'.

First, there would be *uncertainty* as to what the rules were, or the proper scope of the rules once they were identified. In order to remedy this defect, he says that we must analyse law so as to include a rule or rules of 'recognition' that would identify with certainty what the rules of obligation are. His definition of the rule of recognition is as follows:

> 'This will specify some feature or features possession of which by a suggested rule is taken as a conclusive affirmative indication that it is a rule of the group to be supported by the social pressure it exerts.'

Secondly, he says, in a simple regime of only primary rules of obligation, there would be another defect. This would be that the community would remain *static*, because the only way the primary rules of obligation could change would be by decay or by a very slow process of growth. Furthermore, there would be no means by which individuals could release other people, or themselves, from the rules of obligation.

This defect would be cured, he says, by the introduction of secondary rules of 'change', which would enable legislators to repeal or enact new laws, or private citizens to create rights and obligations in the form of wills, contracts and so on.

Thirdly, he says, a simple regime of only primary rules would be an *inefficient* system, because there would be no means by which disputes could be settled. In order to cure this defect, he says that we must introduce secondary rules of 'adjudication', which would confer power on certain people to adjudicate and would also define the procedures in accordance with which adjudication would take place.

Hart then says:

> 'The remedy for each of [the] three main defects in this simplest form of social structure consists in supplementing the *primary* rules of adjudication with *secondary* rules which are rules of a different kind. The introduction of the remedy for each defect might, in itself, be considered a step from the pre-legal into the legal world.'

This, then, is Hart's characterisation of the central set of elements that make up his answer to the question 'What is law?'. It describes a modern municipal legal system, with its rules of obligation, and various other rules relating to the identification of the rules of the system, the system of law-making and repeal by both private citizens and by a legislature, and the system of courts.

10.2 The rule of recognition

Hart next examines in Chapter 6 in greater detail the rule of recognition, pointing out its very great importance in matters of constitutional law. The rule of recognition is identified as a matter of empirical fact and this proposition is one of the most important in the whole book for it is by his special means of identifying law that Hart establishes the positivistic (ie separated from morality) nature of his thesis. The important distinction between the 'internal point of view' and the 'external point of view' is analysed. The internal point of view is that of the officials who accept the rule. Hart also defines the existence conditions of a legal system. A legal system exists when it is effective and at least the officials accept certain standards (the rule of recognition) as constituting the criteria of recognition of the law.

It is useful when studying Hart to distinguish a narrower, 'professional' question from the general question that Hart sets himself at the beginning of *The Concept of Law* which is, 'What is law?'. The narrower question is, 'What is *the* law?'. It can immediately be seen that this question is a professional one because it needs a more precise specification of the issue on which knowledge of the law is required, and (very important) a specification of the legal system to which the question relates. Someone might ask, for example, 'What is the law concerning mortgages in England?', and be put off by the reply that it is the 'union of primary and secondary rules', considering it, of course, to have no relevance.

However, there is a reply to this sort of question in Hart. It consists of his theory of legal validity. Briefly, his answer is that the law on a particular topic in a particular legal system is that which it is according to the rule of recognition in that system. We need, therefore, to examine more closely what Hart means by his rule, or rules, of recognition.

Incidentally, if you are bothered by the question whether there is only one rule of recognition, or whether there are several, the writer can confirm that he has asked Hart this very question. Hart's reply was that there is 'no importance' in the issue. We can loosely refer to several rules, such as, in the United Kingdom, 'What Crown-in-Parliament enacts is law', or 'What the common law courts decide is law' and so on, or we can simply bundle them all together in one more complicated rule such as 'What Crown-in-Parliament enacts and what the common law courts decide and ... is law'

Hart defines the rule of recognition as:

> 'This will specify some feature or features possession of which by a suggested rule is taken as a conclusive affirmative indication that it is a rule of the group to be supported by the social pressure it exerts.'

A rule of recognition, therefore, is simply a rule whose function is to identify whether or not *another* rule is part of the legal system. Now Hart distinguishes between what he calls a *supreme* criterion and an *ultimate* rule of recognition. The supreme criterion is part of the rule of recognition and is the part which dominates the rest. So the supreme criterion in the United Kingdom legal system is Parliamentary enactment, and if the common law, or local or general custom conflict with Parliamentary enactment, that enactment prevails. The ultimate rule of the system is the rule of recognition *itself* because you cannot go back further than it. It is ultimate in the sense that Kelsen's basic norm is because we cannot trace validity back any further. So we can trace back the root of title or validity of a bylaw to an Act of Parliament but here, says Hart, 'we are brought to a stop in inquiries concerning validity'.

Hart uses this distinction between a supreme criterion of validity and the ultimate rule of recognition to criticise Austin's attempt to say that all law is the result of legislation (remember Austin's theory of the 'tacit consent' of the sovereign). This sort of confusion, Hart says, is caused by supposing that the supreme criterion of validity within the rule of recognition is the rule of recognition itself, that is, in the case of the United Kingdom, supposing that the only rule of recognition is 'What Crown-in-Parliament enacts is law'.

The existence of the rule of recognition is a matter of *fact*, to be determined by looking to the actual practice of the *officials* of the system. But Hart says that this is not to say that the rule of recognition is explicitly declared. In fact he says that 'in the day-to-day life of a legal system its rule of recognition is very seldom expressly formulated as a rule' and that 'for the most part the rule of recognition is not stated, but its existence is *shown* in the way in which particular rules are identified'.

10.3 Hart's and Kelsen's theories of validity

Nevertheless, the existence of the rule of recognition is a matter of fact, and it is important to appreciate this when Kelsen's basic norm and Hart's rule of recognition are compared. There are four main distinctions drawn by Hart.

First, Kelsen's basic norm is not identified as a matter of fact but is, rather, a 'presupposition' that certain rules are valid. Kelsen explains the ultimate test of validity by saying that we, or possibly the legal scientist or 'jurist', presuppose laws to be valid. This leaves open the possibility of not presupposing the validity, say, of a revolutionary regime. We can simply decide not to interpret the laws of the new revolutionary regime as legally valid whether or not they are effective. This cannot happen with Hart. If the officials of a legal system use a rule of recognition to identify valid law, then that *is* the test of validity of that particular system. So that, for example, if there is a revolution, we do not have to decide whether to interpret the laws of the new regime as legally valid by presupposing a new basic norm as Kelsen would have us do, we simply look to the practice of the officials of the system. If they use new criteria such as compliance with the new constitution, to judge what is legally valid or not, we say simply that the rule of recognition has changed. And the question of whether it has changed or not is again entirely a matter of fact.

It is necessary to emphasise that the rule of recognition is, for Hart, a matter of *fact* and was introduced to 'cure the defect' of *uncertainty*. If the rule of recognition is a matter of fact, then the validity of all the other rules of the system can be identified only as a matter of fact. So Hart says:

> 'To say that a given rule is valid is to recognise it as passing all the tests provided by the rule of recognition and so as a rule of the system ... The rule of recognition exists only as a complex, but normally concordant, practice of the courts, officials, and private persons in identifying the law by reference to certain criteria. Its existence is a matter of fact.'

So the first major point of difference between Hart's rule of recognition and Kelsen's basic norm is that Hart's rule of recognition is a fact, and Kelsen's basic norm is a presupposition, existing, as Kelsen says, in the 'juristic consciousness' that something is valid.

Secondly, the rule of recognition need not be 'presupposed' to be valid. Hart thinks that is a waste of time. All we need do is point to the rule of recognition's factual existence as a test of validity. It is a waste of time or pointless to talk about its being 'presupposed as valid' because questions about its validity are identical to questions about whether it exists or not. It is not necessary to ask ourselves whether the rule of recognition 'What Crown-in-Parliament enacts is law' is *itself* valid or not. All we need do is say that it is in fact *accepted* as the test of validity by the officials of the United Kingdom legal system. Hart means that this is how we normally think of validity. We think of it as a quality imparted *by something else*, some form of standard or test, and not as a quality existing in itself.

Usually, we think of validity as something imparted by *rules*, so we would say that something was a valid argument because it was in accordance with the rules of logic, or we would say something was a valid move in chess because it was in accordance with the rules of chess, and so on.

Hart's point is that it is an odd question to ask whether, say, the rules of logic or the rules of chess were themselves valid, although we could ask ourselves other questions about them. For example, we could ask whether the rules of chess resulted in an interesting or difficult game, or whether the rules of logic were based on experience or intuition.

The basic norm has, in a sense, always the same content. It is that the constitution should be obeyed or, in the Kelsenian way of expressing it, 'coercive acts ought to be applied in accordance with the constitution'. On the other hand, Hart's rule of recognition sets out the factual test of legal validity in any particular system, so it will differ in content from legal system to legal system.

The fourth point is a rather minor one. This is that Hart says that he does not ascribe at all to Kelsen's theory that the basic norm, as Kelsen says obscurely, 'contains within it the principle of non-contradiction'. In other words, Hart is not of the view, as Kelsen *is*, that the ultimate test of validity of a legal system in some way prevents laws of the system from conflicting with one another.

10.4 Judicial positivism

The following chapter in *The Concept of Law* is relatively little read but is a very important chapter in relation to Hart's view of legal reasoning. In it we come across the idea of *judicial positivism*. He stresses the open-ended character of many legal rules and discusses his famous distinction between the core and penumbra of settled rules of the legal system. He attacks the view that law can be reduced to a set of propositions about what judges will do (his attack on American legal realism) and points to the fact that, at times, the identification of the rule of recognition itself can lead to very great difficulties.

This different version of positivism focuses specifically upon the judge and is a theory of judicial reasoning. In Ronald Dworkin's terms, this version is a theory of 'strong' discretion, according to which a judge is not bound by law to come to any decision when the question of law is genuinely controversial.

No positivist has clearly enunciated this theory, although it is implicit, and occasionally explicit in Hart. It could be a doctrine that happens to be associated with the central core of legal positivism. Or, it might be a necessary consequence of regarding law as identified only through its sources. While Hart notably drew attention to the distinction between the 'core' and 'penumbra' of the expressions of legal rules, he did not deal directly with the question of what the judge was bound to do in the area of his discretion.

Both Austin and Kelsen thought that judges had legislative powers but both, too, saw these as confined within wider, legal, principles of constraint. Austin thought that the judges were only empowered in accordance with sovereign intention. Kelsen appears to be dogmatic about the question for he asserts that there are no 'gaps' at all. If a judge is authorised to decide a given dispute where there is no 'general norm' covering the matter, he is acting validly in adding to the existing law an 'individual norm'. But this occurs, not because there is a gap, but because the judge considers the present law to be 'legally-politically inadequate'.

But it may follow, as Dworkin says it does, that a theory of strong discretion is entailed by these influential theories of positivism, whether the theorists realise it or not. He thinks that judicial positivism is a consequence of at least the Hartian type of positivism. In short, according to Dworkin, positivism says that the law ends at the beginning of uncertainty about shared meanings or understandings about the identification of law. For Dworkin, judicial positivism identifies law with the ascertainable clear practice of the law to the extent that rules and so on that are not identifiable as a matter of the empirical facts of official practice cannot, under the theory, properly be called 'law'.

An important book by Waluchow, *Inclusive Legal Positivism* (1994), takes issue with any idea (see particularly Fuller and Dworkin) that positivism has a theory of judicial reasoning that is unconvincing. He propounds the view that not only can positivism accommodate the invocation of moral principles by judges, as Hart can allow, by explicit or implicit incorporation in terms of a master rule or rule of recognition, but also that the *master rule itself* can include moral values (thus 'inclusive' positivism can include moral judgments as the title of his book declares).

Let us first get clear what legal positivism means for Hart. In Chapter 9 of *The Concept of Law* he says that 'it is in no sense a necessary truth that laws reproduce or satisfy certain demands of morality ...'. This thesis is, of course, in the same tradition as Bentham (the distinction between 'expository' and 'censorial' jurisprudence) and Austin's well-known statement that the existence of law is one thing but its merit or 'demerit' is another. This traditional form of positivism is a form which Waluchow dubs 'exclusive' positivism and he thinks it is wrong. Instead, 'inclusive' positivism is right and this thesis declares that moral reasons can be included as part of the formal criteria of validity. An example of this occurs when a written constitution explicitly states that moral reasons will be determinative of legal validity. Mostly the argument for this supposed halfway house between Hartian positivism and natural law is by empirical example, particularly by way of reference to the new Canadian constitution.

Waluchow captures quite neatly the feeling that natural law never quite grapples with the reality of law, namely, that we have no difficulty in day-to-day life in seeing that law is made up, for the most part, of the intentional acts of legislators and judges and can be identified using reasons of the non-moral kind (eg 'it was *in* a statute' or 'the Court decided'). Waluchow says that the Canadian constitution can be identified in a positivistic way since it is empirically discernible as the master rule; nevertheless, there are explicit moral factors identified within that constitution which the courts are permitted or required to apply. Then, the application of these moral standards *determines the legal validity* of regulations made under the constitution:

> '... the conditions for legal validity accepted within the Canadian legal system include moral conditions. That such moral conditions count as conditions of validity can be determined independently of moral reflection. But the conditions themselves require moral reflection for their understanding, interpretation, and application.'

My view is that Waluchow draws attention towards the reality of the moral reasons that pervade the courts in determining questions of legal validity (go into any court, in any legal system, to observe this) but does not quite establish that positivism is still consistent with this way of looking at things. A reference to the Nazi-style 'wicked' legal system is useful here. Imagine that we have an utterly immoral constitution which states categorically that no person of a particular race shall enjoy equal rights of citizenship with other races (cf the Nuremberg laws) and that, in determining whether any contracts, corporations, regulations, bye-laws, etc, contravene this constitution, the judges 'shall take into account any such circumstances the court considers appropriate and just in the circumstances' (a phrase in the Canadian constitution to which Waluchow refers). Clearly the meaning of 'appropriate and just' here is coloured by the overall wording *pedigree-defined*. A judge cannot say: 'I may now apply morality to these acts in the law and I find that this discriminatory bye-law is therefore invalid' because it is clear that 'the morality' she must apply is that supplied by the social aims and policies of the constitution and that, to quote Hart whose theory of law Waluchow is at pains to support, 'is compatible with very great iniquity'. (See *The Concept of Law* Chapter 9.)

10.5 Morality and law

Chapter 8, too, is relatively little read. Both it and the following chapter deal with the questions of morality that arise in relation to law. Hart is really explaining why law and morality have so much to do with each other but nevertheless can be distinguished in the way his positivism requires. His general excursus into the idea of justice, so importantly related to law, is one of the best introductions to this difficult area. In particular, Hart distinguishes between that sort of justice that attaches to law, 'procedural' justice, or 'justice according to law', and that justice that attaches to 'substantive' law, or 'justice *of* the law', saying that it is the latter concept that is more important from the moral point of view.

The next most important chapter for understanding his theory is Chapter 9 on natural law. Here Hart defines legal positivism as the theory that says there is 'no necessary connection' between law and morality. He then discusses the origins of 'natural' law, which says that there is such a connection. In defence of his own theory of positivism he asserts that the fact that law and morality share a common vocabulary ('ought', 'must', 'duty', etc) and a common content (rules against murder, rape, theft, etc), is only a 'contingent' fact or a matter of 'natural necessity'. Given that men want to survive, are vulnerable, approximately equal in power, vulnerability and so on, are reasonably altruistic, have limited understanding and strength of will, and that there are limited resources, it is not surprising, he says, that any set of social rules that men set up will reflect these characteristics. From these facts about people we can say that there is a 'minimum content' common to both law and morality, but not enough above this minimum (because of men's many and conflicting other purposes) to make much sense of the grander claims of natural law. In any case, there are good moral reasons, those of clarifying complex moral issues such as the Nazi informer cases, why we should accept a wider conception of law that *can* include immoral laws over a narrow one that excludes them.

In the last chapter of *The Concept of Law*, Hart returns to the definitional themes of his first chapter by showing how the problems of international law should be treated in the light of his thesis. International law is neither law nor not law: it is to be assessed in so far as it is dissimilar from and similar to the central case of law as he has set it up describing the modern municipal legal system. He applies his idea of the union of primary and secondary rules to the phenomenon of international law and thus this chapter gives him the chance to review the whole of his theory as it applies to a special case.

10.6 The internal and external points of view

As you should know, Hart's criticism of the command theory focuses upon the idea of rule-following. Hart says that there are vital differences between merely habitual behaviour, that is, doing things *as a rule*, and rule-following, *making it a rule* to do something. He says that it is wrong to describe rule-governed behaviour as merely regular and habitual behaviour. Instead, there must be some kind of acceptance of that regular behaviour as being a *reason* or *standard* for behaving in that regular way. So, he says there must be 'a reflective critical attitude to this pattern of behaviour'. And he describes the way courts and so on, in identifying various legal rules, accept rules of recognition. He says that they:

> '... manifest their own acceptance of them as guiding rules and with this attitude goes a characteristic vocabulary different from the natural expressions of the external point of view. Perhaps the simplest of these is the expression, "it is the law that ..."'

These sorts of statement, which we all make, are to be contrasted with *external* statements about the law, which do not signify that the speaker himself accepts them. In these cases, we say, not that 'It is the law that ...' but such things as, 'In the United Kingdom, *they recognise* as law ...' and so on. Thus Hart says that this is an external statement:

'... because it is the natural language of an external observer of the system who, without himself accepting its rule of recognition, states the fact that others accept it.'

Students should bear in mind the above analysis when considering the rule of recognition because, of course, it is itself subject to the same analysis. The analysis is important for understanding the relationship between effectiveness and validity in Hart's theory. Hart says that it is 'pointless' to talk of legal validity unless the legal system referred to is generally effective. He says that sometimes it might have a point, say, when teaching a subject like Roman law. The Roman legal system is no longer effective, yet, he says, a vivid way of teaching it is to discuss the validity of the particular rules in that system as if the system were still effective.

But this sort of example aside, he says that generally when we talk of legal validity in a particular legal system we presuppose that the system is generally effective. So he says:

'One who makes an internal statement concerning the validity of a particular rule of a system may be said to *presuppose* the truth of the external statement of fact that the system is generally efficacious.'

The criteria, in Hart's opinion, for the existence of a legal system are as follows:

First, the *officials* of the legal system must have the internal attitude towards the rule of recognition of the system, and it *not* necessary (although it might be so) that private citizens have the internal attitude towards the rules. (They might obey simply out of fear, as in the command model.) So Hart says:

'What is crucial is that there should be a unified or shared official acceptance of the rule of recognition containing the system's criteria of validity.'

Secondly, the valid legal rules of the system must generally be obeyed by both officials and the private citizens. So Hart says:

'So long as the laws which are valid by the system's tests of validity are obeyed by the bulk of the population this surely is all the evidence we need in order to establish that a given legal system exists.'

There are a number of criticisms of Hart's theory of the rule of recognition and the secondary sources adequately provide reference to them. But two important criticisms should be noted by candidates. One is Finnis' criticism in *Natural Law and Natural Rights* (1980), Chapter 1. A shorter version is to be found in his 'Revolutions and Continuity of Law' in *Oxford Essays in Jurisprudence, Second Series*. His criticism is that Hart leaves insufficiently specified the sort of attitude towards the rule of recognition that the officials have. Finnis says that there are a number of attitudes that could be described by this phrase and that – and here he employs Hart's own definitional technique – there must be a 'central set of elements' that constitute an official's acceptance of the rule of recognition. Finnis' own view, which is a complex variant of natural law, is that the central set of elements constituting an official's acceptance of a rule of recognition is a *moral* acceptance of the rule. In this way, Finnis claims to have found a conceptual, logical link between validity and morality. A similar sort of criticism of the rule of recognition is to be found in the final Appendix to MacCormick's *Legal Reasoning and Legal Theory* (1978). Students might note, too, that there is a strong connection between Finnis' thesis and Dworkin's thesis that a proper legal theory must explain the 'moral force' of law and that a proper interpretation of law requires us to 'make the best moral sense' of our legal practices.

10.7 Raz's theory

Raz goes a long way to answering Hart's critics. He identifies three main features of analytical jurisprudence. One concerns the special features of the judicial process and of judicial reasoning. The second encompasses the discussion of legal concepts such as rights, duties, ownership, legal persons, and so on, and of types of legal standards such as rules and principles, duty imposing standards and power conferring standards. The third range of problems revolves round the idea of a legal system and the features which distinguish such systems from other normative systems.

10.8 The demarcation of law

In *The Problem about the Nature of Law* (1982) Raz draws a useful distinction between moral and legal rules. This centres on the difference between the legislator's duty and the judge's duty. When we are deciding what rule to adopt, we are concerned to ask what general reasons there are for adopting it. This is a purely deliberative phase, characteristic of the legislator's job, although judges are equally faced with it at times.

However, there is a transition from deliberative to executive behaviour. Once it has been resolved to adopt a decision in a legal system, then it becomes regarded as settled or decided. An appeal to law is thus an appeal to something that has been settled or laid down. Practical reasoning of the deliberative kind is then excluded. We no longer ask what are the reasons for this rule, we simply ask, 'what is the meaning of the rule?'. The fact that a rule has been decided excludes or overrides any further general consideration of the reasons for the rule, whether they be of a moral or practical nature.

Raz employs the concept of a rule of recognition and, like Hart, his view is that a rule of recognition is a question of fact. If people actually recognise and apply the rule of recognition in that they adopt only rules made in a certain way, then it exists. The rule of recognition represents a legal rule by which it can be determined, first, what sources of law are and, secondly, what the hierarchy of legal sources is.

Raz also quite sensibly asserts that for a legal system to exist, it must be effective. Therefore, we look to social facts to verify whether a legal system exists. Thus, he says:

'Whether a legal system is in force depends on its impact on the behaviour of people in the society ... [N]ormative systems are existing legal systems because of their impact on the behaviour of individuals, because of their role in the organisation of social life. Consequently, when we look at legal systems as systems of laws ... we should look for those features which enable them to fulfil a distinctive role in society. These will be the features which distinguish legal systems from other normative systems.'

Raz concedes that this is an assumption, and a not uncontroversial one at that. However, the institutional approach, coupled with a sense that law has a distinct purpose, is one that avoids requiring that legal systems be identified by their content or by their morality. It is thus a clearly positivist approach. However, as already noted, 'those features which legal systems must possess to fulfil their unique social function entail that they also have certain moral characteristics'.

As a consequence of this second criterion of function, which is determinable by reference to the institutions required to achieve it, Raz asserts that one of the defining features of law is its institutional system. He determines that the institution that most readily indicates the existence of a legal system is a 'primary institution'. A primary institution is recognised by the way that it performs its function, which can be divided into four categories:

1. those which are concerned with authoritative determinations or decisions;
2. those making these decisions about normative situations, namely, those situations where the question may be 'ought he have done it?', or 'should he do it?';
3. those that apply pre-existing rules or norms; and,
4. those in which the determinations are binding.

The most obvious example of a primary institution is a court, though this is not the only thing that a court does. Yet these features are critical, says Raz, for it to be said that a legal system exists, rather than any particular form of institution, such as a court.

Simply speaking, law must actually provide a method for settling disputes, but also provide guidance, because institutions must decide on the basis of pre-existing rules. This means that their decisions will be regular and therefore predictable. Thus, legal systems are not systems where officials can settle problems in whatever way they think is fit. Law is distinguished from absolute discretion.

It is possible that two sets of rules may contend for the title of legal system in one society. In such a situation, reference must be made to purely societal facts and attitudes, as well as to the effectiveness of constitutional law, that is, whether it is obeyed, in order to decide which one is the prevailing system.

In conclusion, efficacy and demarcation are very strongly linked because what demarcates law from other things is that it achieves its unique social role. In other words, it is effective in carrying out its purpose. In many ways, therefore, Raz is approaching the formulation suggested by Fuller that the existence of a legal system is a question of achievement of purpose, although Raz emphasises the issue of societal effect.

10.9 The 'uniqueness' of law

As we have seen, Raz asserts that law has a unique social function to perform. He employs the following criteria that amount to exclusive and necessary characteristics of law.

Legal systems are comprehensive

Most normative systems do not claim authority to regulate every aspect of life; however, law does. Morality has nothing to say about what colour to paint my house, yet a legal system could so decree. Cricket rules apply only to cricket, not to tennis or driving. A legal system, however, claims to have the authority to determine what we say, what we do in bed and, in terms of *mens rea* in criminal cases, even judges us by our thoughts and intentions.

Raz makes two critical points, however.

1. A legal system need not actually regulate all aspects of social life, but simply claims authority to do so.
2. Not all systems that claim authority to be comprehensive are legal systems; it is simply one necessary feature of a legal system.

Legal systems claim to be supreme

As a logical *sequitur* of the above, a legal system must also claim to be supreme. All legal systems are mutually incompatible at least to a certain extent. Legal systems may adopt the norms of other legal systems, may co-exist with other normative systems, but must, if they are to be comprehensive, reserve the right to exclude the binding application of any other rule.

Legal systems are open systems

A feature of legal systems is that they can, to a certain degree, be open. What this entails is the adoption of norms, already present in society, to which the legal system gives binding force. An example might be the societal institution of the promise which is a normative convention that most legal systems adopt and enforce, under given circumstances. The more of such societal and other norms that a legal system adopts, the more open it is.

From this analysis, Raz concludes that: 'law claims to provide the general framework for the conduct of all aspects of social life and sets itself as the supreme guardian of society'.

10.10 Raz's formulation of validity

As we have observed, there seems to be a concern, particularly among lawyers, to have a vision of what makes law valid. Raz's formulation of validity is a complex one to be found in detail in *The Concept of a Legal System*. He sees three levels at which we can view legal validity.

1. At one level, a legal system is valid if it is effective. This makes more sense if we remember that, for Raz, effectiveness is the achievement of law's unique social purpose. The achievement of that purpose depends on primary law-applying institutions determining cases on the basis of the rules.
2. This requires that there be an acceptance of these rules as valid on the part of the primary institutions. This may be for three reasons:
   a) The members of the institution morally endorse the value of the rule, that is, it is valid because it has moral authority. Obviously, it would be factually unrealistic to suggest this applies to all rules.
   b) There may be a rule of recognition which states that all rules made in a certain way are to be treated as valid. Therefore, although a rule might not have moral authority in itself, it may be valid because it is of a class of norms recognised as being valid. It is therefore valid because it belongs to a valid legal system.
   c) A rule may be alien to the legal system, but in an open legal system, as defined above, this will be a valid rule, even though it does not belong to the system, if it is enforced by the legal system. Therefore, although private international law is not part of the English legal system, its rules are nonetheless treated as valid.

      (b) and (c) have, according to Raz, 'systemic' validity because they either belong to or are enforced by the system. A type (1) rule may also be valid because it belongs to the system, but it has the additional authority of a moral endorsement.

      The question therefore becomes: 'What is validity, if it is not a moral endorsement?' Raz then asks, 'What does it mean to say that a legal system is valid?' To explain his complex reasoning we might contrast the following reasons why a woman refuses to marry a man:
      a) 'People do not get married these days!' Now, this is not a valid argument. Just because other people do not do something is not (at least in the usual case), in itself, a reason for not doing something. The statement is not a valid argument because the question is a normative one: 'Why should we not get married?'
      b) 'I am already married. If I married you as well I would be a bigamist!' This does not mean that the woman does not want to get married, but there is an exclusionary reason, a particular rule, which prevents further action. The argument is a valid argument and gives a reason why she cannot get married.

However, it is not necessarily a reason that she morally endorses. She might believe that having more than one husband is perfectly moral, but she accepts that there is a rule that prevents her from having two husbands.

c) 'I am a radical feminist and believe that marriage is an instrument of sexual oppression!' This is a valid argument because it is based on a moral belief. It is also an exclusionary reason.

All of these are answers to the normative question: 'Why should we not get married?' The first statement is only a valid argument if there is a further reason why she should behave like other people. As such it is a statement that is *conditional on the existence on a valid reason*. The second statement gives a valid reason that is based on an exclusionary rule against bigamy, but does not commit the speaker to a moral acceptance that the rule is a correct one. The rule is valid in the sense that the person feels bound by it, but not necessarily because of moral endorsement. It is therefore *morally detached*. The third answer is a *committed statement* in that it morally endorses a reason that the speaker not only feels bound by, but also agrees with.

How does this help us understand validity? To state that law is valid is tantamount to saying that there is a good reason why it should be obeyed. This is to be differentiated from saying that law is effective, which is tantamount to saying that law is obeyed. The former statement is normative, in that it says that it should be obeyed. The latter is descriptive in that it says that law is obeyed.

Raz concludes that to say law is valid is a normative statement, either of a detached or committed kind. However, as we have already seen, for rules to amount to a legal system, they must be effective. So to say that law is valid is a normative statement, implying that there is a good reason for obeying it. It is also a statement dependent on the existence of social facts, namely, the adoption of rules by primary institutions. And, finally, to say that law is valid does not necessarily mean that the speaker is morally endorsing the law, but simply that there is an exclusionary reason for obeying it.

10.11 The position of rules

Raz sees problems in Hart's adoption of rules. Most significantly, the requirement for criticism and support of rules that is central to Hart's theory leads to an ambiguity, according to Raz, between moral and non-moral reasons for action. Usually, language employed to criticise other people's behaviour is on the basis of moral claims (whether genuinely felt by the speaker or not).

As we have just seen, Raz seeks to distinguish between morally committed normative statements and morally detached statements. To explain people's response to law, we can only really talk in terms of the reasons upon which they act. These reasons are not always spoken, so Raz formulates a theory of reasoning to explain this fact. This speculation about what people think, as opposed to what they say or do, is termed a 'heuristic approach'.

Practical reasoning and norms

'[I]ntuitively, it is always the case that one ought to do whatever one ought to do on the balance of reasons.' This is the core of Raz's theory of practical reasoning. For Raz, reasons can be separated into first and second order reasons. An example of the way in which these things work is the following.

1. 'I have bought some 1934 champagne. Because I like champagne I have a first order reason for drinking it. However, there is a second order reason why I should not, in that I promised my friend I would buy it for him to drink.'
2. 'People have an obligation to keep their promises. This entails that they are not at liberty to break their promises whenever they find, all things considered, it will be the best thing to do so. But this does not mean that they ought to keep promises come what may. The presence of reasons of another kind will justify breaking the promise.'

Thus, although a promise might be a second order reason that excludes further deliberation as to whether I want to drink the champagne (I should not, since I promised it to my friend), it may be that there is another obligation involved. For example, the doctor has ordered my friend not to drink, so that keeping my promise would result in harm to him.

For Raz, the existence of a legal rule gives us a second order reason that tips the balance of reasons why I should or should not do something. Second order reasons are weightier than first order reasons and fundamentally affect the way in which we decide what to do. However, laws are not the only second order reasons, for moral rules are equally to be regarded as second order rules. Thus, Raz comes to an interesting conclusion for a positivist. Courts, when they adopt valid rules in order to decide a case, apply legal rules because of the rule of recognition, which is a second order reason to exclude other non-legal rules. However, the rule of recognition is not the only second order reason that the court considers. Ultimately, a judge may be faced with a law that he should apply because it is validated by the rule of recognition, yet he considers that it is too immoral to apply. This is tantamount to saying that there is a stronger second order reason of a moral nature.

In consequence, Raz contends that the acceptance of rules of recognition is a moral decision, not just a matter of fact as Hart asserts. It must be made clear that obviously people do not always act in accordance with the rules that they should obey and as such this acceptance need not be morally right, it simply has a moral dimension.

Reasons and rules

Raz contends that normative statements are statements that imply or express the existence of second order reasons. By reducing statements to this, Raz is able to unravel some critical questions.

1. Not all normative statements are expressed as rules: there are also principles, imperatives and permissions.
2. Not all reasons for action are expressed, yet they are commonly obeyed because the reasons are self-evident. For example, we need not be told to avoid pain.
3. The fact that people do behave in a certain way is not in itself a reason why people should behave in a certain way.
4. A good reason may exist for someone not to do something, notwithstanding that he always does it. A reason is a concept and does not require that it be acted upon for it to exist.

Thus, Raz rejects Hart's narrow concept that law is a system of rules and instead employs the concept of the norm, which is essentially a second order reason for action. Principles, rules, imperatives, permissions and even personal maxims are norms. Second order reasons are reasons in themselves. As such we do not ask, 'Is there a good reason why the law imposes a duty of care?' We simply think, 'I have a legal duty to be careful.' When a rule passes to the executive stage it becomes fixed and there is no point considering the deliberative reasons for which it was made when deciding whether to obey it.

Although norms are the product of practical reasoning, such as the laws of negligence, they are in themselves to be regarded as secondary reasons, because they have been determined or fixed when the norm passes from the deliberative to the executive stage. Raz goes on to elucidate and individuate the various kinds of legal norms.

Mandatory norms, which include rules

These are norms that provide exclusionary reasons for behaving or not behaving in a certain way. They often are expressed as conclusive reasons for behaviour as in the example of the girl who will not marry, because she is already married. She might have equally said because the law prevents me.

Permissions, consisting of:

Weak permissions. If there is no legal norm that either permits, forbids or empowers a person to act, the person may be said to have a weak permission to do something. There is thus no positive reason for doing something entailed by a weak permission.

Strong permissions. If there are second order reasons, such as rules that prohibit an action, a strong permissive norm allows one to ignore the rules against doing something. Thus, there is a positive norm that allows one to do something.

Power conferring norms

Raz indicates that there are powers to create and abolish norms and also powers to change the way in which norms apply to individuals. For people to have power, that is, for them to be able to do things that alter the nature or application of norms, there must be a second order reason why they, as opposed to other people, can do this. These second order reasons for the power to change existing norms are therefore termed power conferring norms. These include the power to legislate and the power to make contracts.

10.12 Raz and Dworkin

Raz has recently come out with an important attack on the Dworkinian position in his 'The Relevance of Coherence', Chapter 12 of *Ethics in the Public Domain* (1994). This is very carefully and fully argued and represents Raz's current thinking on the nature of adjudication. The basic criticism goes as follows. Raz draws a fundamental distinction between coherence and integrity. He says there is nothing in *Law's Empire* which supports the idea of interpretation and integrity to require anything in favour of coherence. Instead, the arguments only support one aspect of integrity, which is that judges should act on principles which may never have been considered or approved, either explicitly or implicitly, by any legal authority and which are not up to the 'best standards' of morality or justice. Raz has in mind decisions which have to be made in accordance with well-established lines of authority and which meet the Dworkinian tests of 'fit'.

The objection Raz raises to this approach, which does accurately portray what Dworkin requires of integrity, is that not only is it not grounded in any moral view but it derives:

> '... from a desire to see the law, and judicial activities, as based to a larger degree than they are in fact or should be in morality, on an inner legal logic which is separate from ordinary moral and political considerations of the kind that govern normal government, in all its branches.'

Raz's point is that first, Dworkin's idea of integrity is not a 'morally coherent' one because of the reliance on 'fit' and, secondly, that the appeal of the law's 'speaking with one voice', which is on what Dworkin purports to base the 'morally best' interpretation, is really an appeal to blind faith in an 'inner logic' of the law 'working itself pure'.

You might care to link this criticism to Fuller's position on the 'inner morality' of law. Fuller believed that, as he said, evil aims 'lacked logic' and that if evil rulers were required, by his eight principles, to be open and consistent in their dealings with those they governed, then evil aims would gradually become less evil and the law would 'work itself pure'. But Fuller nowhere defended this claim in great detail and it is reasonable to suppose his belief was founded on belief alone (eg 'Professor

Hart seems to assume that evil aims may have as much coherence and inner logic as good ones. I, for one, *refuse* to accept that assumption ... I shall have to rest on the assertion of a belief that may seem naive, namely, that coherence and goodness have more affinity than coherence and evil.' 'A Reply to Professor Hart' (1958) *Harvard Law Review*.

10.13 Evaluation of Raz

Even this fairly involved account of Raz does not adequately give a picture of the complexity or sophistication he has brought to Hart's approach. Raz's concept of practical reasoning is not derived from linguistic philosophy, but actually contributes new ideas to it. MacCormick views Raz's theory as unquestionably the best defence yet for the positivist thesis. Some observations might be offered.

Raz allows that a legal system can co-exist with another legal system, but at the same time suggests that there is a potential that these may be mutually exclusive. He does not provide the jurist with a formula by which he might determine which legal system he must obey. Instead Raz suggests that the choice of which rules to recognise is a question of political morality.

Raz asserts that lawyers make a moral choice to accept the rule of recognition (this is a simplification of his position). This may be falsified by the existence of coercive forces that are external to the legal system. Take, for example, a country controlled by secret police and clandestine coercion. Superficially, the judiciary may be applying the law through choice, but fear may be their motivation for doing so. Social and political coercion is very real in certain countries. Does this affect the validity of law? Just as moral and legal rules might be second order reasons for acting, might not duress also be so?

Although he goes a long way towards differentiating legal from other normative systems, a certain element of his differentiation is an assumption that legal rules are unique. But none of his criteria of comprehensiveness, supremacy and openness clearly differentiates law from all other normative systems. Even when we apply the matter of authoritative determinations and look for effects on behaviour, the same could have been said of the Catholic Church a few centuries ago. Perhaps Raz would regard the rules of the Catholic Church as a legal system but it seems doubtful. However, to be fair, there are not that many other normative systems with the features that Raz identifies.

A related question is whether legal norms are generally to be regarded as weightier second order reasons that moral norms. This is a critical question. By a legal system's claim to be supreme, it would seem that legal norms should be viewed as superior second order reasons. Raz is not particularly clear on this issue, since he suggests that the judiciary is still able to take account of other second order reasons.

Raz's book *Ethics in the Public Domain* (1994), consisting of a set of essays which cover both his normative theory of justice as freedom and his theory of positive law, is given a helpfully clear review in *Modern Law Review* (1995) by Richard Lucy. Particularly useful is the overall description which Lucy provides of Raz's liberalism (the main theses of which were first published in his widely admired work in 1986 on normative jurisprudence entitled *The Morality of Freedom*). The view which is now becoming generally accepted amongst jurists is that Raz's legal positivism – as opposed to his liberalism – suffers from its location in historical facts of power. To understand this idea, which has its roots in Austin, we need to appreciate that physical power, for Raz, is the source of law's authority (and, indeed, all authority). Raz's analysis is in many ways compelling; 'authoritative' statements are those which have a 'peremptory force' (see Hart *Essays on Bentham* Chapter 10, 'Commands and Authoritative Legal Reasons') which means that they require obedience (or conformity) without the need for giving reasons other than that these statements are issued *from a particular source*. An easy way to this source idea is through the authority of an expert; for example, we have no intuitive difficulties, as laypeople, in saying that something is so and that we must comply, simply because it was said with the authority of, say, a clinical medical consultant ('doctor knows best'). In the case of law, the authority arises from the historical location of power; the law of theft is 'law' by virtue of the authority of 'the sovereign's having made it so' and its authority arises from no other reason.

But, as Lucy points out, Raz does not really answer the question, posed by so many jurists (Duff, Simmonds, Finnis and Shiner for example) as to why judges would recognise the authority of a particular sovereign. Raz is not an Austin, or Bentham, and he takes the Hartian line that rules of recognition must be accepted by judges. These specify the criteria of legal validity (and thus explain the normative quality of law in its efforts to match human behaviour with commonly accepted standards). These, in turn, locate the source of law in the sovereign. But why should a judge accept the rule of recognition? Fear? Self-interest? Humanity? A full theory of law would specify the criteria of acceptance and the short list I have drawn up suggests that humanity would/should be ranked earlier than fear and self-interest. If that is the case, the road to the anti-positivist, natural law camp is clear and Lucy rightly points out that Raz, in this latest set of essays, has failed to confront his critics on this crucial point.

Christopher Morris has written a long and thoughtful review of Raz's *Ethics in the Public Domain* (1994) in *Ethics* (1996). It is a difficult read in some ways but it has the advantage of explaining clearly what Raz's theories of law and morality are basically about, in particular, in very useful summaries of Raz's main positions. Morris expresses the view, shared by a number of philosophers, that Raz's positions are powerful intuitively but stand in many instances in need of further justification: 'Raz articulates well what I tend to believe, but I do not, after a certain point, know what to say in defence of some of the central theses.'

10.14 The idea of a 'hard case'

Dworkin has popularised the idea of a 'hard case'. In general, his use of the term refers to those issues faced by a judge or a lawyer which are contentious and potentially litigable. Specifically, a hard case is a situation in the law that gives rise to genuine argument about the truth of a proposition of law that cannot be resolved by recourse to a set of plain facts *determinative* of the issue.

Let us take Hart's famous example of the statutory provision prohibiting vehicles from the park, where there are no statutory definitions and no judicial decisions that guide interpretation. Does it include roller skates? His answer is that the rule about vehicles is just inherently unspecific about whether roller skates are included and that a judge could settle matters by declaring a result one way or another, thus making the rule in relation to the roller skates a 'plain fact' for the future. Every rule, he says, has a 'penumbra' where its meaning is uncertain. Nevertheless, we would not have an idea of what the penumbra was unless we first had a firm grasp of the idea of the core.

It is useful, first of all, to consider whether there can be 'plain facts' of linguistic practice. There clearly are. But this fact does not entail a view that there are 'acontextual' meanings. For example, we can dispense with a sceptical response to my assertion, by saying that, in ordinary circumstances, the word 'vehicle' includes a 20 ton lorry. That is so, by virtue of our linguistic practices, meaning simply that an empirical observation of the way in which 'vehicle' is used shows that it is consistently applied to 20 ton lorries. *It is not an odd idea.* Dictionaries record current usage in precisely this way, and dictionary definitions are right or wrong measured against, speaking widely, empirically observable practice.

According to Dworkin, therefore, legal positivism is the appealing theory that law is identifiable with the clear empirically identifiable facts of legal practice. The law is expressed in language and must rely on plain – clear – meanings. It must, therefore, rely on clear dictionary meanings in the large part. It follows that these penumbral meanings do not come within the law. Why? It is that since, by hypothesis, they are not defined either in statute or in a subsequent judgment, they are not *plainly* vehicles within the dictionary definition. And so, according to the plain fact account, they are not vehicles for the purposes of the statute. In other words, if the law is not clearly identifiable it is clearly *not* law. This is so, if we take the central characterising feature of positivism to be its insistence upon clarity.

Many critics do not like this conclusion. Neil MacCormick, for example, says that it is simply not true. Law, he says, is identifiable by criteria of recognition and these may use predicates like 'honest' or 'reasonable' or 'fair' and so forth. Further, rules of adjudication may require or permit judges to 'take account of' moral values in their interpretations. None of this, says MacCormick, is excluded from Hart's definition.

On penumbral issues, there is no uniform practice amongst the officials. In Hart's terms, there is no 'concordant' practice, no concordant acceptance of rules of recognition. Is there law there nevertheless? At first sight, on Hart's own terms, there is not. What if there was a split in official practice? That could mean two things. There might simply be *no* practice here, because judges have such widely different views, say, on the question of the extent to which, in the United Kingdom, arguments drawn from the European Convention of Human Rights are relevant in identifying rules of law of the United Kingdom.

But there may be differing *practices* where, say, judges and other officials are equally divided on the question of whether the United Kingdom Parliament could bind itself in law. According to the view of positivism here discussed, what is the law? Either it is both the law that Parliament can bind itself and the law that it cannot, or it is not law at all. On a weakened view of official practice, ignoring Hart's reference to the 'concordance' of the practice, we obtain a virtually nonsensical result for law. In a nutshell, neither rule follows from the rule of recognition.

10.15 The implications for judicial reasoning

What implications, in Dworkin's view, does legal positivism have for judicial reasoning? He says that when judges are faced with a case in which there is no empirically identifiable law, no law determines the issue. It follows that, in exercise of his clear legal duty to come to a decision one way or the other, the judge must make his decision on grounds other than legal ones. The phrase so often used in this context is that 'the judge must exercise his discretion' in order to come to a decision.

What are the consequences for adjudication on this account? The positivist has two possibilities: he can either deny that there is any law in these unclear cases, or he can say that there is law there but it requires a different method for its identification. These two possibilities may be considered in turn.

Is Dworkin correct in saying that the judge either legislates or he does not? Let us focus in on this claim. The point about these difficult sorts of cases is that it really is unclear what the law is or should be. If the plain fact view of law is the correct one, then it follows that there is no law at all where there are no plain facts of the matter which tell us what the law is. Therefore, a judge who comes to a decision in one of these penumbral type cases is not applying law in the predetermined plain fact sense. The judge is not applying law, because the only law that exists is that of the empirically identifiable sort.

It may further be objected that it is not correct to call the judge a 'legislator' since this goes the further step of saying that positivism speaks to the role of the judges. This is an important objection. If the judge is not applying law in the penumbral cases what is he doing? Is he bound by law? The answer, it seems, is that he is not. If the statute is not clear on the question whether a person has committed a criminal offence by taking a skateboard through the park, then there is no law on the matter. What is the law that binds the judge? There is plain fact law on the question whether a person has committed a criminal offence if he takes a bicycle through the park. Does this have any bearing on the question whether a skateboarder has committed an offence? The answer, for positivism, taken to be the theory that the law is plain fact law only, must be that it has none at all. The idea of 'bearing on the question' is insufficiently clear as to determine the question whether our skateboarder has broken the law.

10.16 The doctrine of the separation of powers

If this account is right, the judge must act in a similar role to the legislature, because he must make new law. There is none on the skateboarder question, so he creates new law on the matter. It is 'new' law because there was nothing in the previous law that guided, or constrained, or impelled him to his decision. This conclusion must, then, speak to the judicial role. It means that every time a judge decides one of these cases, which, of course, are the characteristic sorts of case in the appellate courts, he is as unconstrained as the legislature is in creating new law.

But is Dworkin right in concluding that judges should be controlled in their decision-making? The obvious and most general answer is that a judge has a unique constitutional role. This role centrally concerns adjudication. The judge has therefore great power by virtue of his access to initiating acts of state coercion. He is characteristically unelected and he is not, at least directly, responsible to an electorate. Indeed, it is often thought to be a virtue of the judicial office that the judge should not be swayed in his decision-making by popular demand. Rather, it is thought, the judge should be swayed solely by his sense of justice as to the merits of the case before him. In Lord Scarman's words:

> 'The judge, however wise, creative, and imaginative he may be, is "cabin'd, cribb'd, confin'd, bound in" not, as was Macbeth, to his "saucy doubts and fears" but by the evidence and arguments of the litigants. It is this limitation, inherent in the forensic process, which sets bounds to the scope of judicial law reform.'

Further, the judge has a special role *vis-à-vis* the legislature. The legislature is the institution in a democracy through which the will of the electorate (to use a popular metaphor) is expressed. The judge, not being elected, must not substitute his own will as against the legislature. To do so would be to 'usurp the function of the legislature'. The judge is, instead, concerned with matters which are subsidiary to the legislature's role, such as adjudicating on the precise merits of disputes in individual cases.

So Dworkin's criticism here points us to a dilemma. He says that it is supposed to be a virtue of positivism that it clearly shows us when a judge is out on his own, as it were, independent of the constraints of law. On the other hand, in the explicit recognition that as a result the judge is making new law, like the legislature, we are forced to the conclusion that the judge's characteristic form of adjudicating is directly counter to what we consider an important feature of our democratic procedures – the doctrine of the separation of powers.

10.17 The way lawyers and judges talk

There is another problem, according to Dworkin, in the idea that the judge acts as legislator. Judges (and lawyers whose role is parasitic on the judicial role) do not talk as though they were performing the same function as legislators and, further, if they are legislating, this means that their legislative decisions are being applied retrospectively. Let us consider both these ideas in turn.

Certainly, judges speak judicially of their being 'bound by law'. This is apparent from courtroom language and the reports of judgments, even in the most innovative of cases. Take, for instance, Lord Atkin's introduction to his famous statement of the neighbour principle in the law of tort: 'Who in law is my neighbour?' It would have sounded odd had he asked: 'Who in law *ought* to be my neighbour?' Lawyers make submissions in court about what the law is. The judges come to decisions about what the law is. Always there is the background matrix of law from which both judges and lawyers draw their arguments. At times, when a judge decides that there is no argument that he can extrapolate from this background matrix, he will make a pronouncement about the appropriateness of his judicial role to decide such a matter.

An idea to consider is why it is that judges and lawyers talk in this characteristic way. One reason could be that judges, certainly in the United States, and probably in the United Kingdom, although admittedly that is not so clear, have been or are conscious of the doctrine of the separation of powers. They endeavoured, at one time, anyway, to express their judgments in terms appropriate to that doctrine: they did not make the law, they only declared what it was.

This explanation, according to Dworkin, forces us to reconsider the difficulty which we came across when we considered the role of the judge as a legislator. The obvious response is that if we do not think judges should legislate and they do not talk as if they legislate, this is a very good reason for supposing that not only do they not legislate but the doctrine of the separation of powers is alive and kicking in our legal system.

10.18 Retrospective legislation

According to Dworkin, yet another problem remains. If judges make up the law and apply it to the parties before them, it must follow that the law is being made after the events occurred and that the parties are made subject to law that was, by hypothesis, not in force when the events occurred. The law is thus applied retrospectively. Strong positivism acknowledges this consequence as an unfortunate but unavoidable consequence of the indeterminate nature of rules. When a state of affairs occurs where there is no rule in the clear sense required for the plain fact theory, the judge simply has to legislate and thus create a clear rule.

But is this fair to the party who loses out? He can say, very plausibly, that he did not break the law because there was no law at the time. That is a powerful argument. There is only one counter to him, an argument which, in my view, is specious. This is to say that, since this was an unclear, penumbral case, and it was by virtue of this fact that there was no law governing the matter, he had no reason to be surprised by a decision either way.

So what has he to complain about? Assuming that he wanted to conform to the law regarding the skateboard, he could not know with certainty whether taking the skateboard through the park was in conformity with law or not. All he can do is take the risk. What difference does it make to his position that he was subsequently fined? The risk was one of which he was or should have been aware.

There is more to the principle of *nulla poena sine lege* than the protection of reasonable expectations. A citizen has a complaint that even though he was not surprised by later retrospective legislation there was no liability at the time he did the act. The principle connects significantly with the idea of the rule of law, which requires that official acts be in accordance with law. This latter principle speaks to accountability, not clarity. If the citizen is being made retrospectively liable, it is because there was no law at the time that made him liable that places the special duty upon the legislature to justify retrospective legislation.

10.19 Conclusion on Dworkin

Dworkin's view is that positivism wrongly omits to characterise as part of its model, the role of moral principles in legal argument. Since, as he observes, such principles appear to be a significant and important part of legal argument, especially as it is carried on by lawyers and judges in the day to day practices of the courts, legal positivism should provide and adequate characterisation of it. With the idea of principles of law (moral in content though they be) inherently involved in the hard cases, the above three dilemmas faced by the positivist account are solved: there *is* law there, albeit in the form of principles. So, the judges are *judging*, not legislating; they are not retrospectively legislating, and they are not cynically 'covering up' what they are, in fact, doing quite legitimately. But more about this in Chapter 24!

10.20 Hart's posthumous postscript to the second edition of *The Concept of Law*

Posthumously, a second edition of *The Concept of Law* by Hart was published in 1994. It is predominantly the same but for a 'Postscript' that has been added. In this postscript Hart shows that he is not really prepared to shift his ground in spite of the attacks particularly of Ronald Dworkin; in particular, he defends himself against Dworkin's attack on his version of legal positivism and his perceived attack on Hart's method of legal theory.

1. Hart thinks Dworkin is wrong to suppose that there is such a sharp distinction between rules and principles. There is a difference since principles are less specific and embody non-conclusive reasons for decision-making, and also perhaps involve reasons which are of a particularly important kind. But he thinks Dworkin exaggerates the differences and refers to the *Riggs* v *Palmer* (1889) decision which Dworkin famously uses to show how principles decide cases (see *Taking Rights Seriously* Chapter 2). Hart thinks this decision shows clearly not a clash between two principles but between a rule and a principle. Hart just asserts that there was a clear rule of succession that a murderer could inherit from the estate of the person he murdered; Dworkin denies that there was any such rule but that there was a general principle, outweighed by another in that case ('no man should profit from his own wrong'), that the clear words of a valid will should be closely adhered to.

2. Hart rejects any kind of view which says that moral judgments about what people's rights are are part of the identification of their legal rights. He says that the reason simply is that legal rights and duties are the point at which the law protects or restricts individual freedom by allowing individuals the power 'to avail themselves of the law's coercive machinery'. Thus they are independent of the 'moral merits' of the law; presumably because they are only expressive of your 'right to take the matter to court'.

3. Hart maintains his belief that the Nazi-type legal system, while undeniably of moral wickedness, is nevertheless law since the various features it shares with other modern municipal legal systems are too great for a 'universal-descriptive' legal theory, such as he claims his theory to be, to ignore. He points to Dworkin's suggestion that such a legal system might be described in a 'pre-interpretive sense' but then says that Dworkin's concession there about the flexibility of legal language strengthens rather than weakens the positivist's case because it allows the positivist's assertion here to make use of the flexibility of language too:

   '... it does little more than convey the message that while he insists that in a descriptive jurisprudence the law may be identified without reference to morality, things are otherwise for a justificatory interpretive jurisprudence according to which the identification of the law always involves a moral judgment as to what best justifies the settled law.'

   Hart's conclusion here that, in characterising the Nazi legal system, he and Dworkin are really talking at cross purposes seems very reasonable.

4. On the perennial questions raised by the existence of judicial discretion, Hart addresses the question of how such cases might best be resolved. He thinks that there clearly are cases where judges exercise their judicial discretion by acting as 'judicial law-makers' and he does not think that this poses a great threat to democracy. Nevertheless, it seems to me that it is difficult to agree with Hart's following statement:

'... the delegation of limited legislative powers to the executive is a familiar feature of modern democracies and such delegation to the judiciary seems a no greater menace to democracy.'

This remark draws insufficient attention to the very great differences of role and function between the executive and the judiciary. The executive must govern the community as a whole but we do not think that judges are like that at all. *We think* that they should concern themselves with the merits of the dispute relating to the respective rights and duties of the parties before them.

Hart also disagrees with Dworkin that it is a defect of legal positivism that judicial discretion in hard cases is retrospective in effect, something it seems, Hart must concede if he allows for judicial law-*making*. Hart simply says that if there were law *there*, in the cases, or the arguments, or whatever, as Dworkin supposes, it would not be retrospective but it would be as equally surprising to the defendant what decision the judge came to, as in the positivist position whereby the law is 'made' by the judge. Can't Dworkin be defended here? If we are to choose between two theories about what happens in hard cases, we are bound to choose the one that says that, characteristically, the judge is punishing acts which *at the time that they were done* were against or within the law. The defendant who is surprised by a decision that is the result of retrospective legislation is worse off in this sense than the defendant who is surprised at a decision about the law existing at the time he did the act. It is a simple matter of the rule of law: no one should be punished, or whatever, unless there is a law which prohibited (or whatever) the act at the time that it was done. This principle is frequently referred to as the *nulla poena sine lege* principle ('no punishment without law'). We could remember in this connection that it was this principle which Hart so effectively invoked in the important Chapter 9 of his *The Concept of Law*!

5. It appears that Hart sticks to his view that his theory was intended to be both descriptive and general (cf 'an essay in descriptive sociology'), in the sense that it is not tied to any one particular legal system. By 'descriptive' he says that he intended it to be 'morally neutral' and with no 'justificatory aims' and further he says that this is 'a radically different enterprise' from that envisaged by Dworkin. Dworkin's theory, he says, is 'in part evaluative and justificatory and "addressed to a particular legal culture" '. Then he says that because of these differences, he and Dworkin are not in conflict; it is just simply that they are each writing with different aims in mind. But he does take issue with Dworkin's claim that positivist legal theory can be restated as an interpretative theory. Hart thinks that view is 'mistaken'.

Hart's view here is unfortunately not as clear as it could be. It amounts to saying that we can understand legal systems from the moderate external point of view, namely, the point of view of someone who understands that some people accept certain rules (ie adopt the internal point of view) *who does not himself accept* those rules. Hart concedes that such a person must understand what the internal point of view is:

> 'It is true that for this purpose the descriptive theorist must *understand* what it is to adopt the internal point of view and in that limited sense he must be able to put himself in the place of an insider; but that is not to endorse the insider's internal point of view or in any other way to surrender his descriptive stance.'

6. Hart vigorously denies that he is guilty, as Dworkin says, of having committed the cardinal sin of the 'semantic sting'. That criticism, which Dworkin makes in Chapter 1 of *Law's Empire*, is that no adequate account of law can be based on a description solely of how people speak and what the linguistic practices are which they share when talking about law. Hart denies that he ever had such a theory and says that the charge 'confuses the *meaning* of a concept with the criteria for its *application*'. He appears to refer by this phrase to the distinction, current in much contemporary political philosophy and made much use of by Dworkin, between a 'concept' and a 'conception'. Hart clearly thinks that his theory allows for the elaboration of a conception of law. This is interesting in the light of the way the first four chapters of *The Concept of Law* develop for there one would certainly be led to believe that Hart's aim *was* in fact to capture 'linguistic practices' that are a 'plain fact' about the world. However, it becomes clear by the end of the book, especially in the very important Chapter 9, that Hart is *choosing* between concepts.

7. Hart just denies Dworkin's claim that the point or purpose of law or legal practice is to justify coercion:

> '… it certainly is not and never has been my view that law has this as its point or purpose.'

Hart refers, for example, to his invocation of the 'pre-legal' world and says that the proposed introduction of the secondary rules, of adjudication, of recognition and of change, was not intended to answer any question about the justification of the application of the coercive powers of the state.

This is an interesting assertion for it raises the question of what Chapter 9 is about. There, it will be remembered, Hart justified his legal positivism on the grounds that it made clear that (to quote his oft-quoted remark):

> 'What surely is most needed in order to make men clear-sighted in confronting the official abuse of power, is that they should preserve the sense that the certification of something as legally valid is not conclusive of the question of obedience …'

The rule of recognition's point is to *make certain* what is law and what is a matter for personal conscience. This was to place constraints on the power of the state. For example, the 'evil' that had to be balanced against the 'evil' of letting the Nazi grudge informer go free of punishment was the 'evil' of the use of retrospective law-making. Hart's interests are therefore in some way (perhaps more subtle than Dworkin's) connected with the abuse of state power. Actually, in the construction of his theory that laws can be identified independently of personal moral judgment, Hart is very concerned to justify this on the ground that it shows – for good moral reasons – why we should think of legal justifications *having no moral content*. Although this argument requires further elaboration, it seems reasonable to suppose that Hart's concerns are logically dependent upon concerns about the way we should view the justifications that are advanced for applying law.

8. Hart thinks that Dworkin's arguments that not all legal rules can be identified by referring to a social practice (see *Taking Rights Seriously* Chapter 3) shows a serious misunderstanding of what the rule of recognition was intended to be about. Hart claims that Dworkin assumes that the rule is supposed to determine completely the legal result in every case. Not so, he says:

> '... the function of the rule is to determine only the general conditions which correct legal decisions must satisfy in modern systems of law.'

This is the argument to which reference has been made earlier that the rule of recognition is designed to cure the defect of uncertainty. Hart is simply saying that the uncertainty is cured by seeing that the law identified can be incurably ambiguous. After all, under his theory the law is 'vehicles are prohibited, etc ...' and it is asking too much to expect that there should be determination of the ambiguity inherent in the word 'vehicle'.

Understanding this point requires looking closely at Dworkin's criticism in *Taking Rights Seriously* of the idea of the existence of social rules being necessary to identify judicial duties. He argues that they are not necessary since it is possible for us to assert the existence of duties, in general, without it being necessary to point to a social rule to that effect. A good example is that of slavery abolitionists who asserted that we all had duties to release our slaves, even though there was no social rule saying that we ought to so free our slaves (and, in fact, there was a clear social rule saying that we *may* keep slaves – and for the more fundamentalist of the slave-owners, a Bible-sanctioned duty that we do keep slaves).

Dworkin then moves to saying that there is therefore nothing wrong with asserting that, in hard cases, judges are bound by duties *which cannot be identified by reference to social rules* (viz the social rule of recognition). One possible objection he considers to this is the idea that the social rule theory of duty only applies to law for, after all, the slavery abolitionist only invoked a moral duty in us all not to keep slaves. But Dworkin dismisses that argument, which is a common one, by saying that it is equivalent only to the following bad argument:

> 'In general, duties can exist either as the result of a social rule, or as existing in some other way independently of social rules; but in the case of law a social rule is required; that social rule is a rule of recognition which declares affirmatively whether a rule is a valid rule of law imposing a legal duty.'

That is a bad argument, Dworkin says, because it is just an assertion of positivism and that theory cannot refer to itself in support.

The answer given by Hart is two-fold. First he concedes that Dworkin is right to maintain a distinction between rules accepted socially as a matter of convention and rules which have the appearance of being conventionally accepted but, instead, only represent a consensus of independently held convictions. This distinction is crucial for understanding Dworkin's position. The distinction can be illustrated as follows. In Britain, everyone accepts a moral rule prohibiting physical assault; there is a coincidence of our views. Each view, however, is supported by independent reasons each of us has for our conviction that physical assault is morally wrong. So, if asked, you would say 'invades physical integrity; causes pain; etc, etc'. They are your independent reasons for saying why physical assault is wrong. Compare murder with the rule that men must take their hats off in church. There we might well say that the rule is there just because everyone accepts that rule ('it is the accepted convention'). The difference is striking when we consider what a conventional justification would sound like for physical assault. It sounds wrong to give as the reason for thinking physical assault wrong that 'it is the convention' or 'everybody thinks it's wrong' because these sorts of justification aren't strong enough. The fact that other people think that something is wrong is insufficient justification for why you should think it wrong. You have to make up your own mind. This distinction is, incidentally, very similar to the distinction that both Bentham and Austin draw between positive and critical morality. (See above Chapter 8, the part of section 8.3 headed The province of jurisprudence: the different sorts of law.)

Secondly, Hart says that Dworkin's account of social rules is too strong for:

> '... it seems to require not only that the participants who appeal to rules as establishing duties or providing reasons for action must believe that there are good moral grounds or justification for conforming to the rules, but also that there must actually be such good grounds.'

But Dworkin's reply could simply be that it amounts to positivism citing itself in its own support. If judges and lawyers argue as if there were good legal grounds that are at the same time good moral grounds then that fact must be one in support of a legal theory that accounts for it (as Dworkin's theory purports to account for how judges and lawyers argue then it must be a better theory). However, Hart continues to maintain that, despite the controversial nature of law in hard cases, it is wrong to suppose that the rule of recognition can answer 'completely' any question of law, saying that:

> '... the function of the rule is to determine only the general conditions which correct legal decisions must satisfy in modern systems of law.'

9. Hart thinks that his theory is one which Dworkin would term 'soft positivism', although this is contrary to at least one generally understood interpretation of his

theory, which relies heavily on the idea of the rule of recognition supplying certainty in hard cases (ie the certainty that the judges are not applying law but are, instead, law-making). 'Soft' positivism is the view that there are controversial – uncertain – rules of law; so, for example, soft conventionalism allows for the following two rules to be captured by a rule of recognition which recognises the rule 'Vehicles are prohibited in the park': 'skateboards are prohibited' and its contradictory 'skateboards are permitted'. This is the area of the penumbra. Dworkin's view is that (a) since a decision has to be made between these rules, and (b) because in legal practice there clearly is use made of non-rule standards (he calls them 'principles' – see below Chapter 25), there is much more sophistication to legal argument than even soft positivism could allow.

It has never been quite clear (until his Postscript) what Hart's view was since in Chapter 7 of *The Concept of Law* he endorses a much more sophisticated account of legal reasoning in hard cases than appears to be implied by his rigid criteria of what counts as law. Remember: the rule of recognition 'cures the defect' of uncertainty.

10. Hart thinks that while 'large theoretical differences' exist between Dworkin and himself on the question of the relationship of law to morality, nevertheless, they both share the view that there are certain basic facts of legislative history which each of them thinks limit the application of law by judges:

> '… his explanation of the judicial identification of the sources of law is substantially the same as mine.'

But the main difference, he says, lies in the fact that there are few legal systems outside the United States and the United Kingdom in which legal reasoning takes the form of the all-embracing kind ('holistic') that Dworkin says is involved in the idea of constructive interpretation.

10.21 Hart and post-modernism

There is an interesting and, in some ways, extraordinary article by Allan Hutchison in the *Modern Law Review* (1995). Hutchison has been prominent in the critical legal studies and post-modernist movements for well over a decade now (and a prominent protagonist of the theory of Ronald Dworkin). A consistent feature of these movements has been their denigration of liberalism and of Anglo-American legal philosophy, particularly that kind espoused by Hart, Dworkin, Finnis, and so, on the (very spurious) ground that it is narrow, male-focused, individualistic, ignorant of important developments on the Continent, unsceptical, uncritical and so on (perhaps even because it has a centre in Oxford). But in this article, without appearing to realise it, Hutchison gives the game away. He concludes, as if it were an insight for everyone, not just him, that law is not just a set of rules, but that it is open to all sorts of imaginative possibilities. In elaborating his criticsm, he says it is wrong to suppose that jurisprudence is just about analysing language and that exploring legal discourse is about reflecting on social activity. Thus he says:

> 'Understanding language, therefore, is not about abstract reflection, but it is about social activity. The key relation is between speakers rather than between words and things.'

But, for goodness sake, most philosophers abandoned these ideas as late as the 1960s. Indeed, Wittgenstein was saying these things in the late 1940s and it is wrong to suppose that strands of these ideas are not in Hart. This insight into a prominent 'critical' thinker is most illuminating since it corroborates a growing sense amongst many jurists that the critical legal studies movement is energetic, yes, and is mostly well-meaning, but founders miserably when it comes to sustained intellectual rigour or commitment to proper legal scholarship (had Hutchison not read Wittgenstein's *Philosophical Investigations*, nor read those bits in Hart's *The Concept of Law* where Hart says that certain crucial questions are not to be determined as 'matters of linguistic propriety'?). Not convinced? Compare the following in Hutchison with what you know about Dworkin's analogy between the superhuman intellectual ruminations of the ideal and superintelligent and hard-working judge Hercules, and the construction by a group of authors of a chain novel, an analogy which has been the object of great derision amongst critical legal thinkers:

> '... political players are capable of imagining and opening themselves up to possibilities other than those presently available. They are not actors in another story, but they are committed to be "joyful poets of the story that continues to originate what they cannot find".'

11

Natural Law

11.1 Introduction

Despite a recent revival, natural law theories have been frequently scorned by jurists, for a mixture of methodological and philosophical reasons. There seem to be three major areas of criticism of natural law theories. First, the method used to derive rules of natural law appears to make an illogical jump from questions of fact (what is) to questions of obligation (what ought); secondly, natural law theories have frequently been employed to justify the status quo and to validate what would seem to us to be unjust regimes; and third, natural lawyers have failed satisfactorily to explain what effect the difference between natural law and human law has. These three criticisms are not necessarily applicable to all natural law theories, as we shall see.

11.2 What is natural law?

Professor d'Entrèves, whose *Natural Law* contains a considerable survey on the subject, says that many of the ambiguities of the concept of natural law must be ascribed to the ambiguity of the concept of nature that underlies it. This is not surprising, because the search for a coherent set of natural law principles spans about two and a half thousand years. As a result, the content and the role of natural law are varied. However, the core assertion is that, rather than all moral rules being *created by* reason, there are some moral rules that exist independently of reason, but may be understood by it. The way in which man should live is locked up in his nature and the nature of his universe.

This may sound a little crazy to the non-religious student. Indeed, many natural law theories have relied on the will of God to justify the idea, but this is not necessary for the theory to work. There are essentially three questions that need to be satisfied by the natural lawyer in order to justify his position.

1. Are there pre-determined patterns of behaviour in nature and in human nature? For a while, under the influence of thinkers such as Condillac, the idea that humans were born with any pre-determined ends was denied. However, it is clear from, for example, genetic theory, as well as ecological theories, that human behaviour and the human race have certain innate characteristics. Thus, a human being is born with the urge for sexual reproduction, with social instincts such as the protection of offspring. This leads us on to the next question.

2. Why should a human being follow the pattern of behaviour with which he has seemingly been programmed? Since human beings have free choice, a person might easily decide to be celibate or not to have children. The fact that people usually do have children does not mean that an individual should. It is therefore a matter for his or her own choice and so self-interest or personal preference might constrain such a decision. The only justification above the rational, is the moral. We say a person should follow a pattern of behaviour, in moral terms, because it is good. This leads to the problem of whether (1) there is a difference between what is good and what is expedient in the light of desires or enlightened self-interest, and whether (2) we can ascertain a criterion for determining what is good that is of universal application.

3. How do we know that it is good to follow the natural patterns of behaviour and, even if it is, might it not sometimes be better to go against them? This is the hardest of the questions that natural law has to answer. An independent concept

of good has to stem from some person's non-rational preference. There are two alternatives. First, if we can show that all men think that a particular thing is good, then we might say that natural law is self-evidently good and needs no rational justification. Second, there is a superior entity who requires us to do what is good and has ordained these laws.

The latter proposition usually is not employed to stand by itself. We obey God, rather than the Devil, because God is good. Thus we are returned to the question of how we get to this proposition of good. The former proposition of the self-evidence of good denies that there is basis of the concept in normal reasoning. Finnis explains it as follows:

> 'When discerning what is good ... intelligence is operating in a different way, yielding to a different logic, from when it is discerning what is the case (historically, scientifically, or metaphysically); but there is no good reason for asserting that the latter operations of intelligence are more rational than the former ...'

The three questions, of what the content of natural law is, what the nature of the obligation is and why it is a moral obligation, are necessary to overcome the criticism of the empiricists. The empiricist criticisms of natural law follow the pattern of these problems.

The content of natural law

According to the different theories the content is varied and sometimes contradictory. Thus, while the Greeks thought that slavery was a naturally justified institution, we disagree. There is a continuous struggle to nail down the content of natural law. Most thinkers prefer to assert the existence of principles from which a variety of rules can be derived, rather than asserting the rules themselves. On this basis, thinkers such as Stammler can safely assert that while the principle of justice is universal, its application is varied. While this overcomes the problem of moral variance, it also limits the usefulness of the concept. Natural law thus becomes reduced to universal platitudes.

The obligation to obey natural law

Empiricists criticise the fact that even if universal patterns can be demonstrated, this does not show that there is an obligation to follow them. Just because people do something, does not mean they ought to do this. There are alternative answers to the question.

1. People and things have a purpose and are part of a definite order, established by a benevolent creator.
2. The universal principles are motivations, rather than patterns of behaviour and as such they are automatic preferences. This then requires that bad motivations be separated from good motivations.

3. The principles are only rather obvious facts which practical reason dictates we should obey. For example, when faced with the fact that a road is peppered with land mines we do not need to ask why we should not go over it. Similarly, Hart appears to assume that the fact of human vulnerability means that it is self-evident that we should not hurt or injure some human beings. However, this approach provides us with reasons for doing something on grounds of expedience, or self-interest only, rather than principles for action that are to be followed for moral reasons. Morality and self-interest do not, at first sight anyway, appear to coincide.

Is there a moral obligation to obey natural law?

Empiricists find it hard to understand why there is a need to subjugate individual morality to a universal morality, since in the absence of objectively provable moral norms one can only know one's own conscience. It would seem to be a moral contradiction if one were to ignore one's own conscience in order to obey some universal moral law.

11.3 Natural law and legal validity

The student of law might ask why she should be concerned with people's attempts to say what the law should be. Let us take Hart's concept of law, which describes what law is if it is effective. Such an attitude begs the question of why law should be effective. Alternatively, we might describe law, as Kelsen does, in terms of detached statements, which assume that law should be obeyed, because it is assumed to be valid. This leads to an uncritical formula which does not necessarily place law in any social context and leads to the mindless formalism that distances law from practical and moral considerations. Finally we might use *committed* statements which assert that law is valid, but obviously require good reasons, perhaps of the moral sort.

All three types of statements are descriptive, but uncritical. If a scientist were to describe scientific phenomena in terms of the accepted theories, without necessarily testing whether those theories are valid in the light of facts, science would not have progressed from the flat earth of the Middle Ages. Similarly, the advocate, judge and legislator are embarked on a practical course of controlling human behaviour. The lawyer is likely to be more successful in this pursuit if he can not only say what someone should do, but give reasons that will encourage a person to obey. Merely threatening the use of sanctions and employing bribery is not enough to ensure adherence to the law.

The natural lawyer is seeking to offer an authoritative guide to what human nature thinks it ought to do. Thus, although positivism insists on what lawyers actually do and say in order to define the concept of law, natural law seeks to understand what the unifying idea and ideal of law is.

11.4 The origins of natural law

Introduction

The origins of natural law are obscure. However, clearly the human concern to understand an apparently arbitrary world in terms of order would be a starting point. Although certain natural phenomena seemed to conform to definite patterns, human nature did not always, the difference being that humans seemed to have free choice. While natural things seemed to conform to a regularity, as if they were ordained to do so, man did not. Without the complex faith that we have in cause and effect, the idea of some inscrutable purpose of a mysterious creator seemed the obvious way in which things could be accounted for. However man, with her free choice, was not behaving in a clear and uncomplicated way. Man had obviously gone wrong somewhere, since she did not seem always to fit into the order of things.

This is mere speculation, but accords with the tenor of ancient theological theories that form the premise for some natural law theories. The appeal of such theories is an appeal to an order that is above the order that can be attained by individual human cognisance. Plato advocated that society should be ruled by contemplative philosopher-kings, whose inward reflection would allow them to comprehend the divine truths locked in their own hearts. But this did not mean that there was, for early Greek philosophers, a necessarily consistent truth for all people, or one that was for the common man, rather than merely the wise ruler. Natural law was an ideal.

The Romans

It was left to the practically minded Romans to utilise the concept of natural law. Greek stoic philosophers speculated that a man who lived naturally was a man who lived by reason. Since reason is common to all men, then there are universal laws that can be derived by reason by which man could live. The Romans employed this concept in implementing their laws within the empire, while Cicero employed natural law as a legal argument for striking down laws that did not favour his case. The dedication of the Romans to the idea of natural law was a matter of expediency, since it was an ideology that justified the homogeneity that Roman imperialism required. Thus, while some insist that the Romans were guilty of a naturalistic fallacy of confusing what they applied universally with what is universally valid it was, more probably, a shrewd use of a useful ideology.

Thomas Aquinas

Aquinas, a thirteenth-century theologian and philosopher, made probably the most rationally compelling justification of natural law. His followers in the Middle Ages are termed Scholastics or Thomists. Aquinas still influences modern natural law theories.

Aquinas sees law as being binding on people's actions. However, people act according to their reason therefore 'will, if it is to have the authority of law, must be regulated by reason when it commands'. The compulsion of law, though it might be backed by sanctions, relies on reason for it to have an effect on the will. What must compel humans reason is, for Aquinas, the promotion of the collective good. The power of the legislator therefore stems from a duty to promote the collective good. It is because the legislator is under such a duty that the subject has a duty to obey the law.

Aquinas' emphasis is on society subjugating individual interests to the good of the whole, the force of law being that it is a superior institution to other institutions where rules may be made. Thus, although the head of a family may lay down prescriptions for its members, for the good of the whole, this gives way to the good of a whole community. In conclusion, law 'is nothing else than the ordering of things which concern the common good; promulgated by whoever is charged with the care of the community'.

Aquinas divides law into four categories. Eternal law is the reason of the creator of all things and is revealed, in part, in the scriptures as Divine law. Natural law represents the attribute of humans that allows them to make choices and follow their inclinations towards good. As such, a man may use his reason to help himself progress. As a result of speculations about what is good, people seek to reason practically as to how to attain this. The sum of practical reasoning is human law.

Consequently, Aquinas sees temporal law consisting of a dual order. The precepts of natural law are speculations about the truth of how humans should behave. Primarily, there is an inclination towards the good, which, to Aquinas, is the fulfilment of the Divine purpose. However, the inclinations of man are towards the preservation of human life, and other instincts that he shares with other animals, such as sexual relationships and the rearing of offspring. However, there is a category of natural law that is specific to human beings alone, such as the social nature of man and her urge for truth, which Aquinas views as stemming from religion and God. The reason employed in coming to know the precepts of natural law is distinct from practical reason employed for the attaining of specific rules. While the former is the pursuit of absolute truth, the latter is concerned with the facts of human behaviour, but is subject to the perversions of human reason, motivated by the evil desires of some.

Human law is justified as providing order, which is itself simply justified in that 'man, unlike all animals, has the weapon of reason with which to exploit his base desires and cruelty'. In addition to human law that is inspired by precepts of natural law, such as the prohibition of murder, laws also contain practical derivations of how to enforce natural law. To take an example, natural law does not require the wearing of seat-belts but such a law serves as a way of protecting human life and so is a precept of natural law. Since human law is thus partly a question of how best to achieve the enforcement of natural law principles, the content of human laws may change from time to time and place to place.

Aquinas believed that human laws that do not correspond to the natural law are corruptions of law. These are human laws that lack the character of law that binds moral conscience. Because of the imperfections of individual reason and the need for order, disobedience to law is not however necessarily justified, even if human law contradicts natural law.

Note that the paradigm of Aquinas' theory is the existence of God's universal purpose as the foundation of all truth about how people should act. Thus, ultimately, Aquinas' view is that we must obey natural law because God so wills it. However, the major contribution of his theory is that Aquinas attributes to humans the ability to determine truth from falsehood by speculative reasoning. Furthermore he asserts that there are absolute moral values, but the fact that we do not always see them does not eliminate their truth. Moreover, natural law precepts are inclinations, rather than the result of practical reasoning. This final distinction is one that Finnis develops.

Grotius and others

Thomists and subsequent adherents of the natural law theory employed the concept as a justification for the barbaric practices of the Middle Ages. Efforts were made to distance the concept of absolute justice that natural law entailed from the dictates of monarchs and the stranglehold of the Catholic Church. Additionally, thinkers, such as the Dutch Protestant Grotius, advocated the logical independence of natural law from Divine will. Because man could reason, he could discover principles that are absolutely proper for all people. To this end, Grotius created a theory of a law of nations, built upon peaceful co-existence between sovereign states. Grotius viewed law as necessarily binding because subjects of the law surrender their freedom in return for security. Grotius thus advocates that obedience to the law is a natural facet of social organisation, validated by a social contract between the citizen and the ruler.

Once again the natural law element is the ideology that allows Grotius to universalise his concepts of international law, rather than the impetus for doing so. The importance attributed to Grotius, justly or unjustly, is the secularisation of natural law. The assertion that, irrespective of the existence of God, natural law held good.

Philosophers such as Locke, Rousseau and, to a lesser extent, Hobbes looked to the concept of natural law as a way of justifying minimum principles of rights in their social contract theories. The student should read about these theories. Their contribution to natural law thinking is relatively small.

11.5 Hume's attack on natural law

Hume's contribution to natural law theories may be likened to the contribution of Attila the Hun to Roman civilisation. Hume's empirical attack against natural law theories was two-fold.

1. Hume asserted that natural law theories were bedevilled with the cardinal sin of deriving normative statements (oughts) from factual ones (is statements). See his *A Treatise of Human Nature* (1739) Book III, Section I:

    'In every system of morality, which I have hitherto met with, I have always remark'd, that the author proceeds for some time in the ordinary way of reasoning, and establishes the being of God, or makes observations concerning human affairs; when of a sudden I am surpriz'd to find, that instead of the usual copulations of propositions, *is* and *is not*, I meet with no proposition that is not connected with an *ought*, or an *ought not*. This change is imperceptible; but is, however, of the last consequence. For as this *ought*, or *ought not*, expresses some new relation or affirmation, 'tis necessary that it shoul'd be observ'd and explain'd; and at the same time that a reason should be given, for what seems altogether inconceivable, how this new relation can be deduction from others, which are entirely different from it.'

    Whether this criticism is justified, and Finnis asserts that it is not, the stigma has remained.

2. Hume secondly denies that there is any difference between moral judgments and other judgments:

    'Having found that natural as well as civil justice derives from human conventions, we shall quickly perceive, how fruitless it is to resolve the one to the other, and seek, in the laws of nature, a stronger foundation for our political duties than interest, and human conventions; while the laws themselves are built on the very same foundation.'

    He does not deny the existence of natural law, but his view is a strongly empirical one. Natural law consists simply of the consistent values that are the spontaneous product of societal life and as such the invention of a naturally inventive species. This sociological and psychological approach, founded on an assumption about the nature in which human reason functions, signalled a change in the way law was to be considered.

    The fruit of Hume's empiricism is the broad spread of theories labelled positivist. Most positivists are more concerned with the first of the criticisms of natural law, which has been labelled the naturalistic fallacy. However, perhaps due to the growing search for a foundation for justice and rights in the twentieth century, natural law has been revisited, not only by the idealists, but even by positivism.

11.6 Some conclusions

In most human activities the urge for the best leads to critical processes that seek to exclude the worst practices by theoretical justification, in order thereafter to eradicate the practice. For example, nineteenth century medicine sought to demonstrate with scientific theory that traditional herbal medicines lacked scientific basis. The concern was to demonstrate that doctors should use methods that could be scientifically explained. This was perhaps the best way of removing quackery from medicine, although it did not mean that herbs did not have medicinal effects, as has been accepted in modern times. Equally, natural law seeks to find a coherent theory that will purge us of unjust legal systems. Just as quack medicine lacks scientific justification, unjust law lacks moral justification. This does not mean necessarily that neither works.

The problem with employing natural law theories is that they can denounce legal heresies in the same way as medicine denounced medical heresies. This confirms a tendency towards being conservative or even reactionary. If we had adhered to the Greek concept of natural law we would probably still retain slaves. Moreover, most moral reforms in law have stemmed from individuals acting against the contemporary societal mores.

The positivist assertion that you cannot derive what you ought to do from the way things are is to a great extent a philosophy that rejects conservatism and retains for each individual the sovereignty of his own conscience. This is not to say that the assertion is not independently without a logical foundation.

The value of natural law is, however, to remind us of two things. First, law cannot be conceived purely from the point of view of what lawyers say is law, but from the broader perspective of collective human endeavour. As a result Alf Ross dubs natural law as a harlot at the disposal of any political theory. Secondly, natural law reminds us that law is a social endeavour, rather than a static fact. Most law students take law to be simply posited legal statements, but what is also critical to law is that people act on legal norms. It is thus an insight to see that law seeks to do such and such rather than to say that the law is such and such. Positivism has always been concerned with the neutrality of the content of legal rules, but there seems to be something intrinsic in the nature of the legal enforcement of will that itself seems to be purposive.

Stalin demonstrated adequately that the employment of terror and punishment secures cheaper, quicker and more absolute compliance to will. Law actually pre-warns the subject, risking that a person will take measures so as to avoid being caught doing a wrongful act. Whereas a political regime could quite easily force people to comply, why should it endeavour that people should choose to behave in a certain way and accept the validity of a requirement? Natural law theory at least attempts to explain this problem. As we shall see this is not necessarily true of positivism.

11.7 Positivism as a reaction to the naturalistic fallacy

The term 'positivism' has acquired two features. First, it covers a multitude of various theories with a limited amount in common and, secondly, it carries with it almost the same pejorative sense as the naturalistic fallacy. Drawing upon Hart's famous article in the *Harvard Law Review* (1958), we might identify five different meanings to 'positivism'.

1. Positivists view valid laws as the expression of the wills of human people, as opposed to the manifestation of any greater purpose, such as Divine will.
2. There is, for positivists, no necessary link between law and morality. This does not mean that positivism denies that law should be moral.
3. The analysis of legal concepts is deemed by positivism as distinct from other disciplines such as sociology, anthropology and history. The identification of legally valid laws is thus perfectly possible without reference to morality.
4. As a result of the previous point, some writers have asserted that, to positivists, law is a 'closed' system of logic and therefore all legal decisions are deductible from posited legal rules and require no external justifications of a moral or social nature. It is doubtful if anyone, even Kelsen, claimed this sort of primacy for the discipline of legal reasoning.
5. Positivism, of a different sort, 'moral' positivism, claimed that moral judgments cannot be objectively verified by indicating demonstrable facts. Legal positivists, such as Kelsen, deny that there are objective moral values.

It is clear that the radical difference between positivism and natural law is that while positivism states that the concept of law is simply what the legal system in a given society recognises as law, naturalism considers law to be an ideal, commonly shared by human societies. The ideal of law is order, preferably good order, irrespective of the variance of moral values. Positivism cannot ignore the normative nature of law, but does not regard this as a moral premise. For many, it is regarded, rather, as a social technique.

There are two aspects, therefore, that emphasise the contrast between positivism in its caricatured form and natural law theories. First, law is exclusively the premise of the legal caste (including legislators). This deprives law of any spurious claims of intrinsic morality and ensures the individual's right to his own conscience, while reserving the legal system's right to punish him for transgressing. Secondly, it allows for precise statements about the nature of valid law which approximate to the lawyers' experience. This final point might, for the student, be the clinching factor.

Kramer (1999) provides a defence of positivism, against the claims of idealistic positions, such as those of natural lawyers. Capps (2000) and Dyzenhaus (2000) are useful for their account of this work and the critique that they offer of it.

11.8 The attributes of being a human being

Although Hart denies any implicit link between law and morality, he does recognise a broad category of legal rules of moral derivation, and recognises that the human condition requires certain protections. He posits the one indisputable goal of human society, that of survival. Social institutions must therefore accommodate a realisation of certain criteria which have an effect on survival. He cites the following sociological/psychological facts:

1. humans are vulnerable;
2. humans are approximately equal;
3. humans have limited altruism;
4. humans are subject to limited resources;
5. humans have limited understanding and strength of will.

Hart concedes that even if these facts were accepted by a legal system, they would not necessarily make it more just and fair. Moreover, he acknowledges that many legal systems do not necessarily even take cognisance of any of these. Nor are these themselves the rules of natural justice, but simply the considerations that must be taken into account as a basis of an ideal legal system. What Hart does is to posit an indisputable factual end to which most societies will aspire, namely, survival, and remind us of the obstacles to achieving that goal, in the form of his five human weaknesses.

He takes it as self-evident that in order to circumvent these weaknesses there is a necessity that there be some protection of property, persons and promises. Hart's starting point of the assumption of the validity of survival has been criticised by Fuller. That people need to survive in order to do any other thing seems right. But we may take issue. Take, for example, the Jonestown community which committed mass suicide on the basis of religious belief, or the Jewish community of Masada, which extinguished itself rather than submit to the Roman Empire. But these extreme cases are the exception rather than the rule (that is why we say they are 'extreme'). Survival thus becomes a generally understood common goal, rather than a necessary premise for a society.

Hart acknowledges that an overwhelming majority of men do wish to live, even at the cost of hideous misery. Fuller's criticism is that truths about man's desire to survive represent only a lowest common denominator of aspiration. He paraphrases Aquinas: if the highest aim of a captain were to preserve his ship, he would keep it in port for ever. The concern of natural law is to produce not only guarantees for individuals, but to find the morally correct balance for society. By ignoring this he ignores the collective aspect of the human condition. One could posit additional considerations that are necessary for the survival of society. The need to sacrifice or punish the individual for the good of the whole. The need to allow individuals to profit from their contribution to society as a recognition of their usefulness to society; the allocation of status to those with particular abilities.

D'Entrèves is more concerned with the extreme noncommittal nature of Hart's natural law principles. For all their evasive sociological premises they are practically useless, because Hart will not commit himself to any moral or factual interaction with law-making.

11.9 The Nazi informer case

Hart has another defence of positivism, this time against the criticism from a school of thought about law that sprang up in Germany after the Second World War. In particular, Hart takes on the criticism of a German jurist called Radbruch. The history of Radbruch's thought about law was that he was originally a positivist. After experiencing Germany of the 1930s and during the war, his views radically changed and he became convinced that legal positivism was one of the factors that contributed to Nazi Germany's horrors. Among other things, he said, the German legal profession failed to protest against the enormity of certain laws they were expected to administer. In the light of this, Radbruch claimed that a law could not be legally valid until:

1. it had passed the tests contained in the formal criteria of legal validity of the system, and, more importantly;
2. it did not contravene basic principles of morality.

This doctrine meant that, according to Radbruch, every lawyer and judge should denounce statutes that contravened 'basic principles of morality' not just as immoral, but as *not having any legal character*, that is, being legally invalid, and therefore irrelevant in working out what the legal position of any particular plaintiff or defendant was.

Hart is critical of Radbruch's thesis. He thinks it is naïve to suppose that what occurred in Nazi Germany was to a degree caused by a general belief that law might be law even although it contravened basic principles of morality. At the very least, Hart says, it is necessary to ask why this general belief in other countries was accompanied by opposing liberal attitudes as, for example, in England with Bentham and Austin. More importantly, though, Hart thinks Radbruch's conception of law is confused. Hart refers to the use of Radbruch's conception of law by West German courts after the Second World War in which certain Nazi legislation was deemed to be void because it was contrary to morality.

A general argument was used in several West German criminal cases involving allegedly criminal acts of informing on other people during the war and thereby securing their punishment by the Nazis. The form of the defences to these alleged offences was that such actions were not illegal according to Nazi laws in force at the time they were done.

It is very important that students understand both the decision and the facts in this case, because it is often completely misunderstood. The facts were that in 1944 the defendant, who was getting bored with her husband, denounced him to the Gestapo for having said something insulting about Hitler while at home on leave from the German army. The man was arrested and sentenced to death in accordance with a Nazi statute that made it illegal to make statements detrimental to the German government. In 1949, the wife was charged, in a West German Court, with having committed the offence of 'unlawfully depriving a person of his freedom' a crime under the German Criminal Code of 1871, which had remained in force continuously since its enactment. The Nazi statute that had made it illegal to make disparaging statements about the German government was, of course, repealed by this stage.

The wife pleaded in defence that what she had done was lawful in 1944 when she did it. That is, she had not unlawfully deprived her husband of freedom, because it was made lawful by those Nazi statutes in force *then*. When the case came to the appeal court, although the woman was allowed her appeal on other grounds, the court accepted the argument that the Nazi statute would not have been valid if it were 'so contrary to the sound conscience and sense of justice of all decent human beings'. If so, it would have followed that this statute did not make it lawful to deprive people of their freedom when they denounced Hitler, so that, at the time the defendant informed the Gestapo about her husband's remarks, she could have committed an offence under the German Criminal Code of 1871.

This reasoning is, of course, along the lines proposed by Radbruch. The Nazi statute had met the formal tests laid down by the criteria of legal validity of the Nazi legal system, but was nevertheless not 'law' because it contravened 'fundamental principles of morality'. Hart is critical of the argument, which was apparently followed in a number of similar cases. His short criticism is that this is 'too crude a way with delicate and complex moral issues'. The better way, he says, to deal with the problem of punishing the Nazi informers under the law would have been by retrospective law declaring the Nazi statute to be invalid. Then the woman in this particular case would have been criminally liable *not* because *when* she did what she did it was illegal, but because a later statute made it illegal retrospectively.

This way of looking at the problem of legally justifying punishing the woman, Hart says, brings to view the full nature of the moral issues involved. His suggested way of dealing with the matter brings another element into the equation of justification. This is that, although we think it was wrong to do what the woman did, we also think it wrong to punish a person when what they did was permitted by the state, that is, was lawful. The moral principle here, and one endorsed by many legal systems, is that of *nulla poena sine lege* ('no punishment without law'). The rationale of this principle is that if you are acting within the law at any one time then it should not be later declared that what you were doing was against the law.

Hart is not saying that this principle can *never* be sacrificed to some other moral principle, but rather that a transgression of that principle is part of the equation, and must be taken into account in determining whether the woman should be punished. Hart says, for example:

> 'Odious as retrospective criminal legislation and punishment may be, to have pursued it openly in this case would at least have had the merits of candour. It would have made plain that in punishing the woman a choice had to be made between two evils ...'

The two 'evils' he refers to are first, letting the woman go unpunished and secondly, introducing retrospective legislation. The Radbruchean, natural law approach, just simply says: 'What the woman did was wrong and she should be punished, and it is irrelevant that she thought that she was doing what she was permitted to do, or that when she did it, it was permitted by the enacted law.'

11.10 Hartian positivism as a moral theory

So it does not follow that Radbruch and Hart have different views about the outcome of the case, but just that they would have approached it in different ways. Why, then, does it matter if the outcome is the same? Well, the argument is that the outcome could have been different. Hart's justification for punishing the woman by a retrospective law is a result of a better mixture of justification: it involves a weighing up between the rightness of punishing a Nazi informer and the wrongness of retroactively enforced decisions. Radbruch's approach cannot allow the wrongness of retroactively enforced decisions as relevant for, by definition, if the law is morally bad, then it is not a law at all and so cannot be extinguished by retroactive decision. It would be possible, therefore, by Hart's and Radbruch's methods to come to different decisions simply because the judgment Hart recommends is a more complex one than Radbruch's, having an extra ingredient in the argument, and merely having the extra ingredient in the argument *could* turn the decision in another way.

But Hart goes further than just saying that we should be candid about our approach to the problem of how to deal with the Nazi informer. He says also that to adopt Radbruch's approach would be to obscure a very powerful form of moral criticism, that of being able to criticise legislation. He says that to state plainly that something can be a law but too evil to be obeyed is to rivet people's attention. That is, such a statement makes, as he says, 'an immediate and obvious claim to our moral attention' for it raises the whole question of what our obligation to obey law generally is. On the other hand, it is obscure to say that immoral laws are *not* laws at all. In fact, many people would simply disbelieve that as a dubious proposition.

Note that here Hart appeals to the way *we actually think* about law. To repeat his point: we understand his viewpoint because we accept, in our thinking and the way we speak, that one can criticise laws in this sort of way. Now this point of Hart's is a little unfair to Radbruch. Hart just appeals to current thinking, that we do in fact draw the distinction. Radbruch could presumably just answer it by saying we do *but should not*. Remember that it was his belief that thinking in this sort of way contributed to the rise of Nazism. That is, Radbruch was not just describing the way we actually think but making a prescription for the way we ought to think. So it is Hart's *prescriptive* point that Radbruch's proposal blurs over the various moral issues involved that is the better one. It meets the morality of Radbruch's point head on.

Hart openly admits that the choice between Radbruch's natural law approach and his own is to be settled by choosing morally between them. He says that we could choose between two rival conceptions of law:

1. there is the wide, positivist conception of law that considers as law all rules which are valid by the *formal* tests of a legal system, even though some of them might offend against society's morality or our own morality; and
2. there is a narrow, Radbruchean conception of law that considers as law only those rules, passed as formally valid, that are not morally offensive.

Hart prefers the first conception. The first reason he gives is that it is, as he says, descriptively better to think of law in this way. It is fairly clear that he means by this that it more accords with the way *we actually think* about law. He says:

> '... nothing is to be gained in the theoretical or scientific study of law as a social phenomenon by adopting the narrower concept: it would lead us to exclude certain rules even though they exhibit all the other complex characteristics of law.'

The second reason he gives is that the first conception 'grossly oversimplifies' the variety of moral issues.

It seems that Hart is right at least in pointing to three kinds of confusion that could be created by adopting the narrower conception.

1. First, if we train ourselves to think of laws as essentially moral then, since we have different views about morality, some laws will be valid for some people but not for others. For example, some people would consider that they did not have a legal obligation to pay taxes. If the narrower conception of law were adopted how would the courts decide whether people had legal obligations, say, to pay income tax? The narrower conception of law could only operate if there were not only one set of true moral standards, which is at least a debatable proposition (although not as strange as it might appear since we all talk that way!), but a set of true moral standards that was *objectively ascertainable.*
2. Secondly, if we train ourselves to view law in this narrow way, then we might become indifferent to the fact that Parliament passed legislation affecting us. That is, the narrower conception of law trains us to concentrate only on the particular action that we judge to be morally right and this sidesteps the major issue of whether we have some sort of obligation to obey (even if only *prima facie*) just on the ground that Parliament produced it. Surely, in any matter of civil disobedience, that Parliament has said something in a statute must be an *ingredient* in any judgment whether to obey it. But it would follow from Radbruch's narrow conception of the law that you could not commit civil disobedience against an immoral law because such a law does not exist, in fact, it cannot.
3. A third sort of confusion would be that thrown up by the Nazi informer case. We might, in short, ride rough shod over the important principle of *nulla poena sine lege* to which reference was made in paragraph 10.17 in relation to Ronald Dworkin's attack on legal positivism.

Hart's arguments can be summed up in his own words. What follows are his *moral* reasons for preferring the wider conception of law that separates law from morality by declaring all rules formally identifiable by reference to the factual test of the rule of recognition *ipso facto*:

> 'What surely is most needed in order to make men clear sighted in confronting the official abuse of power, is that they should preserve the sense that the certification of something as legally valid is not conclusive of the question of obedience.
>
> A concept of law which allows the invalidity of law to be distinguished from its immorality enables us to see the complexity and variety of these separate issues; whereas a narrow concept of law which denies legal validity to such rules may blind us to them.'

This section in *The Concept of Law* gives insights into Hart's approach, his 'methodology'. The title of his book, *'The' Concept of Law*, and his Preface (in which he claims he is writing an 'essay in *descriptive* sociology') suggest he aims to describe. But this section indicates that, whether he is aware of it or not, he has other than descriptive grounds for 'choosing' the wider conception of law over the narrow.

Clearly, Hart's theory has been constructed along moral lines. It is a highly sophisticated relationship *not* between the meaning of 'law' and 'morality', but between the meaning of 'theory of law' and 'morality'. That is, although Hart's conception of law is one that separates 'law' and 'morality', the strong suggestion is that he thinks that this conception – the wider conception – is *morally* better than the narrower one. We could argue, therefore, that he connects law and morality in the necessary sense that a theory of law must serve a moral purpose and that we must view as law only those rules that are law according to the morally best conception of law. This view is not far from Dworkin's, in Chapter 3 of *Law's Empire*, or Finnis' in Chapter 1 of *Natural Law and Natural Rights*.

11.11 Introduction to Fuller

Law and purpose

Fuller identifies a dichotomy of views as to the proper purpose of legal study. On the one hand, there is the positivist contention that law must be treated as a manifested fact of social authority to be studied for what it is and does. Such a position is certainly proper for the study of substantive law, for a law student would learn precious little unless she treated individual legal materials as categorical. However, this does not mean that the method is apt for the study of law as a general phenomenon.

On the other hand, Fuller's argument is that the theoretical concept of law cannot be understood without attributing to it the purpose of subjecting human conduct to the guidance and control of general rules. Such a view is clearly right. However, he goes on to assert that without this idea of purpose one cannot judge the degree to which a legal system has succeeded in meeting its goals. Fuller considers that one might term the goal of all legal systems the ideal of legality.

When positivists like Kelsen set down a criterion such as efficaciousness as a required element in the definition of law, they are thus stating that if law fails to achieve its purpose then it is not law. There is a qualitative difference between Kelsen's view and Fuller's. Kelsen suggests an all or nothing view of law, begging the question how many people need to disobey a legal system before it ceases to be efficacious and hence ceases to become law? On the other hand Fuller sees the legality of a system of rules as a question of degree. His criteria for legality we will explore in a moment.

A critique of positivism

Fuller claims, in his criticism of legal positivism, that some things taken as legal facts are merely achievements of legal aspirations. For example, we say Parliament is supreme, but this is not a datum of nature, it is a manifestation of a tradition of agreement that it legally should be so regarded. This 'should' is not in itself a moral evaluation, but a result of the success of a rule. To state the nature of a legal system in terms of 'is' statements is to endorse that a legal system is what it says it is, which creates a problem if a society rejects a legal system. For example, when Parliament passed the Southern Rhodesia Act 1965, it considered that it was the supreme legal authority for that country. However, the country declared independence and simply ignored Parliament.

According to Fuller, law can only be said to be binding if people believe or act as if it is. Some people certainly do not feel that law is binding upon them. They may disregard the rules, fail to observe them and many evade punishment for breaking them. If it can be said that the laws of a particular system are binding, that is an appraisal of the success or adherence to the rule. Fuller's contention is that when a person seeks to describe a legal system as it is, he is actually evaluating the degree of success it has achieved in pursuing its purpose. To summarise, law is not a binding set of rules, but something that aspires with some degree of success to be binding.

So Fuller's point is that a genuine *working* legal system cannot be understood merely by looking at the rules consciously created by lawmakers. He cites as an example the fact that the American Constitution, from which all American legal authority flows, never mentions a requirement to legislate. This has not stopped Americans from making laws, because this is an activity implicit in the pursuit of legality. Thus, a statute made in 1700 may still be enforceable in 1992. To Fuller, the judiciary are charged with an implicit duty to be the 'curators' of statutes, so that if those plants regarded as weeds change over the decades, the judge invests the Statute of Weeds with the new, more appropriate meaning. Such implicit rules of legality serve as a bridge between the legal world and the social world. This idea has great insight and provides the basis for his very original view of the relationship between law and morality.

11.12 Procedural morality

Moralities of aspiration

While this critique of positivist methodology is important, the student might find it remote from the issue of law and morality. But Fuller does not seek to prove that substantive morality is bound up with law. He is aware that there are perils in seeking to prove a relationship between a relativist, content-based concept of morality and a content-neutral, universal conception of law.

Fuller bases his view of the relationship on the following logic. If morality must be seen as being relative rather than absolute, then if we seek to relate morality to law, that morality must be one specific to the nature of law. Therefore legal morality is a particular type of morality to be found in the nature of law itself, rather than being abstracted from other moral norms.

Fuller's conception of law is that of a purposive activity which aspires towards the ideal of legality. As such it is not surprising that Fuller's concept of morality is founded on practical criteria which are goals to which the legal system should aspire. For example, one of his legal-moral criteria is legal clarity. This morality of aspiration is thus largely a question of degree. Obviously, things are usually more or less clear, although occasionally we may say something is incomprehensible. However, Fuller's morality is not a morality of duty, which is normally expressed in terms of the rules of a substantive morality. An example of a morality of duty is illustrated by the 'rule thou shalt not kill'.

The difference between moralities of aspiration and of duty is largely one of formulation. We might employ a rule 'do not kill', but this can be equally expressed as voicing respect for human life. The former gives us the ability to judge individual acts individually, whereas the latter allows us to give a judgment of degree. If a legal system does not completely prohibit killing then it has broken the spirit of the rule, but it may be shown that to a greater or lesser extent it accords with the principle.

The second aspect of moralities of aspiration is that they do allow for complete censure, if there is no satisfaction of the criteria. Rules of substantive morality carry with them absolute obligations, while Fuller's morality of aspiration is founded on the desire of the legal system to achieve an ideal of legality.

The internal morality of law

The only problem is that Fuller is concerned to relate a morality that is linked to his content-neutral concept of law rather than following the conventional approach of asserting that law respects certain substantive moral values. As such, the content of the internal morality of law looks remarkably like common-sense rules of good craftsmanship. Indeed, Fuller's contention is that there is an inherent logic to the subjugation of human conduct to legal rules, which if ignored will lead to failure.

Fuller asserts that the eight principles of the 'inner morality' of the law are as follows.

1. A legal system must be based on or reveal some kind of regular trends. As such law should be founded on generalisations of conduct such as rules, rather than simply allowing arbitrary adjudication.
2. Laws must be publicised so that subjects know how they are supposed to behave.
3. Rules will not have the desired effect if it is likely that your present actions will not be judged by them in future. As such, retrospective legislation should not be abused.
4. Laws should be comprehensible, even if it is only lawyers who understand them.
5. Laws should not be contradictory.
6. Law should not expect the subject to perform the impossible.
7. Law should not change so frequently that the subject cannot orient his action to it.
8. There should not be a significant difference between the actual administration of the law and what the written rule says.

These criteria are in the form of the moral rules of duty. Fuller expresses them as principles or goals; generality of laws; promulgation of laws; minimising the use of retrospective laws; clarity; lack of contradiction; possibility of obedience; constancy through time; consistency between the word and the practice of law.

Fuller's evaluation speaks for itself:

'Though these natural laws touch one of the most vital of human activities they obviously do not exhaust the whole of man's moral life. They have nothing to say on such topics as polygamy, the study of Marx, the worship of God, the progressive income tax, or the subjugation of women. If the question be raised whether any of these subjects, or others like them, should be taken as objects of legislation, that question relates to what I have called the external morality of the law.'

Fuller shows how the Nazi regime suffered a progressive decline in its adherence to these principles of legality. Furthermore, he concedes that even if these standards are adhered to, it would not *guarantee* that they will prevent law being the instrument of oppression. Even disregard of these principles does not necessarily make a system not law, *just further away from the ideal of legality*. In essence, Fuller states that the internal morality of law is neutral towards the law's substantive aims.

There are, however, aspects of the internal morality of law that he claims are not so neutral. The urge for legal clarity fights against laws that direct themselves against alleged evils that cannot be defined, such as discrimination on the basis of race. He cites the 1948 decision in *Perez* v *Sharp* (1948) where a statute preventing the marriage of a white person to any Negro, mulatto, Mongolian or member of the Malay race was held unconstitutional on the basis that the constitution requires clarity.

The legal approach to human nature

Interestingly, Fuller asserts that the purpose of law embodies an inalienable view of humanity:

> 'To embark on an enterprise of subjecting human conduct to the governance of rules involves of necessity a commitment to the view that man is, or can become, a responsible agent, capable of understanding and following rules, and answerable for his defaults.'

If we revisit Fuller's inner morality of law in this light we obtain a better perspective of why he considers it appropriate to term these criteria as being moral in nature.

By making laws general and predictable, a choice is given to the subject, the opportunity to predict when he will be punished, for example. By making laws known people may know on what basis they will be judged and how they must act so as not to fall foul. By this, Fuller is stressing that law is, to a certain extent, a partnership between the legislator and the subject. An illustration of this is the principle of taxation law that although a person may not evade his tax obligations, he has the right to act so that he can minimise the amount of tax that the law requires him to pay. So Fuller has some idea of 'fairness' or 'consistency in dealing' between government and citizens.

Hart's criticism

What Fuller succeeds in doing is setting up what amounts to an optional morality that has little to do with questions of right or wrong. Has he actually made any contribution to asserting that there is a link between law and morality? Certainly one has to view law itself as a morally acceptable thing, rather than a necessary evil, as Nozick might view it, or an instrument of class oppression, which is a Marxist attitude.

However, one of the more unfair criticisms of Fuller is based on his assertion that beyond the satisfaction of a very minimal standard, the legality of a system is a matter of degree. The criticism is put as follows. Who talks about a legal system existing more or less? A legal system either exists or it does not and it cannot 'half-exist'. The second element of the criticism is that if a legal system can exist to a lesser degree, how can we decide when we do or do not have an obligation to obey it?

This (frequently used) argument is nonsensical and ignores Fuller's chief insight. When we talk of the existence of a legal system it is not like talking about the existence of a piece of steel. It is either steel or not steel. A legal system is a social fact which depends on the degree of co-operation achieved between its members and its subjects. The advocates of the all-or-nothing point of view do not answer the question: how many people need to disobey a legal system for it to cease to be a legal system? The assertion that a legal system either exists or it does not stems from the lawyerly desire to have clear yes-or-no answers. This has to do with the human need to know when one must obey a legal system and when one no longer has a legal obligation.

Hart's well-known criticism of Fuller's equally well-known eight principles of the 'inner morality' of law must be understood. These principles, which loosely describe requirements of procedural justice, were claimed by Fuller to ensure that a legal system would satisfy the demands of morality, to the extent that a legal system which adhered to all of the principles would explain the all-important idea of 'fidelity to law'. In other words, such a legal system would command obedience with moral justification.

Fuller's key idea is that evil aims lack a 'logic' and 'coherence' that moral aims have. Thus, paying attention to the 'coherence' of the laws ensures their morality. The argument is unfortunate because it does, of course, claim too much. Hart's criticism is that we could, equally, have eight principles of the 'inner morality' of the poisoner's art ('use tasteless, odourless poison'; 'use poisons that are fully eliminated from the victim's body'; etc). Or we can improvise further. We can talk of the principles of the inner morality of Nazism, for example, or the principles of the inner morality of chess. The point is that the idea of principles in themselves with the attendant explanation at a general level of what is to be achieved (elimination of non-Aryan races) and consistency is insufficient to establish the moral nature of such practices.

What has been unfortunate about Hart's criticism is that it obscured Fuller's point. This was that there is an important sense of legal justification that claims made in the name of law are morally serious. At the least, the person who makes a genuine claim for legal justification of an immoral, Nazi-type legal system *must* believe that there is some moral force to his claim. At its best, we believe that when we make some claim about our law it carries some moral force. It is not enough simply to deny this. At least some explanation is required for our belief that this is so if, in fact, we are wrong.

Kramer (1998) provides another version of Hart's criticism of Fuller. He concludes that, in the end, the idea that Fuller's theory captures a moral 'reciprocity' between rulers and the ruled ultimately fails. The force of this idea of reciprocity is that however much we can imagine 'evil' legal systems of a highly efficient kind which appear to comply with the 'inner morality' of law, evil legal systems built on such lines can still exist.

An 'inner morality' of carpentry which was neutral on the question of whether torture racks or hospital beds were being made, would not be moral. Thus it would be perfectly possible to have a legal system in which the officials followed the procedural rules with precision but did so with evil aims in mind. Seen in this light, Fuller's principles are amoral and as Hart noted they are compatible with great iniquity. Kramer is inclined to agree with the supporters of Fuller to the following extent. That Fuller's theory emphasises the values of procedural fairness and the autonomy of citizens, and these ideas are bound up in the notion of the rule of law that his theory is often thought to support. And so he thinks that the Fullerian procedural rules would encourage officials to be 'impelled' by a mixture of prudential and moral factors. Nevertheless, in a wicked system, officials would be impelled only for purely prudential reasons, and in this situation officials could well be meticulous in carrying out plans that have no moral content at all. They would, in other words, be engaged in 'scrupulousness without scruples' and so, Kramer concludes, the logical connection that Fuller wanted to draw between the form of his legal system (compliance with the eight principles of the inner morality of law) and ultimately its moral content, is unsuccessful.

General comment

A useful addition to the debate about the point of Fuller's theory of law is to be found in Brudney's article 'Two Links of Law and Morality' in *Ethics* (1993). The first part of this article, where Brudney discusses the famous Hartian criticism, is the most helpful, although there is a useful comparison drawn by Brudney between Fuller's theory and a similar one, that of Soper in his book *A Theory of Law* (1984). The article amounts to a limited defence of Fuller against the criticism that Fuller's eight principles are compatible, in Hart's terms, with legal systems of 'great iniquity'. The thrust of article makes a very practical point: when all is said and done about the 'conceptual' or 'logical' relationships between 'law' and 'morality', the application of the eight principles to actual, living rulers would be to make them be more careful about making immoral laws. Why? Because the rules would create a climate of 'transparency' in decision-making in the sense that laws could not be enacted in secret, had to be general in scope, non-retroactive, etc. Given that human beings are volitional creatures, of a particular kind of psychological make-up, then it seems reasonable to assume that imposition of the eight principles would make human beings who are rulers behave in an acceptable manner.

There are, of course, difficulties with this idea, which Brudney acknowledges. These are, however, of an empirical sort; do human beings in fact 'knuckle under' to the pressures of having to make transparent decisions? Brudney is keen to point out that if it is not clear that human beings are that keen to make morally acceptable decisions it is also not clear that they are *not*. He therefore calls for an empirical investigation into what human beings are actually like:

> 'Such investigation could be of two kinds: inquiry into the law-constraining properties of human beings as such, or inquiry into the law-constraining properties of some restricted group of human beings. The former seems a doubtful enterprise. History exhibits too much legalised evil to think it likely that there are immutable human properties that constrain the moral content of law. The latter inquiry might seem too local to be of interest. The fact, for example, that a particular royal family always trains the next ruler in its line to be morally enlightened would hardly be an informative empirical link of law and morality. But suppose there are law-constraining properties which (i) are characteristic of members of our culture, and (ii) cannot be easily and quickly eradicated (as princely training could). Such links of law and morality might shed light on the nature of our institution of law.'

This passage suggests ways a student might consider the practical application of

Fuller's theory; that has always posed a problem, not so much with the 'really evil' system, such as the Nazi legal system, as with the half-way house such as the South African legal system. The answer, Brudney suggests, lies in the correct empirical description of those responsible at the time for the production of the laws.

11.13 Finnis

Hart says of Finnis' restatement of natural law that it is of very great merit. By drawing upon the works of natural lawyers such as Aquinas and Aristotle, Finnis attempts to dispose of what he regards as two cardinal misconceptions about the theory.

1. Finnis denies that natural law derives from objectively determinable patterns of behaviour, but instead asserts it is ascertainable from inward knowledge of innate motivations.
2. Natural law does not entail the view that law is not law if it contradicts morality.

In *Natural Law and Natural Rights* (1980) Finnis seeks to distance his own position and that of his philosophical predecessors from these much-vaunted criticisms. Natural law may be the set of principles of practical reasonableness in ordering human life and human community, but he asserts that they are pre-moral. By this he means that they are not the product of logical deduction, nor are they merely passions verified with reference to something objectively regarded as good. The latter position represents the view of the empiricists such as Hume, and is that all moral values are subjective whims that have the extra force of validity because others accept them as being good.

To the extent that the empiricist criticism of some natural lawyers might be right, he states that there is no inference from fact to value. Therefore the goods that Finnis speaks of are not moral goods, but they are necessary objects of human striving. The peculiar nature of this view is that these goods are subjective so far as they require no justification from the outside world, but are really objective since all humans must assent to their value. Finnis argues that these are the result of innate knowledge.

There is a strong affinity between Finnis' view of natural law and that of Aquinas. However, the major difference is that, for Finnis, the existence of God is only a possible explanation for the comparative order that he seeks to project on human values, not the necessary reason. Finnis instead states that his goods are self-evident. This is demonstrated by, though not inferred from, the consistency of values that are identified throughout all human societies, such as a respect for human life.

Finnis' process of reasoning is to address any individual with the question, 'X is good, don't you think?' He maintains that it is because of the consistency of these basic values of human nature that one gets one's ability sympathetically, though not uncritically, to see the point of actions, life-styles, characters and cultures that one would not choose for oneself. This argument about the consistency of human nature is a compelling one. We can read, with understanding, the recorded life of a tax-gatherer in ancient Egypt or a mediaeval monk with the freshness of a report in a modern magazine because in fundamental human strivings, in human nature there is an undoubted consistency. Often we refer to the writings of Shakespeare whose observations about humanity are as relevant today as they were when he was writing. Finnis can certainly say with justification, that, as a speculative truth, human nature seems remarkably constant.

11.14 The basic goods of human nature

Finnis' seven basic goods are as follows.

Life

Finnis is well worth reading, if only because of the poet in him, which sets him above most other jurists because he writes as a human, rather than as a tired old machine. To Finnis, life is not bare material existence, but is a matter of quality, so that mental and physical health and comfort are necessary aspects of living. The striving and lust for life are brought out in his examples: 'the crafty struggle and prayer of a man overboard seeking to stay afloat until his ship turns back to him; the team-work of surgeons' and even 'watching out as one steps off the kerb'.

Allied to life as a basic good is its propagation. As most schoolboys know, life, like death, is a sexually transmitted disease. However, Finnis separates the good of procreation from the more complex sexual and paternal and maternal urges. Such urges can be diverted to other goods. Thus, sex can be a recreational activity (play) or a cementation of relationships (sociability, friendship). As Hume might put it, the diversion of the urge for copulation to these other ends may be another invention of a naturally inventive species.

Knowledge

Finnis sees curiosity and the quest for truth in itself as a manifest human good. He hastens to add that 'it is knowledge, considered as desirable for its own sake, not merely instrumentally'.

Play

Everyone, asserts Finnis, engages to a greater or lesser extent in activities that are pointless except for their own sake, from sports and games on the one hand, to mischiefs and diversions such as toying with one's pen as one writes. 'An element of play can enter into any human activity, even the drafting of enactments.'

Aesthetic experience

Although linked to play, and indeed to life and knowledge, the appreciation of forms and spirits of beauty is, Finnis asserts, equally a common and self-evident human good.

Sociability (friendship)

To be in a relationship of friendship with at least one other person is a fundamental form of good, is it not? The bonds of human community, even at the level of pure self-interest, are involved with this good, but Finnis obviously views friendship as its flourishing.

Practical reasonableness

The ability to reason provides a level of personal autonomy, since it is the measure of active choice and free will as well as providing the potential of self improvement by ordering one's thoughts. Through reason comes therefore, in Finnis' view, peace of mind as well as self-determination.

Religion

Finnis seems reluctant to use this word, but employs it 'summarily and lamely' for want of a better choice. Finnis suggests that all humans are concerned to know both how things came to exist as they do and whether there is not something greater and more powerful than human intellect, to which humans are subject. Finnis' explanation is obviously imbued with his own faith, but these questions are also universal concerns and in the absence of explanations that are proof positive that God does not exist or that the Big Bang actually happened, we choose theories to cling to, or at least search for them, and our adherence to them is a matter of faith.

Finnis makes two further relevant points.

1. These are not the only goods but, simply, all other goods may be reduced to being means by which these basic goods are attained. Nor are they the only common urges or inclinations. He does not deny that some people, perhaps all, have an urge for gratuitous cruelty. However, this is not self-evidently good.
2. None of these goods can be reduced to a mere extract of another, since they are ultimate ends in themselves of equal value and importance when one focuses on them individually.

It may be seen that Finnis' list, although it has some peculiarity, is not radically different from the lists of others, such as Aquinas. The difference Finnis asserts is that these goods are not the result of speculative reason. They are not good *because* of anything, they are just good. The problem is that they are, according to Finnis, 'primary, indemonstrable and self-evident'.

The student may be tempted to view life as a necessary material pre-condition to all of the others. You cannot play cricket or study law if you are a corpse. However, Finnis, with his emphasis on life as being a good rather than an empirical necessity, forestalls this criticism. The value of life is nothing without the other goods *in some measure*. Simply, the student must ask herself: 'Do I believe that any one of the seven goods is intrinsically good?'

It is difficult to argue with Finnis' example of the seven goods and it would be foolish to do so, since he offers no logical proof concerning them and indeed says they are not demonstrable. Much fruitless pursuit of logical criticism has been expended on Finnis' goods, the most obvious being based on the principle that since Finnis offers a logical justification of knowledge, he is defective in not providing logical justifications for his other goods. Finnis states, quite rightly, that even a man who denies knowledge, relies on his knowledge to deny its value. As MacCormick puts it, 'Why should ... anyone ... care to know that knowledge is not worth having unless, after all, at least that knowledge is worth having?' It is a neat argument, but is divorced from the premise of Finnis' argument. Finnis may provide empirical explanations, say from anthropology, to illustrate the prevalence of these values, but he does not employ them as proof.

On these poetic foundations, Finnis seeks to rebuild the edifice of natural law. He argues that the concept of law has a focal content that is based upon the convergence of legal systems with the various facets of a central definition of law. These facets are concepts that law is the following: made, determinate, effective, communal, sanctioned, rule-guided, reasonable, non-discriminatory and reciprocal. However, to Finnis, as to Hart, the concept of law is a common-sense category that is applied to varied institutions that have roughly, though by no means exactly, the same function in society. So a 'tight' definition of law is a fool's errand. It is rather like giving a substantive definition of weeds:

> '[T]he intention has been not to explain a concept, but to develop a concept which would explain the various phenomena referred to (in an unfocused way) by ordinary talk about law ... and explain them by showing how they answer (fully or partially) to the standing requirements of practical reasonableness relevant to the broad area of human concern and interaction.'

Finnis accepts that lawyers are concerned with categorical statements about what is valid law. This varies from society to society and from time to time. His theory:

> '... cannot be assumed to be applicable to the quite different problems of describing and explaining the role of legal process within the ordering of human life in society, and the place of legal thought in practical reasons effort to understand and effect real human good.'

What Finnis is suggesting is that the moral success or failure of a law is not the test of whether it is law. His concern is not to posit what he wants law to be, but rather to evaluate what expectations there are of law, in order critically to evaluate law itself. To Finnis, the focal meaning of his concept of law is not intended to explain what law is, but what moral expectations are made of it. So the purpose of law is to work for the common good. This does not, however, mean that laws that work against the common good are not laws and should be relegated to some other discipline. What such laws amount to is an imperfect or fringe meaning of law in its focal meaning.

An example of this is the man who walks into a restaurant and orders Bombay Duck (curiously, a fish dish). When the waiter brings his dinner he might say, 'I ordered the Bombay Duck, but this is not a duck.' The waiter is not deceiving him, but his own expectations are not satisfied. Similarly, Fuller would not deny the appellation of law to what a legal system claims to be law, but his focal meaning is concerned with expectations rather than classifications.

The legal system must thus, to some extent, satisfy the common requirements of human good, although there are no very precise yardsticks for assessing this.

Equipped with the knowledge that Finnis has shown us what he thinks the natural absolute values are, as well as his conception of law, we might seek to understand how these two relate to each other. The objects of human striving are the seven basic goods, but they are best and perhaps only achieved through communal enterprise. This is the result of the application of one of the goods themselves, practical reasonableness, to the question of how best to attain the others. However, it is not sufficient for life, play, and so on, that people act collectively. Rather they should do so in an organised manner. This requires that the individual works for the collective good. Now Finnis does not deny that there might be varying conceptions of what the collective good is. It is just that these are simply aspects of the ongoing process of reasoning to find the best way to promote the collective good. Certainly, organised communal activity for the collective good can be furthered by the employment of law.

However, practical reasonableness must also be applied to ensure that the individuals within society can attain the basic goods that they seek. Finnis articulates nine methodological principles for practical reasoning. These include the need for a coherent plan in life, no arbitrary preferences amongst values or people, detachment and commitment, an evaluation of the relevance of consequences, the requirements of the common good, and following one's own conscience. This is the foundation of justice and rights. Justice and rights represent a tension between the common good and human goods.

However, our present concern is the link between positive law and natural law. Finnis cites the easy case of murder. The law of murder is derived from the general good of the value of human life, interpreted by another good, that of practical reason. The force of the law against murder thus doubly derives from natural law. The process of doing this is, however, a complex one. Finnis' explanation of the nine requirements of practical reasonableness and their interaction with legal reasoning is very sophisticated. It cannot be fully described here. But the application of practical reasonableness is the determinant factor of law. Obviously, reason allows the choice of a multitude of means to be thought up in order to achieve ends. But Finnis' conclusions are of interest to us.

1. Natural law is concerned to prove that the act of positing law is an act that can and should be guided by moral principles.
2. Moral principles are derived by practical reasonableness from objective principles, not from subjective whim or custom.
3. Law itself, its structure and the institutions that it creates, such as contract etc, is justified by moral norms.

Finnis is not satisfied merely to say that history shows that law normally reflects contemporary morality, but seeks to determine what the requirements of practical reasonableness really are in order to have coherent standards for legislation.

11.15 Evaluation of Finnis

By employing the principle that goods are self-evident, rather than derived from objectively observable facts, Finnis not only avoids being accused of deriving an 'ought' from an 'is', but also deprives us of any attack on his methodology. Since we cannot show precisely where values come from, we are reduced to attacking the paucity of analogous arguments. However, this reduces us to shadow-boxing and is in no way dispositive of his method. All we are able to do is face Finnis on his own grounds, answering the question as to whether we agree with him or not. However, we can ask whether we agree because of our learned instincts, our reason, rather than because what he says is self-evident. The Humean criticism would be to grant that these goods are aspects of passions and urges we all recognise but that there is no more to them than just that.

Finnis' concept of play, for example, could cover any human activity from pulling wings off insects to watching a person being burnt to death. It is the direction of his methods of practical reasoning that essentially makes these goods seem good.

A controversial aspect to his theory is his inclusion of practical reasonableness as a good. Obviously, it is expedient and useful to reason, and it has beneficial side-effects that Finnis notes. However, the essence of practical reasoning is that it is concerned with moving to practical solutions from general inclinations or urges. His methods of practical reasoning are laden with value considerations, which unlike the broad propositions of the seven goods are not necessarily the self-evident methods of practical reasoning. He asserts that practical reasonableness dictates that the promotion of the common good and justice are necessary aspects of our existence. This leads him to focus on law from the point of view of practical reasonableness imbued with moral priorities. The criteria of practical reasonableness still allow a vast diversity of systems to be justified. However, Finnis' focus is on a concept of law that is assumed to be differentiated from other normative social orders because there is a *prima facie* moral obligation to obey it. The reason there is such an obligation is that legislators are assumed to be acting in the interests of the common good. And that they are so assumed to act is because it is a necessary dictate of Finnis' norms of practical reasonableness.

Finnis criticises Hart's focal concept of law, centred on the internal aspect of rules, on the basis that it does not focus on the main reason for the adherence to legal rules, namely, the promotion of the common good. Finnis is self-avowedly seeking to define what the requirements are for a practically reasonable legal system.

A criticism frequently advanced is that Finnis advocates what is essentially a materialist, capitalist society, which may have its virtues as a political institution, but which need not promote these ultimate goods. The by-product of this kind of society is the reliance on materialism for the achievement of goods. On the other hand, it is arguable that the wise man chooses not to be diverted by maximisation of material, but seeks these goods in a simple life. Indeed this is the assertion of many idealists, who regard political society as an aberration (Rousseau) and law as a diversion from the human achievement of good (Marx).

11.16 Dworkin's 'grounds' and 'force' of law

Dworkin does not like the idea of being branded a 'natural lawyer' because his view is that the term 'natural law' covers too many different theories. But his theory is often described as one of natural law, simply because of his integration of moral arguments into legal arguments. He does, too, like most natural lawyers, view evil systems, such as the Nazi system, as not properly to be described as 'law'. He distinguishes between what he calls the 'grounds' of law and the 'force' of law. The grounds of law are obtained by looking interpretatively at the legal practices of some community from the point of view of a participator in those practices. It would be possible, from this standpoint, to work out how a judge in Nazi Germany might decide a case. We can call him Siegfried J. Imagine some horrific hard case under the Nuremberg Laws, say, to do with sexual relations between Jews and German nationals. We could take account of widely believed theories of racial superiority to provide detailed arguments about which way the case should be decided. We could learn how to argue a case by learning the 'ground rules', as it were, of an evil legal system.

Law as moral justification of the use of state coercive power

But to produce an argument from the 'grounds' of law is not thereby to endorse it. A full-blooded political theory, according to Dworkin, requires an explanation not only of grounds but of the moral 'force' of law. He adds that philosophies of law are usually unbalanced because they are usually only about the grounds of law. So, we can judge Nazi law from Siegfried J's point of view, in the sense that we can predict what he will do, in the same way as we might imagine how a magistrate, in Roman times, would decide a point of Roman law.

It is easy to fall into traps here. Some critics, Hart notably, have supposed that Dworkin has merely created an amended, and confused, form of positivism. By the addition of 'principles' and 'underlying theories' of law, perhaps to a positivist account such as Hart's, all that was necessary in order to understand and argue hard cases was to talk of 'Nazi principles' and 'underlying theories of racial superiority'. According to this understanding, because Dworkin unites both legal and moral rights, any rights arising should have a very weak *prima facie* moral force which would be overridden by a strong background morality. Thus, with some vehemence, Hart says:

> 'If all that can be said of the theory or set of principles underlying the system of explicit law is that it is morally the least odious of morally unacceptable principles that fit the explicit evil law this can provide no justification at all. To claim that it does would be like claiming that killing an innocent man without torturing him is morally justified to some degree because killing with torture would be morally worse.'

Dworkin's answer involves an appeal to the fact that a problem of law is that we do ascribe some moral force to laws which we believe to be morally bad:

> '... the central power of the community has been administered through an articulate constitutional structure the citizens have been encouraged to obey and treat as a source of rights and duties, and that the citizens as a whole have in fact done so.'

It must follow from this, says Dworkin, that the decision whether a statute gives rise to a moral right is a moral question. 'We need,' he says, 'the idea of a legal right, which someone might have in virtue of a bad law, in order to express the conflict between two grounds of political rights that might sometimes conflict.'

The idea is much more easily understood in the later light of the development of Dworkin's theory of law as an interpretive concept. The interpretation of law is addressed to a set of legal practices in a particular culture. The essential point about the interpretation of evil legal systems is that the best moral sense that can be made of them is just that they have no moral force. In an important respect, it distorts this project to say simply that the laws are 'there' but should not be endorsed.

It is only when we introduce the history of 'natural' law that problems arise. The history of that idea is a long one. In recent times, it has become a debate about the 'conceptual' connection between different uses we make of language. At times, it centres on the structural nature of legal systems, at others, upon the validity of single rules. It mixes with requirements of the laws of the international community. At times, it reports necessary conditions of 'human flourishing', at others it claims that human attributes are merely accidental.

Nevertheless, there are people who want a clear line on the question whether Dworkin is a 'natural' lawyer. If the question is whether Dworkin believes that making moral judgments is part of the question of determining whether the community has a right or duty to use its coercive powers, then he is a natural lawyer. If the question is whether he believes immoral legal systems are not law, then he is *not* a natural lawyer. If it means whether he thinks that there is a 'natural' answer, 'out there', which supplies an 'objectivity' to moral and legal argument, he certainly is not a natural lawyer. The message should be clear by now. It is not at all helpful in this area to run together, under the one term 'natural law', so many different kinds of theory.

Ronald Dworkin and contemporary case law

The contribution of Ronald Dworkin to contemporary legal theory should not be underestimated. His views, like his predecessor Herbert Hart, may have an eventual effect on the English judges. He is widely taught in United Kingdom law schools and the freshness of his emphasis on the importance and value of understanding real live issues of a practical nature is of importance.

Let us compare, however, the decisions in the Court of Appeal and the House of Lords, of much topical interest, to allow medical treatment to be withdrawn from an irreversibly comatose patient who had been in that state for three-and-a-half years since the Hillsborough disaster. The Court of Appeal decision is *Airedale National Health Service Trust* v *Bland* (1993), and the most interesting judgment is that of Hoffman LJ who not only adopts an avowedly natural law approach (see Chapter 3, section 3.4) but also refers to Dworkin's book *Life's Dominion*, obviously the sister book to his *Law's Empire*. Here is a flavour of Lord Justice Hoffman's judgment:

> 'This is not an area in which any difference can be allowed to exist between what is legal and what is morally right. The decision of the court should be able to carry conviction with the ordinary person as being based not merely on legal precedent but also upon acceptable ethical values ... I tried to examine the underlying moral principles which have led me to the conclusion at which I have arrived. In doing so, I must acknowledge the assistance I have received from reading the manuscript of Professor Ronald Dworkin's forthcoming book *Life's Dominion* and from conversations with him and Professor Bernard Williams.'

Williams' book (along with Smart) entitled *Utilitarianism: For and Against* (1973) is recommended reading for the chapter on the moral theory of utilitarianism (see Chapter 6).

But let us compare that decision in the Court of Appeal with that in the House of Lords (immediately after the Court of Appeal decision). The most interesting from the point of view of testing jurisprudential theories is Lord Browne-Wilkinson's judgment. He says, first:

> 'Where a cases raises wholly new moral and social issues, in my judgment it is not for the judges to seek to develop new, all-embracing, principles of law in a way which reflects the individual judges' moral stance when society as a whole is substantially divided on the relevant moral issues ... For these reasons, it seems to me imperative that the moral, social and legal issues raised by this case should be considered by Parliament.'

Here are some questions. Is Lord Browne-Wilkinson making a judgment here of political morality about the doctrine of separation of powers? (It seems so.) Is he saying that judges should not decide general issues (policy?) on matters on which there are moral divisions? Is he saying that judges can never take a moral stance? (Presumably not, because he has just taken one on the proper relationship between the judiciary and the legislature.) One wonders what his Lordship would have said had he been on the consenting sado-masochistic acts case, recently decided in the House of Lords, of *R* v *Brown and Others* (1993). There, Lord Templeman is reported to have said:

> 'The slogan that every person had a right to deal with his body as he pleased did not provide a sufficient guide to the policy decision which must be made ... Society was entitled and bound to protect itself against a cult of violence ...'

Lord Browne-Wilkinson then went on to say that he thought that 'The answer to the [moral question as to whether feeding should be withdrawn] must of course depend on the circumstances of each case and there will be no single "right" answer.' It is not, however, possible to see any argument for that conclusion other than that doctors will disagree. It must, too, be a non sequitur to say that, just because people disagree therefore there is no right answer, since that would allow no possibility for people ever to be wrong. In any case, the right answer might simply be that, because people disagree, the right answer is something such as (and this was what Lord Browne-Wilkinson proposed): 'the court's only concern will be to be satisfied that the doctor's decision to discontinue (feeding) is in accordance with a respectable body of medical opinion and that is reasonable.' But this smacks of a fudge: what is 'respectable'?; what is 'reasonable'? A criticism of Lord Browne-Wilkinson's approach is that this is buck-passing the question of deciding right and wrong issues of morality to doctors; one wonders whether he would have been prepared to do this had he been sitting in judgment in the sado-masochistic case of *Brown and Others*.

Dworkin's Life's Dominion

Dworkin's book, just referred to, is important in two respects. It introduces a new way of looking at the abortion debate, by denying that foetuses have rights albeit having a 'sacred' or 'inviolable' status, and it applies this moral understanding about abortion to the contemporary debates in American constitutional law about the future of the famous and controversial 1973 decision of the US Supreme Court in *Roe* v *Wade*.

The book's full title is *Life's Dominion: an Argument about Abortion and Euthanasia* (1993) and it divides into three parts. In the first, Dworkin argues that we misunderstand both sides of the abortion debate if we take it to be about whether the foetus is, from the very early stages of pregnancy, a creature with rights and interests that abortion would violate. In order to make sense of what most people on both sides of the debate actually believe, Dworkin says, we must see them as taking seriously a quite different moral idea, which he calls the sanctity of life. The second part of *Life's Dominion* is devoted to the constitutional jurisprudence of abortion, specifically to the argument that, given what the abortion debate is really about, something very close to the position taken in *Roe* v *Wade* is the correct constitutional standard for laws regulating abortion. Finally, in the last two chapters of the book, Dworkin applies the distinctions he has drawn between rights, interests, and the intrinsic sacredness of life to the difficult case of euthanasia.

Of great importance is his denial that foetuses have rights. He says that, until the third trimester of pregnancy anyway, they do not have sentience and so cannot sensibly be called persons or sensibly described as having interests. To characterise pre-third trimester foetuses in this way, he says, would be like saying that Frankenstein's monster had a right, or interest, in Frankenstein's throwing the switch which would bring the various body parts together. On the other hand, it is going too far to say that foetuses have no status whatsoever. Dworkin thinks that the status is sacred. Foetuses have an intrinsic, inviolable character akin to the importance and inviolability of the environment, or of about to become extinct species, or the great works of art. This idea of the sacred expresses better, he believes, the wrong that all, liberals as well as conservatives, feel is wrong with abortion, even to save the mother's life.

But if the foetus is not seen to have rights the differences between liberals and conservatives is smoothed out considerably. The liberals and conservatives differ only over the relative importance they accord the foetus. Conservatives place more emphasis on the 'natural investment' that has gone into the creation of something as unique as each individual foetus; liberals, on the other hand, place more weight on the 'human investment' that has gone into a life. Thus a liberal might compare the wrongness of destroying an early term foetus against the wrongness of coercing a young women to go through a pregnancy that she – really – does not want to go through with. Here the 'human investment', by which Dworkin means the result of all those decisions and attitudes and intentions by which a person plans to live a certain kind of life, would be seriously frustrated.

The chapters (Chapter 4 – 'Abortion in Court: Part I'; Chapter 5 – 'The Constitutional Drama'; and Chapter 6 – 'Abortion in Court: Part II') which follow attack the idea propounded by many constitutional lawyers in the United States who are 'pro-lifers' that the US Constitution does not grant a right to abortion because the Constitution does not mention such a right. Here there is a clear and condensed version of the arguments in Chapters 9 and 10 of *Law's Empire* and it is a useful reworking of the ideas, familiar to readers of *Law's Empire*, of judicial interpretation of law according to the virtue of integrity and the imaginative application of the ideas of 'fit' and 'substance'.

Legal and Social Theory

12

Sociological Jurisprudence

12.1 Introduction

12.2 Sociological jurisprudence (idealist)

12.3 Sociological jurisprudence (evaluative)

12.4 Socio-legal studies

12.5 Sociology of law

12.1 Introduction

Although this section passes under the heading of sociological jurisprudence, there are several approaches, with differing labels that are subsumed under this heading. They encompass various schools of thought. All of them share the attribute of applying methods of social enquiry in order to elucidate the role of law in society. We can divide the ideas conceptually into three strands of approach.

Sociological jurisprudence (idealist)

In this area should be included those thinkers who either:

1. base their analysis of society on idealist historical information;
2. base their analysis of society on an economic or political theory.

Sociological jurisprudence (evaluative)

This section includes those thinkers who are primarily concerned with whether law is sufficiently reflective of societal needs.

The sociology of law

This section includes those thinkers who are concerned to apply social scientific methods to explain laws and the reasons for laws in their social context.

These groupings, particularly the first two, are necessarily arbitrary. There are numerous other ways to view the sociological approach, but these groupings are intended to marshal rather diverse subjects into manageable categories.

12.2 Sociological jurisprudence (idealist)

Auguste Comte is credited with inventing the term sociology, denoting the scientific analysis of society. The student will already be aware that the belief that scientific method was the one appropriate to the study of all phenomena flourishes to this day. However, the study of society did not necessarily start with Comte, although he represents a good starting point for our purposes.

Comte's espoused theory was that the appropriate method for study of society was by observation, experimentation, comparison and historical method. This is not dissimilar to the broad principles of modern sociology, although it has been somewhat refined. A fundamental problem that plagued early sociology was the poor state of historical knowledge, based on official versions and broad and somewhat idealised views. This necessarily prejudiced the works of early sociologists.

Scientific theories, developed in the nineteenth century alongside crude economic ones, also influenced the views of sociologists, with Herbert Spencer espousing social Darwinism that contrasted with the historical idealism of other thinkers, but was based on little more truth. Equally, based on the idea that self-interest dictates social responsibility, the *laissez-faire* attitude that economic and social forces will necessarily order society for the better, was adopted by Adam Smith, Ricardo and, to a certain extent, Bentham. The followers of such theories were less interested in legal control as in deregulation of trade, which was viewed largely as the answer to most social evils.

Bentham, followed by von Jhering, adopted a utilitarian approach, based on the satisfaction of human wants. Law, by means of coercive methods, would be the instrument of order by which society could balance the needs of the individual with the needs of society.

Ehrlich placed considerable emphasis on the diversity of social institutions with coercive or normative force, directing attention towards institutional rules and practices that are parallel, but not part of the law. These almost constitute private legal systems. This insight is a useful one and its reflection is to be found in the growing interaction between legal institutions and social ones. For example, we might now find that professional rules and standards are widely reflected in judgments in the law of negligence. Equally government has begun to delegate legislative powers to agencies, even of a private nature. The Financial Services Act 1986 delegates the power to legislate and make rules on investment practices. The holders of these powers are private limited companies that are the evolutionary forms of independent professional investment bodies.

However, Ehrlich took his analysis further. Although he conceded that the law had its own professional approaches to social problems, he emphasised that true law was living law, that is, the interests and practices in society, and as such most legal reform was simply the accommodation of living law into these rules. Ehrlich urged the lawyer to gain his understanding and weight his judgments by the interests of society, thus moulding book law to the living law. But Ehrlich overlooked the fact that legislation itself has an effect on practices and seeks itself to balance interests. However, we cannot be excessively critical of him, without taking into account the rapid progress and complexity that was a feature of his times.

All the above theorists share a fairly remote and instrumentalist view of law. Law was seen as subservient to greater social forces that would set the legal agenda. The concept of social progress and the rightness of the forces within society seem to reflect the economic and political changes in the nineteenth century. However, such approaches contribute little to our understanding of law's place in society. Indeed, it is possibly dispensable.

It may be noted that historical and empirical fallacies are not confined to this section. Durkheim, who will be considered a little later, based much of his argument about the role of law on assumptions and somewhat dubious historical data. His concept of society bears closer resemblance to an organism, with collective thoughts expressed through law. Equally, Weber, whose importance is significant, still, as Lloyd points out, remains bound to the *laissez-faire* ideal. It seems hard for a sociologist to approach the status of law in society without bringing with him unfounded preconceptions or quasi-empirical theory.

12.3 Sociological jurisprudence (evaluative)

The informal group of social scientists considered in this section are primarily, though not exclusively, concerned with the effectiveness of law. Principally their aim is to focus on the gap between law-in-theory and law-in-action. The reason for this concern was largely a reforming instinct. A second concern relates to the nature of society. Does society have a common interest expressed through law, or does it represent conflict within society?

There are three thinkers whose importance is predominant in this area: Pound, Weber and Durkheim. Pound is to be regarded as synonymous with the term sociological jurisprudence. Weber's contribution is indisputable, since his methodological improvements and refocusing seem to pave the way for a true sociology of law. However, Weber must be viewed in the context of responding to the legal sociology of Marx. For practical reasons, it is therefore necessary for the student to refer to Chapters 17 and 18, since Marx's concept of law and state, although properly a sociological and economic analysis, deserves special attention. Finally, Durkheim is an appropriate figure of focus. Marx, Weber and Durkheim should be categorised together as legal sociologists, marking the transition to a sociology of law, away from the traditions of sociological jurisprudence.

An introduction to Roscoe Pound's theory

The extensive writings of Roscoe Pound, which are spread over a long period of time, represent the culmination of the legal thinking of the past. Pound was an academic lawyer and an advocate for socio-legal studies. His concern was to examine law in action as opposed to the topic of law in books. Again it should be emphasised that his primary concern was with law reform and his theory ought to be read with this in mind. He wished to develop a technology to redraft the law to take account of social reality. He saw law as a social phenomenon which translated into policy, and meant that in the making, interpretation and application of laws, due account should be taken of law as a social fact.

The following represents, in his view, the task of the purposes of the legal order.

1. Factual study of the social effects of legal administration.
2. Social investigations as preliminary to legislation.
3. Constant study of making laws more effective.
4. Study, both psychological and philosophical, of judicial method.
5. Sociological study of legal history.
6. Allowance for the possibility of a just and reasonable solution of individual cases.
7. A Ministry of Justice to undertake law reform.
8. The achievement of the purposes of the various laws.

In order to achieve these purposes of the legal order it would first be necessary to achieve the recognition of certain interests which operate on different levels. These levels are the individual, the public and the social.

Secondly, it would be necessary, Pound thought, to arrive at a definition of the limits within which such interests will be legally recognised and given effect to. And thirdly, the securing of those interests within the limits as defined was necessary.

What, according to Pound, would be required in order to achieve this? He listed (Pound was very fond of lists!) the following as necessary.

1. The preparation of an inventory of classified interests.
2. A selection of interests which should be legally recognised.
3. A demarcation of limits of securing the interests so selected.
4. Consideration of the means whereby laws might secure the interests when these have been acknowledged and delimited.
5. The evolution of the principles of valuation of the interests.

As stated above, in doing this rather protracted task Pound sought to harmonise law in books with law in action. It is not at all clear that he has succeeded in this aim or indeed that anyone could have succeeded. However, in order to give due regard to his attempt we shall examine his efforts further. In particular we shall examine his concept of social engineering and the balancing of conflicting interests and the use of his jural postulates in the achievement of the balancing act.

The models of conflict and consensus

In order to understand the working of Pound's theory it is necessary to discuss the broad distinction that runs through sociology of law and sociological jurisprudence.

This is whether society is essentially a reflection of the consensus or of the conflict model. Although this may appear rather a general discussion in the middle of Pound's theory, it is the first point in the text where we come across this matter and it is one to which we will regularly return.

A consensus model is one which sees society as having shared values and traditions, whereby law serves the interests which are to the ultimate benefit of society. Law is thus seen as a value consensus, representing the shared values of the society, and adjusting conflicts and reconciling interests to match with the consensus. Such a model may be seen, explicitly or implicitly, in the works of Pound and Durkheim.

It is also the basis of the framework provided by Parsons and developed by Bredemeier. Parsons views the legal system as having a function of integration, of preventing via the set of rules the disintegration of social interaction into conflict. He splits the legal from the political system. In the former, the courts hold centre stage with their work of interpretation; in the latter, the legislature formulates policy. Pound put it in this way: The success of any particular society will depend on the degree to which it is socially integrated and so accepts as common ground its basic postulates. Such a view postulates that law adjusts and reconciles conflicting interests according to the requirements of social order. The problem with this view of society is that it seems to represent society as more stable and homogenous than it really is. It seems a very cosy view.

A conflict model, on the other hand, suggests that society involves not a value consensus but a value conflict and that law, rather than reconciling conflict interests in a compromise, instead imposes one interest at the expense of the other. Such a model is expounded by Quinney and, of course, the Marxists.

Which is a correct reading of the English legal system? Both views can claim support from particular pieces of evidence; either showing a social consensus (major crimes, civil liberties protection?) or rules that are the product of conflict (rules of property and contract).

Is the conflict a simple one, with one ruling class of which judges are a part? (See, for example, Griffith's *The Politics of the Judiciary*.) Or is it more complicated, with competing interest groups possessing varying amounts of power? Writers differ on these points. It should be pointed out that if the latter position is accepted, the question arises as to how far different is the conflict/consensus position?

Social engineering

Following on the consensus model of society and in explaining the process of the balancing of conflicting interests, Pound has used an analogy with engineering. He sees the task as one to build as efficient a structure of society as possible, which requires the satisfaction of the maximum of wants with the minimum of friction and waste. Thus by identifying and protecting certain interests the law ensures social cohesion.

The idea of the balancing of conflicting interests was derived from Ihering and can be stated as the giving effect to as much as possible of conflicting claims which men assert *de facto* about which the law must do something if organised societies are to endure. It has been observed that Pound's theory is not a fully developed theory of justice. Harris, for example, has stated that Pound's theory equates justice with quietening those who are banging on the gates, in that achievement of one's interests depends on articulation of those interests. Those interests are subject to manipulation through advertising campaigns for example. Incidentally, the role that advertising plays in shaping desires is well discussed by Stone in Chapter 9 of his *Human Law and Human Justice*.

Balancing of conflicting interests

It would be appropriate to examine further the notion of the balancing of conflicting interests. In doing so Pound looks at actual assertion of claims in a particular society as manifested in legal proceedings and this of course includes rejected as well as accepted claims. Again there is more classification involved. It is worth learning the three different levels on which Pound identified interests operating, shown below.

1. Individual interests. These are claims as seen from the standpoint of individual life. The following are examples:
   a) personality, such as interests in person, honour, privacy;
   b) domestic relations, as distinct from social interests in institutions, such as family or parent;
   c) interests of substance, such as property, freedom of association.
2. Public interests. These are claims asserted by individuals but viewed from the standpoint of political life. They are less important but would include:
   a) interests of the state as a juristic person; looking at the personality of the state; and
   b) interests of the state as guardian of social interests.
3. Social interests. These are the most general and, according to Pound, the preferred level on which to balance conflicting interests. They are claims as viewed in terms of social life or generalised as claims of the social group. This includes the social interests in:
   a) general security, that is, to be secure against threats to existence from disorder, and matters such as health;
   b) security of social institutions, which acknowledges the existence of tension and the need to protect religious institutions;
   c) general morals, including such matters as prostitution and gambling which are said to be offensive to moral sentiments;
   d) conservation of social resources. This is comparable to Rawls' just savings principle and is in conflict with the individual interest in one's own property;
   e) general progress, which would cover free speech and free trade (but nonetheless ignores the tendency towards resale price fixing); and

f) individual life, according to which one should be able to live life according to standards of society.

These are just examples. The important point according to Pound is that these must be balanced on the same level otherwise the decision would not be neutral. It would dictate the outcome of the supposedly scientific exercise in balancing out these interests. It is noteworthy that Ihering did not insist on this when he spoke of balancing conflicting interests. Are you convinced by Pound's insistence on balancing conflicting interests in a neutral fashion? But Pound has not paid much attention to ways in which one conflicting interest is to be compared with another. Lloyd summed it up thus: 'Unlike Ihering, who assumed that social and individual interests should always be directly compared, Pound insisted that a fair balancing of interests could only be achieved by examining a conflict on the same plane or level.'

The 'jural postulates'

In circumstances where an accommodation of interests is not possible there is, according to Pound, no objective way of resolving disputes. To meet this defect Pound developed the notion of jural postulates as the means of testing new interests. These jural postulates are the presuppositions of legal reasoning which embody the fundamental purposes of the legal system. They are in effect the basic assumptions upon which society is based. We can conclude that Pound was using a new term to describe something that was already well recognised.

Pound's methodology was that of incremental legal reasoning. This method of legal reasoning, which is well known to common law lawyers, would allow new claims only if claims of that sort are already recognised. The speech of Lord Buckmaster in *Donoghue* v *Stevenson* (1932) represents one of the most famous adoptions of incremental legal reasoning. In essence Lord Buckmaster was saying that unless Mrs Donoghue could show that in a previous case a claim such as that she was bringing to the court was admitted, then whatever the particular merits of her case her claim would have to be rejected.

According to Pound these jural postulates may conflict, although he insists that his do not. Furthermore they may change and would do so relative to the stages in social evolution. It is helpful to remember this before dealing with a criticism that was made by the Scandinavian realist Lundstedt to the effect that Pound's jural postulates were nothing more than natural law allowed in through the back door. Lundstedt is wrong in that these jural postulates do not possess the characteristics of natural law. They are not absolute, nor are they universal and indeed, as has been stated, nor are they unchanging.

Critical evaluation of Pound

There is much written by Pound and more written about him. It really is not possible to raise all the critical evaluations that have been made; here, however, is a selection.

1. Patterson, in *Jurisprudence: Men and Ideas of the Law* (1953), describes Pound's catalogue of interests as a rationalisation of the actual.
2. Lloyd and Freeman state that Pound's classification of interests reads rather like a political manifesto in favour of a liberal and capitalist society even though for Pound it were seen as objective. A socialist would insert other interests. They add that the classification of interests suffers from excessive vagueness.
3. With regard to the recognition of interests Dias has argued that there are graduated levels of recognition and cites the case of *Van Duyn* v *Home Office* (1975) which involved the denial of access to this country of a citizen of the EEC who was a member of the Church of Scientology. This would normally be a breach of the rules on freedom of movement within the EEC but, as Dias points out, while the Church of Scientology was not outlawed it was however officially condemned.
4. Dias raises further criticisms when he states that the whole idea of balancing is subordinate to the ideal that is in view. The march of society is gauged by changes in its ideals and standards for measuring interests. Dias is of the opinion that the listing of interests is less important than judicial attitudes towards particular activities. According to him weight will depend on ideal.
5. Note that the recognition of a new interest might be created as a matter of forward-looking policy as opposed to being a jural postulate that can be extrapolated from the matrix of the law.
6. Dias has criticised the engineering analogy as being false in that engineering projects are based on a plan, whereas the reality is that society changes and that the building must always be erected on shifting ground. Perhaps there are limits to which analogies can be taken. Dias does, however, argue with some force that law is not a planned enterprise and, rather, attempts, in an *ad hoc* way to cope with situations as and when they arise.
7. Pound asserts that claims pre-exist law, whereas often claims are based on law. An example would be with regard to welfare benefits where claimants base their claim on existing rules and regulations.
8. It is clear that Pound asserted that the nature of a society is one of consensus, yet it is not particularly clear whether or indeed how balancing of interests will produce a more cohesive society. Further, the process of using law as a tool of social engineering would depend on the credibility accorded to the law. This can be seen in the examples of political trials such as the trial of the Chicago Eight or the Oz obscenity trial where the aim of the defendants was to discredit the court. The experience of the trials of IRA suspects in Northern Ireland also makes the same point. There the defendants seek to deny all legitimacy to the proceedings. In such circumstances social engineering breaks down.
9. The law concerns considerations of people's needs as well as their interests. This is especially the case with regard to paternalistic laws such as the law on the compulsory wearing of seat belts in cars. The very idea of satisfying people's interests conflicts with a paternalist view of society. The laws forbidding the

display of pornography run counter to the satisfying of people's interests if interests are defined as desires, yet there exists powerful argument from a paternalistic point of view to the effect that such laws are necessary.

10. It has been shown, and this point is discussed above, that post-Pound socio-legal research doubts whether law is the result of value consensus. The findings of Quinney tend to confirm that society is better described as founded on a conflict model rather than any consensus.

11. Overall it can be stated that Pound exerted a considerable influence on jurisprudence in that he laid the foundation for post-traditionalism. However, according to Alan Hunt in *The Sociological Movement in Law*, Pound used sociology when he saw fit; he cannot be regarded as having developed a sociological theory of law.

Weber's response to Marx

The writings of Marx proposed a revolutionary theory that sent capitalism scurrying for cover. As with any revolutionary theory those at the focus of the revolutionary attack will seek to provide a response. This can clearly be seen with regard to von Savigny's response to the adoption of the French Code Napoleon in parts of Germany (see Chapter 15). In the more modern frame this is also exemplified by the response of the Gulf States to the revolution in Iran. Weber offered a response to the Marxist challenge to capitalism. In assessing the response of Weber it would be appropriate to discuss the nature of that challenge.

Marx thought that capitalism was in crisis. He saw the brutal exploitation of labour in the Lancashire cotton mills and drew a conclusion from this that capitalism was in its last stages. He developed his Marxist theory on the premise that capitalism would not survive for long and that it would inevitably be replaced eventually with a classless society. As part of his attack on capitalism he noticed that the greatest revolutionary potential was the working class and that in order to bring about that revolution and the arrival of the stage of socialism, what was needed was to raise the revolutionary consciousness of the working class. This would be done in Marxist terms by dispelling capitalist ideology which he saw as a false consciousness that mystified the working class and legitimated the capitalists' control of the means of production. Marx therefore saw everything in terms of economic determinism whereby the state and the law served the interests of the class that controlled the all-important means of production. This crude class instrumentalism was the focus of Weber's remark that authority strives for acceptance, not submission.

Marx thought that the state and the law which represents authority was a tool of oppression in the hands of the ruling class in seeking to dominate the working class. While this view has been reneged by more modern Marxists seeking to enter the political agenda of today, at the time Weber was writing he was dealing only with the original works of Marx and Engels. It would not therefore be a legitimate criticism to say that Weber did not take account of something that did not exist at his time. In response to that class instrumentalism Weber observed that the search for a single primal cause was futile. He was thus critical of Marx for the view that economic factors were the sole determining cause of the nature of the society. While saying this, Weber recognised that economic factors are important. But the criticism was ill founded. Marx merely said that in the final analysis economic factors determine the nature of society. Thus Marx recognised that other factors were important also.

Marx's dialectical materialism viewed the history of all hitherto existing society as the history of class conflict. According to him, law was the instrument of those controlling the means of production in the maintenance of their domination over the relations of production. That control was effective by both appearing to accord legitimation to the state and by mystifying the oppressed class. The mystification operated through the exploitation of the surplus value of labour, and the legitimation was through simple power disguised by the state's ideological and repressive apparatus, such as the legitimate state use of force and the false consciousness that sought to preserve the status quo. One such form of false consciousness was religion which Marx saw as the opiate of the masses because it dulled their senses about the reality of their exploitation.

If there exists a single thread that runs through Weber's work, it is his response to Marx whom he regarded as fundamentally wrong. Weber thought Marx was dogmatic and vague and he rejected Marx's views about the false authority of the law. In response to the idea that the state was the tool of the dominant class, Weber sought to speak of legitimate authority. The legitimate authority would strive for acceptance, he said. This Weber attempted to prove by examining the question why people feel obliged to obey law.

Legitimacy and authority

Weber addressed himself to the problem of the nature of order. He saw society as a system of ordered action where almost invariably the particular order is claimed to be right or, as he put it, it was 'legitimised'. Weber believed that no society could exist for long on a set of static or unenforced norms and it would therefore be necessary to have power or command to change and enforce these norms. For Weber, power meant the possibility of 'imposing one's will on the behaviour of another person'. What is new in Weber is that he identified power as a reciprocal relationship and this is the crux of his debate with Marxism. The Marxist views power as the consequence of control of the means of production and the means of preserving that control.

Weber identified two types of power relation, both of which were reciprocal. These are monopoly power and power by authority. In monopoly power the seller fixes the price but the buyer wants to pay it. There is thus mutual self-interest, where power is based on a constellation of interests. In power by authority the parties, namely, the ruled and the rulers, accept the relationship as legitimate. Focus is directed at the meaning that the ruler and the ruled place on the relationship between them, that is a relationship of legitimate authority. It would then be appropriate to examine the three types of legitimate authority identified by Weber. These are: the traditional, the charismatic, and the legal rational.

1. By 'traditional authority', Weber spoke of the according of legitimacy to that which has always been. This is characterised by a belief in the sanctity of age-old rules. An example would be the aristocracy.

2. By 'charismatic authority', Weber meant a revolutionary situation where the followers attribute special powers to the leader. It involves an automatic break with the past. Legitimacy is founded in the belief in the authenticity of the leader's mission. An example of this would be Mahatma Gandhi in India. He held no formal office and was certainly not a manifestation of traditional authority and yet he was widely obeyed. In that example the obedience was certainly not through any domination by naked power. There is a problem with the question of succession to authority in such a situation, although it could be observed that religious leaders have been more successful than their political counterparts in ensuring the succession, a problem faced by, among others, Napoleon Bonaparte. Having said that, it is recognised that there are some notable exceptions.

3. The third type of authority was the most important for capitalism, according to Weber. It is 'legal rational' authority. It was important for the development of capitalism because it provided certainty in the law of contract, for example. By this type of authority, the authority vests not in the person but in the office held. It corresponds to our conception of the rule of law in which all people are subject to a uniformly administered system of rules and in which all people are subject to the law. The quotation by Lord Denning, directed at the Attorney-General, of the words of Thomas Fuller: 'Be you ever so high the law is above you' in *Gouriet* v *UPW* (1977) illustrates the sentiment of this type of legitimate authority. It is the office which holds the authority, not the person, and obedience is given to norms not to the person. When Mrs Thatcher ceased being prime minister she lost her authority not because she was no longer Mrs Thatcher but because she was no longer prime minister. Simply, she no longer held the office to which authority attaches. According to Weber, in such a system the law serves to repress a conflict of wills by coercion and rationality.

Thus Weber thought that on occasion the ruling class could act in the national interest. That is certainly the language that the government uses. It never states that the measure is designed to serve the interests of the ruling class at the expense in terms of labour of the working class. Yet what of measures such as the welfare state, which so clearly are at the expense of those who control the means of production? Marxists today would explain this in terms of the 'relative autonomy of the state' and would view many laws that serve the interests of the working class as actually also serving the interests of the ruling class in ensuring a satisfied and healthy work force which will produce better products.

According to Weber, in order for capitalism to thrive, law has to be systemised so as to ensure the predictability of economic relations. In essence this is the point made by the new Marxists who stress the relative autonomy of the state. So long as the state protects economic relations it need not do anything else as far as the ruling class in Marxist terms is concerned. The problem with this idea is that it does not accord with the sequence of events in England where capitalism first took root. Weber acknowledged this and referred to it as an exception to his rule. There was no complete legal codified system in England then and there is not, of course, now.

Weber's typology of law

Weber was a trained lawyer who, as stated, was interested in explaining the development of capitalism in western society in terms of the growth of a rational legal order being required to facilitate such a development. He also thought that capitalism developed as a consequence of the practice of what he called the Protestant work ethic to the effect that people would work hard and save some of the proceeds of their labour. These proceeds would then be invested to build up capital and hence encourage the rise of capitalism.

We might take issue with that hypothesis by considering that, in all probability, much of the capital required came less from such savings and more from the profits of global trade. The point, though, is not central to the law aspect of Weber's work. The premise that underlies Weber's theory is what he called *verstehen*, by which he meant that a social action could only best be understood by reference to its meaning, purpose and intention for the individual. Hence the remark that, in Weberian terms, a wink is different from a blink because it is social. A blink is not interpreted to have any meaning, whereas a wink is so interpreted.

Weber offered a definition of his typology of law:

'... an order will be called law if it is externally guaranteed by the probability that coercion, whether physical or psychological, to bring about conformity or avenge violation, will be applied by a staff of people holding themselves specially ready for that purpose.'

In pursuing this he developed a scheme of lawmaking and adjudication that can be represented in the diagram overleaf.

Note: The substantive/formal aspect relates to the extent to which the system possesses the rules and procedures required for decision making within the system. The rational/irrational aspect relates to the manner in which the rules/procedures are applied in the system.

The legal rational form of legitimate domination is impersonal. Obedience in such a system is not owed to the person but is rather owed to the legal order. The legitimacy of the type of political domination is drawn from the existence of a system of rationally made laws which stipulate the circumstances under which power may be exercised. Because the system is rational it is supported. This is, according to Weber, the source of all state authority in modern societies where legal domination is not dependent on the extent to which the law reflects the values of the people who accept the legitimacy of the system. Obedience does not depend on agreement with the content of the law but with the rationality that lies behind its creation and enforcement. This is an important point of much relevance to our study. A good question to consider is whether we would agree that it is an accurate reflection of the nature of the relationship between the subject and the government in Britain today.

	Rational	Irrational
Substantive	**Substantively rational** There is no separation between law and morals	**Substantively irrational** Cases are decided on their own merits without reference to general principles
Formal	**Formally rational** The legal system contains answers to all legal problems	**Formally irrational** Decisions are made on the basis of tests beyond the control of human intellect, eg trial by ordeal

Evaluation of Weber

Although Weber's writings are almost a hundred years old there is much that is still very informative as regards modern capitalist society. Weber's distinction between power and authority and his emphasis on the reciprocal relationship acting as a constraint is most illuminating. Further he can be seen as an early advocate of the value-free social sciences, a tradition that is widely accepted in this country. The Marxist would, however, dispute that such is a possibility. What Weber was saying was that it is possible for the sociologist to carry out value-free sociology while at the same time realising that the sociologist has his own value judgments. The sociologist is entitled to exercise his own value judgments in selecting the area of research but having done so the research must be carried out in a neutral way. This is a further manifestation of the separation of the 'is' from the 'ought'.

Nonetheless there are some aspects that are difficult to piece together in Weber's theory. Perhaps Weber took too restricted a view of the relationship between law and domination. He appears to have reduced the relationship to one of a personal nature as between the ruler and the ruled. It is suggested that the process of domination is much more complex than is clear from its formal legal manifestation.

Weber appears to have a good answer to Marx's point on naked domination but more recent responses have been to suggest that Marx is largely irrelevant in modern Britain. While Weber's views on authority as legitimate, not seeking to oppress but ruling by agreement, are applicable it is suggested that in modern Britain with a share-owning population owning their own homes and so on, the Marxist analysis is no longer relevant. Weber should therefore be seen in his historical perspective as an early but effective response to the challenge of Marxism.

When Weber stated that the search for a single primal cause was futile he was, of course, criticising the Marxist reliance on the relations of production, yet the criticism is somewhat misapplied. As we shall see in Chapter 17, Marx did not actually say that the relations of production were the only causal factor. What he did say was that economic determinism operates in the last instance and as such he clearly recognised that other factors are of some importance.

Weber's attack on the Marxist use of models also provides us with a valuable insight. Weber believed that models are heuristic devices against which we might test reality. To the extent that reality does not accord with the model the task of the social scientist is to change the model (if you take the view that there is an 'unalterable brute reality' 'out there'). Marx took the opposite view. According to Marx, if reality did not correspond with the model then the task was to change reality. Hence we have the revolutionary nature of Marxism. This point is developed in more detail in Chapter 17.

In his concept of *verstehen* Weber may have placed too much emphasis on the individual mind in an attempt to understand social action.

In his legal rational domination he speaks of the norms being impersonal. But since they are perceived as impersonal that might be due to factors such as social conditioning and blind acceptance. If so, these factors should be examined. An interesting thought is whether the media, advertising and so on, play a role in 'impersonally' but non-legally fashioning the norms in society.

His view of the rationality of the bureaucracy probably ignores the role of senior civil servants. They have considerable influence even to the extent of persuading government ministers on the content and timing of legislation. If this is so because these discussions are not open and thus not subject to proper debate and the public check of truth, that aspect of rationality is lost. If one is to give credence to the television series 'Yes, Prime Minister', wherein in a humorous manner the civil service are seen as manipulating their ministers to pursue civil service policy rather than the policy on which the government may have been elected, the argument gains even more force. Bureaucracy also has a tendency to create inertia and as such cannot be regarded as always efficient.

Emile Durkheim's social solidarity

Emile Durkheim drew much inspiration from the work of Charles Darwin. He was one of the first to insist on studying law in both its social and historical context. He subscribed to a consensus model of society and developed his theory that there exists a connection between law and the forms of social relations. Durkheim was not primarily concerned with law *per se* but was more interested in the study of society. His relevance is that he attributed a central importance to law in the developing of an understanding of social life in general. Durkheim has been labelled an anti-individualist. He spoke of the primacy of the social and of the collective conscience. He meant by this that thoughts have an existence separate from the person thinking them. His concept of the collective conscience is important to an understanding of his theory and to what he said about law.

Durkheim engaged in primitivist reductionism using anthropology to assist understanding. He attempted to reduce matters to their most primitive form and in his important study entitled *The Division of Labour in Society* (1893) he joined issue with the Marxist contention on the conflict society, stipulating that the social bond is not one of domination but of cohesion. Throughout his writings it is clear that he adopts the consensus model which presumes value consensus in the society.

In his study on the division of labour he identified the extent of the division of labour as the way to classify society and in so doing stated that the type of law prevalent can be used as an indicator of the type of social organisation. Hence, law is to be seen as the external index which symbolises the type of social solidarity. To study society's solidarity, he said, we study its law. Something needs to be said about his use of the term 'social solidarity'. According to Durkheim, social solidarity is a completely moral phenomenon and law plays a central role in the transition from mechanical to organic solidarity. These are the two polar forms of social solidarity and are identified by the degree of the division of labour. In the 'archaic' society, which he also called the mechanical solidarity society, there is no division of labour. In these circumstances the people have shared life experiences. Everyone lives a life almost the same as everyone else. In these circumstances Durkheim thought that since people were self-reliant they would not depend on each other to a great extent and that therefore there would be no problem in carrying out severe punishments on those who violated the code of conduct. Law would be repressive and because everyone shared the same life experiences their reaction to deviation from the accepted code would be passionate and knee-jerk. In a mechanical solidarity society, Durkheim maintained, the collective conscience would be both strong and uniform.

On the other hand, in a more advanced society which Durkheim labelled one of 'organic solidarity' there would be a clear division of labour with a high degree of job specialisation. In such a society the people would have different life experiences. There would be considerable social interdependence as the plumber would need the electrician, the lawyer, the taxi driver, and so on. In order to preserve cohesion the law would need to maintain an equilibrium. The collective conscience would be noticeably narrower and possibly considerably weakened when compared with a mechanical type solidarity. The type of law would be predominantly restitutive. That is not to say that there would not still be repressive laws. These would however be purely functional, designed not as a passionate reaction because that would be meaningless where beliefs were not commonly shared, but rather simply and functionally to preserve social cohesion.

In his study Durkheim stated that every precept of law can be defined as a rule of sanctioned conduct. Within that he identified sanctions as being of two kinds. These are:

1. repressive sanctions, whereby there is suffering or loss inflicted;
2. restitutive sanctions, whereby there would be a re-establishment of troubled relations to their normal state.

This process with regard to law is an indicator of the change and development of society. As stated, reference is made to the division of labour and in particular to the degree of specialisation in the economy. This is not, however, the only change in which Durkheim was interested. He also showed that there would be a corresponding shift from religion to secularism, from collectivism to individualism, and from penal sanctions to restitutive sanctions. It is this last shift that is of primary interest to our study.

With regard to the connection between law and morality Durkheim concluded that these were virtually synonymous. He maintained that law is derived from and is an expression of society's morality and that this explains how punishment may be seen as the expression of collective sentiments by which social cohesion is maintained. Again, this reflects his consensus model of society.

In an important passage Durkheim declared that: 'An action does not shock the common conscience because it is criminal: rather it is criminal because it shocks the common conscience.' On a practical level, this leads to interesting conclusions. As society progresses the form of punishment becomes less violent because the basic function of the state is to legalise norms. The state is the central focus of attention and is therefore influenced both by public opinion and by occupational groups. The method of enforced compliance engaged in by occupational groups is a further interesting area of Durkheim's study and one that has inspired more recent research into the role of the occupational group as a substitute for the socialising function of the family.

A question arises as to why there is still a predominance of repressive law in an organic society such as modern Britain. By a predominance it is meant that there is more than is necessary to preserve social cohesion. The answer which Durkheim would provide is that the division of labour has deviated from its original course.

There has been a breakdown of 'socialisation', meaning that the occupational groups are not performing their socialising tasks effectively enough. This is explained by Durkheim in a study on suicide as being made up of a series of different factors.

1. Egoism, whereby the individual is isolated and the bonds which hold the group together are loosened.
2. Altruism, whereby the individual relates to goals above those of the society and therefore becomes too heavily institutionalised.
3. Anomie, which is a state wherein the individual feels his life lacks meaning and guidance. In his explanation of this Durkheim focuses on man's activity as governed by norms. These norms ought to be integrated and non-conflicting in order that the individual can be properly adjusted to his society. Where these norms are not integrated or where they conflict with one another, the individual will lose his moral guidance because there will be no norms against wrongdoing which make sense to the individual. In this state the individual is said to be in a condition of anomie; he has no identity.
4. Alienation, where the individual who feels that the society is not there for him and indeed is there to exploit him will not identify with the aims of that society. Recent happenings in inner city areas in England may illustrate this point.
5. Inequality. This is self-evident and reinforces the above.

The view exists that it is not the individual but rather society which is at fault with regard to crime. It is a failing of us all if an individual is not sufficiently socialised and has to resort to crime. Not surprisingly this point leads to some strongly critical evaluation of Durkheim's thesis. What of individual opportunity and propensity? Are all people in a state of anomie potential or actual criminals? How does one explain crime committed by those who are most certainly fully integrated, such as stockbrokers found guilty of insider dealing? Such people would never consider robbing a bank even though there remains no clear loser when a bank vault is rifled. It is difficult to explain why we still do not regard insider dealing with the same opprobrium as we do burglary.

Durkheim has a point about punishment that has perhaps been taken too far. He observes that punishment performs a useful integrating function in society by providing a scapegoat through which the public can identify with the norms. The criminal broke the norms and therefore ought to be punished because that will act as a cohesive factor with regard to the other citizens. Hence Durkheim is able to argue that if we didn't have crime we would have to invent it to keep society together.

Evaluation of Durkheim

Durkheim's work is important in many respects in spite of what will be suggested are some rather fundamental flaws. He has identified the importance of punishment as a socialising force. He has emphasised the importance of viewing law in a sociological perspective rather than in terms of a pure analytical enquiry. However his treatment of law as a completely moral phenomenon does, it seems, neglect the extent to which law and morality often conflict. There are other points which can be made about his thesis. Empirical evidence tends to refute the assumption that in a primitive society there is no division of labour. Even as between the sexes there was a division of labour whereby women tended the home and men hunted. Their life experiences were therefore quite different. It is therefore disputable whether there ever was a true mechanical solidarity society as Durkheim understands the phrase.

Even without this point it would appear that Durkheim has provided no adequate account of how law becomes increasingly restitutive. He has given no description of the intermediate stages between primitive and industrialised societies and has assumed that the change was swift. This is misleading. As we shall see, anthropological studies show that repressive law is less important in primitive society. A good example is Gulliver's study of the Ndendeuli in Tanzania, in which he demonstrated that a group in which each individual relied on his fellows extensively, and had a widely shared life experience, developed a sort of bargain model as their dispute resolution mechanism. Leon Sheleff has demonstrated in *From Restitutive Law to Repressive Law – Durkheim's The Division of Labour in Society Revisited* (1973) that while Durkheim relied on Maine to say that primitive law is repressive, actually Maine said the reverse.

This view of punishment and the role of the law regards the state as the expression of the collectivity, that is to say an instrumental organ being the means by which offenders are punished. This is not the only view of the role of the state in these matters. The difficulty with such a consensus model is the contention discussed in the previous chapter that the state may not be neutral. If one were to accept the conflict model, then a different view of the role of the state would emerge. Durkheim assumes that everyone will identify with occupational professional values, which is simply not the case. He takes insufficient account of power, conflict and change, preferring to presume a value consensus without proving its existence.

More narrowly, his view of punishment as retributive ignores the deterrent, rehabilitative and reformist aspects of sentencing and also ignores the punitive aspect of the civil law in the form of exemplary damages. As has been stated above, Durkheim's view of crime negates the element of individual choice in crime.

Taking a Marxist perspective, Karl Renner has demonstrated the need to distinguish between the form and function of law, a distinction which Durkheim blurred.

12.4 Socio-legal studies

It may be seen that the approaches of Pound, Weber and Durkheim differ radically. Sociological jurisprudence in the manner of Pound has had certain adherents who are worthy of mention. Pound's jurisprudence finds certain resonances in the writings of the early American Realists. But his reformist approach was to be taken up in the writings of Lasswell and McDougal, who espoused the virtues of social progress and enunciated aims and social expectations that should be adopted by lawyers. Once again their thoughts are more like a manifesto of social policy than a concrete and applicable formula.

However, the empirical approach that emphasises questions of effectiveness and the law-in-action thesis, has been subsumed into the broader category of socio-legal studies. These empiricist studies, mainly centred on the idea of achieving social justice, are often based upon positivist sociology, which largely denies any intrinsic normative consistency to law. Law is thus defined as a procedure whose content and effectiveness may be critically evaluated. There is little in the way of a theory of law, but rather it is concerned with need and effect. It is clear that the instrumentalist view of law implicit in the work of those engaged in socio-legal studies is positivist in nature.

Lloyd is particularly critical of experiments such as the Chicago jury project that contrasted lawyers' predictions with jury acquittals. Particularly, the project is criticised as giving insufficient appreciation to the complex role of juries. Ultimately, the approach is the legacy of sociological jurisprudence that is concerned with law as a tool that may be employed for harm or good.

The fruits of the socio-legal pursuit have been noticeable, though, including the Bail Act 1976 and considerable concentration on the provision of legal advice. However, the jurisprudential theory that underpins it is largely an assertion that all that legislators need to know is what the subjects of the law respond to. Law is seen as an instrument, as a catalyst for change, but not an independent phenomenon to which much theoretical attention need by paid.

12.5 Sociology of law

Selznick marks out three stages in the application of social sciences to law.

1. 'The primitive, or missionary, stage is that of communicating a perspective, bringing to a hitherto isolated area an appreciation of basic and quite general sociological truths ...' He quickly points out that lawyers have been quite capable of doing this without the help of sociologists.
2. 'The second stage belongs to the sociological craftsman ... He wants to explore the area in depth, to help to solve its problems ...' This probably amounts to the socio-legal studies movement.
3. The third stage should be categorised as the stage of the sociologist of law when he 'addresses himself to the larger objectives and guiding principles of the particular human enterprise he has elected to study'.

He concludes by saying that the sociologist can not only give advice to the lawyer, as the socio-legal studies movement has sought to do, but can learn from law and legal systems in a search for an understanding of the broader context of society.

Stone observes that the early reformist drive of sociological jurisprudence was a phenomenon of its time, when legal reform was most needed. The new approach might be more reflective of law as an institutional part of society rather than as a panacea for societal ills. He points out that a more coherent, less ad hoc, approach may improve the methods of societal control through law.

Thinkers such as Black, who advocates a sociological positivism that is not interested in lawyers' reasons, but is more interested in lawyers' behaviour, may be seen as complementary to the positivism that, for example, Austin and his disciples advocate. However, there is a dichotomy of views on whether there can be a sociology of law that can accommodate such notions. Nonet insists that sociology must be informed by jurisprudence, observing further that jurisprudence itself is informed by policy. Disputing the mutual ignorance of the two disciplines, Nonet exhorts:

'We need a jurisprudential sociology, a social science of law that speaks to the problems, and is informed by the ideas of jurisprudence. Such a sociology recognises the continuities of analytical descriptive and evaluative theory ...'

This seems to be the tenor of a new approach to legal theory through sociology. However, its fruits are, as yet, not as substantial as its rhetoric and methodological argument.

13

American Realism

13.1 Introduction

As with many new attitudes and schools of thought, the American brand of realism was a reaction to an earlier school. In its case that earlier school was formalism, which concentrated on logic and a priori reasoning, and was thus thought to be only theoretical and not practical or pragmatic. Formalism, so the realists thought, had no regard to the facts of life experience. Realism attempted to be both practical and pragmatic, rejecting theoretical and analytical approaches to jurisprudential questions, and attempting to look at what it perceived to be the reality in the question: how does law work in practice? One of the factors that may have contributed to this approach in the United States is the rather different traditions of their judiciary. Indeed one of the pioneering realists in jurisprudence was Mr Justice Holmes, a Justice of the US Supreme Court (who was not approved of by President Roosevelt: 'I could carve out of a banana a judge with more backbone'). Holmes' famous statements include: 'The life of the law is experience' and 'The prophecies of what the courts will do ... are what I mean by law'.

This concentration on the courts is, of course, partly a reflection of their more important role in the United States, where they have the power to declare legislation unconstitutional and therefore invalid, and are not as strictly bound by rules of precedent as in the United Kingdom. Much more of the law is open to judicial alteration, and even momentous issues of great political significance can be decided on by the court (for example, the case of *Brown* v *Board of Education* in 1954,

199

declaring that the provision of separate but equal educational facilities for negroes violated the Equal Protection of the Laws amendment to the Constitution, and thus outlawed segregation).

Here we shall discuss the two main approaches of the American realists, namely, that of the rule sceptics and that of the experimentalists or fact sceptics. This chapter will also consider the schools that have emerged from American realism (jurimetrics and judicial behaviouralism) and finally will note the many criticisms of the realists' work and attempt to disentangle the extent of the contribution, if any, that they make to modern legal theory. A comparative evaluation of the Scandanavian realists is made in the following chapter.

13.2 The realist approach

Briefly, the realist approach was to attempt to look at the facts of the legal experience, and not at those things, such as the legal rules and doctrines, which were in theory held to be important. The two most important facets of the realists' writing seem to be their rule scepticism and their concentration on the courts' role in settling disputes. The essence of their approach was that there is more to law than the mere logically deductive application of rules. They are not saying that there is no value in the logical application of legal rules to fact situations, merely that if a more accurate prediction of the likely outcome of the case is desired, as the practitioner ought so to aspire to provide, then the mere logical application of rules will not provide a sufficiently accurate prediction.

The technique in which most students are trained in law schools in this country is logical application of legal rules to fact situations. The student learns the legal rules during the year (although, paradoxically, in the examination is given the hypothetical fact situation to which the rules do not clearly apply). What the American realists are saying is that the process is too simply understood. Their approach prefers rule analysis plus a sociological approach. It takes the law as it is posited and addresses the question of the factors that will influence those engaged in the application of the law. This is a feature of their approach, namely that they place lawyers centre stage in that they are primarily concerned with the role and behaviour of officials in difficult, court-centred cases. It is proposed to examine the two approaches of rule scepticism and fact scepticism.

It is useful always to compare the American realist approach to law with the approach to law in the United Kingdom. In a recent article (*Current Legal Problems* (1996)), the main part of the 1996 Bentham Club Presidential Address, Lord Steyn, recently elevated to the House of Lords, considers the question of the degree to which law is now considered to be merely a set of formal rules. He rightly identifies the origins of formalism on this side of the Atlantic in Bentham, who doggedly insisted that judges were mere judicial 'functionaries' who could only act within a severely limited role and that the way to a happier state, via social progress, was through legislation.

Lord Steyn distinguishes two senses of formalism. One is the use of the 'inner logic' in the process of legal reasoning and a tendency to assimilate all types of such reasoning to that form (although he recognises that lawyers do not use 'logic' either precisely or to refer solely to deductive reasoning). The other is the use of judicial language by which conclusions of law are expressed. This is an interesting idea. He means by the latter 'the unconscious tendency to express judgments is in purely formal language although consequentialist arguments and policy factors also play a part in the decision'. The former, and narrower, type of reasoning he dubs 'substantive' reasoning. Lord Steyn concludes that in the last 25 years there has been a shift away from using formalist techniques, particularly as a result of the two great contributors to non-formalism: Lords Denning and Reid. Interestingly, he says that the House of Lords judgment in *Pepper* v *Hart* (1992) (see Chapter 24) was, while admittedly bold, yet 'simply a culmination of a more realistic approach to the interpretation of statutes'.

Introduction to rule scepticism

By way of a brief introduction it can be stated that the rule sceptics acknowledged that it was not possible to deny that lawyers, judges and onlookers described the legal system and the substantive laws in terms of rules. About one minute spent looking at a legal textbook or a judgment would show this to be the case. What the rule sceptics denied was that rules were, in fact, the main operative factor in legal decisions. Other factors, for example, the background and prejudices of the judge, were important. Hence, because most judges are conservative, judgments in the political field will follow the conservative viewpoint; and so on for decisions on trade unions, students, etc. And, of course, each judge will have his own individual beliefs which will, consciously or not, influence his decisions.

As a consequence, rules cannot be viewed in the normal way (as reasons for decision, authoritatively laid down, or as binding commands of a sovereign, for example). Instead, they should be seen merely as predictions of what the courts will do. The rule that theft is dishonest appropriation of another's property and so on, is, in reality, a prediction that in the given circumstances the court will punish an offender for theft.

Gray

Perhaps the rule sceptics went overboard in their concentration on the courts and what they will do. If a descriptive formulation of a rule in a textbook does not accord with court practice, it is not a rule at all. In fact, Gray in *The Nature and Sources of the Law* went as far as to suggest that until a statute had been enforced by a court, it was not law at all, but only a source of law. This approach denies the facilitative function of certain statutes, such as, for example, the Companies Act 1985. One does not go to a court in order to incorporate a company, yet the procedure and requirements for doing that are prescribed in statute. Cardozo J, a critic of realism, has observed that if Gray's thesis is carried to its logical conclusion then 'law never is, but is always about to be'.

Oliver Wendell Holmes J

Holmes, in his *The Path of the Law*, took the concept of 'our friend the bad man' who 'does not care two straws for the axioms and deductions', but 'does want to know what the Massachusetts or English courts are likely to do in fact' and what he predicts will happen if he does certain things. However, it may be asked why Holmes takes no account of 'our other friend, the good man'. According to Holmes, then, the law *is* the rules which the courts lay down for the determination of legal rights and duties.

Fact sceptics

Jerome Frank went further than other realists in suggesting that it was not in fact possible to predict what courts would do. In each case, everything depended on how the court decided the facts.

It is not only the actual writings of the realists that are important. The encouragement of systematic and detailed study of the areas they concentrate on has produced much research, and many results. The realists themselves did not, on the whole, engage in such research (Llewellyn's main research, for example, was anthropological), but two new directions, judicial behaviouralism and jurimetrics, can be seen as the outcome of stressing empirical research and predictions of what the court will do.

13.3 Karl Llewellyn's rule scepticism

Llewellyn was a mainstream realist, a rule sceptic. It was he who suggested that rules, apart from being predictions of what the courts will do, are merely 'pretty playthings'. Alongside this general approach, we can place his more detailed analysis of the functions and techniques of law. Many of his ideas seem rather more theoretical than scientifically or empirically researched, and the conclusion that he reaches, that appellate decisions can be predicted accurately in 80 per cent of cases, seems surprising, but much of what he says is significant.

According to Llewellyn, the basic functions of law are, first, to aid the survival of the community and, second, to engage in the quest for justice, efficacy and a richer life.

To fulfil these two functions, there are a number of 'law jobs' which the institution of law has to do. Llewellyn saw an institution in terms of an organised activity which is built around doing a job. The important aim is to ensure that these jobs are well performed. These law jobs are then the basic functions which the law has to perform. He lists these law jobs in *My Philosophy of Law* as follows.

1. The disposition of trouble cases, which he likened to garage repair work. The continuous effect was to be the remaking of the order of society.
2. The preventative channelling of conduct and expectations so as to avoid trouble and looks at the purpose of new legislation.
3. The allocation of authority and the arrangement of procedures which mark action as being authoritative.
4. The net organisation of society as a whole so as to provide integration, direction and incentive.
5. Juristic method as used in law and the settlement of disputes.

His analysis of these is found in his book *The Normative, The Legal and The Law Jobs: The Problem of Juristic Method* (1940) in which he identifies the basic aspects of law jobs and claims that these law jobs are implicit in the concept of any group activity. The first of these he sees as the most important yet he does not tell us about their interrelationship. He says that these law jobs are universal, and the emphasis upon universality leads to his arguing on a high level of abstraction.

Llewellyn was concerned to find the best way to handle 'legal tools to law job ends'. Although he suggests that his framework provides a general framework for the functional analysis of law, his theory suffers from a defect common to other examples of functionalism by under-emphasising the dimensions and structure of power.

According to him, the institution of law consists of rules, principles, concepts, as well as an overall underlying ideology, and of various techniques of argument, such as precedent, and practices. Within the set-up of the institution is the body of specialists who carry on the law jobs, and who pass down the skills or 'crafts' necessary to the working of the institutions.

In his concept of juristic method developed in his *Common Law Tradition* he outlines his theory of craft. Here he identifies his period style of judicial reasoning. He identifies two polar positions within this period style and says that judges will fall within that spectrum. This idea was based on empirical research that he and his students engaged in by looking at the performance of the courts at different times, hence his 'period' style. He claimed that courts could be classified according to the different ways in which they used or 'manipulated' precedent. At the one pole is his 'grand style' in which judges are less strictly self-constrained by the rules of precedent and in his 'formal style' the judge considers himself bound by the rules of precedent entirely.

In the grand style the judge will follow what Llewellyn calls a 'situation sense' in order to ensure that a reasonable result is achieved. By identifying a judge's propensity it may be possible to achieve the aim of the American realists, namely, the prediction of the outcome of the case. If we know what approach a judge takes we may be able to predict how he will handle a particular dispute.

The most relevant of these crafts, in view of the realist concentration on the courts, is the juristic method of decision-making. As has been pointed out, 'reckonability' in case law is high. This, according to Llewellyn, is the consequence of various attributes of the system which tend to provide stability.

Llewellyn has made the important point that law is not just about rules, and that the prediction of the outline of cases is an important and useful function. However, law is not solely concerned with the prediction of what the court will decide about a particular dispute. It is also about giving guidance to individuals. Lloyd and Freeman observe that Llewellyn's law jobs overlook the dimensions of structure and power in society. Further Twining, generally favourable, observes that Llewellyn's period style is 'a relatively simple theoretical model'.

As is clear from a brief summary, Llewellyn realised that judges do use rules, and also realises that dispute settlement is not the sole function of laws. In adjusting to meet possible criticisms in these areas (the general realist approach ignores any function but dispute settlement in the courts, and derides the use of rules; both of these points can be effectively criticised) the impact of the realist attack is weakened. Law is only partly about predictions of what the court will do (dispute-settlement), for it is also about giving guidance to individuals. Rules may be predictions, but they are also used by judges. One of the surest ways of predicting what a judge might do, after all, is to look at the rules and principles of the law to which he will refer. The lawyers recognise this because they put a lot of effort into producing arguments, *to persuade judges*, in a court of law. It is true, however, that a really good lawyer will do a little homework on the particular personal predilections of the judge who will hear a trial. If he is known to be 'down on drink' or bad tempered, it might be wise not to allow certain emphases to be made.

A fellow American realist, although from the fact sceptic faction, Judge Jerome Frank, took the view that Llewellyn's work was focused on the appeal courts and took no real account of the work of the trial courts in which it was not the application of the rule that was important in predicting the outcome, but where the uncertainty about the fact finding process was the key.

A strong criticism levelled at both the rule sceptics and the fact sceptics is that they engage in over-generalisations in order to make a valid point. Furthermore, as pointed out, the judges do use rules to explain their decisions and the judge is judge by virtue of a rule that says he will decide disputes. These points are considered unimportant in Llewellyn's law jobs theory. To this extent his analysis is defective.

13.4 Frank and the experimentalist approach

Jerome Frank expounded a theory more extreme than the general approach we saw in section 13.2. He termed the views of Llewellyn *et al* 'rule scepticism'. They were concerned to show that the enunciated formal or paper rules did not prove reliable as guides to judicial behaviour, so that uniformities of such behaviour should be studied to achieve certainty of prediction. Frank considered that such certainty was impossible in relation to trial courts and that the writings of the rule sceptics concentrated on the upper courts, not the 'sharp end'. In the lower courts, prediction of the outcome of litigation was not possible. The major cause of uncertainty is not the legal rule (either the proper or the real version), but the uncertainty of the fact finding process. Much depends on witnesses, who can be mistaken as to their recollections; and on judges and juries, who bring their own beliefs, prejudices and so on, into their decisions about witnesses, parties, etc.

These prejudices are idiosyncratic to the particular judge and jury, and cannot be standardised or predicted. Take, for example, the trial of Clive Ponting, the senior civil servant charged under the Official Secrets Act 1911 for disclosing to an unauthorised person (an MP) official secrets connected with the sinking of an Argentine ship by British forces during a conflict in the South Atlantic. It was not in dispute that he had so leaked the information. His own defence counsel, according to a book the defendant himself wrote afterwards, advised him on the day the jury were due to return their verdict that he should bring a new toothbrush as he would need one in prison. As we know the jury returned a verdict of not guilty. We do not know the reasons for this (it would be an offence to attempt to elicit from the jury their reasoning or their deliberations) but it may be speculated that they did not wish the matter of sentence to be left to the judge and so removed that function from the bench by returning a verdict which, in view of the evidence and interpretations of the law brought out at trial, was quite unexpected.

Further uncertainty can also be found in the process by which a judge determines a particular fact to be a *material* fact. On the basis of the determination of material facts the legal rule will self-apply. This extreme version of realism does make an important point. The decision in any specific case does depend on findings of fact which can be affected by the preconceptions and prejudices of the judge and jury members. Recent controversies over jury vetting (checking by the security services of the prospective members of a jury, to see if a challenge should be made against individual members), the common opinion that a jury is better than a judge for trials involving motoring offences, and challenges to certain types of jurors (for example, challenging women jurors in rape cases) are all evidence that practitioners are aware of influences on decisions.

Frank does, however, seem to go too far. Many of the objections to realism set out in paragraph 13.6 below apply with added force to the Frank version, particularly the concentration on the courts, and the denial of any place to the relevance of formal rules.

Moreover, it simply is not the case that all questions of fact are unpredictable as Frank describes. Within the bounds of the rules of evidence, a professional adviser can make a fairly firm prediction in most cases of what facts the court will accept as proved, and what rules of law are to be applied to them. Could a thief caught red-handed by two independent witnesses really be told that all depended on what facts a judge or jury found? Further, many cases never really get to the stage of disputed facts. How is fact scepticism then relevant to a defendant pleading guilty in a criminal case or only contesting quantum not liability in a civil case? And what of the many cases which go to judges on a basis of agreed fact, to see what the legal rule is? A famous example would be *Donoghue* v *Stevenson* (1932). As perhaps with mainstream rule sceptical realism, an interesting and important point about the legal process is spoiled by over-generalisation.

13.5 Jurimetrics and judicial behaviouralism

Jurimetrics

The term 'jurimetrics' was coined by Loevinger in an article in 1949 to mean the scientific investigation of legal problems through the use of symbolic logic and computers. The latter play a significant part in the legal world. Many law firms and chambers now rely on computer retrieval systems to discover relevant precedents (several systems, including Lexis, are available). Key words are typed in ('company' 'director' 'fiduciary duty') and the computer finds the cases where these words occur within a set number of words of each other.

Computers can aid some complicated legal processes, such as tax planning, where the relevant information is fed into a programme designed to ascertain the most efficient tax plan. This can save many man hours of calculations.

Computers can also take part in investigations, the proper field of jurimetrics, where the data can be quantatively analysed. For example, research on the true realist concern, whether there are regularities of judicial behaviour which could give us patterns to help make predictions.

Computers can deal very quickly and effectively with logical patterns. When used as an aid to prediction of the likely outcome of a case, the computer is fed with a plethora of information about the court and behavioural models on which to base its prediction. The behavioural models will look at the group approach of a multi-judge court and identify the task leader, whose self perception is as the efficient solver of a given problem, and the social leader, who provides the friendly atmosphere conducive to solving the problem. This group approach, however, looking as it does on the inner workings of the group, requires a consistency in the membership of the tribunal. That is not provided by the court. Further, in order for the computer to detect a logical pattern, a precondition would be the existence of consistency in decisions and attitude of the court. Here lies the central flaw. Judges are not logical machines; indeed that is the essence of what the realists are saying. Judges have moods, they change their mind and are subject to all the other weaknesses, or strengths, of the human condition.

What realism has done is lead to a systematic gathering and processing of data about the court which in Britain remains only at the level of gossip and rumour. The purpose behind this approach is clear. It is to aid the advocate. He will ascertain the preferences of the judge and tailor his argument to meet those preferences. This is, of course, done by better advocates on an *ad hoc* basis. What the jurimetrics application seeks to do is to make this approach more organised.

These developments have led to criticism, and fear of machine justice. Such fears are exaggerated. Computers are useful tools of memory and research, and cannot at present be conceived of as replacing human roles in the judicial process. Probably the real danger from computers now is the threat to privacy posed by computer data-banks. Lawyers have a part to play in controlling this development, but should not be hindered from using computers.

Judicial behaviouralism

This can be seen as the logical follow-up to realist theory. It involves actually carrying out research into how judges behave. A mixture of realist encouragement for such studies and social research techniques is regarded by judicial behaviouralists as necessary. The research is patchy, and on appellate court decisions alone, some obvious results, notably those predicting decisions after the cases themselves have been decided, and more surprising ones. Schundhauser, for example, found that judges who had sat on lower courts before getting to US Supreme Court level were more likely to overrule than those who had not.

An interesting English writer's work on judicial decisions adopting a judicial behaviouralist approach is John Griffith's *The Politics of the Judiciary*. He takes the view that judges are too conservative and 'pro-government' to be capable of giving fair decisions. Lon Fuller has observed that a defect in this kind of approach is that the behaviouralists put consistency at a premium which leads to the judicial process being seen as a formalised game of 'snap'.

13.6 Contributions and evaluations

Returning to the general approach of the American Realists, we must evaluate it and determine what, if any, contributions this brand of realism has made to legal theory.

To recap briefly, the approach we are examining is as follows. Legal rules are not the mainly operative factor in legal decisions. Because of other factors playing a part it is important to look behind these paper rules for the real rules, namely, the uniformities and regularities of judicial behaviour. The formal paper rules are now only useful insofar as they are predictions of what the court will do.

Is this picture of rules, predictions, judicial process right? The most obvious general point is that it involves a change in the way we talk and think about law. Textbook writers, judges, practising lawyers and students all view law in terms of rules and exceptions applicable to fact situations. While this is not in itself a damning criticism of the realists, it is clearly a strong indication that there are faults in the realist theory. Is everyone engaged in the law perpetrating, or the subject of, a mass delusion?

Imagine, first, that you are an individual approaching a solicitor on a non-contentious matter. You want to form a company, perhaps, or carry out properly your duties as executor of a will. If, when you ask what law is relevant to your case, the solicitor talks in terms of predictions of court behaviour, you might be surprised. After all, you intend to fulfil your legal obligations and not end up in court at all (failing to form the company properly will merely result in invalidity, not illegality or an offence). Surely the law and its rules are as much about these non-contentious matters as about cases that go to court? Non-contentious questions of obligations (as with a trusteeship) and the facilitative power-conferring rules both public and private seem to be obscured by the realist dismissal of rules. This is the first specific criticism.

Much of the law, and much of the importance of legal rules, relates to guiding people's behaviour by allowing them to avoid a failure, to live up to their obligations and duties, and to take advantage of the various facilitative devices, such as wills, contracts and company formation, that the law provides.

Next, place yourself as a litigant in a contentious matter. Let us say as a plaintiff in a road accident case. Again, if advice was given as prediction of judicial behaviour, something would seem to be missing. Of course, especially in a case involving disputed facts, an element of prediction is involved in any complete advice. Considering the evidence that the court is likely to hear, is it likely to find the defendant liable? What level of risk can be expected? But this is not the complete picture. We assume that, given that certain facts can be proved to the court's satisfaction, the defendant is liable and not just that the court will *probably* find him to have been so. In fact, the reason why the court is likely to find him liable is because he is liable, because he was under an obligation to drive non-negligently, which he has breached.

To take another example, we think it perfectly correct to say, in an appropriate case, 'I'm sure X is guilty of theft, but the police cannot prove it and so he will be found not guilty', or 'he was negligent, but there were no witnesses', and so on.

Rules impose obligations and duties upon people. They have a normative aspect in that they guide behaviour. When they are breached, the question of whether or not a court will enforce the rule is a separate question from whether or not it has, in fact, been breached. Law is then not only about dispute settlement but about behavioural guidance as well.

A further minor point could also be made here. If our contentious litigant was told that there was no rule imposing liability on the defendant, because rules were only predictions, and in his case the defendant would probably not be liable, he might turn his mind to other questions. All is said to depend on the courts and the judges. But *who* are they? It seems that they are only official because the legal rules and principles give them their authority.

Since the emphasis is on the courts, we should next try to look at things from the viewpoint of a judge. The cases cited to him in argument do not bind him, they are merely predictions of what he will do. This ascribes too restrictive a view to the nature of legal rules. Rules bestow authority on judges. They are judges by virtue of a rule that says they are. They are to decide cases by virtue of a rule that says they are to do so. Their decisions are to be carried out by virtue of a rule that says so.

Frank, who was a judge himself, suggests that a judge must be conscientious, but this is not helpful. How is he to decide in which way his duty lies? With regard to fact scepticism in general the approach is of no application when there is no dispute as to facts. Take, for example, the interlocutory proceedings in *Donoghue* v *Stevenson* where the court assumed the facts as alleged by the plaintiff and addressed the legal question as to whether those facts disclosed a cause of action.

Again we must move back to our criticism that the predictive explanation has missed out the normative aspect of rules, the obligation imposed by them. Furthermore, judges are not only bound by the rules, they have the Hartian internal aspect: they accept the rules as a standard and a guide to their decisions. They will decide in a way following the rules, because they accept those rules as a standard to be followed. As Hood Philips has stated, habits enable external prediction whereas rules provide a justification for acting in conformity and grounds for criticising those who deviate.

Hart has said that the fact that the judge has the last word does not imply that there is no rule. He uses an analogy with a soccer game and states that where a player who gets the ball into the net is offside a referee may still award a goal. This does not negate the offside rule but merely means that it was not applied in that case.

There are cases that do not have a settled rule covering them, and in those cases the judges must make new decisions: almost inevitably, personal viewpoint as well as institutional material will enter the new decision. These are the exceptions for, in general, a judge will apply a settled rule, and this brings us to a closely related point.

Although there is a degree of uncertainty about the law, there is also a large area which is certain, in which rules are the heavily operative factor in a judge's decision. If a judge circumvents a rule, on the rare occasions that it is possible, he may be able to do so in a manner that conceals the fact of his doing so, and furthermore legal rules act as a brake on capricious or whimsical decision-making.

Next, it has been said with much justification that realism is less a philosophy than a technology. The realists sought to approximate the methodology of the natural sciences to an examination of the workings of the law. However as Glendon Schubert, a judicial behaviouralist, has argued, the realists failed to achieve their objective in that they lacked both theory and method. Of course, as a behaviouralist Schubert was concerned with motivations and attitudes behind judicial decisions.

There are some more minor points that can be mentioned here drawing on the critical literature. Stone, who is quite critical of the American realists, says that they offered nothing more than a mere gloss on the sociological approach. From a Marxist perspective, Ackerman in *Reconstructing American Law* (1984) writes that realism was a culturally conservative theory designed to insulate the common law discourse from the New Deal, thus viewing the theory as a response to the economic crisis of the time.

So what of the contribution of the realists? The points made above seem to destroy the realist approach. In view of some of the points and criticisms made, the realists towards the end of the movement became less extreme and distanced themselves from their earlier views. Llewellyn, for example, talks about the behaviour-guidance function, and discusses the normative aspect of rules: while situation sense is one operative factor in judicial decisions, the legal rules are another.

Without getting bogged down in too much detail, it is probable that the intention was never to get rid of rules altogether, but only to show that there was more to the use of the law than the mere deductive application of legal rules. They have not rejected technical legal analysis but have merely emphasised that it is not enough if we wish to understand how the law works or how to improve the law. From that point of view, many of the realists' ideas are now commonplace. Empirical and scientific studies of law in action and particularly judges in action, scepticism about fact-finding processes by judge and jury, realisation that the prejudices and personal predelictions of judges do play a part in litigation and decisions, and that judges do have a degree of discretion in some cases. Further, behaviouralism and jurimetrics are two positive off-shoots.

The idea of rules as predictions, the concentration on dispute settlement and the neglect of normative aspects of legal rules, may have been rejected. But in lots of other ways, however, the American realists have influenced and made contributions to our grasp of legal theory: perhaps to such an extent that Alan Hunt in *The Sociological Movement in Law* wrote that: 'In a very real sense we *are* all Realists now if only in the most general context of recognising the need to view law in its social context ...'.

13.7 Patterns of American jurisprudence

Duxbury's *Patterns of American Jurisprudence* (1995) is an intelligent and remarkable new study of the development of American jurisprudence since the middle of the nineteenth century to the present day. Not surprisingly, his view is that the developments in America, as distinguished from jurisprudential development in the United Kingdom, were largely influenced by the Realists. Duxbury thinks that American jurisprudence is much more coherent than commonly supposed and does not consist of a collection of disparate, unconnected schools of thought about law. One of the reasons is, of course, the background of the United States constitution which supplies explicitly moral reasons for lawyers to engage with in the courts. So it is not odd, or embarrassing, for a lawyer there to advance his or her convictions about what is required by the idea of *moral equality* in a case concerned with a citizen's equal protection under the laws. The great landmark case of *Brown* v *Board of Education*, decided in 1954, was one such case; the lawyers disputed at great length over the obviously moral question of whether respect for this requirement of the US constitution of 'equality' allowed or forbade equality by 'separate but equal' treatment (ie black schools and white schools co-existing). This kind of Socratic dialogue in which lawyers debate moral issues was brought to the fore in the case-law method specifically instituted by Dean Langdell of the Harvard Law School, mainly as a reaction to a perceived wrongful formalism of more formal teaching methods which tended towards law students thinking of law as a set of doctrinally fixed rules. Duxbury, in his chapter entitled 'The Challenge of Formalism' early on in his work, goes into some depth in picking out what precisely was the 'animal' of formalism which Dean Langdell attacked.

There are obvious connections between this sort of way of approaching law – by seeing it as an 'argumentative attitude' (see Chapter 2 above) and the way espoused by Dworkin's model judge Hercules: the judge looks to the requirements of the constitution in a way which gives the constitution 'best sense' in terms of abstract and background moral rights. Naturally, since propositions about such rights are controversial there is room for the Socratic dialogue to take place. Not only that, there is room for a healthy scepticism about the proposed extension of purported propositions of law and that scepticism, not often recognised in jurists such as Dworkin, is similar to the scepticism displayed within the Critical Legal Studies movement. In a chapter entitled 'Uses of Critique', Duxbury both takes the Critical Legal Studies movement to task for its frequent self-conscious and self-indulgent stances and attacks those who would see nothing whatsoever in the movement. Like the Chicago Law-and-Economics school, which he says combines the American desire for promoting individualism with a distinctively modern form of rationalism, the Critical Legal Studies movement has been part of the American jurisprudential movement of modernisation, or practical problem-solving and for recognising 'reality' when it sees it; nevertheless, he also takes the view that much of the 'crit-bashing' has been an idle sport:

> 'Exposing the myriad vices of "the crits" – the fuzzy reasoning, the abstruse jargon, the moral impoverishment, the double standards, the political naivety, the unworldly ideals, the legal incompetence, and so on – has become a popular pastime among clever-dicks, reactionaries and attention-seekers.'

The interesting thing about Duxbury's book is his optimistic conviction, well-supported in his argument, that American jurisprudence forms a distinctive, rational pattern of overall coherence, although very surprisingly, given this conclusion, he devotes almost no attention to the great American jurist of our time, Ronald Dworkin!

14

Scandinavian Realism

14.1 Introduction

14.2 General approach

14.3 Hagerstrom

14.4 Olivecrona

14.5 Evaluation of Olivecrona

14.6 Ross

14.7 Evaluation of Ross

14.8 Comparison with American realism

14.1 Introduction

The other movement of realists consisted of a group of Scandinavian philosophers and jurists. As with the Americans, an overall similarity of approach conceals a difference in detail and emphasis in the writings of the various theorists.

We shall look at the identifying characteristics of the movement's approach, and then concentrate on the three major figures: Hagerstrom (1868–1939), and more recently Olivecrona and Ross. A consideration of the contribution made by the Scandinavians will be followed by a section comparing them with the Americans: do the realists form one movement, or two?

14.2 General approach

It would not be true to say that all the Scandinavians talked about, or even agreed with, the following points, but they are the characteristic ideas we can associate with the movement as a whole.

Empirical realism

In a more philosophical way than the Americans, the Scandinavians considered themselves to be realist. They were interested in the legal system as a whole rather than the narrow area of interest of the courts adopted by the Americans. In essence, they were talking about law as observable fact, which makes them similar to positivists such as Austin (although not Kelsen, of course) as part of the world of cause and effect, and therefore legal science as a science of 'causality'. They rejected formalism because, in their view, it had no regard to the empirical world. In their rejection of *a priori* reasoning they declared that the method for the enlargement of knowledge was through empirical observation. This is what they meant by viewing law as an observable fact. As we shall see discussed in more detail below, the proof of the existence of law was ascertained through the psychological effect.

Against metaphysics and confirmed the 'verifiability principle'

This realism led them to reject as metaphysical anything which did not exist on the level of cause and effect, of empirical reality. They subscribed to the verifiability principle of the logical positivists (nothing to do with the *legal* positivists) whereby if a statement cannot be proved by empirical evidence, it is meaningless.

The importance of this principle to an understanding of law is obvious and fundamental. In talking about law, we continually use statements and concepts which do not seem to be 'verifiable' in this way. Many legal rules are based on views of what is 'good', 'bad', 'just', and 'right', and so on. The rules themselves are phrased normatively, in terms of 'ought', and not 'is' and we think of legal concepts such as 'right', 'duty', 'ownership', arising from these rules. All of these ideas are non-verifiable, it seems, referring to a different realm of thought from empirical reality, a realm or science of 'ought', not 'is'. Simply they are not rooted in the actual sense experiences.

Such a realm of thought is rejected as being metaphysical. We should here contrast the Scandinavian realist position with that of many natural lawyers, for whom such a realm of thought does exist and in fact controls our moral and legal rules. Unless all legal thought and experience is to be rejected as metaphysical, some other explanation of the concepts and rules which constitute it must be given. This is the task that the Scandinavians have set for themselves.

The argument was that it is to be found in the mind of the individual, in psychology. There is no objective criterion of good or bad or just, only different subjective views. The normative effect of rules of law comes from their effect in psychological terms; and notions such as right and duty can be explained only as psychological feelings. A right as a sensation of power, and a duty as a sense of constraint or compulsion. The exact explanations differed from theorist to theorist. Lundstedt, in particular, was extreme in condemning as metaphysical even the idea of normativity. Ross and Olivecrona were less extreme in this respect. For them, normative statements are clearly a form of language with an important function, which need to be re-evaluated in the light of verifiability.

Normativity: psychological occurrences

The meaning of a normative statement according to the Scandinavian view, then, is psychological: X ought to do something because he feels bound to, or he has a right because he has a feeling of power, and so on.

The concepts of normativity, of the binding quality of law, of the validity of law, are all explained with reference to psychological occurrences. Law takes place through the psychology of individuals. People who have rights feel they have power and people who are under an obligation feel they have to act in a certain way. These concepts are considered in detail by both Olivecrona and Ross, below.

Other points

The points set out above are the main tenets characterising this school. There are other points made in the theories, not perhaps as important, which we should mention before considering the individual writers:

Law as rules about force

A recurrent theme is that the legal system has a monopoly of force, and that all laws are ultimately backed by the threat of force. We must not confuse this with the view that a sanction is a necessary condition for a valid law: Ross, for example, expressly rejects that. Nevertheless, sanctions and force are central to an understanding of how law works. Without the monopolisation of the use of legitimate force psychology would not be effective.

Legal rules as predictions of officials' behaviour

This, of course, is a strong element of American realism rule scepticism. In the present context, the point is subtly different. While it seems that rules will not be valid unless they are effective predictions of how officials will behave, unless they are followed in practice, another aspect must not be forgotten. To be valid, a rule must also be felt to be binding, and therefore be the motivation for obedience. This latter point is not to be found in the American theory.

Magic words, legal ritual

Both Hagerstrom and Olivecrona are concerned with the effect of legal formulae in changing the legal position.

14.3 Hagerstrom

Hagerstrom has been referred to as the spiritual father of the Scandinavian realist movement. The others in the movement took up his ideas and built upon them. It is therefore by way of background information that a brief outline of his views is here discussed.

Hagerstrom rejected the idea of a non-natural sense in which things could exist. So goodness and badness are subjective notions, and similarly there is no reality to the concepts of rights and duties, beyond their actual effect in the real world.

An insight into his thought can be gained by looking at his explanation of the rights created by imperative laws. When a legislator, for example, declares that a person has a right, he has in mind the likely consequences of that declaration, based on his knowledge of the effectiveness of the legal system. Those consequences are two-fold. First, that when certain facts exist, the person with the right will generally enjoy certain advantages against another and, second, that legal proof of relevant facts in court will enable the person with the right to get at least an equivalent of those advantages.

A legislator will generally also consider that his declaration has the effect of producing a right in a supernatural sense, providing an obligation which exists in some way even if neither of the two consequences above occur. For example, if the person with a contractual right gets neither the advantages (the other side does not perform) nor the equivalent in court (since he cannot prove the relevant facts, such as the formation of an oral contract). We think it perfectly coherent to say that there is a contract, and therefore contractual rights, but I am unable to prove it. Hagerstrom rejects this analysis because it does not reflect reality in the empirical world.

Another interesting aspect of Hagerstrom's work emerged from his study of Greek and Roman law, and concerns the legal use of magic words. He suggests that formal words, such as those in the *mancipatio* ceremony in Roman law for the acquisition of property and those of livery of seisin in a medieval feoffment were taken to have a magical effect in the real world. Perhaps there is something to this view in modern law. Provided the appropriate formula of words is uttered in the appropriate ritual a magical or legal consequence flows. The marriage ceremony is one such example. Uttering the words 'I do' in a marriage ceremony has the effect in the real world of changing your legal status. No actual change takes place. The change is not real but is a change in attitudes. The parties, namely, the bride and the groom, will treat each other differently. More importantly, from this point of view, other people will treat them differently and all because they uttered these magic words in a ritual.

The law too will treat them differently. For example, the husband will be responsible for paying his wife's poll tax, so there can occur the rather ridiculous situation at the moment that where a married woman writes to her local authority the reply is addressed to her husband. That this law dates back to a previous era (1806) when the status of a woman was quite different must be obvious. Another example is the incorporation of a company. Where the appropriate procedure is correctly adhered to (the ritual) the Registrar will incorporate the company (the magic words). The legal effect of this is to create a new legal person. Perhaps Hagerstrom has something to tell us about the importance of psychology in this regard.

This view has been questioned in relation to the ancient laws, and is not obviously the case today. One cannot deny the importance of form and language in law as, for example, using a seal instead of consideration for a contract, or the words of the marriage ceremony, but we no longer believe in any magical effect. The forms of language fulfil an important function, which is discussed by Olivecrona (on performatives, below). There is a suggestion that there is a middle ground in the use of language where the language of rights and duties is a separate and legitimate use of language. The argument goes as follows. There is a body of rules which establishes standards. Statements made with reference to these standards are an explanation of rights and duties. These statements take their validity from the sense that they are part of an acceptable body of standards. This is not metaphysics because it is not being said that the body of standards exists. This has been described as a possible middle ground. The extremes are firstly where rights exist in an objective fashion. A view that there are objective human rights, for example, and at the other extreme where a right is a feeling of power. The popular view today is that rights exist irrespective of whether they are accepted. The Scandinavians did, perhaps, 'throw out the baby with the bathwater'!

14.4 Olivecrona

Olivecrona was concerned with how laws played a part in the world of cause and effect. He also, as did Hagerstrom, rejected metaphysical ideas surrounding the laws. Instead he considered the factual circumstances of the law. These circumstances were that a state, which was not a metaphysical entity in any way but *just* a group of people, and which has a monopoly of force, passes legislation which results in psychological pressure being felt by individuals, who because of that pressure obey the law. The reality is how legal concepts work in relation to constellations of facts, so that a right would have no objective existence but would merely describe the relationship between a set of facts.

According to Olivecrona, a legal rule has two elements, the ideatum and the imperatum. The ideatum is the imagined pattern of conduct, which the rule is meant to bring about. Traffic regulations, for instance, are intended to produce a smooth and safe flow of traffic. To supply a motive, sanctions are directed for non-compliance. The rules relating to these sanctions contain a pattern of conduct for others such as the police, judges, and so on, who will enforce the original rule.

The imperatum is the form of expression of the ideatum, namely, the imperative. The addressee is told to follow the particular pattern required. These imperatives are independent imperatives. They are like commands, but no one actually commands them, because Olivecrona rejects the idea of the will of the state is rejected as a metaphysical concept. They merely issue forth from the accepted procedures for lawmaking.

Even power-conferring rules on the Hartian model are imperative, according to Olivecrona. They are 'performatory imperatives' or 'performatives' because they require that something should happen. The imperative form is used. 'If so and so happens, a contract shall be formed ... property shall pass...the parties shall be married.'

The above exposition of a legal rules content comes from the 1971 edition of Olivecrona's *Law as Fact* and is particularly interesting because Olivecrona clearly identifies the individual citizen as the addressee of the independent imperatives. This contrasts with his own earlier view that laws were addressed to officials, and were chiefly about the exercise of force. It may be concluded that he drew heavily for his inspiration on the writings of Hans Kelsen (see Chapter 9). Although force is often kept in the background, all laws are ultimately executed by force. Criminal laws by imprisonment, civil laws by execution of judgments through seizure of goods and imprisonment and so on. The relationship of force and law is that the law consists chiefly of rules about force, rules which contain patterns of conduct for the exercise of force. Hagerstrom argued that a duty arises out of an individual's psychological response to coercion. By this he meant, clearly, those laws addressed to officials, to ensure that they enforce the patterns of conduct expected of individuals. In this version, these latter patterns of conduct are only aspects of the rules about force, which are for Olivecrona primary. In this way Olivecrona sought to explain the attitudes and responses of those to whom the law is directed.

The later shift from officials to individuals as the addressees of laws should not obscure the importance of force to law. A necessary condition of effective legislation is an organisation to execute laws by force if necessary, and laws are about the exercise of that force.

As we have seen already, the Scandinavian view of normativity is a psychological one. A valid rule is one that is binding and a rule is binding in terms of the compulsion felt by individuals. Olivecrona considered the psychological processes involved in the legal experience. It is instructive to take account of three such processes.

Legislation and judge-made rules

Both legislation and judge-made rules are effective because officials and individuals feel bound by them, although the effect of judge-made rules, because of the uncertainty inherent in them, is less formalised and certain. For statutes, the fulcrum is the act of promulgation. Since officials accept the constitution, rules which are passed according to the proper procedure are automatically accepted as binding. In fact, officials will generally rely on the conscientious collection of official copies of statutes and so will not in fact check to see if they have been properly passed. In English law, judges must rely on the correctness and validity of an Act of Parliament which expresses the correct passage and is kept in the correct places, *BRB* v *Pickin* (1974), and individuals will simply accept the appellation of law.

Judge-made rules, which must be seen as legislation and not as inferences of what law is, depend for their effectiveness on whether, because of the judge's renown and reasoning, courts and writers are prepared to accept them as law.

The law and fear of sovereigns

The law and the fear of sovereigns, which is the force which ultimately enforces the law, are the main source of our moral standards. Rather than in each instance making a calculation about whether or not obedience to the law is worthwhile, the independent imperative form of law is absorbed into our minds as we grow up. The situations then enter our minds with an imperative symbol stamped on them of the form: you shall not steal! This is wrong! This process is internalisation.

Performatives

The performatives, or power conferring rules, seem to work in the same way as legislation. The expression of the words of marriage, according to the proper procedure and in the proper place, change the status of the couple by producing psychological effects in them and other people. In short, people treat them and think of them as married, and that is the reality of the married state.

14.5 Evaluation of Olivecrona

It is not possible fully to evaluate Olivecrona without critically considering the overall Scandinavian position, and that consideration is left to paragraph 14.8. However, some specific criticisms must be made. Most importantly, Olivecrona's generalisations were the result not of research but of guesswork. Do we really have our moral standards formed in that way, as a result of legal rules? Most of us would think of the process in reverse. It is because murder is thought immoral that it is a crime, and *not* because it is a crime that it is thought immoral. Also, if we all live in the same legal system with the same laws, how do people's views come to differ? Hard core pornography is banned in this country, yet some people consider it morally acceptable to be permitted to read it.

Another criticism relates to the importance of force in the theory. Saying that all views are about force seems to be a misleading exaggeration. Laws are about providing a standard of conduct for the people in society, and the rules of enforcement are to uphold that standard. Perhaps this explains Olivecrona's later shift to considering individuals as the addressees of law when he said that rules to individuals are not secondary, but primary. A similar criticism has been made of Bentham and Kelsen and will be made of Ross shortly.

Finally, it does not seem to be correct to treat performatives as just another form of imperative. This criticism is similar to one concerning the flaws in Austin's theory whereby he thought that all laws could be reduced to the status of commands or duty-imposing rules. It under-emphasises, in Hart's words, the 'facilitative aspect' of the power-conferring rules of law.

Olivecrona spoke of the internalisation of norms which leads to the development of moral standards. According to him, law is valid because it is felt to be and the binding force of law is a reality only in the minds of the subjects. This places great emphasis on the importance of psychology without an accompanying account of that discipline. It does not seem, at first blush, that psychological study really could uncover the effect that 'right', 'duty' and so on have in the legal system, and provide us with a full understanding of these important terms in the law.

14.6 Ross

Ross has provided what is generally regarded as a better developed explanation of law than that of his colleagues in the Scandinavian school, and one that is strikingly similar to that of Hart. Much influenced by logical positivism and therefore rejecting metaphysics and attempting to explain law as a social fact in a positivist way, Ross again attempts to explain the normative quality of law in psychological terms. Ross' work can be read in *Towards a Realistic Jurisprudence* (1946).

Scheme of interpretation

Using the analogy of a chess game, Ross sees the rules of both chess and law as explaining behaviour which is otherwise inexplicable. Ross takes this from the viewpoint of a third person, namely, a spectator. There is no reality apart from the experiences of the two players. The moves themselves mean nothing. Ross sees the primary rules as directives which are accepted by both players as socially binding. It is important to distinguish between the rules of the game and the rules of skill. A bad move may still be a permitted move within the rules. The effectiveness of these rules of the game are established by observation. However, like Hart, Ross is also interested in the extent to which the rules are regarded as binding. Here Ross would adopt the introspective method which is, to him, concerned with the psychological state of mind of *feeling* bound. In Hart's *The Concept of Law*, the internal aspect may coincidentally involve feeling bound or compelled, but it is coincidental and not necessary. The internal aspect performs an altogether different function that is providing both a reason for following the rule and for criticising those who deviate from the rule. Why should a particular move in chess cause the removal of a piece from the board, and, applying the analogy, why should a particular document, plus certain factual circumstances, cause a judge to order compensation?

The explanation is in terms of law as a scheme of interpretation. Valid law is that set of normative ideas which can be used to interpret law in practice. So, the judge orders compensation (law in practice) because of a particular normative idea (for example, a breach of contract followed by damages, an ought). All such normative ideas together constitute valid law. This interpretative scheme enables us to explain the behaviour of judges, and to predict their decisions. Thus, like the game of chess where one knows the rules, one can comprehend the actions. What had previous to comprehension appeared to the external observer to be mere regularities of conduct.

Valid norm

A specific norm exists if it is both followed and felt to be binding, and followed *because* it is felt to be binding. Logically, this obedience is obedience by judges. As with Olivecrona, Ross sees laws as concerned primarily with the exercise of force, and therefore as primarily addressed to officials to order the application of that force. In his later work, *Directives and Norms*, he does accept that psychologically, as against logically, there are norms addressed to individuals which are grounds for the reactions of the authorities. On the other hand, the secondary norms addressed to officials to give legal effect to the primary norms addressed to individuals, contain all that is contained in those primary norms, and as such are the ones strictly necessary.

Not behaviouralist

The notion of predicting in terms of the system, and exercise of force in terms of an individual law could lead to a misunderstanding, namely, that Ross holds the American realist line that rules are, if anything, the predictions of what a judge will do in the particular case. Such a behaviouralist approach is rejected by Ross. He gives the traditional but strong argument that it cannot cope with the difference between a punishment and a tax demand. The important point to emphasise is that valid law enables predictions of the judge's behaviour to be made because the judge feels the rule to be binding. This element is lacking in American realist explanations.

Why are rules felt to be binding?

The reason that judges feel the rules to be binding is their allegiance to the constitution and the accepted sources of law. Individual citizens obey the primary norms addressed to them from a mixture of motives, fear of the sanctions to be imposed and belief that they should obey the law.

Norms of competence

Ross does distinguish some norms, those of competence, divided into private and social, or public, which do not purport to obligate the subject, and instead give him the competence to do something. These are what we have so far identified as power-conferring laws. However, these norms as well are seen as directives to the courts, and therefore as fragments of laws imposing duties as in Kelsen's and Bentham's theories.

14.7 Evaluation of Ross

There is much more in Ross that could be explained, but we have concentrated on the main lines of argument. We can note how strongly in some respects his theory resembles Hart's. Hart has identified as the necessary characteristics of a legal system, the general obedience to the rules by individuals, and the internal acceptance of the secondary rules by officials. Ross also sees a distinction between individuals, who will obey for mixed reasons, and officials, particularly judges, who obey out of allegiance to the constitution and the accepted sources of law. Hart identifies laws which do not impose obligations, as does Ross. Ross thus makes a notable advance on Olivecrona, who refers even to performatives as imperatives. Hart also identifies and emphasises the internal aspect of rules, the clear outline of which can be seen in Ross. The rule for Ross is felt to be binding. For Hart, the internal aspect of a rule involves it being taken as a standard for conduct, an internal statement being one from that point of view.

Several criticisms can be made. Ross takes no account of law that has never been applied by the courts because it is universally obeyed. A major flaw in Ross as well as the other Scandinavian theorists is that they seem dogmatically to follow the tenets of early logical positivism which has been demonstrated to be defective. The idea that there are only two forms of meaningful statement, namely the logical (analytical) and the empirical, must be too restrictive. The heavy reliance on the verifiability principle which has been stated by Schlick as, '(the) meaning of a proposition is the method of its verification' failed to produce a logical criteria for verifiability. The verification principle is neither analytical nor empirical and therefore, as it exists in the realm of metaphysics, by their own standard the Scandinavian realists must reject it.

Ross' theory can further be criticised. As with Olivecrona, law is seen as rules about force, which ignores its function of setting standards of behaviour. The misrepresentation inherent in the rules about force view is reinforced by seeing laws as norms addressed to officials, and a similar misrepresentation of power-conferring laws as part of the same pattern ignores their different function.

A further aspect of his theory and approach can be seen in Ross' claim that jurisprudence should be rooted in empirical study of official behaviour, not norms that ought to be obeyed but those norms likely to be applied by the court. In this way he was similar to the American realists, although this aspect is discussed in more depth below.

Yet another criticism of Ross' theory is that his approach does not take account of how courts justify their decisions which, according to Hart, is explicable in terms of the rule. Ross merely states that an understanding of the rule is necessary in order to comprehend the judicial process and to predict the likely outcome of the case. If we know the rules we know what the judge will apply. As Hart has amply pointed out, the concept of a rule involves it being taken as a standard of conduct and not just that it is felt to be binding. Lloyd and Freeman point out a further difficulty with regard to the place of the judge in Ross' theory. The observer will not know if the judge is applying the rule because of the experience of validity or simply through fear or indifference. The theory itself is of no assistance to the judge. When judges read their own decisions they are not predicting their own behaviour.

Ross attempts to pre-empt this criticism by drawing a distinction between statements *about* the law and statements *of* law. His discussion about validity relates only to statements about the law. In response to criticism which he felt to be misdirected Ross asserted that the use of the term valid in his account was really a mistranslation of in force or existing law. If this is so, then Ross has weakened rather than strengthened his argument, as he is now in danger of using a tautological definition which goes something like, 'a rule of law is in force if it is applied by the courts' Ross went in search of the impossible. He sought a norm that was not normative. He sought to derive validity from application. This was doomed from the start.

It is impossible fully to assess the Scandinavians' contribution, as their works are referred to relatively infrequently in the rest of Europe, and then they are often dismissed briefly. Their main point, that law produces psychological feelings and compulsion and that this is its place in the world of cause and effect, seemed at first to be new and extreme, denying, as Lundstedt did, even the possibility of normativity. Despite their detailed faults, Olivecrona and Ross are to our eyes more acceptable. Their interpretation is still a psychological one, but an explanation of normativity within the system is provided, with results that, in Ross, mirror closely the most mature results of Anglo-American positivist analysis. The psychological point is made, watered down, and becomes a useful and acceptable insight.

In other specific ways, there are contributions and speculations that give support to other positivists, by saying the same thing.

The parallels between Olivecrona and Kelsen, for example, are worth noticing, too. Both see law as imperatives issuing from the system rather than an individual, both see law as rules about force, with laws addressed to officials, and both see the acceptance and validity of laws within the system as resulting from acceptance of a constitution. The emphasis on reality as against metaphysics finds echoes throughout positivism, and the support for empirical study obviously echoes American realism and other sociologists. It has a breath of fresh air about it.

The Scandinavians may now be silent and not generally accepted. But in various ways their ideas and contributions remain in our legal theory. In an illuminating chapter on their theory, Finch has appreciated that they engaged in a radical and iconoclastic approach to the traditional problems of legal theory This description would also apply to the American realists and therefore a brief comparison is discussed in the next section.

14.8 Comparison with American realism

The student can be expected to make detailed comparisons of his own after reading the last two Chapters, to answer the question whether there is one school of realism, or two schools accidentally joined by a common name. Two main strands can be identified as an opening to this comparison. First, in their different ways the Americans and Scandinavians were realists in trying to reject metaphysical, or 'theoretical' explanations of law like natural law, and trying to explain the law in terms of observable behaviour, in terms of cause and effect. For this reason, research is important and encouraged, although the Americans must be regarded as having the stronger hand on that.

Second, to different extents, there is a concentration on judges. Both Llewellyn's rule scepticism and Frank's fact scepticism result in a closer look at what the courts do. On the Scandinavian side, Olivecrona and Ross both suggest that rules are addressed to officials. This similarity must not be allowed to mask the fundamental difference. For Ross, judges follow rules because they are binding and cover the case in question determining its results. For the Americans, seeing rules as determining cases in this way is incorrect.

Finch has stated that: 'Both the American and the Scandanavian Realist movements are radical and iconoclastic in their purpose, and this attitude is reflected primarily in their respective attitudes to legal rules.' This is an interesting statement, an examination of which would enable a comparison between the two to be made. By way of a summary this comparison could be made as follows.

Both the American and the Scandinavian realists can be seen as a reaction to the rule formalism that preceded and to a certain extent has succeeded them. Their point was that too much emphasis was placed on the rules and not enough on the reality of the legal experience.

Thus the Americans thought that there was more to the legal experience than the mere logical application of legal rules. Placing the lawyer at centre stage the Americans indeed did smash some widely accepted models of legal reasoning. The rule sceptics denied that rules were the main operative factor in legal decisions. Indeed, one of their number, Gray, went so far in his *The Nature and Sources of the Law* to argue that a statute is not law but is merely a source of law. When it is applied by a court it is law but then thereafter it reverts to being a source of law for another court. This led Benjamin Cardozo to observe that for Gray law never is but is always about to be. What cannot be denied is that the approach of Gray is certainly radical and iconoclastic. His fellow travellers in the rule sceptics did not go quite as far along that road as he did. Gray ignored the facilitative function of law, yet Oliver Wendell Holmes, considered by most to be the grand old man of the American realists, thought that the law is what the bad man thinks will happen if he does certain things. The law for Holmes was the rules which the courts lay down in the determination of legal rights and duties. Similarly Karl Llewellyn thought that rules are mere pretty playthings in the hands of the lawyers, although in his later work he moderated this stance. He thought that the law is what officials do about disputes.

From an entirely different perspective but no less radical and iconoclastic was the experimentalist approach of the major fact sceptic Jerome Frank. In his volume *The Courts on Trial* he argued that the rule sceptics suffered from a craving for certainty.

He emphasised the need to look at the work of the trial courts as opposed to the appellate courts on which Llewellyn concentrated so much of his attention. Whereas the rule sceptics saw the rule as of assistance in the prediction of the outcome of the case, Frank thought that the rule was of no use in the predictive process. The rules according to Frank are fixed. What leads to uncertainty are the difficulties in the fact finding process both with regard to witnesses and the juries and also with regard to the process by which the judge determines particular facts to be material. Thus there would be no point in examining the rules as this would not give any indication as to how the matter would be decided if it came before a court.

Our own law schools have failed to take this into account. In substantive law topics the examination calls for the logical application of legal rules to a hypothetical factual situation in order to advise the parties to the dispute. The American realist in answering that type of question would want to introduce matters such as the background of the judge and other personal factors which he would say would also contribute to a decision.

The American realists' approach to rules while not universal is certainly very radical and iconoclastic. It is a major departure from anything that went before. It has also given rise to jurimetrics and to studies involving judicial behaviouralism. It has emphasised an important matter, namely the emphasis that a potential litigant will place on the prediction of the likely outcome of the case. Unlike the rule formalist, the American realist will not arrive at that prediction solely through the mere logical application of legal rules.

Such an approach is not without its critics. A prediction of the court's behaviour would not be appropriate in non-contentious matters. Furthermore, rules have a normative aspect in that they guide conduct. Thus law is not only about dispute settlement but is also about behavioural guidance. This side of the law's function is ignored by the American realists. Hart has observed that the fact that a judge has the last word does not imply that there is no rule. He draws an analogy with a soccer match in which in spite of the fact that a player is offside the referee may not see it and still award a goal. The award of the goal does not negate the offside rule. The point was made by Hood Philips that habits enable external prediction yet rules provide a justification for acting in conformity and grounds for criticising those that deviate. This is similar to Hart's observation of the presence in a rule of a critical reflexive attitude. Within the limits of the courtroom I would concur with Hunt who observed that we are all realists now.

The approach of the Scandinavian realists while quite different from their American namesakes is nonetheless radical and iconoclastic. The Scandinavians had a deep mistrust of the metaphysical and insisted on verification of any metaphysical notion in the real world of cause and effect. Lundstedt in his *Legal Thinking Revised* argued that legal rules are mere labels and become meaningless if taken out of context. He argued that it was not possible to stipulate that because of a rule a duty arises, because this would be to support a metaphysical relationship that cannot be proved in the world of cause and effect.

Olivecrona saw two parts of the rule, namely the ideatum and the imperatum. By the ideatum he identified the imagined pattern of behaviour that the legislature wants to bring about and by the imperatum he identified the expression of the ideatum. His was essentially an imperative approach although he did not see imperatives in terms of the wish of any person, as Austin so required. For Olivecrona the imperative was independent of the wish of anyone. He viewed his performatory imperatives as a type of power conferring rule, yet it is submitted that this is wrong. Power-conferring rules are not just another form of imperative. In essence what Olivecrona was writing about was that law is valid because it is felt to be. The binding force of law is a reality only in the minds of the subjects and this is its manifestation in the real world, through psychology. For this reason, Olivecrona had to change his idea of who were the addressees of law. In his book *Law as Fact* he was similar to Kelsen in saying that laws were addressed to officials. But this did not enable him to explain how individuals had feelings of power and of obligation as a consequence of a rule. This would mean that the rule was meaningless. Therefore, Olivecrona altered his position and spoke of laws being addressed to officials in the primary sense and to the public in the secondary sense.

By use of an analogy with a game of chess Alf Ross shows in his work *On Law and Justice* that there is no reality apart from the experience of the players. He approaches the question of verification in a sophisticated psychological way. He distinguishes legal rules from rules of skill and maintains that the effectiveness of a rule can be established by observation. He then addresses the question of why rules are felt to be binding and concludes that the normative quality of law can be understood in psychological terms. Thus for Ross, rules act as schemes of interpretation for particular actions and it is this that enables the explanation and prediction of judicial behaviour. On the basis of the paper rules it is possible to predict what the judge will do. This is because the judge feels the rules to be binding upon him as he has accepted the sources of law and has allegiance to the constitution. The general public feel bound by a variety of reasons.

Law, for Ross, produces psychological feelings of compulsion and this is its place in the world of cause and effect. Thus a valid law for Ross would be that set of normative ideas that enable us to interpret the actions of officials in applying sanctions. Hence a realistic jurisprudence ought to be rooted in the empirical study of official behaviour and not in norms that ought to be obeyed but rather in those norms that are likely to be applied in a court. In one important respect Ross is similar to Hart and that is that he regards law as a social fact. For him a norm is a directive that stands in a relation of correspondence to social facts. We need to know the rules before we can understand what is happening.

15

Historical Jurisprudence

15.1 Introduction

The so-called historical school of the nineteenth century, led by the very different theories of von Savigny and Maine, shows us that law cannot be fully understood until its historical and social context is studied and appreciated. The natural law emphasis on universality and reason, and the positivist emphasis on law as it is, might blind us to this fact.

In its historical perspective there were two main reactions against the natural rights doctrine that arose during the age of enlightenment. We have already examined in detail the reaction that was positivism and the reasons for that reaction. In this chapter we shall examine the other main reaction which may be called romanticism.

It is possible to identify several pressing reasons that lay behind the romanticist reaction against the natural rights doctrine, as follows:

1. a reaction against the unhistorical assumptions of natural law which it will be recalled asserted the supremacy of unchanging principles;
2. a reaction against nationalism which promoted the excesses of the French Revolution and the wars that followed that event;
3. a rejection of the idea that the legal system is founded on the basis of reason;
4. a xenophobic reaction against anything French, which was particularly true of von Savigny; and
5. a desire to re-emphasise tradition as emerged from a leading anti-French Revolutionary work by Edmund Burke entitled *Reflections on the Revolution in France* (1790).

For the purposes of this Chapter, we shall take the theories of von Savigny and of Maine together. They represent two very different approaches to an understanding of law and the legal process. They have in common the reaction against the natural rights doctrine and a desire to emphasise the historical perspective, although that is as far as their similarity goes. Very generally, we may identify these theories as 'organic' for Maine and 'mystical' for von Savigny, following fairly widespread use.

15.2 Maine

Background

In the second half of the nineteenth century, Henry Maine's writings concentrated on law in a historical context, stripped of the mysticism of von Savigny's *volksgeist*. The early positivists, while rejecting natural law, still sought a universal analytic definition. Political philosophers considered present-day political obligation, and any references to history to bolster their arguments tended to be history read backwards. For example, they would read the later developed idea of a contract into the state of nature, and they would suggest laws as the commands of a supreme law-giver while ignoring the historical priority of custom over legislation. Maine pioneered a new approach, studying the history of different legal systems and the legal set-up of primitive societies, to enable a full understanding of law.

A great influence on his work was Darwin's *Origin of Species*, the theory of evolution, which dominated thought in every field in the late nineteenth century. In Professor J H Morgan's view, Darwin demonstrated that our legal organisms are as much the product of historical development as biological organisms are the outcome of evolution. This connection with Darwin is most clearly seen in the evolutionary stage model of development.

Theory

Studying the early law of Greece, Rome, and the Old Testament, and Indian law and using as well his commanding knowledge of English law, Maine said that the development of legal systems followed a pattern of six stages. Static societies passed through the first three stages; progressive societies then moved through at least some of the latter three. Maine stated that the origins of legal development can be traced to religion and ritual. This can be seen in societies that never developed literacy, at least so far as the majority of their population are concerned. There ritual is used as a means of education in circumstances where it would be futile to reduce instructions to writing. Examples of ritual washing may demonstrate this point. From this initial pool of ritual and religion flowed the stream of the development of the law. The pattern of development that Maine was so concerned to identify, along the same lines as Darwin identified for the development of species, was as follows.

Royal judgments

Royal judgments, divinely inspired, were the first stage. This has also been described as the stage of Themistes, after the Greek goddess. This should not be confused with the command of a sovereign idea as it was not deliberate law-making, merely dispute settlement. In fact, Maine suggests that Bentham's and Austin's description tallies exactly with the facts of mature jurisprudence, but more primitive law is more difficult to fit into the Bentham picture. An example is the story of King Solomon and the two mothers, proposing to divide the live baby in two as the mothers could not agree on who was the real mother. There was no principle or rule that King Solomon was applying. Within the context of Maine's theory it can be observed firstly that it was to King Solomon that the parties turned for a resolution of the dispute and secondly that the decision was divinely inspired in order to draw out the real mother who would rather have her child live but away from her than dead. While this is a good example to illustrate the concept of divinely inspired judgments, it can also be used to defeat the historical and chronological aspect of Maine's thesis. The point is that King Solomon existed after the law had been codified and not before, as Maine's developmental process would have maintained.

Custom

Custom and the dominion of aristocracies follow royal judgments; the prerogative of the kings passes to different types of aristocracies (in the East, religious; in the West, civil or political), which were universally the depositaries and administrators of law. What the juristical oligarchy now claims is to monopolise the knowledge of the laws, to have exclusive possession of the principles by which quarrels are decided. Customs or observances now exist as a substantive aggregate, and are assumed to be precisely known to an aristocratic order or caste. This is the stage of unwritten law; knowledge of the principles is retained by being kept by a limited number.

Interestingly, it appears that the aristocratic order or caste in England was the judges. It is quite true that there was once a period at which the English common law might reasonably have been termed unwritten. The elder English judges did really pretend to knowledge of rules, principles, and distinctions which were not entirely revealed to the bar and to the lay public.

Codes

Next we arrive at the period of the codes. This is when written and published laws replace usages deposited with the recollection of a privileged oligarchy. This is not an era of change, but rather a period at which, because of the invention of writing, the usages are written down as a better method of storage. In Roman law, the Twelve Tables, and in England the gradual move to written law reports, represent the codes stage.

Static societies stop there, and only progressive societies move on. The major difference of the next three stages from the first three is that they are stages of deliberate change. Most of the changes in the content of law in those first stages were the result of spontaneous development. In that time, and to Maine's possibly paternal eye, very few progressive societies made deliberate attempts to alter the law. Social necessities and social opinion are always in advance of the law. To attempt to close the gap there are three instrumentalities. While one or other may be omitted, their historical order, according to Maine, is always as follows.

As stated, it is at this stage that static societies cease their legal development. Further, according to Maine, the progression through the foregoing three stages will be spontaneous. Any further development will require definite acts. Maine identified three further stages, taking account of the development of law to the stage at which he was writing. These are as follows.

Legal fictions
That is any assumption which conceals, or affects to conceal, the fact that a rule of law has undergone alteration, its letter remaining unchanged, its operation being modified. Examples would be false allegations in writs to give a court jurisdiction (for example, the growth of contract actions from assumpsit pleas) and the Roman fiction (a false averment by the plaintiff which the defendant may not traverse). This device is now not needed, according to Maine, since its day is long since gone by.

Equity
The development of a separate body of rules, existing alongside the original law and claiming superiority over it by virtue of an inherent sanctity, is a second mode of progress and change. Such a body grew up under the Roman praetors, and the English chancellors.

Legislation
The final stage of the development sequence. It is the enactments of a legislature in the form of either an autocratic prince, or a sovereign assembly. These enactments are authoritative because of the authority of the body and not, as with equity, because of something inherent in the content of the principles. In modern terminology, the authority of the enactments is content independent.

This six-stage development is of the form of law. Maine saw a parallel movement in the context of law in progressive societies from status to contract, thus his statement that:

> 'The movement of the progressive societies has been uniform in one respect. Through all the course, it has been distinguished by the gradual dissolution of family dependency, and the growth of individual obligation in its place. The individual is steadily substituted for the family.'

In his view, slavery had been replaced by the contractual servant-master relationship. Women and sons were no longer subject to the authority of their husbands or parents, but could enter contracts themselves. Of course, minors and lunatics could not for they were still subject to their status, but only because they lacked the judgment to make contracts.

In his most famous passage, Maine says we may say that the movement of the progressive societies has hitherto been a movement from status to contract.

15.3 Evaluation of Maine

In a single sentence, we may evaluate Maine's contribution to jurisprudence by saying that while his conclusions have not proved, on further examination and evidence, to be correct or to have stood the test of time, his scientific and empirical method was the forerunner of much modern jurisprudence and sociology.

Some doubt the sequential development of a legal system of which Maine wrote. Malinowski in *Crime and Custom in Savage Society* argues that considerable latitude is inherent in the content of primitive people's customary practices. It is not clear that primitive societies move through the first three stages, nor that they are static. Some studies of primitive tribes show use of legislation, for example. Nor is it clear that the Anglo-Roman experience of fictions and equity as the first two progressive stages is universally experienced. An evolution along the six-stage pattern should not be expected for every legal system. Anthropological studies tend to suggest that Maine's conclusions were incorrect, although also Maine's account has suggested that the anthropological accounts need reappraising.

Perhaps the problem was that Maine sought to identify a pattern, a law of the historical development of law, and that he sought such a pattern of legal development through a comparative examination of a few different systems. Of necessity, like much historical research, some of his work had to be second-hand. His study of the Old Testament is an example. However, while some doubt of his conclusions exist, his method provided the framework for the early anthropological studies, many of which set out specifically to prove or disprove his findings. He was an inspiration for anthropology which only really developed into a separate branch of learning after his work pointed the way.

On the status to contract thesis, criticism has centred on modern developments in the law. The rise of the welfare state, employment protection, statutory implied terms in contracts, and so on, are all relatively recent developments. Their existence provides evidence that we have moved back to status. This is not an argument which strikes at the heart of Maine's thesis, of course, because he was talking of developments up to that date. In any case, this growth of legislation in some ways makes people more, rather than less free. If I am contracting with a monopoly and must use their written terms, am I really contracting at all? Was a nineteenth century factory hand really free to bargain with the factory owner? Clearly there has been a change since the *laissez-faire* of the nineteenth century. It does not seem to be too difficult to argue that modern development furthers the movement Maine saw, rather than reverses it.

Finally, we must emphasise that Maine was the start of anthropological and sociological studies of law. His particular conclusions have been criticised but his influence was immense. His view of history was more balanced than that of others of his time. This is particularly so with von Savigny whose 'mystical' theory we shall now consider.

15.4 Von Savigny

Von Savigny was a Prussian aristocrat, writing in the first half of the nineteenth century in reaction to what any aristocrat in Europe would have regarded as the excesses of the French revolutionaries, in particular their method of dealing with the French aristocracy. Von Savigny was therefore a man of his time, influenced by, and absorbing, many current ideas and feelings. This perspective ought not to be lost on those reading his work. (And we might bear in mind that Bentham, too, was radically affected by the same events of the French Revolution.)

Intellectually, the eighteenth century had been dominated by the Age of Reason, and the natural rights doctrine. The reaction against reason took two forms. One, Benthamic positivism, we have already considered. The other was the romantic movement, based on feeling and imagination in the arts, literature and learning.

One writer who particularly foreshadowed von Savigny's thought was Herder, who stressed that each nation and era had its own unique character. This character and the national spirit (*volksgeist*) should not have a universal natural law imposed on it, since this would affect its free development. The idea of a unique national spirit which must be respected is the basis of much of what von Savigny says.

One reason for the reaction against the new Age of Reason was its part as an origin of the French Revolution. Antipathy to all things French was also important in von Savigny's rejection of the idea of imposing the French Code Napoleon on German law. It was to stop this development that von Savigny wrote.

Finally, the long-drawn-out Napoleonic Wars had increased nationalism throughout Europe, and particularly in Germany where anti-French feeling was strong. His *On the Vocation of Our Age for Legislation and Jurisprudence* contains a powerful argument against codification and in particular the proposal by Thibaut to adopt the Code Napoleon in Prussia. Briefly, his argument was that the character and national spirit, or *Volksgeist*, should not have a universal natural law imposed upon it. Von Savigny's central idea was that law is an expression of the will of the people. It does not, he said, come from deliberate legislation but arises as a gradual development of the common consciousness of the nation. He expressed it as follows: The spirit of the people gives birth to positive law. In another passage, he says: The nature of any particular system of law was a reflection of the spirit of the people who evolved it.

Von Savigny saw the historical development of law as follows.

1. Law originates in custom which expresses national uniqueness. The principles of law derive from the beliefs of the people.
2. At the next stage, juristic skills are added, including codification which does no more than articulate the Volksgeist but adds technical and detailed expression to it.
3. Decay then sets in.

More important than his idea of this historical development are the underlying implications of his theory. These are that law is a matter of the subconscious; that law-making should follow the course of historical development; that custom is superior to law; and, importantly and significantly, that the *Volksgeist* cannot be criticised for what it is, namely the standard by which laws are to be judged; and, finally, if law was a reflection of the *Volksgeist*, law could *only* be understood by tracing its history.

It would be appropriate to examine his theory in more depth. Since von Savigny was opposing codification, a good starting point is his attitude to reform and codification. He was not opposed to either reform or codification, but for them to be successful the strands of development and continuity in the country's laws had to be understood.

A major feature of his theory was that the law was the expression of the spirit of the people, the *Volksgeist*. Law did not come from deliberate acts of legislation, but from a gradual development of the common consciousness of the nation, which is reflected in judicial decisions, and should be reflected in legislation. The time for codification is when the legal system has added the technical skill of specialist lawyers to the nation's convictions.

Such views are strange to the English reader, schooled at the forepangs of positivism, and it may therefore be appropriate to include here a few extracts from von Savigny in order that, as it were, he may speak for himself. Thus he wrote:

> 'In the general consciousness of a people lives positive law and hence we have to call it people's law. It was by no means to be thought that it was the particular members of the people by whose arbitrary will, law was brought forth ... Rather it is the spirit of a people living and working in common in all the individuals, which gives birth to positive law, which is therefore to the consciousness of each individual not accidentally but necessarily one and the same ...
>
> When we regard "the people" as a natural unity and not merely as the subject of positive law, we ought not to think only of individuals comprised in that people at any particular time; that unity rather runs through generations constantly replacing one another, and thus it unites the present with the past and the future. This constant preservation of law is conditioned by, and based upon, the not sudden but ever gradual change of generations ...'

From his study of Roman law and its history, von Savigny concluded that law originates in custom, with the work of lawyers a later step. In fact, for both law and nations he saw a three-stage developmental process. First, principles of law deriving from the convictions of the people; second, law reaches its pinnacle, with juristic skills added to these convictions. It is at this stage that codification is desirable, to retain the perfection of the system. The third stage is one of decay.

The juristic skills in the second stage do not, according to von Savigny, pull law away from its customary roots. The jurists are an actual part of the people, and represent the whole:

> 'The law is in the particular consciousness of this order, merely a continuation and special unfolding of the people's law. In outline it continues to live in the common consciousness of the people, the more minute cultivation and handling of it, is the special calling of the order of jurists.'

As has been noted, legislation does not play an important role. It is in fact inferior to custom, and often is just a speeding up of the gradual process of assimilation of real norms and institutions into the legal framework.

15.5 Evaluation of von Savigny

We should not doubt the important point inherent in von Savigny's version of historicism. The particular history, situation and values of a country do manifest themselves in that country's laws in many ways. In the UK, for example, one thinks of rules about the monarchy, the House of Lords, the Privy Council. In fact, for many countries, their constitutional laws and conventions will have been shaped by history and political values. Many other examples could be found.

However, it is clear that this truth is obscured by the flaws in von Savigny's discussion of the *Volksgeist*. The whole concept of the *Volksgeist*, the spirit of the people, is difficult to accept for any less than homogenous, or pluralistic, society. Nineteenth century Germany may have fitted the concept, but it is relatively rare to find societies of which the same can be said. Some fundamentalist Muslim societies might fit his model. One can see how positivism accommodates the pluralistic society and this fact serves to emphasise the close connection between the growth of early positivism and liberal doctrines.

Many countries have groups of different races and different cultures, different religions or totally different political persuasions. Differing spirits exist even in countries with strongly totalitarian governments such as in Poland. While von Savigny allowed for inner circles of groups and localities within a country, his theory cannot accommodate these many countries where a choice of spirits exists.

To be more specific with examples. When Jim Crow legislation discriminating against negroes in the United States flourished, was that part of the *Volksgeist*? Is the apartheid legislation in South Africa part of the *Volksgeist* too? The strongest churches in Europe seem to exist in Eastern Europe. Is the legally imposed atheistic communism part of the spirit of the people? What would von Savigny have made of the laws of Nazi Germany?

Further points of criticism may also be mentioned. According to von Savigny, the technical law which is the result of the juristic skills is as much part of the *Volksgeist* as the common convictions of the first stage of development. It might be easy to fit laws against murder into the mould of common consciousness, and other types of laws, such as family laws, for example, which permit divorce but not abortion. Note, however, that some of these laws appear to be universal and so not unique to one *Volksgeist*. Only the details differ from society to society. Can the same really be said for technical institutions, such as the fee simple, the secret trust, promissory estoppel, bills of lading? And tax legislation? Also, and many laws seem, at times, to be contrary to the common consciousness, such as the abolition of capital punishment, the decriminalisation of homosexuality, those setting up the UK's entry to the EEC.

Of course, von Savigny's reply might simply be to say that they corrupt the proper historical process, as deliberate lawmaking out of tune with the common spirit is a mistake. But deliberate lawmaking by both legislature and courts can lead public opinion in new directions *and* introduce technical laws about which the common consciousness is unconcerned. This is an aspect of our legal experience, particularly of modern systems, which von Savigny's theory underplays. For example, the abolition of capital punishment can be seen as an attempt to educate people, and change the customary way of thought. Similarly, the legislative introduction of the welfare state changed people's attitudes, their *volksgeist*.

Perhaps there are laws which reflect the constitution and which represent a political development. Take the example of the personal status laws in the Republic of Ireland. There that country has a strong Catholic tradition and the vast majority of its citizens are observant Catholics. Its laws forbid divorce, abortion and contraception. Is this a particular manifestation of that country's *Volksgeist*? Perhaps the concept of the *Volksgeist* identifies a continuity in tradition in any society.

However, it suffers from very serious consequences. It assumes that 'people' is an identifiable entity possessing a separate metaphysical personality. From the practical point of view, this conception could have disastrous consequences for humanity. It allows for those who would argue that the involvement of those *outside* the *volk* leads to a corruption of the sacred *Volksgeist* and enables those people so arguing to call for the exclusion or worse of those perceived of as corrupters. The examples of Nazi Germany's treatment of the Jews and of South Africa's treatment of non-whites demonstrates this point. It is not here argued that von Savigny was a racist in the modern sense of the word but it can be attributed to his writings that they laid the intellectual groundwork for racial purity theorists that were to follow him.

Several more specific points in critical evaluation of von Savigny's mystical theory should be mentioned. One could identify many universal laws, such as the laws against murder which are not unique to a given *Volksgeist*. Further,to explain certain technical laws as being developed by juristic skills from a revelation of the *Volksgeist* is too mystical an idea. Does it really describe the functions of a modern legislative drafting department?

Von Savigny extrapolated his *Volksgeist* notion into a sweeping universal but then treated it as discoverable. There exists some evidence which shows that codes have been transposed without difficulty such as, for example, Egypt's adoption of French codes which seem to work well there, yet the two peoples cannot be more different in background and culture. Relevant here is Lipstein's study of the reception into Turkey of Western laws under Kemal Ataturk. These points do not, however, entirely defeat the argument that von Savigny was making. He is making more than just a descriptive point about actual legal systems. He is, after all, trying to make sense of history. The political sense of that history was a deeply conservative one. He stated that reforms that went against the stream of the *Volksgeist* would be bound to fail. In the same way, following the analogy that a body will reject an organ that is transplanted but which is incompatible with the body system. He was not engaged in a rejection of all reform. Indeed, he allowed reform if it was based on historical research that showed that it would be compatible with the *Volksgeist*.

It is not clear who the *volk* are whose *geist* determines the law nor is it clear whether the *Volksgeist* may have been shaped by the law rather than vice versa. This theory ignores the point that law has an educative function such as the Sexual Offences Act 1967 among other measures of the first two Wilson governments that were designed to change perceptions and attitudes, as in the example cited towards homosexuality. In pluralistic societies such as exist in most parts of the world today it really seems somewhat irrelevant to use the concept of the *Volksgeist* as the test of validity.

Von Savigny venerated the past without regard to its suitability to the present. To take an example. In Roman law the notion of privity of contract would not admit negotiable instruments. Generally, although Romanticists look to history their concern is with the present. Perhaps the essence of their point is that the national character influences some types of laws more than others and in particular those concerned with personal status.

16

Anthropological Jurisprudence

16.1 Introduction

16.2 The anthropological school

16.3 Evaluation

16.1 Introduction

One of Maine's great contributions was to prompt others to study the law of primitive societies, to see if they reflected his, or another, pattern of evolutionary development. Maine was only correct if study could show that primitive, static societies did in fact go through his first three stages of development, and then progressed no further. As we shall see, many of the studies that have followed have cast doubts upon Maine's sequence, but that does not deprive him of the achievement of being the first in a new and important field.

Maine was a forerunner of social jurisprudence, the historical and anthropological approach emphasising that law differs with different societies, and at different times gave an impetus to consideration of how society affects law, and what part law plays in society. Further, the pattern of development in the two fields bears an overall similarity. Early pioneers in the field, leading to studies often very much from a legal point of view overtaken by studies from a wider viewpoint and attempts to answer the general questions which caused the interest in the first place.

There are two points to bear in mind as we look briefly through the history and development of the anthropological school. Does looking at law in primitive societies help us to understand them? Perhaps, more important, does it help us to understand our own societies and to be better able to analyse properly our own concept of law?

Harris in *Legal Philosophies* identified two approaches to the study of primitive law. First, to study primitive society using conceptions of law derived from our own society. Secondly, to mould a conception of law broad enough to encompass the ways in which primitive peoples themselves see their own arrangements.

16.2 The anthropological school

No attempt will be made to cover all the writers, viewpoints and contributions of the school. Rather, an overview of major figures and the sequence of development will be attempted.

Maine and others

Maine and other early anthropologists in Germany and the USA were much influenced by the evolutionary fervour produced by Darwin's *Origin of Species*, and produced grand schemes of development of law, with different systems for different types of development (cf Durkheim, Chapter 12). While most researchers in the period immediately following Maine depended mainly on secondhand knowledge, not actually observing *in situ* themselves, two things were discovered of great importance. In even the simplest societies, regularities of behaviour could be observed, and yet often these societies had no visible means of enforcement. These discoveries open up the questions still central to legal anthropology; how does social control work in such societies? Do different forms of organisation and control go with certain stages of development or certain types of societies?

The basic answer of early researchers such as Rivers was that obedience to the regulations or customs was automatic and unthinking. Later anthropologists have criticised this conclusion. It seems at least strongly affected by ethnocentrism, ie a bias towards the forms and customs of one's own culture, in this case, our own English-type law, with courts, Parliament, statutes, etc. Ethnocentrism, for this author, means looking at the situation in primitive societies through the eyes of an Englishman, and attempting to recognise courts, rules, prisons, or their equivalents. Often, in these early and later times, a definition of law was chosen, in an attempt to categorise and arrange the material provided by the primitive societies.

Anthropology is not just about law, indeed law represents a very small part of anthropology. It should therefore be borne in mind that we are examining a relatively minor part of a very wide discipline.

The two approaches

Ethnocentrism was a great problem with early theorists, and has remained so since. It has two distorting effects. First, if we define law in order to decide which aspects of a society to study and write about, we will tend to distort those aspects by taking them out of context, ignoring their relationship to other normative material in that society; and second, when we try to fit the data into categories to explain it, we will again distort it, by arranging it in ways that suit us rather than the way it is used by and appears to the society itself.

An early example of this was Evans-Pritchard's study of the Nuer people; he said that they had no law because there was nothing to fit the definition of law as social control through systematic application of force by society: no one had the authority to adjudicate. By looking for western institutions and concepts via that definition of law, Evans-Pritchard's view of the material was distorted.

Malinowski's study of Trobriand Islanders, *Crime and Custom in Savage Society*, was a major step forward. He studied the islanders by personal observation, so that his material was authentic; and he strongly criticised ethnocentric factors in earlier works. His own conclusions have themselves been criticised; from his studies, he concluded that the observable behaviour came about not automatically, but via continuous control mechanisms, especially the ever-present possibility of the withdrawal from reciprocal economic arrangements which were central to the islanders' livelihood. Such reciprocity he classified as the identifying characteristic of law.

Simon Roberts, in his introduction to legal anthropology, *Order and Dispute*, has identified two main approaches following Malinowski: law-centred studies inspired by western jurisprudence is one approach, and wider studies of order and dispute is the other.

The first approach

The law-centred studies are those which attempt to define law, and how the simpler societies fit into that picture. Obviously the criticisms of ethnocentrism already discussed could well apply. Apart from Malinowski's definition mentioned above, Bohannan sees laws as institutionalised customary norms (custom redefined in legal institutions), Gluckman sees laws as recognition by judges, Hoebel sees laws as coercive enforcement, and so on. It is proposed to examine these in more detail and then to draw a general conclusion.

Malinowski

In addition to the foregoing about Malinowski, it can here be added that while primitive communities generally do not have any specialist vocabulary which distinguishes legal from non-legal rules in the manner of the language of an advanced society, Malinowski in *Crime and Custom in Savage Society* sought to identify some crucial feature of primitive life by applying some distinguishing characteristic of law which for him was reciprocity. He identified the following characteristics.

1. Rules are felt and regarded as obligations and rightful claims.
2. Rules are sanctioned not by mere psychological motive but by a definite social machinery of binding force.
3. Social machinery is based upon mutual dependence and realised in the equivalent arrangement of reciprocal services.

Bohannan

Bohannan in *The Differing Realms of Law* (1965) has criticised Malinowski's approach as being too undiscriminating between customary norms as a whole and law in particular. He preferred to define law in terms of institutionalised customary norms. According to him law comes into being when customary, reciprocal obligations become further institutionalised in such a way that society continues to function on the basis of rules.

Thus, according to Bohannan, for law to work there must be:

1. a way of disengaging disputes from a particular institution and engaging them in a legal institution;
2. a framework for handling the dispute and coming to a decision;
3. a way of re-engaging it into a previous non-legal institution.

Bohannan maintains that this process of double institutionalisation explains why law is behind contemporary thought in society. The problem with this explanation is that there is no central focus in primitive society to facilitate this re-institutionalisation.

Gluckman

Gluckman in *The Judicial Process Among the Barotse of Northern Rhodesia* (1967) shows that it is obedience which is contemplated, not disobedience, in a society that rests on reciprocity but also possesses a mechanism to deal with disputes; such a society, he observed, had developed the 'reasonable man' test quite independently of the English judiciary. This assertion has given rise to much dispute and is discussed below. Gluckman's study identified the process of dispute resolution for the Barotse as involving:

1. reconciliation rather than ordering of sanctions;
2. sanctions, which will be applied only where reconciliation has failed or is not possible.

The obedience to the custom rested on the reciprocity of services.

Pospisil

Pospisil in *Anthropology of Law* suggests that primitive law is essentially a matter of degree which can be isolated by reference to a cluster of differentiating criteria among which he listed:

1. authority;
2. universality;
3. the sense of obligation;
4. sanctions.

He did however focus on the disposal of disputes rather than behavioural guidance.

Hoebel

Hoebel in *The Law of Primitive Man* saw coercive enforcement as the sole badge of law. He observed that the more civilised man becomes, the greater his need for law. Law is but a response to social needs.

In another illuminating passage he stated that without a sense of community there is no law. Without law there cannot for long be a community.

Hoebel listed the four functions of law for primitive man as:

1. defining relationships amongst the members of society;
2. taming naked force and directing it to the maintenance of order;
3. the disposition of trouble cases;
4. the redefinition of relationships as the conditions of life change.

Harris finds this list more illuminating than those concentrating on the content or the institutions of primitive law. Hoebel criticises both Maine's and Hart's view of the static nature of primary rules (due to the absence of a secondary rule of change). In a customary society of the ideal type there would be no perceived tension between what is practised and what is thought to be right. Harris further observes that there would be no self conscious creation of rules. This is however an ideal type from which the real world differs.

It has been pointed out that if the community being studied does not distinguish law from other customary norms, then why should the observer? Barkun in *Law Without Sanctions* argues that our notion of law is too professionally orientated. In a manner similar to Ehrlich's living law approach, he sees law as a product of the society and does not confine it to the courtrooms.

The extent to which these studies are ethnocentric and thus flawed, varies. On the one hand can be put studies prepared for the practical purposes of informing western officials, who had the job of enforcing local customs and laws, what those laws were: these studies tended to be lists of laws in English type categories, and therefore very much subject to the second pitfall of ethnocentrism (distorting information by putting it in inappropriate western categories). On the other hand, even some studies which confined themselves to law and what were seen as legal institutions were of value and interest.

Malinowski studied why people followed the patterns of behaviour in the society studied; Gluckman and the Llewellyn-Hoebel study *The Cheyenne Way* looked at what happened to disputes and conflicts. From the latter, we can see that even primitive societies do alter the law (as a result of disputes); Gluckman's study of the Barotse in Northern Rhodesia explored how rules actually affected decision making.

In considering language Bohannan maintains that one cannot juxtapose one language to another; since there is no possibility of true translation this would have the effect of negating the use of language. Bohannan denies the possibility of cross-cultural knowledge and in order to reinforce this descends into the pessimism of infinite relativism. Bohannan then speaks of the use of a folk system relying heavily on the use of folk terminology. Gluckman developed an analytical model in an attempt to avoid stagnation, to engage in comparative studies and educate against ethnocentrism. In doing so Gluckman may have been presumptive in that his descriptions are not total (is it possible to have total descriptions?) and that therefore his analysis is engaged too early. Further, his description stage suffers from the problem of ethnocentrism as in the eyes of the describer rests the description. This can be represented on the following diagrammatic representation of Gluckman's analytical model.

The second approach

If a wider approach is taken to avoid the danger of ethnocentrism created by using a definition of law (which danger does not always, as we have seen, actually occur), a similar problem is reached. Some boundary to our study must be set: if we are not imposing our own limited view of law, we must still decide which features of the simple societies we want to study. Roberts suggests that the best framework is to look at order – the way order is preserved in society; and disputes – how disputes are considered and solved. Freed from the corrupting influence of our ideas and rules, courts and coercion, a more complete and correct picture of primitive societies can be acquired, without distortion.

Studies following this wider approach have found wide variety between societies. Various factors push them into considering the processes of the society and how they affect the individual and how he views them; particularly, disputes are seen as a necessary part of society, and are considered from a longer-term perspective: attempts to compromise, various forms of outside intevention, and how the society returns to normal. In some societies, discussion is not used to settle disputes and force is!

These wider studies enable better perspectives to be gained, and ultimately answer the questions of how societies are controlled, and whether different legal mechanisms and organisations are present in different societies.

16.3 Evaluation

The outline of anthropological thought related to law given above is sketchy and brief, but raises interesting topics. The two approaches are complementary. The wider based studies of dispute processes, particularly in societies without institutions and formal rules, introduces an element missed by narrower attempts to study the law and legal system – even those that manage to avoid the dangers of parochialism. It is interesting to ask whether more is learnt about primitive societies or about our own by the various writings. While much can be learned about the societies themselves, a lot can also be learned about ourselves. The wider perspective enables us to see that law is not unique, and that our type of legal system is far from being so. Primitive societies with their wide variety of methods show us that courts and strict laws are not the only, or even the best, way to control society and deal with disputes. Above all, perhaps the importance of negotiation and conciliation found in many studies contains a lesson we could certainly benefit from.

Although there is also a wide variety of content of laws in primitive societies, it does seem clear that something like Hart's minimum content of natural law is a universal feature.

Findings such as Llewellyn's and Hoebel's (that the Cheyenne did create new rules) and the decreasing attention paid to evolution, have led to Maine's actual conclusions not now being accepted. The continuing vitality of the anthropological approach remains as a monument to his innovative work.

One of the main difficulties with anthropological studies is the tendency that they have towards ethnocentricity. This involves the study of others through concepts developed by ourselves. On the other hand, it could be said that on the micro level at least, phenomena of our society also occur in primitive societies. In primitive society the study of these common phenomena may be more simple since they are less likely to be complicated and obscured by the complexities of an advanced industrial society. This view looks to the study of primitive society as if it were a laboratory for the understanding of our own society. The validity of this approach in itself is highly suspect.

Even if this laboratory thesis is accepted, then the anthropologist will still have to develop a mechanism for the avoidance of the tendency towards ethnocentrism by which the scientist will largely invalidate his study, as he takes law out of its context and arranges his observations according to preconceived yet inapplicable notions. Malinowski attempted to get around this defect in his study *Crime and Custom in Savage Society*. Perhaps the only effective way is through the avoidance of translation! In his study of the Barotse of Northern Rhodesia (now Zambia), Max Gluckman came across the notion of the reasonable man which he observed was employed in the same way as in our courts to arrive at an objective test by which to assess the conduct of the defendant. Bohannan isolated the problem as being one of language, hence the point above about translations. He claimed that Gluckman analysed the Barotse according to the doctrines of the common law which is clearly not applicable to them. Bohannan insists that if there is to be any potential for anthropology truly to understand any tribe then it must use tribal terms and not western concepts.

Although Durkheim tried to draw a distinction between mechanical solidarity and organic solidarity type societies, it has to be observed that western industrial society has both restitutive and repressive laws and that both of these are expanding. That fact does not necessarily defeat the usefulness of Durkheim's model in helping us to understand the difference between the two types of laws, but the conclusion drawn by Durkheim has been proved wrong.

If the models used in the anthropological method from primitive societies are applied to advanced post industrial society then that exercise may well enhance our understanding of our own society through sociological inquiry. It is my view, though, that the conclusions reached in the anthropological studies are inapplicable to our own society so far as the institution of law is concerned and I take it that that must be the prime area of interest of the jurisprudence student. In *The Law of Primitive Man* Hoebel has said that the more civilised man becomes, the greater his need for law: law is but a response to social needs. He thought that the institution of law was a necessity. He observed that without a sense of community there is no law and that without law there cannot for long be a community. The Andaman Islanders (in the Indian Ocean) have no suprafamilial authority. There social control is exercised by and within the family. However, in our society the individual is independent of both the family and the clan. Such a mechanism as is applied in the Andaman Islands would be inadequate here.

Anthropological studies can show us that conclusions that are relevant to primitive societies are not relevant in our advanced society. Felsteiner's study, *Influences of Social Organisation and Dispute Processing*, shows that the form of dispute settlement flows from the social organisation. He distinguished between TCRS (technologically complex, rich society) and TSPS (technologically simple, poor society) and observes that cross comparisons between these are of very limited value. Von Savigny had a point in this regard when he noted that each society develops the law it needs and that indeed law is a reflection of the particularities of each society (the *Volksgeist*).

Anthropological studies do have certain advantages not least of which is that they provide us with an understanding of law in societies other than our own. Certain heuristic devices have also been developed through anthropological studies and these may well be useful models for a study of law in our own society. At the micro level anthropological studies have pointed to the working of some aspects of our own society. Gluckman's model of testing not only cases, which undergo a transformation when taken to court, but also looking at rules and praxis (the way people act under the law) does not however explain the purpose of law, but is useful as far as it goes.

Take for example Gulliver's negotiation and adjudication models where he observed that in adjudication the dispute is settled on a zero/sum basis where one party wins and the other loses, whereas in negotiation the dispute is settled on a mini/max principle where both parties minimise their loss and maximise their gain. Perhaps in industrial relations (and in particular the fiasco surrounding the Industrial Relations Act 1971) where the relationship is one of reciprocity a lesson might have been learnt from anthropological studies that in such circumstances adjudication is not an appropriate mechanism for dispute resolution and preference should be given to negotiation. The industrial relations court had an impossible task, not because of the law, but because of the nature of the reciprocal relationship that the law was attempting to regulate in a compulsory adjudicatory method.

Rather than focus considerable attention and resources on anthropological studies it would be preferable to pay greater attention to sociological inquiry into our own society from the point of view of the needs of the jurisprudence student. In particular one would look for an inquiry into the nature of our state; the form and function of law; the source, distribution and location of power in our society and the study of conflict in our society. Admittedly, these are rather parochial issues; however they represent a view that although lessons can be drawn from primitive societies such as that coercive law is not always the best dispute resolution technique, these lessons are already drawn and these anthropological studies merely cloak a conclusion in a robe of authority. Our society had already invented tribunals long before Nader told us that they were a good way of resolving certain disputes.

17

The Origins of Marxism and Its Application in Real Societies

17.1 Introduction

To identify the genuine Marxist attitude towards law is a difficult task. The writings of Marx and Engels have spawned as much diversity and factionalism as the Bible. The Marxist approach might, however, be summed up as being centred on a particular notion that society and history are governed largely by economic and material factors.

In common with other nineteenth century theories based upon social analysis, Marx's own views on law denied that it was autonomous or objectively separated from society. Law follows and reflects the material forces of society to an extent that he views ideas of legal objectivity as simply legal fetishism. For this reason, a brief account of the Marxist theory is needed as a background to understanding Marxist jurisprudence.

17.2　The Hegelian dialectic

Marx's and Engels' philosophy was based on the insights of Hegel who viewed all aspects of civilisation, including law, as having a defined place in the progress of the human mind towards freedom. He used as his model of historical progress the concept of the dialectic. The dialectic theorises that progress is a result of conflicting forces, in Hegel's theory, ideas. The clash of contradictory thesis and antithesis results in a sort of compromise called the synthesis. The synthesis is reacted to by another antithetical idea resulting in another synthesis. Thus, through the process of conflict society progresses towards the truth.

Marx was a law student and initially influenced by the German Historical School, although he moved towards the Hegelian left. The influence of Hess is apparent, who viewed law and morality as disposable when people are freed from their lack or self-awareness. Under the influence of Fuerbach, Marx adopted the view that Hegel had made a mistake in viewing the dialectic as one of ideas; instead ideas were the product of social life and as such the dialectic of history was one of social conflict.

Thus, Marx's dialectic materialism sees history as conflict resulting in a synthesis. Ideas are the awareness of the social situation and as such are a result of social conflict. Social conflict arises from economic differences; thus ideas, including law, are predominantly expressions of the economic conflict in society.

The processes of history see the development of feudalism, which historically resolves itself by dialectic means into capitalism. In feudal times the feudal lords dominated the means of production, land, and were therefore in conflict with serfdom. The development of better means of production results in a shift towards capitalism, where the bourgeoisie, owning the means of production, dominate the working class, the proletariat. Ultimately, this conflict will result in revolution of a violent or non-violent kind that will cause the overthrow of the bourgeoisie and bring about the dictatorship of the proletariat. Thus, the means of production will be returned to the people who produce, resulting in the eradication of repression and a communist state, where neither state nor law will be necessary.

Since ideas are reflections of social conflict, they are incomplete and partisan. Law is simply an aspect of these false ideas or ideology. The makers of law, as with other ideas, are subliminally influenced by social conflict. As a result law rides on the processes of historical materialism.

17.3　Law as superstructure

Marxism sees society divided into base and superstructure. The base is the actual relations between people involved in production, the economic structure of society. The dominant class in a society is the class that is the exploiter in these economic relationships. Superstructure represents the following.

1. A reflection of these relationships in legal and political forms.
2. The dominant class view of the world.
3. The development of awareness of social conflict, resulting in a critique of the above.

Law represents a mirror of inequalities in society, often obscured by the ruling classes' presentation of it as impartial and detached. Thus, Marx speaks of the laws of contract. They seem as if there is an equality of bargaining power. However, the reality of relations of production is that the employer is more equal than the employee. The judge may believe that he is working with objective categories, but they are simply the product of the economic forces. Thus, law is false consciousness.

Consequently, we can expect that in feudal society, where the emphasis is on the retention of land, that this will be the role of law. Equally, in capitalist society, commercial relationships will be much of the concern of law. This view is the crude materialist approach. However, Marx and, to a greater extent, Engels, concede that other factors influence the base, such as tradition, which will be reflected in superstructural institutions such as law. Thus, the material and economic forces are the ultimate, rather than the only, determining factors in the progress of laws.

17.4 Law as ideology

Marx and Engels view opinions and beliefs about law as ideology. By this they mean, as Kolakowski puts it, false consciousness or an obfuscated mental process in which men do not understand the forces that actually guide their thinking, but imagine it to be governed by logic and intellectual influences. Ideology might be the product of the dominant class, who are normally, by virtue of their opportunities, the dominant intellectual class. Thus, Victorian morality might be one classic example of ideology. Equally, the commonly held views about the nature of the world are likely to be ideology, since these will normally be warped by a lack of awareness of social conflict. The broader contributions of the arts and sciences would to a certain extent fall into this category.

17.5 The tension between material forces and ideology

There is, to a certain extent, a contradiction between the influence of economic forces and the false nature of legal ideology. Engels brought this contradiction out in his letter to Conrad Schmidt:

'The determining element in history is, in the last resort, the production and reproduction of real life. More than this neither Marx nor I have ever asserted. If therefore someone twists this into the statement that the economic element is the only determining one, he transforms it into a[n] absurd phrase. The economic situation is the basis but the various elements of the superstructure ... constitutions ... forms of law, and even the reflexes of all these actual struggles in the brains of the combatants: political, legal, philosophical theories ... and their further development into systems of dogma, all these exercise their influence on the course of historical struggles ...'

Thus, law can itself exert influence on the base in three ways.

1. Law has a crystallising effect that maintains traditions, customs and religious conceptions. These are restrictive on the achievement of awareness of class struggles and as such hold up the inevitable processes of history.
2. The more antagonistic the forces in society, the more law seeks to achieve a compromise of conflicting interests.
3. The demystification of law has a critical effect on raising class consciousness necessary for revolution.

Marx was not unaware that he himself was contributing to ideology and that his terms were quite frequently like those used by a feudal jurist.

Thus, by the end of Marx's life, Engels commented: 'We, the revolutionaries, the rebels, are thriving far better on legal methods than on illegal methods and revolt.'

However, although Marx and Engels see law as having a relative degree of autonomy, they scarcely give a definition of law, rather seeing it as an ideological cloak that hides the truth about social conflict either by compromise or conservatism and an aspect of state control. The Marxist perspective of law is dependent on the Marxist conception of the state.

17.6 The state

Marx writes that the state acts as an intermediary in the foundation of all communal institutions and gives them political form. Hence there is an illusion that law is based on will, that is on will divorced from its real basis, free will. The state is thus an illusionary community serving as a screen for the real struggles waged by classes against each other. It is political in character and an instrument by which the real relationships in society can be controlled, either by the ruling class or on their behalf. Because the state arose from the need to hold class antagonisms in check, but because it arose, at the same time, amid the conflict of these classes, it is, as a rule, the state of the most powerful, economically dominant class, which through the medium of the state, becomes also politically dominant, and thus acquires new means of holding down and exploiting the oppressed class. So says Engels in *The Origins of the Family*, prompting the notion that the state, and its means, including law, are instruments of class oppression.

However, where the struggle within society is strong, there may be a need to allow the state autonomy. Thus, the ruling class may, as was the case after the *coup d'état* of Louis Napoleon, place the apparatus of state in the hands of an autonomous bureaucracy. The state is nonetheless a means of coercion and therefore alienates people and is alienated from people.

In summary, therefore.

1. The state is a means for furthering economic domination.
2. The state acts to mediate in class tensions, maintaining the inequalities in society.
3. The state takes on a more or less autonomous role, depending on the relative strengths of classes in conflict in society.
4. The state is thus a means by which people are prevented from achieving genuine freedom.

In his earlier writings, Marx expresses his views on bureaucracy:

'... wherever the bureaucracy is a principle of its own, where the general interest of the state becomes a separate, independent and actual interest, there the bureaucracy will be opposed [to the cause of the citizen].'

17.7 The withering away of the state

The state and its instruments, such as the judiciary, is in Marxist theory, doomed by the dialectics of history. The state is a particular manifestation of the oppression of the ruling class. The ultimate overthrow of the ruling classes by the proletariat might employ the state as an instrument for bringing about total awareness, under the dictatorship of the proletariat. Lenin was to transform this idea when his time approached to apply Marxism. Ironically, Marx claimed not to be a Marxist since Marxism was to be applied revolutionary theory. He was perhaps wise so to distance himself.

17.8 The emergence of dichotomy

Marx's and Engels' philosophical theory was one open to multiple interpretations. Before we turn our attention to the main current of Russian Marxism, it is interesting to see how Marx's ideas had affected both believers and non-believers.

Kelsen, in *Sozialismus und Staat*, criticises Marxism on the basis of its Utopian view that the state could be abolished, since law will be necessary until such time as humans are transformed into angels. In response, Adler, an Austro-Marxist, simply asserts that this is exactly what Marxism entails. It is this aspect of the Romantic ideal in Marxism that is perhaps abandoned in Leninism.

Lenin was faced with the practical problem of applying Marxism. For a while he had been in sympathy with the social democracy characteristic of people such as Kautsky, which advocated universal suffrage. However, certain conclusions became apparent to him, as Kolakowski points out:

If law, for instance, is nothing but a weapon in the class struggle, it naturally follows that there is no essential difference between the rule of law and an arbitrary dictatorship. (When his adversaries were able to point out that he was in conflict with something Marx had actually said, for example, that dictatorship did not mean arbitrary despotism, they were proving Marx's own inconsistency rather than Lenin's unorthodoxy).

Lenin thus began to see the state and laws as means to ends, as instruments of the struggle for freedom. This contrasts with Marx, who saw the ends as predetermined by economics.

The dichotomy mentioned in the heading was thus between those who advocated the gradual reform of capitalism and the utilisation of the legacy of the bourgeois state, and the pragmatists, exemplified by Lenin.

17.9 Lenin's theoretical contribution

Lenin's ideal was a pure democracy, at first conditioned by coercion, but ultimately achieved without restraint. Equal pay and elected officials feature in his Utopian view in *Materials Relating to the Revision of the Party Programme*. The party would be the educating force, bringing the oppressed the self-awareness that would prompt the arrival of the socialist state. This would necessitate a transitional proletarian state. However, it is his approach to law that concerns us. In the proletarian state the judiciary would be elected by the workers. However, Lenin's theoretical attitude to law was already less than Utopian from my bourgeois point of view.

Lenin had the following attitudes to law, which were built upon after the Russian revolution.

1. Categories such as freedom and human value were to be qualified by the question of what class they serve. Thus, bourgeois freedom is a tool of the bourgeois class struggle.
2. International law is not a matter of concern. Lenin would cite Clausewitz that war is simply the continuation of politics in another form.
3. Democracy and its institutions are simply the legal expression of class conflict. In the light of this, the bourgeois state should be smashed immediately to be replaced by the proletarian state that would wither away.
4. The proletarian state is necessary to remove the traces of bourgeois values and as such democracy can only come about when capitalism has been eradicated by the dictatorship of the proletariat. In *The Victory of the Cadets and the Tasks of the Workers' Party* he states, 'Dictatorship means unlimited power, based on force, not on law.' He frequently reiterated this view.
5. The blueprint of this was found in his 1918 party programme:
    Abolition of parliamentarianism (as the separation of legislative from executive activity); union of legislative and executive state activity. Fusion of administration with legislation.
6. In a letter to Kursky after the revolution, Lenin wrote that the courts must not ban terror but must formulate the motives underlying it, and legalise it as a principle.

These principles were carried into action in the Russian revolution. This reformulation of Marxism might best be termed Marxist-Leninism. This doctrine of law was transmitted to Stalin when Lenin died. It is interesting to note that the official support for Marxist-Leninism was only withdrawn in 1991.

17.10 Pashukanis

Pashukanis was the head of the department of legal studies in the Soviet Communist Academy. His *General Theory of Law and Marxism* is thought to be representative of the legal theory of the Thirties. He argues that, not only the content of legal norms, but the form of them, are intrinsically linked to fetishist commodity relations. Law was created, therefore, as an instrument of trade that was extended to personal and other relationships. Legal relationships reduce humans to abstract juridical categories, according to Pashukanis. The continued existence of law in the USSR was, thus, a sign that the society was still in a transitory stage.

A similar approach is taken by Stuchka, who suggests that law is the weapon of class struggle and as such is necessary to fight hostile forces and saboteurs. Stuchka was a member of the Cheka, the Soviet secret police. The task of the Cheka was to fight against the forces that sought to overthrow the proletarian state. To further this end, Lenin had proposed an amendment to the criminal code which permitted draconian punishment for anyone whose statements might objectively serve anti-revolutionary forces. Ultimately, such a law is a strict liability catch-all! Such approaches became the norm under Stalin whose contribution to Marxism was the adding of numbers to a manual on the Marxist ideology and reducing the numbers of Soviet citizens by millions, which was termed socialist legality.

17.11 The post-Stalinist era up to the break-up of the Soviet Union

Until the 1990s, the Soviet Government had not lost sight of the revolution and future communist state. They saw the Soviet Union as an all-people's state, and no longer a workers' state: the internal enemies of the workers are sufficiently under control for the state to be considered classless. The concept of a classless state, even an all-people's classless state, does, however, run counter to the strict reading of Marx (the state comes from class division and inequality). Similarly, there is no justification in Marx for the developed socialist society once claimed in the Soviet Union as a necessary step on the road to communism.

Clearly, a communist state has not arrived in the Soviet Union, indeed the Union itself has now collapsed. Equally, law has not withered away even to the extent foretold by Lenin and Engels. The state remained important, as did law, right up to the collapse of the Union. The Soviets gave many reasons for the continuation of the State and law. They may be summarised as follows.

1. Capitalist encirclement where there is an external physical threat. This was relied on by Lenin and Vyshinsky. The immediate post revolution experience of the Soviet Union and the Nazi invasion lend force to this.
2. Law is an important lever in establishing the foundations upon which communism will be built. This is a notion developed by the rather more sophisticated theorists Ioffe and Shargorodskii and represents a considerable development from beliefs existing at the time of Stalin.
3. Law is a necessary ideological tool enabling re-education of the masses who have been exposed to ideology
4. Parental law, as it was known in the Soviet Union, allowed for the inculcation of communist morality. There is lots of propaganda ensuring citizens are aware of the law, the aim being an internalisation process (cf Olivecrona), the law inculcating the dictates of communist morality. As Lloyd and Freeman point out, the legal process itself has an educational role. Courts go out to the provinces, and there is considerable lay participation. A question which arises here is why is there still a need for this seventy years after the revolution?
5. A more sophisticated and longer lasting explanation was that law is necessary for the administration of a complex society and the central planning of the economy.
6. Because the process spoken of by Marx of the spread of the revolution has not taken place, the Soviet Union maintain that they require the state and law to act as a defence against any reassertion of bourgeois materialism.

17.12 Alternative schools of Marxism

Whether the Soviet experience was applied Marxism or simply a totalitarian empire that adopted an ideology that suited it, is a matter of debate. The collapse of the Soviet empire has shown that, as with the failure of revolution to materialise in the West, the predictions of the Soviet ideologues were to prove to be unfounded. We shall discuss the effects of these changes in the next Chapter.

However, independently of the Soviet development, Marxism was and still continues to be an important analytical framework. It is worthwhile addressing some of the alternative conceptions of Marxism. This we shall do in the next Chapter, since the Marxist trends that have developed in capitalist societies have been of use as critical, rather than political tools. It has been suggested by Lloyd and Freeman that it is possible to use the Marxist attitude towards law as a jurisprudential guide, without necessarily accepting the predictive aspects of the theory. It is submitted that in the light of recent developments, this is possibly the most useful way in which we can employ the Marxist perspective of law and state.

18

Contemporary Marxism

18.1 The failure of applied Marxism

It may well be argued that Marxism, like God, is dead. However, like religion, Marxism claims considerable intellectual support. The experience of Marxism would seem to refute the intellectual adherence to the idea. In Eastern Europe the communist state has withered away in a manner not anticipated by Marx. In China, the crude Maoist Marxist theory is becoming diluted by capitalist reforms, while the recent experience of Ethiopia suggests that the Marxist state is not the reforming success anticipated even in the third world. However, it is easy for Marxists to argue that this is not real Marxism, but the adoption of a label in order to sanction a different political regime. There are certainly contradictions, as witnessed by the Soviet experience.

Ideology and economy

Lenin differed from Marx in his belief that political power, rather than economic forces, could influence the coming of a socialist society. As a result, it might be suggested, the Russian revolution may not have been the outcome of the inevitable forces of materialist history, but an ideological coup. This argument would suggest that Russia was seeking to run before it could walk. Certainly, most Marxist states have developed in societies throwing off feudal or colonial power, rather than capitalist orders. However, Marx was aware in later life that Russia was a likely place for a communist revolution. Ideology, rather than historical materialism, was the dominant force behind most of these revolutions.

The Leninist-Marxism of the Soviet Union further subverted the laws of history by restraining the development of production by centralised planning and under-investment. Much of the means of production in Soviet society has remained the same as it was in the distant past. Such restraint on technology is, to a certain extent, to restrain one of the essential elements in the evolutionary process of history according to Marx. However, it might also be said that the progress of society towards socialism will never happen because the constant advance of means of production through technology means that surplus capital will always be accrued. Thus, if a person in an unregulated socialist society invented a new way of manufacturing food more cheaply, and using less labour, he would exploit this and recreate capitalism. The only reason why Marx does not envisage this happening is because he believes that in a post-capitalist state everyone would act in harmony according to the maxim from each according to his means; to each according to his needs. It must be submitted that this Romanticism is not an accurate reflection of human nature as it is now.

The proletarian revolution

Marx believed that it was only when the proletariat became aware, that the revolution would take place. However, the Soviet revolution happened before such awareness came about. It may even be suggested that such an awareness is not necessarily a feature of historical development into communism. The anti-communist revolution, although spearheaded by intellectuals, such as Havel in Czechoslovakia, is largely a proletarian one.

The development of a bureaucratic caste in Russia was a predictable part of the retention of the state structure. Lenin was aware of this himself, as was Stalin. However, their solution was the imposition of more bureaucracy. It may be submitted that, on the death of Stalin, there was a complete bureaucratic takeover and the subsequent legal reforms and limited rule of law were merely to protect their interests. As we saw in the last Chapter, Marx was well aware that the bureaucratisation of a state adds to, rather than detracts from, conflict in the state.

The Soviet state

Lenin's concept of the proletarian state which protects its own interests is in Marxist thinking inevitably self-perpetuating, particularly when bureaucratised. The identification of the real proletariat with the state is a feature reminiscent of the adoption of natural law theories such as divine right, to sanction older totalitarian regimes. Stalin stated that he was, himself, the proletariat. Furthermore, he believed that the proletariat in Russia were too uneducated to produce their own ideas, but would simply emulate capitalist ideology. Consequently, the state justified its existence as being the conscience of the proletariat, until such time as they became aware, yet intellectual autonomy was prevented, thus stopping the proletariat from developing this awareness. This inevitably became the justification for the continuation of the state.

It is interesting to note that Marx, in his early critique of the German press laws, asserted that censorship can never be in the interest of the state, since it is thereby blinded to the conflicts that threaten it. It may be contended that this prediction was accurate with regard to the Soviet empire.

A further observation is that the state in Hegelian views tends to get stronger with the forces of history. Hegelianism was the foundation of fascist theories of law and state. It may be that the Hegelian notion of the laws of history is a more accurate prediction than the Marxist one. However, the Marxist experience seems to confirm that the state is an alienating feature that falsifies production relations and increases conflict.

The Italian Marxist Gramsci directed this criticism equally at Marxist and fascist states:

'It is regressive when it aims at restraining the living forces of history and maintaining outdated anti-historical legality that has become a mere empty shell … when the party is progressive it functions democratically … when it is regressive it functions bureaucratically (in the sense of bureaucratic centralism). In the latter case the party is merely an executive, not a deliberating body …'

Gramsci rejected the scientific socialism of Lenin, which advocates the indoctrination of the proletariat with the correct doctrine. He saw this as anti-historical and anti-democratic.

International order

It is submitted by many Marxists such as Renner that the worldwide, or even national, revolutions expected by Marx were averted by the effect of colonialism. The modern world is viewed in terms of global, rather than national, economic forces. Even in the post-colonialist world, we still benefit from the effects of economic colonialism, which increases surplus in capitalist societies, thus funding the reform of capitalism.

The Soviet Union as an element in the economic world was, in economic terms, doomed since it continued to have to compete in global economic markets for commodities that were necessary.

The change in necessary commodities

In Marx's time technology promised to be able to deliver the answer to people's basic needs: that of health, housing, food etc. However, technology has the remarkable side-effect of creating new needs. The utilisation of technology for need functions such as communications, transport, domestic efficiency, creates demand for televisions, cars, washing machines, etc, which in the modern world are viewed as necessities. Needs can therefore be seen, in the technological age, to increase at an ever greater rate than means. Thus, the producers' wares are always insufficient to satisfy demand. I feel it is the development of technology that inevitably falsifies the means-needs beliefs of Marxism. If technology can supply a commodity, then it is no good saying that you do not need this, since this is viewed as economic oppression. The consumerist aspirations of those in communist society, as much as the urge for free thought and democracy, must be seen as an important factor in the decline of communism in the Eastern bloc.

18.2 The implications for law of Marxist-Leninist contradictions

1. In the absence of human perfection, law is necessary for the purposes of ensuring the distribution of commodities according to needs.
2. It seems fairly obvious, even from the British point of view, that administrative and executive action requires internal objective regulation and has a tendency towards bureaucracy. Rules are necessary if any kind of normatisation is required, including scientific socialism.
3. Stalin and Lenin thought that social coherence will progress largely from political domination through scientific socialism. The socialist legality of scientific socialism inevitably assumes the continued existence of social diversity and may be said to perpetuate social conflict. Part of the inevitable definition of law is that, as Kelsen pointed out, people do not always obey it. Therefore the claim to have achieved an all-people's state accepts the necessity of continued legal control to achieve socialism.
4. According to Marx the state does not wither away because of ideologies, but as a result of economic forces and the real relations in the base. Thus, the idea that law may be used to stimulate the withering away of law, which is at the heart of scientific socialism, is an obvious self-contradiction.
5. It is clear from the Soviet experience that social deviance is not necessarily a feature of class conflict, but may be related to other social phenomena.

18.3 The failure of the revolution to materialise in capitalist countries

What is particularly damning about Marx's predictions is the failure of revolution to take place in developed capitalist countries. As a result, it is asserted by some Marxists that the reform of capitalism is to be blamed. However, the reform of capitalism may be seen as stemming from a duality of forces. On the one hand, capitalist forces are viewed as bribing the proletariat with reform in order to retain their economic dominance. On the other, some Marxists and socialists have seen the reform of capitalism as the way in which socialism may be brought about. As such, Marxist conceptions have crept into the everyday language of capitalism. We need only to hear the language of current English conservatism to realise that the classless society on the basis of minimising state intervention in economic affairs appeals equally to Marxist ideology and to capitalist *laissez-faire* philosophy. This is, obviously, not to suppose that the Conservative Party are Marxists, but that class conflict and economic oppression are still considered to be real issues. Ironically, socialism seems to advocate the increased use of legal intervention in modern democratic society. It may be suggested that the democratic reforms which enfranchised the working class have instigated a weak instrumentalism in the proletarian use of law.

As a result, there seems to be some point in a continued evaluation of law in the light of Marxist jurisprudence.

18.4 Modernised Marxist conceptions of law

Historical influences on modern Marxist criminology

While Engels saw crime as a result of the demoralising effect of the condition of the poor, Marx was also aware of the parasitic lumpen proletariat that are the criminalised class. A consistent criminology was not, however, a feature of early Marxist thought. Nonetheless, the sociological evaluation of law tended towards an analysis of the correlation between crime and social conditions. Additionally, the feature of social alienation due to economic disparities is to be found stressed in some sociological studies. Consequently, in the last twenty years there has been more interest in Marxist thinking and its application to crime. As a result there has been a rediscovery of non-orthodox Marxist jurisprudence of which the following are influential examples:

Karl Renner, a Marxist, yet also a noted Austrian statesman, began to emphasise the way in which law could be useful in the manipulation of material conditions. His *Institutions of Private Law and Their Social Functions* affirmed that law could mould the social conditions of a society. Renner emphasises that the relationships between law and economy are subtle ones. He views the base-structure distinction as a metaphorical one that illustrates the division in society.

The Frankfurt School of critical theory used Marxism as an analytical tool, but incorporated philosophical and psychological learning in their search for understanding.

Horkenheimer, in *Studies on Authority and the Family*, introduced the conception that law and other political institutions increased in importance as socialising or normatising as parental authority is transferred or declines. All the contributors to this study saw social relationships as being bureaucratised, while individuals were increasingly controlled by law. This was the result of the effect of mass media and other technocratic controls, which sought to create a false culture among the mass of society, using utilitarianism and pragmatism. People were being turned into consumer robots.

Of particular interest to criminologists are the methods of Adorno, who used empirical methods to understand what factors contribute to the obedience of some individuals to authority and what creates deviance.

Similarly, Fromm's post-Freudian analysis of society and the urge for social order is an interesting one. Capitalism liberates creative forces and gives men the awareness of their individual dignity and responsibility. However, they also become aware of the competing and conflicting human interests. As Kolakowski describes his theory:

> 'Personal initiative has become the decisive factor in life, but increased importance also becomes attached to aggression and exploitation. The sum total of loneliness and isolation has grown beyond measure, while social conditions cause people to treat one another as things and not persons.'

Fromm's conclusion is that, to coin a phrase, 'All you need is love'. It might be argued that Fromm over-emphasises the humanist tendencies in Marx's writings; however his views are nonetheless influential in understanding social deviance.

The Frankfurt School consisted of other, very interesting thinkers such as Marcuse. However, the relevance of these is limited for our present purposes. The publication of their journal had a considerable effect in 1960. Its criticisms of institutional values and its emphasis on a revolution of minorities, together with cultural reform and mental reflection were imported into America as a result of the war and have had a considerable effect on both society and the interpretation of society.

Modern Marxist theory of law and state

The new criminology

The approaches of social scientists investigating the nature of crime was beginning to be questioned in the 1960s. The Marxism of the above thinkers led Marxists such as Quinney to view some elements of crime as being proto-rebellion against falsified values. The radical movement that asserted the rights of gypsies, homosexuals, drug-users and so forth required an understanding of the relationship between criminality and the state value system. Thus, Taylor, Walton and Young, in *The New Criminology*, called for a fully social theory of deviance that would demonstrate that criminality was politically, economically and socially induced by material forces. They identified the relationships between law and the means of production as follows:

English civil law is largely centred around the three concepts of:

1. property;
2. rights of possession;
3. contractual obligation.

All these things favour the accumulation and retention of capital.

The criminal law has a preoccupation with property crimes, such as theft, criminal damage etc. The concept of equal treatment before the law means that the existing economic distribution is maintained. This is precisely the Marxist thesis.

However, it has been pointed out by some that the law also protects, to a greater or lesser extent, the working class from having their meagre resources taken by the rich. However, the economic relationship with law is thus tenuously established. The view that the law is somehow impartial and separated from economic forces becomes less tenable. However, this does not exclude the moral element involved in the making of criminal law. This view is rather too simple.

One application of Marxist theory is the suggestion that crime is largely the domain of surplus populations that have no real role in the means and relations of production – the unemployed and unemployable. This lumpen proletariat certainly exists in modern society and is the source of much crime. However, it does not account for the violence of the so-called lager-lout of the mid-1980s, who, rather than being poor and unemployed, tended to be well-paid working class, falsifying the demoralisation as well as the lumpen proletariat thesis.

The function of a capitalist state

Hall and Scraton argue that in modern democracies, the state is viewed as being bound by the will of the people, but urge us to look at what the state does. Their argument is more complex:

The principal purposes of the state are economic ones.

The capitalist state is as its label implies capitalist, that is, committed to individuals being able to make profits if they have the means to. It lives on the extracted surplus of these profits and its health and importance is measured by the production of the country.

Therefore it employs law which will help in the maintenance of this system.

Consequently, employee share participation on the small scale that we see in current English society represents an incentive towards better productivity. Education models the new minds necessary for modern production techniques. Even unionisation allows for easy collective bargaining and normatised protest.

This view is sustainable without any implication of conspiracy. It differs from the Marxist conception of law as purely an economic reflection of the present, but is compatible with the view that law, state and economic activity act in concert to a certain degree. This view is somewhat at odds with the crude class instrumentalism of Quinney who at times viewed law as simply the weapon of the ruling class.

With more subtlety, Miliband argues that the majority of those in judicial positions are of a particular class and inclined towards their own cultural views. This is true, as the profession itself accepts, although the judiciary do have remarkably broad minds considering their backgrounds! However, there is an institutionalised distinction to be found in a system that sends a lawyer who has embezzled client funds to an open prison and a person who steals a car to a more secure one. Presumably the latter is more likely to escape!

The structuralist approach

For Poulantzas, the law and state are the mediators that legitimise existing relationships within society, although not all of them. Thus, dominant economic classes can claim that the law is concerned with the general interest. Contrary to being synonymous with classes, the law treats, according to Poulantzas, everyone as an individual of equal status, thereby blinding us to the economic domination of a class of people. Thus, legal concepts such as citizenship, equality before the law and rights amount to an isolation effect by which people become unaware of the minority that own the majority. However, it might be pointed out that this does not account for the existence of the welfare rights that protect the less fortunate sections of the population. Poulantzas' structuralist approach is therefore limited.

18.5 A critical evaluation of main Marxist conceptions

Marx himself argued that every movement is a product of its own time. Questions have been raised as to whether the same can legitimately be said of Marxism. Was the theory a product of its time?

In his analysis of capitalism in crisis Marx identified certain important issues and offered an explanation of them in terms of a conflict theory (the history of all hitherto society has been the history of class struggle). He developed a science of historical materialism that offered an explanation for everything in economic terms. This was attractive and remains so to some people. The question is to what extent is it still valid. The response could be addressed in Marxist terms by looking at changes in society in economic terms and observing that as our society has changed from the rather naked exploitative capitalism of the mid nineteenth century through the Welfare State, working class participation and more recently the advent of the Thatcherist enterprise culture, the distinction between working class and capitalist class has become blurred. Workers now own shares, if not in the recently privatised concerns then in their own workplaces. The real distinction in Britain today seems to be between those who have a job and those who do not – between the working class and the non-working class.

The explanation offered in original Marxism that the state and law are but parts of a superstructure that is reflective of the economic base – the relations of production – concerned itself to show that the superstructure served those that controlled the means of production. This class instrumentalism is rather crude and more recent studies such as those of Ralph Miliband have sought to update Marxism by showing that the relationship is more symbiotic, resembling more a partnership rather than a position where one determines the other. In essence what Miliband is trying to do is to show that Marxism can explain modern phenomena and is not restricted in time to the last century.

Another modern Marxist, Alan Hunt, has sought to explain modern events in the post industrial society in terms of economic factors and of the conflict theory. This is a clear attempt to show that Marxism is relevant and can enter the current debate rather than address itself only to obscure and historical points. The argument used by modern Marxists is that unless they can offer such an explanation then their theory will lapse into obscurity and they will be excluded from the current political debate. With regard to criminology, Taylor, Walton and Young as Marxists have sought to participate in current debates the agenda for which is not set by Marxists, and have developed an approach to criminology that does not just call on the rather simplistic Marxist explanation of crime but seeks to explain crime in more complex terms whilst remaining faithful to the essence of Marxism as they see it, namely the importance of economic factors and the conflict model of society.

Lloyd and Freeman, who are not Marxists, argue that it is legitimate to accept Marxist analysis without Marxist conclusions. That is to say that Marx identified important factors at work in society and that his explanation of naked capitalism in the mid nineteenth century is essentially accurate. If that is the case then Marxism has only a value in terms of the historical development of ideas whose time has since passed, rather like the explanation of the flat earth society. The student of jurisprudence need not then be concerned with Marxism. Marx would reject such an approach. As has been stated, Marx attempted to provide an explanation for everything. Marx would see ideology as a product of economic factors. He argued that those who control the means of production also control mental production and that truth would not be truth until applied. He would then regard the discrediting of Marxism in economic terms as an ideology or false consciousness designed to mystify the exploited class and to legitimate the position of the dominant class as those who control the means of production.

Hence while it is probably accurate to argue that original Marxism as an analysis of naked capitalism is dated and not therefore of much relevance to the modern student, it is rather the analysis of the modern post industrial capitalist state that remains of considerable importance. Here Marxists, rather than Marx, speak of the relative autonomy of the state, the explanation of which can be found in Poulantzas' *Political Power and Social Classes* wherein it is pointed out that the state which is also the Welfare State and the provider of laws on consumer protection that appear to be in the interests of the working class, remains the state of the ruling class. The Marxist explanation of the separation of state from civil society, which observes that those who govern are not those who control the means of production, points out that in the capitalist mode of production there is no need for those who own the means of production to rule just so long as their rights in capital are protected; the state can otherwise be relatively autonomous. This can be summed up in the phrase of Sigman that the capitalist class rules but does not govern.

Whether these approaches are correct is a matter for considerable argument. The student of jurisprudence must recognise the importance of that argument and therefore there is much in Marxism that is still relevant to the student of jurisprudence. The fact that half the world subscribes to what it terms Marxism, even though Marx might have difficulty in so recognising it, further reinforces the argument as to its relevance.

The theme which therefore runs through this discussion is that while original Marxism may have little to offer by way of explanation of those matters that properly concern the student of jurisprudence today, there has developed a new Marxism that does attempt to offer explanations in Marxist terms of developments in modern British society. If for only this reason Marxism is still relevant.

18.6 Evaluation

We have outlined Marxist views on law in a capitalist society. Briefly, law is one of the institutions of the superstructure of a society; the superstructure reflects the base, the relations of production; this is because the dominant class controls law and state and uses them to oppress the workers. Is this view satisfactory?

Is there a clear base-superstructure division? Is law just part of the superstructure?

In the theory, the base of the society consists of the relationships of production, that is, the relations between the owners of the means of production and the workers; this economic base is reflected in the superstructure of the society, of which law is a part. In fact, the real situation is more complex than this simple model suggests. Law plays an important role, not only in the superstructure, but also in the base. It defines the relations of production and upholds them. In capitalism, one side of the relationship is the owners' side: ownership is a legal concept, with large bodies of law defining it (law of real property, of personal property, of conveyancing) and enforcing it (law of theft, to prevent appropriation; trespass, to prevent improper invasion: conversion, etc). Further, owners frequently rely on forms of combination which are defined and controlled – and to an extent aided, in tax terms – by law (partnerships, companies). Money is raised through institutions controlled (to an extent) by law (the stock exchange, banks); ownership is subject to nullification by law (compulsory purchase, bankruptcy, insolvency).

On the other side, the workers – what counts as an employee, rather than a contractor, is defined by law; combinations of workers are controlled by law (trade union legislation).

The relationship between the two sides is defined by law (contract of employment), and is subject to legal control (employment protection legislation giving protection from redundancy and unfair dismissal; fair wages control; Factories Acts and Health and Safety at Work Acts controlling conditions of work; a complex network of torts and immunities relating to strikes, picketing and other industrial action).

Law, then, is an integral part of the base. Collins suggests that this criticism is not a fatal one: law can be understood as superstructural in that it reflects the dominant ideology; but it closely governs the relations of production (presumably thereby reflecting the relations of production) and so acts in the base.

Law reflects the economic base: class instrumentalism

Law is held to reflect the economic base, and the dominant ideology: this works through a process of class instrumentalism, that is, the law is used by the owners to oppress the working classes. Does this analysis fit the facts?

In some areas of law, it clearly does. Recent Employment Acts removing immunities from strikers fit the model. So does the lack of a required minimum wage, complex company legislation (which allows for flexibility in setting up companies, and by limited liability allows owners to attempt to make profit without risk, allows for access to money via the Stock Exchange, without losing control of the company, and allows, if financial affairs are carefully planned, for lower taxation levels), insurance laws (to allow risks to be minimised), banking laws (to give further access to required capital), commercial laws, and so on. A whole battery of laws exist to permit owners of the means of production to combine and make agreements between themselves and with workers, allowing for the maximum possibility of profit-making with the minimum risk. One could clearly analyse all this as the dominant bourgeois ideology at work.

Other laws, however, are not as easy to fit into the picture of an oppressed working class. Some laws appear to contradict it even in the economic base. Employment protection legislation which gives workers the right to have details of their contracts, and to payments for unfair dismissal and redundancy; the Health and Safety at Work Act, protecting workers at their place of work; and immunities for workers involved in trade disputes from actions for various economic torts, thus in effect giving a right to strike. Other laws, acting clearly in the superstructure, contradict the general picture of a dominant class oppressing the working class: consumer protection legislation including the Sale of Goods Act and similar statutes, and the various provisions of a Welfare State (National Health Service, National Insurance, Social Security).

There are also laws in other areas which seem remote from the class oppression picture altogether – family laws, law relating to crimes of violence, wills, charities, and so on. Another view would be that many laws protect monopoly since they make it more expensive for new enterprise to get started by raising the capital cost of establishment in compliance with safety and consumer legislation.

Can a Marxist properly explain all these laws? Taking the third category first, those laws which appear remote from class conflict, there is a ready Marxist answer for many of them. We have seen that the dominant class ideology will support the retention of the status quo. For this reason, laws against violence and against sexual crimes, and laws relating to family, etc, can be seen as part of the social fabric, preserving the present stable social order and an acceptable level of community morality. They prevent social unrest and disquiet from rising to too great an extent. It is rather more difficult to justify laws regarding charities, or even freer moral laws relating to homosexuality or abortion, on this rationale: perhaps these can be seen as sops to the conscience of various groups in society. The laws of probate and intestacy allow the means of production to be preserved in the families of the dominant class.

The contradictory laws in the superstructure can be explained, by a Marxist, in different ways. They can be seen as proving that the dominant class does not control each and every law passed by the legal system, but allows it relative autonomy, that is, only preventing the passage of laws which would be harmful and ensuring the passage of vital laws, allowing any other laws to be passed. This can be accepted, just about, as an explanation of the Welfare State. Although the owners will have to pay a large part of the cost out of profits, they do benefit, because they and their workers are kept healthy and alive between jobs, and they can manipulate the tax system so that the working classes bear a large proportion of the cost themselves. Whether relative autonomy could be used to explain consumer protection legislation must be regarded as more open to doubt, since it is clearly harmful to the owners of productive means not to be able to sell their products as they wish. A further possible explanation is that these superstructural laws are sops to the working classes, given to keep them happy and to prevent them forming a coherent class consciousness (a necessary prelude to revolution).

This, of course, can be used to explain away any contradictory laws, even those of the first type (that is, those forming part of the base). A third possible explanation is that these laws are concessions wrung out of the dominant class by the developing consciousness of the working class. The dominant class, however, retains overall control of the system. Presumably the recent anti-union legislation can be seen as the dominant class reasserting its position, when the present economic climate makes the concessions unnecessary (a recession obviously works against working class solidarity, since personal concerns such as getting and keeping jobs become more important). The contradictory laws in the base could also be explained thus, as concessions wrung out of the ruling class.

Are these various explanations satisfactory? Can all laws be justified as being oppression – directly or indirectly by preserving the status quo – of the working classes, or instances of relative autonomy, or sops to the working classes, or concessions wrung out of the dominant class?

Obviously these questions are empirical ones. There is at least one counter-interpretation. This view would say that the various types of contradictory law merely show the theory to be incorrect. Whatever the earlier capitalist situation, in a developed capitalist society – by electoral reform and other means – the working classes now play a full role in the law-making process, and the distribution of benefits and burdens in society take their interests into account as well as the interests of the owners. The Welfare State, as well as consumer and employee protection are simply manifestations of the concern of the law-making process with the interests of the working class and the poor. Further, it is a mistake to see law simply in terms of the power balance between the classes. Doesn't law have other functions, such as regulation of law and order and upholding commonly upheld standards of decency and family life?

Class reductionism

One final point of evaluation, and then we can move from discussion of the capitalist state, to the revolution, when law and state will wither away.

This point concerns the Marxist division of the population into just two classes, the bourgeoisie and the workers. In present-day Great Britain, for example, many pressure groups and interest factions play a part in the political and legislative process, lobbying MPs and party leaders. What is more, sometimes those from the same Marxist class will take differing sides. For example, agricultural owners and fishing boat owners will often clash with developers of land and/or seaports; a good case in point is the clash over damage done to the owners of the fishing industry by entry into the EEC (which has imposed quotas), which entry was, of course, supported by most industrialists. Further examples of conflict within the Marxist classes could be given. To avoid the charge of class reductionism (that is, over-simplifying the class position by seeing only two classes), a Marxist would have to argue that pressure and interest groups are just short term, and are not as fundamental as the real classes. Class conflict, in the sense of conflict within the classes, arises because of a lack of class consciousness, not sufficiently developed in the working class and not required at present in the bourgeoisie, who can afford to wrangle and still dominate. Is this answer convincing? Could a Marxist give any other answer?

Charges of class reductionism have another aspect too. The two class divisions can now be seen to be a simplification because many members of the working class now form part of the ruling class. Pension funds and trade union funds, building societies and banks all invest in, own shares in and therefore partly own, companies, etc. The money in these various funds comes from the man in the street, who also sometimes saves more directly by buying shares himself. Most working people own at least some stake in the means of production. In fact, the people at the top of the big companies often own little or no stake therein. The controllers of the means of production no longer necessarily own it. Further, the institutions which might be included in a wider definition of the ruling class (see, for example, Griffith *The Politics of the Judiciary*, especially the last Chapter), the courts, civil service, police, armed forces, etc, cannot really be seen as having a different ideology from the ordinary person: and remember that the ordinary person controls, ultimately, by the power of the ballot box.

Isn't seeing capitalist society as divided into two classes, the owners of the means of production and the workers, thus a gross misinterpretation?

19

Feminist Jurisprudence

19.1 History

19.2 Natural rights and women's rights

19.3 Equal rights versus separate rights

19.4 Sexual discrimination: provocation and rape

19.5 Feminism in perspective

19.1 History

Although anthropologists suggest that many primitive societies were essentially matriarchal, historical evidence from the Roman era till the present time indicates that most legal systems have treated women in an unequal fashion in comparison with their male counterparts.

There have, of course, always been exceptional women who as individuals have overcome many disadvantages to achieve considerable authority. The Empress Theodora, for example, who in 523AD saved the Byzantine Emperor Justinian, when the imperial palace was seized by the rioters and the Emperor was about to flee the city. But although Theodora ruled as joint Empress, the system of law which Justinian codified treated the head of the family (the oldest male) as alone possessing contractual and political rights. Both Roman and Byzantine law, and the civil law of the Middle Ages, relegated women to an inferior status.

The nineteenth century English liberals were among the first jurists seriously to question the position of women in society: see especially J S Mill *On the Subjection of Women*. Mill questioned the traditional, to some extent religious, view that women were inferior beings destined to obey their husbands, which had found expression in the old marriage service, where the woman promised to obey, and in the common law rule that a woman's property belonged to her husband, not abolished until the Gladstonian liberals introduced the Married Women's Property Act in 1882.

Towards the end of the century Marxist writers began also to question the way in which women were treated under the law and economically, championing women as an oppressed class. See for example Engels *The Origins of the Family, Private Property and the State* reprinted in Mitchell and Oakley *The Rights and Wrongs of Women* (1986). See also Safiotti *Women and Class Society*.

In Marxist eyes it is the male capitalist who is the villain. Women and workers are the oppressed and exploited victims. The perception of women as the victims of male political and economic dominance is a theme which recurs from the martyrdom of Joan of Arc by the English in France in the Middle Ages to the murder of Rosa Luxemburg by the Nazis in Germany. So modern writers, such as Zaretsky (*Capitalism, the Family and Social Life*, 1976), attempt to show that male dominance is as much an evil as capitalist oppression. To what extent female emancipation was really achieved in Marxist and post Marxist societies, however, is open to debate. Today there may be more female than male doctors in Russia, but political power remains largely in male hands. See for example Mackinnon *Feminism, Marxism, Method and the State* (1983).

In the West, the suffragettes of the early twentieth century were instrumental in securing votes for women in 1919 and 1929; and educational and career opportunities were gradually equalised as the twentieth century progressed. Since then the question of women's rights has come to present a number of interesting issues in jurisprudence. Claims in Lloyd's *Introduction to Jurisprudence* that the growth of a 'women's' view of law arose naturally out of both the suffragette movement and, more recently, the relatively large influx of women law students (2 per cent in 1960; about 50 per cent today – see Twining *Blackstone's Tower: the English Law School* (1994)). It is pointed out that the approach is more 'concrete' and that the movement:

> '... seeks to analyse the contribution of law in constructing, maintaining, reinforcing and perpetuating patriarchy and it looks at ways in which this patriarchy can be undermined and ultimately eliminated.'

You should note, however, that there is another clear context in which feminist concerns in jurisprudence grew, namely, the critical legal studies movement. That challenged the orthodox way of looking at law so that what was seen as 'just', or 'fair', or as 'establishing equality' was now regarded by members of this movement as at best a superficial gloss and at its worst a cynical disregard for justice, etc, other than from the point of view of those wielding power (the law schools, amongst others ...!). It was an easy jump from this view of things to say: the justice, fairness, etc of the law is male justice, etc. So it would be true to say that a number of fairly obvious factors combined to produce the modern feminist approach to law.

19.2 Natural rights and women's rights

The emergence of the women's rights movement parallels in some degree the rise of natural law. For example, if in Dworkin's terms (*Taking Rights Seriously* (1972)) there are principles underlying the laws that the courts apply, do these principles include the principle that rights should not be abrogated on account of race, sex, language or religion? Dworkin would say yes, citing the 14th Amendment to the US

Constitution. His fundamental principle is, after all, a principle that all people should be treated as equals.

In Rawls' analysis (*A Theory of Justice* (1972)) there are principles of equal rights to the most extensive total system of equal basic liberties, and a principle that social and economic inequalities are to be arranged so that they are both to the greatest benefit to the least advantaged and attached to offices open to all in conditions of fair equality of opportunity.

Notice such American decisions as *Griswold* v *Connecticut* (1967) in which state laws banning the manufacture, sale or use of contraceptives were held to be unconstitutional as an infringement of the right of privacy inherent in the 14th Amendment. Likewise, *Roe* v *Wade* (1973) holding that the anti-abortion laws of the State of Texas infringed the right of privacy, and the right of a woman to decide whether or not to bear a child.

It is significant to compare English developments in the law.

A decision such as *C* v *S* (1987), in which the House of Lords held that, in the matter of abortion, the father has no rights, may be open to the criticism that sometimes the protection of the rights of the woman may involve denying rights to the father or the unborn child.

A decision such as *R* v *B* (1991), holding that a husband may be convicted of rape against his wife, may be justified by saying that in late twentieth century England the principles which underly the relationship of marriage differ from those which existed in earlier generations. Dworkin acknowledges that the interpretation of the principles which underlie the law may change as society develops, and arguably today the principle of equal concern and respect best fits that interpretation which requires a free and continuing consent, in a marriage which is today regarded as a relationship between equals.

The case of *R* v *Thornton* (1992) holding that provocation does not encompass the conduct of the husband in beating his wife, which had occurred some time before the wife killed her husband, raises wider issues about the scope of the defence of provocation of interest to feminists. Note too the case of *Davis* v *Johnson* (1979) in which the House of Lords held that a battered girlfriend was not entitled to the protection of the Domestic Violence and Matrimonial Proceedings Act 1973. It is, perhaps, out of step with a society in which so many couples are unmarried.

Rhode *Justice and Gender* (1989) discusses the question whether the law treats women fairly, and concludes not. See also Smart *Feminism and the Power of Law* and Dahl *Women's Law*.

19.3 Equal rights versus separate rights

Initially, the women's rights movement argued in favour of equal rights based on a principle of equal concern and respect. This is still the mainstream attitude. For example, Phillips *Feminism and Equality* (1987) adopts the widely accepted view that gender should not preclude equal treatment of either sex, and also discusses the question of positive discrimination in favour of women. Such feminist writers as Germaine Greer (born in Australia 1939) and Simone de Beauvoir (*The Second Sex* (1965)) symbolise the generation of women who achieved such changes in the law as the Abortion Act 1967, the Equal Opportunities Act 1973 and the Sex Discrimination Acts 1975 and 1986.

However, in recent times there has emerged a group of women's rights activists who argue that the only answer to male dominance is for women to seek a new society in which men and women are separate and equal. Important here is Alice Walker (born in Georgia, USA, 1944, author of *The Color Purple* (1983)) who discusses the dual problems of being female and of living in the southern United States before the Civil Rights era. She advocates men and women living in separate communities, and visiting one another to reproduce: 'This is the pattern of freedom until man no longer wishes to dominate women and children or always to have to prove his control.' For precedent, she refers back to such mythical Greek societies as the Amazons and the Priestesses of Vesta. Whether separatism is socially practicable or morally justifiable must be open to doubt.

Whereas Germaine Greer and Simone de Beauvoir argue in favour of equal treatment for men and women, Alice Walker takes the different position (similar to that of some Civil Rights activists) that women are not the same, and that separation is the solution. Whether separate societies would suit everyone is, however, a matter for question, and Alice Walker could be interpreted as advocating that women have the right to live separately *if they so choose*. To achieve this it is necessary to put an end to economic, social, domestic and legal dependence.

Richards in *Separate Spheres* (in Singer *Applied Ethics*, 1986) discusses the question whether feminism requires the acknowledgement of the equal but separate spheres of men and women, an argument which has similarities to that of the US Supreme Court in *Plessy* v *Ferguson* (1894) when interpreting the 14th Amendment, which was ultimately rejected in regard to educational segregation in *Brown* v *Board of Education* (1954). Richards is perhaps influenced by the libertarian views of Nozick, and other contemporary American philosophers who have addressed their attention to the 14th Amendment.

Okin (1998) explored the implications of movements towards equality. She points to the fact that the kinds of problem faced by women in trying to obtain for themselves the same status as men can be in conflict with the kinds of claims that minority cultures make for equal recognition. Her general criticism is that, where a minority culture makes a breakthrough in the political arena, it does not follow that intra-culturally the rights of women have been vindicated. These rights might, within that culture, still remain submerged, and although the general argument that that minority culture has rights of equality to all other cultures, it might overshadow the claims of women within it. This is wrong, she says, because:

'... one's place within one's culture is likely to be at least as important as the viability of one's culture in influencing the development of one's self respect and capacities to make choices about life. Establishing group rights to enable some minority cultures to preserve themselves may not necessarily be in the best interests of the girls and women of the culture, even when it is in the men's.' (at 269p683)

Such issues also raise the question whether there is exploitation of women in sexual pornography and in the use of women in advertisements for male orientated goods such as motor cars. Maybe, as in any successful social revolution, there is eventually a possibility of reaction by those whose dominance is being displaced.

Jagger *Feminist Politics and Human Nature* and Einsenstein Z R *The Sexual Politics of the New Right* discuss this topic, and the reaction of the new right who represent a masculine counter-reaction to the separatist movement. Levitas R *The Ideology of the New Right* discusses the relation between this and Republican politics in the United States. Note, for example, President Ford's instructions to the Justice Department in preparing a list of candidates to succeed Associate Justice William Douglas in 1975: 'Survey the field and don't exclude women from your list ... The final choice was between two men ... I pored over their legal opinions myself ... It was a close call ... I selected Stevens (a man) and the Senate confirmed him by a vote of 98 to 0.' Perhaps, significantly, it was Associate Justice Rehnquist, who dissented in *Roe* v *Wade*, whom President Reagan chose as Chief Justice in the 1980s. The way ahead is by no means clear.

19.4 Sexual discrimination: provocation and rape

Law's insistence on treating like cases alike creates the pretence that certain important differences between people (blacks/whites; men/women; advantaged/ disadvantaged) are not real differences: the law thus reinforces unjustifiable differences in treatment. This is the thesis of feminist jurisprudence; for example, it is advanced by Iris Young in her book *Justice and the Politics of Difference* (1991). In fact, many feminists take the view that the virtue of equality in general, not just that equality that pertains to law, is an idea *detrimental* to oppressed groups' interests. This idea has the same force as the idea that certain offices are open to all when we know that, to take the bar and the judiciary, for example, some offices are hardly at all open to blacks, women or the working class.

A more specific example is that of the defence of provocation; the law requires a 'temporary loss of self-control so that the defendant is not for the moment the master of his mind'. Women do not, it is said, react in 'white-hot rage' because it is not in their nature (and there are biochemical reasons why they do not). Decisions whereby women who murder their husbands, after a long period of abuse, are *not* afforded the defence of provocation on the ground that they have not acted in the spontaneous way the law requires, are therefore given as examples where the law fails (and is oppressive) because it treats women as in the same position as men.

It is useful considering criticisms of Young's (and others') approach. Note that if we take a natural law type approach, that is, we assume morality to be part of the law (like Hoffmann LJ in *Airedale National Health Service Trust v Bland* (1993): see 'Ronald Dworkin and contemporary case law' in section 11.16 above) we can discern strains of the requirement, not of naked, computer-like, consistency, but of *moral* consistency – equality – in the application of the idea of the rule of law. The moral argument must then be joined; there are differences between men and women that are morally relevant, say, to the defence of provocation in the criminal law. The law, in the name of consistency, properly understood, can deal with these differences.

Take the case of provocation again; it is not difficult to see that a justifiable difference can be extrapolated from the law. In the case of *DPP* v *Camplin* (1978), the action of a 'reasonable man' requirement was interpreted to include not only a man but a boy, and a retarded sensitive boy at that. The present state of legal argument is not so thin as to disallow the extension of reasonable man to include, in the circumstances of provocation in the context of domestic abuse, the reasonable woman.

There is a triumph for women in the marital rape case of *R* v *R* (1992) in which the House of Lords decided that it was, after all, possible for a man to rape his wife. This was despite the belief, held by many, lawyers included, that the implied consent of the wife, by remaining married to the defendant, provided an adequate defence. It was argued around the Sexual Offences (Amendment) Act 1976 which defines rape to be unlawful sexual intercourse and the argument was that 'unlawful' here meant 'outside marriage'. Lord Keith simply said 'the fact is that it is clearly unlawful to have sexual intercourse with any woman without her consent' and dismissed the idea that the word 'unlawful' added anything. Despite the doubts of John Smith, who wrote the commentary on this case, the reasoning is good. In a nutshell it is this: there is no such thing as implied consent (remember the nonsense we can make of the idea of 'tacit command' in Austin!); rape is therefore rendered lawful by the state of marriage; marriage thus gives men the right to treat their wives as chattels and not persons. That is why the decision is a triumph for women, since the decision will make some men think twice before behaving in a barbaric way.

19.5 Feminism in perspective

There is an excellent introduction to problems of political philosophy in J Wolff's *An Introduction to Political Philosophy* (1996), which is useful in general for obtaining a birds-eye view of problems of political philosophy as they impinge on law. It is particularly clear, however, on problems of feminism and students are recommended to read the admirable Chapter 6, entitled 'Individualism, Justice, Feminism' concentrating on the section on rights for women. At pp229–230 Wolff makes useful reference to a number of classic works on feminism. His account in 'Rights for

Women' is both sympathetic to the feminist movement and intellectually rigorous and it is an impressively clear overall account given the length of the piece.

Wolff points out that, indeed, women have been systematically if not intentionally, discriminated against in the past. For example, in Britain in 1970 before the equal pay legislation, women earned on average only 63 per cent of the average male wage. But he also notes that merely making pay equal between men and women is insufficient in itself to secure the appropriate social advance since there are other relevant differences between men and women, for example, a wrongly perceived difference in physical (and mental) strength, a wrongly perceived difference in attitudes to work, the fact that women but not men bear children, and so on. That is why some feminists say that it is gender differences that are generally irrelevant in determining the just social structure rather than just sex differences, since gender differences are different at different times and in different societies. (Gender difference is, as some say, a 'socially constructed' idea.)

So there are feminists who wish to abolish gender differences by bringing about social change so that, for example, men do not see it as automatic that women stay at home, do housework and look after the children. A discussion of this sort of approach leads Wolff to consider the status of social programmes of reverse discrimination. Those focused on sex discrimination would seem to be the most important projects for feminists to encourage, perhaps through legislation and certainly through other means, by supporting extra justification for appointment to otherwise seemingly equal positions of money and status, to boost the status, income and political weight of women, and so achieving, for example, more woman judges, more woman politicians, more women QCs, more women professors, etc. This line is a natural one to take. If women are in a disadvantaged position for morally irrelevant reasons then social means must be taken to offset the disadvantages.

Wolff usefully discusses the difficulties in this area. Briefly, such programmes can be disastrous in practice, creating stigma and feelings of injustice and that, at first sight, reverse discrimination seems to rely on making discriminations on the basis of sex even though it was sexual discrimination which caused the problem. There is, furthermore, great difficulty in justifying why we should raise the status of women today in order to right wrongs done to women in the past, and perhaps a very long time ago. But he thinks there are answers to be supplied. For example, one can argue that:

1. the equality that really matters is equality of *opportunity* rather than merely making women equal;
2. social policy of long term equality justifies the short-term inequalities;
3. reparation now for injustices in the past is justified because women today are discriminated against by the culture that was brought about in the past; and
4. there is great symbolic power in reverse discrimination which can break the habit of thinking that women are pre-destined to serve only in certain sorts of roles.

However, very importantly, Wolff points out that much of this line of thinking is frowned upon by feminists. One reason is that the social programmes of reverse discrimination, changing and raising consciousness, etc, do not question the general political, legal and economic structures of our society. Reverse discrimination takes place in a generally capitalist, generally liberal-type society (reflected in our democratic procedures and our idea of 'equality before the law'), and that means that the values of this structure are implicitly assumed to be *true*, and *fair*. Therefore, some feminists say that these values must be examined since here the deepest prejudices will be implicit. There are prejudices in favour of capitalism which infuse our discourse about the justice within which reverse discrimination arguments are made. When feminists take this view, they abandon the 'male liberal' endorsement of emancipation by, say, reverse discrimination programmes, and become critics of 'liberal individualism'. In fact, it is in this area that the major amount of writing is now done by the feminists and, unsurprisingly, they focus on the role of the family – in which the woman plays an 'inferior' role – its private 'sphere of influence', its relation to the State and its public area of influence.

The idea that justice is a 'gendered' concept which provides a prejudiced justification for its treatment of men and women through its allocating a private sphere of influence to the family is, says Wolff, an 'astonishing charge' since justice is supposed to be about treating people equally. But it can be given some credibility. He points to the argument by some feminists (notably N Chodorow, *The Reproduction of Mothering* (1978) and C Gilligan, *In A Different Voice* (1982)) that there is a fundamental difference between men and women in the way that they form their relationships with others. Women value 'connectedness' and 'caring' whereas men value 'separation' and 'independence'. If so, the fact that men have been in control of the political institutions for so long means that our way of thinking about justice is weighted towards allocating rights to people which keep them at an 'uncaring' and 'disconnected' distance from other people. Thus the idea of 'private spheres of influence' and a 'right to privacy' – upon which, in the US the right to abortion is dependent (see *Roe* v *Wade* (1973)) – are male ideas which perpetuate insidious gender differences into our political structure.

Carol Gilligan develops the arguments in the debate by claiming that men's different approach to 'caring' means that they argue justice in terms of general rules (eg 'no person *shall*, etc ...') and principles (eg 'no person *should* profit from crime'). The woman's perspective, on the other hand, is to make moral decisions on the basis of a 'case by case' basis. The kind of situation that a woman will want to decide differently from a man will be the one where immediate sympathy 'floods the moment' and casts aside the man's 'stern' reference to the rule and the injustice of making exceptions. Thus Gilligan and other feminists talk in terms of the man's 'perspective of *justice*' as opposed to the woman's 'perspective of *care*'.

Wolff points out how much of these arguments are speculative and, perhaps, draw stereotypes. After all, there are caring men just as there are uncaring women. Further, sometimes rules of justice and the ethic of caring conflict where women would concede that compliance with the rule would come first (eg choosing between not giving your child a Christmas present she wants and obtaining one by shoplifting it). But he also says that there is a sense in which the idea of rights cannot define close relationships, borrowing an idea from J Waldron, 'When Justice Replaces Affection: the Need for Rights' in Waldron's *Liberal Rights* (1993). In this idea, that rights form a kind of protective shield around relationships – acting as a sort of 'fall-back', or 'hands-off' position – while providing nothing of substance within, is the germ of political philosophy which gives sense to the feminist doctrine that 'the person is political'. As Wolff says (at p215) '... individualism seems particularly inept at explaining the moral relations within a family' because family relations are not chosen ('you choose your friends but not your relations') and so seem to impose obligations that are independent of individual choice.

But it is too simple to say (as Wolff hints) that the family and the values of free choice are incompatible. Clearly, we do not just choose our obligations. You have an obligation to another in danger to protect him or her from it when there is little or no cost to you. Another form of obligation appears to arise just from a family relationship as, for example, that of a mother to her baby. But note that there is no duty to love another! Nor is there a special duty towards another merely because that other loves you! In fact, it is not too difficult to say that there is nothing special about family relationships beyond that they are often more complex or demanding than relationships outside the family, governed by principles of liberalism.

There is, therefore, nothing particularly problematic about the family which requires feminists to proclaim that we must start seeing individuals within the family as 'political'. We are all 'political' in the sense that we are owed liberal duties. In fact, if we stop seeing 'the family' so preciously, as so distinct, then it is not difficult to see the injustices perpetrated within it. It is not necessary to espouse a 'critique of man's justice' or of 'man's liberalism' or 'man's concept of privacy' or 'man's discourse of equality', in order to see that child abuse is wrong or that men raping their wives is wrong (and so a good argument for reinterpreting or creating law: see *R v R* (1992)) or the other forms of subtle domination and bullying that occurs within families. Of course, the extent to which the community can protect weaker parties raises a difficult problem but not one that is solved by imagining a 'different discourse' or a 'radical reconstruction' of the 'private/public dichotomy'. Better education, policies of reverse discrimination (if they can be shown to work), fairer wealth distribution and, if necessary, the criminal law, are all standard tools of liberalism for bringing about a better – more just – community culture. As Wolff concludes at p220:

> 'Feminist criticism requires not that we replace the ethic of justice with the ethic of care at the heart of political philosophy but that we apply the idea of justice with an enriched sensitivity to the ways in which our institutions can embody and reproduce injustice ... A society that has a tendency to create ruthless, egotistical exploiters is worse than one with a tendency to produce charitable, altruistic co-operators, even if, in formal terms, both societies can be described as just.'

Justice

20

Arguments about Justice

20.1   Introduction

20.2   The enforcement of morality by law

20.1 Introduction

Utilitarianism has already been discussed as moral theory, setting out a theory of justice, in the context of the early positivists who were also utilitarians. In this section, we shall briefly sketch the outlines of some alternative conceptions of justice, and try to discover their bases and starting points. Many writers have put forward ideas of justice in social arrangements, and it will not be possible to consider them all.

In this section we shall briefly consider social contract theories, natural rights theories and Marxist theories. In fact the first two go together very often, as we shall see; we differentiate them now because two of the modern theorists Rawls and Nozick (Chapters 21 and 22) do not combine them, but use a social contract and natural rights model respectively. We first should make several points about method, bearing in mind the idea of 'reflective equilibrium' discussed in Chapter 4.

There is a universal appeal to justi ce. All persons are aware of the need for justice, yet there is no agreement on the nature of justice or what arrangements constitute a just ordering of society. Hence justice, Hart suggests, is shared as a concept; however, there are many conceptions of justice. Justice, on this analysis, would defy definition. The purpose of this Chapter is to illustrate some of the conventional theoretical approaches to the question of the nature of justice.

David Hume wrote that justice can only be meaningful in conditions of moderate scarcity. In his view, a conception of justice is inapplicable where there would be no resources because the population would be starving and shelterless. The issue would be one of survival, rather than justice. On the other hand, where everyone has everything they want, then distributive justice (as opposed to procedural justice) would be unnecessary. Justice in this sense can be seen as the justification for the distribution of resources in society. Distributive justice is concerned with the distribution of both material resources and legal rights to material resources.

Aristotle sought to draw a distinction between distributive and corrective justice. The former idea is concerned with the fair division of benefits and burdens, that of giving to each according to his just deserts. Corrective justice seeks to ensure a fair equilibrium by redressing any unfair distribution. The latter might be seen to be more properly the occupation of the courts, while the former is more properly an issue of political or social justice.

A further distinction may be made between procedural and substantive justice. Procedural justice might be viewed as expressing the tension between what Herbert Packer terms due process and rule of law. Due process is concerned that people, when faced with the courts, should be treated in accordance with the procedural requirements laid down by a particular legal system. This ensures that the rules are not bent; however, it may allow a mass killer to be set free on a technicality. Rule of law conceptions of procedural justice entail the primary motivation of the courts being the punishment of the wrongdoer if it is clear that he has broken the law, irrespective of procedural technicalities.

However, although this might correspond more strongly with the popular idea of justice, it does present a watering down of the checks that are designed to prevent the innocent being wrongly punished. One might also refer to Fuller's inner morality of the law as providing a theoretical framework for procedural justice. In essence procedural justice is therefore a concern with how legal rules are applied.

Substantive justice, on the other hand, is concerned with the content of a law itself. It is a question of juxtaposing the existing legal system with ideals or standards of political morality. The difference between issues of procedural justice and issues of substantive justice can be illustrated by the contrast between a just decision in a court and the justness of the law that the court has upheld.

Social contract theories

These base the justice of society's organisation on the fact that the individuals in the society have, or would have, or may be presumed to have, entered into a contract agreeing that society should be so patterned. It is often unclear whether the contract or covenant is thought actually to have existed: in its modern exponent, Rawls, it is clear that it is a hypothetical justificatory construct.

Natural rights theories

These emphasise the importance of society being formed in such a way as to protect and not enfringe upon natural rights, rights which people have either from God or from their nature.

The major exponents of social contract theory in its first heyday in the seventeenth century also placed great emphasis on natural rights: because of their different stresses it seems right to consider Hobbes' as a social contract view, and Locke's a natural rights one, but both included the idea of a state of nature including natural rights, and a contract leading to civil society.

Hobbes

Hobbes argued that men had their natural rights in a state of nature. Since men had a tendency to compete and infringe on the rights of others (and, in the famous words, the state of nature would therefore be nasty, brutish and short) they would find this state of nature unsatisfactory, and would therefore wish to join a society where the urge to competition was controlled and restrained by a political sovereign. This sovereign could become so by force or by contract, it didnt matter: people in the state of nature would be prepared to covenant or contract to transfer their natural right to protect themselves, and all their powers to a sovereign. They are then subject to an all powerful unlimited sovereign (cf Austin), subject to political obligation because of a contract they had made or would be prepared to make. On the applied level I think it is clear that Hobbesian philosophy has been and is used by military dictators following a *coup d'état* in order to justify their actions. So long as the absolute ruler (Leviathan) maintains order then his rules shall be obeyed as being just, for he has improved the lot of men by removing them from anarchy. The justification for despotism is obvious. Military leaders do indeed argue that the reason for their takeover is to preserve order or to prevent the country from slipping into anarchy.

Locke

In the state of nature, man had rights including that of appropriation of land. The two limits to this (to prevent waste, and to leave enough and as good for others) can be shown to be removed by the advent of money, leaving an unconditional right of appropriation, along with a right to protection of life, liberty and estate. Man could live in the state of nature, but some will try to gain property by trespass rather than just acquisition. Locke has a more optimistic view of man in the state of nature. There is a need simply to channel men's natural goodness. To protect their property, men will enter into a covenant agreeing to a civil society. This society is there to ensure natural rights, and the state is still subject to them; if the state passed laws infringing these rights, rebellion would be justified. All law then must conform to the standard of natural rights. The application of this theory justifies revolution in the face of tyranny. Locke's discussion of certain rights which cannot be assigned to the state has laid the foundation for the recent re-emergence of the concept of inalienable rights in human rights treaties, such as the right to national self-determination.

Rousseau

A third theorist tying social contract and natural rights was Rousseau, whose work was seized on as a philosophical justification for the French Revolution. By the social contract, a man transferred his rights not to an actual sovereign but to society which was the general will: to obey this was to obey oneself. The state should grant the citizen his freedom and, if it did not, it could be overthrown or revoked by the general will. The state held these rights on trust. The society is just to the extent that it follows the conditions which the contracting members would impose and accept. If it does not do so, like Locke, Rousseau would justify rebellion.

Marxism

We have already considered Marxist theories of law and the state (Chapters 17 and 18). It is not proposed to repeat that discussion here. What will emerge from a discussion of a Marxist conception of justice is that it is a collectivist theory and that it maintains that a just ordering of society occurs when each contributes according to his ability and receives according to his needs. An example of an attempt to organise on such a principle would be the National Health Service in Britain. Those who are earning contribute whether or not they are ill. Those who are ill receive treatment as often as necessary regardless of their contributions, if any.

Since these theories are included for background information it is not proposed to examine them in depth. However, some critical evaluation will point to the content and structure of the more modern theories that do represent a part of the course. At first, difficulty might be seen in relating these theories to our theme of justice, since Hobbes, for example, concentrates on political obligations to the state, not the obligations of the state to conform to standards of justice. Clearly the natural rights stress of Locke does suggest a standard of justice, namely, a society will be just if it respects the natural rights of its citizens (similarly Rousseau). This is the view of Nozick (Chapter 22). However, although Hobbes does not allow the social contract to be used in the direction of obligations of the state, it seems that individuals who were contracting in such a way would lay down conditions to control the state, and determine how it would operate. So the social contract model suggests a standard of justice as well, viz a society will be just if it follows the conditions which contracting members of society would impose and accept. This sort of approach can be seen in the work of Rawls.

Those are only a few of the types of individualistic theories of justice. Others include *perfectionism*, which organises things to promote a particular good or value, and *intuitionism*, which denies that any acceptable complete criteria of justice can be worked out, and therefore results in each decision being made by the intuition of the decision taker. The former is only acceptable if we accept the idea in question; the second only if no complete criterion proves satisfactory.

20.2 The enforcement of morality by law

Introduction

The extent to which courts and legislators should reflect our moral and intellectual interests is a matter of considerable debate. Certainly, we feel that in a democratic society, law should be sensitive to social attitudes. However, one must address the issue as to how far the law should go to protect us from ourselves. The law is, of its very nature, an instrument of restraint frequently associated with the enforcement of more enlightened morality, such as the prohibition of sexual and racial prejudice.

We have, to a certain extent, relied heavily on the critique of morality favoured by Hume. The empiricist view of morality seems to be one that offers us no absolute moral facts. However, when we approach the question of how people should act, there seems to be a convergence of views. Professor Isaiah Berlin suggests that the fact that people do react consistently when they communicate matters of morality would seem to suggest a relative stability in moral values. Moral values may thus be found in the consistency of attitudes, rather than resulting from some empirical or logical process.

The modern view of ethical philosophers shies away from the relativist concept of moral norms. Singer, a notable ethical philosopher, observes that human nature has its constants and there are only a limited number of ways in which human beings can live together and flourish. Now, how ethics has arrived at this view is hard to understand and still harder to explain, but it suggests that it is morally acceptable to make moral judgments about the behaviour of others. If we go further and accept Kantian ethics, which are based on equally difficult reasoning, but are largely regarded as being the right approach, we are bound to enforce moral propositions which would prevent harm to another. This is, of course, all theory.

The enforcement of morality debate is essentially a moral or ethical one; whether we prohibit homosexual activity is not a legal issue. Law either prohibits it or it does not. Unlike murder, which has a clear formula of evil intent and destruction of human life, not all moral issues easily provide pragmatic reasons for censure. Even if life had no value, the malicious killing of a slave, as property of economic value, would be wrong. Most settled issues of morality that English law enforces can be reduced to attitudes to property, especially if you reduce people to being mere chattels. Rape becomes as easily accounted for as trespass, even to the extent of the former fiction that marriage provided a sort of easement over a wife's body and therefore excluded the concept of marital rape. Thus simplified issues of enforced morality can be easily if not satisfactorily accommodated by the law.

However, the process of modern development confuses society and the state. Social cohesion is built up on moral institutions and values. The things that make it work are factors such as reliability, trustworthiness, affection, loyalty and so on, and most human endeavours are founded on these aspects of mutuality and consistency. Equally, it carries with it taboos, which do not fit easily into the legal framework. Law seeks to superimpose rules of behaviour on this matrix and to tinker with it, without destroying the links that make society work. Law is a social fact, but if society breaks down so does law. John Stuart Mill was concerned with social progress, but with a formula for legislation that did not allow the destruction or substitution of these fundamental social values with theoretical ones.

Mill was much influenced by Bentham, but like our contemporary ethical philosophers he was a believer in the synthesis of the seemingly irreconcilable doctrines of utilitarianism and Conservative idealism. He presents the dilemma of democracy in his essays contrasting Bentham and Coleridge. On the one hand [he] is deeply impressed with the mischief done to the uneducated and uncultivated by weaning them of all habits of reverence, appealing to them as a competent tribunal to decide the most intricate question, and making them think themselves capable, not only of being a light to themselves, but of giving the law to their superiors in culture. On the other hand the pursuit of self-interest by the ruling elite has been generally to a ruinous extent (and the only possible remedy is pure democracy, in which people are their own governors). Having seen the latter achieved (after a manner) by the passing of the Reform Bill in 1832, he turned his attention to the former problem, that of the tyranny of the self-serving interests of the numerical majority.

In *On Liberty* he addresses himself to the protection of individual rights and minority interests from the popular opinion in a democratic state. However, his concept of individual rights is often seen as a charter for the permissive society. This is to take his views out of historical context. The Reform Act enfranchised the industrial middle and artisan classes, so that the interests Mill saw as a threat were largely those of the rampant capitalists. Linked to his concern is his detestation of utilitarianism as a substitute for societal values:

> 'A philosophy like Bentham ... can teach the means of organizing and regulating the merely business part of social arrangements ... it will do nothing (except sometimes as an instrument in the hands of a higher doctrine) for the spiritual interests of society; nor does it suffice even of itself even for the material interests ... All he can do is but to indicate means by which, in any given state of national mind, the material interests of society can be protected; saving the question, of which others must judge, whether the use of those means would have, on the national character, any injurious influence.'

This reflects Coleridge's concern that 'we shall ... be governed ... by a contemptible democratic oligarchy of glib economists'. Mill saw a distinction between the public realm of morality and the private realm, employing the harm principle as the acid test. The only purpose for which power can be rightfully exercised over any member of a civilised community, against his will, is to prevent harm to others. His own good, either physical or moral, is not sufficient warrant. This is an insurance against the danger of cultural and societal decay which he fears is the result of throwing out societal values. Bentham's idea of the world is that of a collection of persons pursuing each his separate interest and pleasure. To Mill an alternative institution should protect societal mores because he was unsure of what sort of guardian of morality the electorate would make.

Critique of Mill

The formula therefore becomes more complicated in a democratic society. Law has an educative and regulatory role; however, true democracy requires that laws be made by the people who are subject to them. Law made by the wishes of the numerical majority may result in misery for the minority. Mill, in his later work, advocates the dualism of political self-determination through the instrument of law, but elite determination of moral and cultural values. Not surprisingly, Marx criticises Mill for trying to reconcile the irreconcilable.

Other critics of Mill, such as Stephen J, in *Liberty, Equality and Fraternity* (1873) doubt that a distinction can be truly made between acts that harm others and acts that harm oneself. Individuals are, to a certain extent, what St-Exupéry called knots in the web of society. Society must be free to judge what is harmful to itself. In the present democratic system this would mean the will of the majority, which returns us to the tyranny of the electorate.

Fortunately, or unfortunately, we do not really exist in the sort of pure democracy where the electorate makes moral decisions. Parliament reserves the right to vote paternalistically on matters of conscience, such as hanging or the preservation of Sunday trading laws. Equally the courts consider, 'There is in the courts as *custodes morum* of the people a residual power, where no statute has yet intervened to supersede the common law, to superintend those offences that are prejudicial to public welfare' (Viscount Simonds *Shaw* v *DPP* (1962)).

However, even if we grant that institutions exist that might enforce and retain a static content of morality, the problem is far from solved. The credibility, or efficaciousness of a legal system in a democratic society depends on its treading a tightrope. On the one hand, the legal system should not be seen as over-paternalistic and interfering, while on the other, it must retain a relativity to society. A legal system cannot take for granted that because it tolerates something, society will as well, for forces in society that see unrestrained deviance may be prompted to take action independent of the law. The law is placed in the situation of a schoolmaster who cannot use corporal violence, but must nonetheless maintain discipline. Law cannot dictate, but neither would it be acceptable for it to ignore society's maladies. The problem, therefore, takes on a legal dimension.

Reasonableness as a test

One attempt at solving this equation was the Wolfenden Committee's *Report on Homosexual Offences and Prostitution* (1957). The committee deployed the arguments of the harm principle and a proposition similar to that of Mills: there must remain a realm of private morality and immorality which is not the law's business. Both prostitution and private homosexual acts were determined to be unharmful to non-participants and, as such, outside the proper ambit of legal restriction. That the findings were correct, in the historical framework of societal mores, is not widely disputed. However, the employment of the harm principle was seen by some, such as Devlin in *The Enforcement of Morals*, as being unduly restrictive. Instead he appeals to the widely employed legal fiction of the reasonable man (also see Chapter 4, on the nature of morality). Devlin, in the true spirit of democracy, supports the view that law should not tolerate that which the reasonable man finds disgusting. Society needs a moral identity, because it is the moral values of society that make it cohere. For Devlin, even private acts of immorality can weaken the fabric of society if they are sufficiently grave.

The balance that Devlin seeks to achieve is placed in the context of the political morality of contemporary society, where toleration is itself a prime moral principle. Thus, there 'must be toleration of the maximum individual freedom that is consistent with the integrity of society'. Devlin's justification for the legal enforcement of morality is an extension of the harm principle to a perceived threat to society, rather than harm to other individuals. This seems quite a reasonable proposition. However, his test is one that masquerades as (1) a relevant test for the principle, and (2) an objective test. Devlin's reasonable man is not asked in sociological terms what immorality is actually threatening to society. He is asked, instead, what he feels disgust at. Most Englishmen think that eating frogs' legs is disgusting. That does not mean that they consider it harmful food. An appeal to aesthetic sense is to rely on preferences to answer what should surely be a rational question.

Furthermore, while the reasonable man test is employed as a way of alienating a courtroom issue from the subjective opinions of parties to a particular legal issue, it does not necessarily have the same effect in this situation. Devlin employs the term reasonable man to give the impression of objectivity. However, it is a fiction to suggest that there is a reasonable man when it comes to more difficult moral issues. The reasonable man of legal fiction is one who employs practical reason and due consideration when acting. However, all the practical reason and due consideration in the world will not change the preferences and prejudices that embody disgust. On the issue of homosexuality, many people intellectually feel that people's sexual orientation is not a matter for legal intervention, but they nonetheless find homosexual acts to be repellent. The reasonable man test is thus a spurious validation for prevailing societal aesthetics, rather than a test of what society feels to be threatening.

Devlin's fundamental thesis is one of conservatism. He advocates maximum privacy, freedom and toleration, subject to the overriding principles of societal harm and public outrage. Law should be slow to change since it protects the institutions that are the fabric of society. To subvert the morality of a democratic society by attacking these institutions is, to Devlin, tantamount to treason.

For a liberal, such as Dworkin in *Taking Rights Seriously*, Devlin is seeking the legislation of a sort of moral majority that can veto change to the moral environment, when it opposes that change. For Devlin, the individual in the eyes of the law is ultimately a part of society, and, as such, is morally accountable if he is, in himself, grievously deviant.

Hart's Law, Liberty and Morality

In *Law, Liberty and Morality*, Hart recognises that there does not seem to be any real widely shared morality, and there can be no freedom if we are compelled to accept only those things that others approve of.

Hart notes that there are certain constants of the human condition, which he terms the minimum content of natural law, such as the vulnerability of human beings. If we disregard these sociological facts it would be tantamount to suicide. But beyond these facts, society is faced with a choice of what rules to adopt in order to protect us from the frailties of the human condition. Hart seems to assert that since the development of a society is a collective odyssey, the values that a society has adopted for its preservation and progress constitute a shared morality of sorts. This does not mean that the norms that a society has accepted and retained are ones that are logically necessary for the achievement of social preservation. However, they are instrumental in the maintenance of social cohesion. For this reason he would not accept Devlin's analogy of deviation from moral norms with treason against society. It may be that a change in morality can result in friction, but it need not result in the collapse of society.

Hart also adopts the harm principle, but denies that consent can be used as a mitigating factor. In the case of a minor, for example, the fact that the child consents to something does not necessarily mean that the law should not protect it from harm. Equally, immoral acts in public may be harmful to others and, as such, open to legal censure, whereas acts in private should not be a matter for the law. His justification is that while the first is the legitimate prevention of harm, the latter is the enforcement of societal will over the individual. Hart finds paternalism justified, but not enforced morality, per se.

The use of rationalistic theories to justify the enforcement of morality is somewhat undermined by the arbitrary application of those principles. Most sports are not subject to moral censure, yet there are many sports harmful to participants and non-participants alike. Arbitrariness of this nature betrays the fact that the legal enforcement of morality is a matter more settled by tradition than reason. Perhaps it may be more honest to approach the problem from an alternative perspective that the law should enforce those moral norms that it has traditionally enforced, unless it cannot be morally or rationally justified.

The danger of this is well illustrated by the situation occasioned by the offences of blasphemy, which the law still prohibits within the context of the Christian religion. The Law Commission report on *Offences Against Religion* (1985) (No 145) recommended the complete abolition of blasphemy offences, a recommendation that has not been acted upon.

An introduction to thinking about the foundations of liberalism

It is important to appreciate the intellectual difficulties of liberalism. It is intended to be more than a set of discrete beliefs, say, about rights to personal freedom, or to the treatment of people as equals, or to the exercise of personal morality. Liberalism is these things, true, and can be loosely summed up as tolerance. But it aspires to be a justified doctrine of beliefs. No liberal, like no conservative, wishes to hold a set of beliefs that could be shown to be contradictory, for example, or could be shown to have unacceptable consequences.

The problem of liberalism is that it appears two-faced. It seeks a moral justification for ignoring certain sorts of immoral conduct. It is helpful to give a short review of ways in which answers have been sought to the problem.

One very common view is that liberalism follows from the perceived impossibility of the objectivity of moral reasoning. The argument goes (I emphasise that this view is extremely common): 'My moral view is my own personal opinion only, and therefore I have no right to enforce it upon another person. It follows that everyone is entitled to his own personal point of view. It further follows that the state must be tolerant towards everyone's views.'

Another view, not common now, but very common among young people in the 1960s, is a variant of the view just expressed, and shares, like it, the liberal intuition about tolerance. Instead of accepting the dilemma that you might not approve of conduct that must be tolerated, you were urged to approve it. What you did was to be tolerated not just because it was an exercise of your freedom, but it *was actually good*. Hippy liberalism does, however, escape the crude assumptions about the subjectivity of moral opinions, and its amiable and attractive side includes both the injunction that we should, at least, take an active and approving interest in the activities in which other people engage. That is an endorsement of the imaginative possibilities of liberalism, in which we must view our lives as experiments in living.

Influential critics of liberalism have been a group of philosophers known as the 'communitarians'. They have criticised liberalism on a number of grounds, several of which can be described generally as follows. Liberalism, in preaching the virtues of tolerance, relies too heavily on 'the priority of the individual and his rights over society'. The criticisms focus on the idea that individuals cannot, for a variety of reasons, some 'metaphysical', some solely moral, be thought of as 'atomistic' beings independent of their existence within a community. The idea is that, in some important sense, an individual's good life cannot be separated from the good of the community (and vice versa).

The arguments are too diffuse to be examined in detail here. For what is not clear is that liberalism depends on any idea that community values are not important (depending, of course, on what they are) or that, in any society, individuals can only be seen as 'atomic' units. Nor is it clear that people's having rights is inconsistent with community goals.

An elegant attempt at defending liberalism against the charge that it is neither concerned with the quality of individual lives nor provides an adequate account of community, is made by Raz. His attempt denies the primacy of rights to liberalism, but it does, too, accord very special weight to the idea of personal freedom. He argues that the possibility of an autonomously led life requires that there exist within society an 'adequate' range of options. If there is only one option, or only an extremely limited range of options, then lives cannot be lived autonomously. Raz offers as an example of a life where there are clearly inadequate options that of a man who is kept in a pit. He is given sufficient food to survive. He is free to do what he likes except that he is not allowed to get out of the pit. Another example Raz gives is that of the 'hounded woman'. The woman lives on an island and there are sufficient resources to survive. Unfortunately, there is a large and ferocious animal on the island, too, who hunts the woman, so that she has to spend most of her time and energy escaping from it.

Raz's view is that valuable lives consist in the pursuit of projects and commitments to various 'forms of life' and, since such projects and 'forms of life' are frequently supported and identified by public institutions, the state has an integral role in the enhancement of autonomy. The state *is*, then, concerned with 'perfect' forms of living but not with particular ideals, for that would offend the principle of autonomy.

But forms of life incompatible with the driving principle of Raz's scheme cannot be tolerated, surely. Imagine an autonomous choice to choose a non-autonomous life (as in some ways of living as a nun). There is clearly a difficulty here. How can the endorsement of autonomy permit a non-autonomous life within one comprehensive view? Raz senses that his form of liberalism withers where it is most needed, for he rules out certain incompatible forms of life. We are not required, in his view, to tolerate forms of life that are 'repugnant'.

It is not surprising that he leaves the argument there, for he must sense that his theory, while providing a coherent and comprehensive view, does not solve the central and pressing problem of liberalism. On what grounds must we support the toleration of conduct that is repugnant to, or 'discontinuous' with our own personal ethical convictions? (See, also, Dworkin's theory of liberalism, Chapter 23.)

A practical problem

It may well help the student, in his search for a meaningful evaluation of the law and morality debate, to consider a problem issue. Much has been written on the issue of the rights of homosexuals. The problem is a useful one, since its paradigm is the clash between Judeo-Christian and liberal moralities. The debate seems to be hottest in America, where the lack of explicit constitutional safeguards and the federal system of legislatures has placed the courts in the invidious position of making what is, essentially, a moral choice.

In *Bowers* v *Hardwick* the American Supreme Court was faced with the question of the constitutionality of Georgia's anti-sodomy laws. It was argued that the broad provisions of the American Constitution should be read as being applicable to gay men. The majority of the court found the Georgian state laws to be constitutionally valid.

Bowers presents an interesting situation. On the one hand, since *Brown* it has been clear that the courts may apply the constitution as if it were higher law. The gay case was that, by reasonable implication, the constitutional protection of private life applied equally to homosexual men as to any other minority group. The state case was that the explicit legislation was designed to prevent acts, that of their nature took themselves outside the normal protection of constitutional rights. In legal terms the choice was between implicit higher law and explicit lower law. Thus, legally speaking, the court was faced with six of one and half a dozen of the other.

The moral problem may be formulated in many ways, depending on one's attitude towards the issue. Whichever way the court had decided, one could argue with equal vigour that the law was seen to be settled on moral grounds or pragmatic grounds. The situation is thus an interesting one, for it presents us with what is essentially a moral dilemma. The dilemma is one of construction of a concept that is a moral rather than factual issue. In his consideration of the case, Mohr in *Gays/Justice*, posits the idea that the notion of homosexuality as a phenomenon is a sociological judgment, rather than a biological fact, one that is derived from the stereotypation of sexual roles.

Certainly there are those who do not agree with him on this, such as Moran. However, the law is asked to consider gays at the same time as a special case and not a special case. The criminalisation of sodomy itself is not the issue in *Bowers*. It is the restriction on the freedom of sexual expression and privacy of gay relationships that is being criticised. As such, to a certain extent, the argument is that gays are a special case. On the other hand, there is an appeal to broad constitutional provisions, that gays are equally as entitled to privacy in their private lives as heterosexuals. The vital question becomes what the nature of being gay is.

The Georgian laws do not seek to prevent a homosexual disposition, for this would be almost impossible. The effect of the law is to label homosexual activity as aberrant. By the same token, to deny equal constitutional treatment of homosexual men is either to deny homosexuality as a normal practice, to judge it to be aberrant, or simply to ignore it altogether.

Now, we might seek to apply some of the theoretical knowledge to this practical problem. The positivist view of this issue would certainly be that the law is what the law is. The only problem with this approach is that before *Bowers*, and even after *Bowers*, what the law is seems very hard to tell. The tradition of constitutional construction is one that derives fairly complex decisions from very static norms. There is no real guarantee that a differently constituted court would not make a different decision in the same circumstances.

Positivism has a view of law based on the assumption of validity of legal statements. Thus, if Georgian law states that sodomy is illegal, then it is illegal. However, to state that law prohibits such and such is to say what legal statements have been made in the past and then to presuppose that such statements will be valid in the future. But law is something more than the history of legal statements. The vital elements in a living legal system involve advocates and advisers evaluating the probability of certain legal arguments being successful. In addition personnel of legal institutions are not only required to decide what the law requires them to decide in terms of posited norms, but also to make rational judgments in the light of these norms in detailed factual circumstances that are unlikely to have been exactly determined by existing legal norms. However, practical reasoning is seldom free of moral considerations, whether it be of a personal, political or societal nature. This is, incidentally, precisely Dworkin's theory of correct reasoning in hard cases.

This view, too, would certainly be endorsed by Fuller, who appreciated the implicit nature of law as a human activity. However, Fuller's procedural morality of the law would have little to say about the problem faced by the court in *Bowers*.

In contrast there seems to be a tension between Hart's view of what law is and what he believes its role should be. Hart justifies the positivist separation of law and morality, not just on empirical grounds, but also on moral grounds. He reminds us that law is not morality and should not supplant it. He also recommends that law should be paternalistic in the prevention of harm. His concept of harm principle would censure certain classes of homosexual activities on the ground of corruption. This seems to be at issue with his advocacy of the separation of law and morality.

On the other hand, Devlin's disgust test would be of critical difficulty for the judge. The judge would have to decide whether the reasonable man can only be a heterosexual. To assume this would be almost certainly to preclude any answer other than the legitimation of state censure of homosexuality. Since the majority in America are taken to be heterosexual, this is the validation of moral standards on the basis of numbers. In the past, slavery and segregation have been regarded by the majority as morally right at the expense of the minority.

Mill's harm principle, coupled with his moral libertarianism, would isolate the problem from the danger of the moral majority, but would require an empirical and/or sociological justification for legal prohibition. This remains the subject of controversy since most empirical and sociological studies of the subject evoke emotionally charged criticisms of homophobic premises.

Still more controversial would be the application of Dias' principle that moral deviance should be cured. Previously in England, before the relaxation of controls on homosexual activity, a harsh regime of aversion and diversion therapies had been employed to cure homosexuals. The results were mixed. It seems from the body of scientific research that there is an element of conditioned rather than innate homosexuality. But to justify curing conditioned homosexuals would be to justify sexual conditioning to fit in with a perceived sexual normality. The premise would once again seem to require a pre-judgment on moral grounds.

Distinguishing 'sport' from sado-masochism

R v *Brown and Others* (1993) raises the issue of whether the State through its criminal law should enforce matters of private morality. The facts are sordid. A number of homosexuals committed sado-masochistic acts on each other in 'torture chambers' (and videoed what they did, which was how the activities became known to the police). Small cuts and bruises to genital areas were intentionally inflicted by the defendants in the course of acting out torture scenes. There was no real torture because there was consent (apparently) and no permanent injury (amazingly, given the descriptions of what was done). Nevertheless, the House of Lords said that the consents given did not amount to defences to the assaults. The House of Lords took the view that people could not consent to an assault that caused visible physical harm. The only exceptions would be where there was social utility, a category in which they included competitive sports, surgery and tattooing. It seems that people are not permitted to make *their own choices* as to what they want to do in their spare time. Can you think of a way of distinguishing these two sorts of activity which is consistent with the view that we should be free to do what we like provided we do not interfere with the freedom of others?

Here is a real test for you to decide what your liberal inclinations are. Quite apart from whether judges should come to these sorts of decision, do you think that society ever has the moral right to do what these judges did? That is, do you think that outlawing this sort of activity by statute, say, could be justified? After all, the people in the Brown case actually consented. And since they did, they were exercising their personal autonomy so highly prized by liberalism; they were not interfering with the personal autonomy of others. Why, then, prohibit?

The test is whether you think that the prurience you feel at what they did is a sufficient ground for outlawing. Is it not the case that the real difference between the so-called 'manly sports' and the torture session is that of plain dislike – a plain feeling of, to use Lord Devlin's phrase, 'intoleration, indignation and disgust' of the acts? After all, we all like watching a game of rugby: it is 'clean', it is out in the open, and, of course, people get scratched, gashed, concussed and their bones are broken. But homosexual scratching and gashing is somehow horrible. Is that the right way to look at things? Here is one difference: the scratching and gashing was intentional, albeit consented to, but that should not make a difference because we can consent to quite severe gashing when we consent to an operation to having our appendix removed, for example. Why are medical operations justifiable, but not torture sessions? One thing about this sort of case is that there are no easy answers, although it should be clear that a simple appeal to intuition is insufficient.

Conclusion

What the arguments provide is rational justifications for preconceived moral attitudes. Conversely, the fact that such a debate exists, and the nature of the problem faced in *Bowers*, emphasises that moral judgments cannot be excluded from legal discourse, since legal discourse is simply a specialised form of human discourse. What it does reinforce, is that although there is no firm moral content to law, the nature of the legal pursuit is to regulate human behaviour. Some of the most important areas of human activity involve moral issues. A legal system that does not address the moral facet of human behaviour is one that inadequately comprehends human nature and therefore is almost certainly doomed to failure. This is not to say that the legal system's morality needs be convergent with that of its subjects, but it requires the legislators and judiciary to be aware of the moral impulses that propel individuals.

21

John Rawls

21.1 Rawls' theory of justice

The most complete argument for a theory of justice is possibly that provided by Rawls, who argues for his two principles of justice in *A Theory of Justice* (1972). His theory is of justice as fairness, accepting those principles that would result from an 'original position'. In this 'original position', the parties set out, subject to conditions considered reasonable and fair, to agree the principles by which their society should be organised. It is thus a social contract position, although the contract is a hypothetical one.

Method

Rawls accepts Hart's distinction between concepts of justice and conceptions of justice. He agrees that any theory of justice must deal with both of these. By a concept of justice Rawls means the role of its principles in assigning rights and duties and in defining the appropriate division of social advantages. This is essentially an objective phenomenon. By a conception of justice he means the interpretation of the role of these principles in particular situations. He acknowledges that this is much more subjective.

Rawls' theory in its own terms is designed to cope with situations where mutually disinterested persons put forward conflicting claims to a division of goods and services under conditions of moderate scarcity. His theory is of no application in conditions of total scarcity, for example, Mozambique.

His method is to test all the previous theories and from their defects to extrapolate a superior theory. While he states that his is the best (not surprisingly) he acknowledges the existence of other theories. His starting point is a rejection of utilitarianism.

Rejection of utilitarianism

The first half of the book is directed at a rejection of the earlier theories. We shall concentrate on his comments with regard to utilitarianism. Classical (total) utility is easily dismissed, since it supports an increase in population even if average utility would be thereby decreased. Average utility is more of a problem; Rawls has criticisms of it. Some of these are general, in terms of allowing sacrifice of persons for others: we have already discussed utility in this light. Some criticisms are specific to the original position (OP) and show why parties to the original position (POP) would not choose average utility. The veil of ignorance denies them knowledge of the probabilities of being at any particular economic/social level in the society. To choose average utility is to take a risk on whether or not one's position is a good one; it is the logical choice if the principle of 'insufficient reason' is followed, and the probabilities for each position are regarded as equal. Rawls says that the POP would reject such risk-taking and would, as we shall see below, adopt a 'maximin' strategy, that is, one that maximises good only so far as a minimum of good is maintained.

Rawls states that utilitarianism suffers from two major defects.

Utilitarianism ignores the distinctness of persons. The utilitarians assume that just as rationality requires making small sacrifices for larger gains, so it also requires a trade-off of the welfare of some against the welfare of others. This idea of trading off the welfare of some against the welfare of others conflicts with our moral intuition. In Simmonds' book *Law, Justice and Rights* the author uses the analogy of having a toothache and going to the dentist and suffering great pain for a few moments in order to have the toothache cured. This is a utilitarian calculation and it is submitted it is a legitimate utilitarian calculation because one is talking about sacrifices for oneself. One is undergoing the pain in order to gain the pleasure for oneself. As indicated in the previous Chapter the problem with utilitarianism is that it speaks of sacrificing the pain of others for the pleasure of oneself.

Furthermore utilitarianism merely regards people as mechanisms to measure pain and pleasure and as receptacles in which welfare is to be maximised with the greatest possible efficiency.

Utilitarianism seeks to define the right in terms of the good. Utilitarianism begins with an account of good and defines as right that which brings about the good. Herein is the anomaly, because utilitarianism takes account of unjustly obtained happiness. According to Rawls,

> 'Justice is the first virtue of social institutions in the same way as truth is the first virtue of thought. And like truth, justice is uncompromising …'

Characteristics of a theory of justice

Having rejected utilitarianism, Rawls goes on to consider the conditions which any theory of justice must satisfy before it is a useful theory of justice, as listed below.

1. The theory must be general.
2. The theory must be universal in application.
3. The theory is public in the sense that the population must know about it, there being no point in having a secret theory of justice.
4. The theory must impose an ordering on competing claims.
5. The theory must have finality.

Content

According to Rawls, justice is prior to happiness. It is only when we know that happiness is just that we regard happiness as having any positive value. Is Rawls then affording us a neutral conception of justice? Rawls believes that justice represents the framework within which different individuals have a fair opportunity to pursue their own goals and values. His theory seeks to meet the criticisms that he levelled against utilitarianism and attempts to employ the criteria of rational prudence in a manner consistent with both the distinctness of persons and the priority of the right over the good.

In his book, Rawls uses a complex mixture of two forms of reasoning: deductive and inductive; and of two bases for argument: the contract and reflective equilibrium. We will look at the two bases in turn.

Contract

As we have said, Rawls envisages an original position in which, in conditions of equality (discussed below), the parties agree to the principles to judge society. A contract model is used for two reasons:

Exposition. As a nice framework within which to explain the various conditions which can reasonably be imposed on such an agreement 'the conditions we accept as "fair"' and to show how the principles can be reached from these conditions.

Justification. The contract is not supposed to have been made *in fact*, but the device is used to show 'to emphasise' that the principles chosen are 'fair', ones we would accept given a fair starting point. Anybody at any time can enter the original position and if they did and were rational they would arrive at the same conclusion, the same principles of justice, that Rawls arrives at. For this reason these principles are said to be objective and would be binding on the members of the society. He has thus, it is submitted, overcome the difficulty with the earlier social contractarian theories that could not account for how the contract was binding on those not party thereto. The contract model is thus justificatory, in support of the principles and giving them some degree of legitimacy, as well as expository.

Having established the conditions of the contract, the argument is both deductive and inductive. Rawls attempts to show deductively that the principles would in fact be chosen by the parties, and why they would be chosen. They would value liberty very highly, as the first principle chosen shows: they would then adopt maximin as in the second principle. The two principles result from the conditions of the original position and that deduction.

The main argument, as Rawls calls it, is of another kind. It involves looking at a list of other conceptions of justice, particularly variants of utilitarianism, and seeing why the two principles should be preferred. This argument is not deductive. Nor is it a complete argument: there may be further conceptions of justice not yet disclosed which would win, and anyway Rawls' list is not complete re present conceptions.

In our discussion of Rawls, we concentrate on the deductive argument from the original position.

Reflective equilibrium

How are the conditions in the original position decided upon? Basically, they are conditions we accept as reasonable to impose on (people choosing our) standards of justice; for example the veil of ignorance encourages impartiality. There is, however, another important aspect, that of trying to reach reflective equilibrium.

Rawls outlines the derivation of principles, following a process whereby reasonable conditions are used, and the principles that result are discovered. These principles are tested against our considered judgments in particular situations. If they run counter we must either, after thought, reject our considered judgments, or alter the conditions of the original position. The results of those altered conditions emerge, are checked against our considered judgments, and so on. Eventually, by modifications at both ends, reflective equilibrium emerges between the principles emerging and our considered judgments. We have then reached the best version of the original position, which expresses reasonable conditions and yields principles matching our considered judgments. The starting point, the conditions of the original position, is tinkered with until correct principles emerge.

This argument is clearly not deductive. It also makes the original position itself redundant, if one is being harsh. Why not just put up possible principles and modify them with regard to our considered judgments, without referring to the contract idea at all? We must refer to the earlier points (contract as exposition and justification) to see why Rawls uses a contract even though it is not strictly a necessary part of the argument.

The original position

The parties

Rawls does tell us who the parties will be; they are various representatives, all of the same generation. We will not consider who they are in detail: it is pointless since one or all come to the same conclusion. The conditions are meant to be such that the two principles are the 'correct answer', to which everyone will agree.

What choice?

The parties are to choose general principles by which society should be organised, principles of justice for that society. It is interesting throughout to consider how various other possible theories are eliminated by Rawls. We discuss this below.

As pointed out above, the choice is made primarily by arguing against other conceptions, but also by a positive deductive argument for the various facets of the two principles.

What motivation?

The parties agree to principles that we term 'principles of justice', but it is important to note that from the point of view of the parties the principles are not principles of justice, but the terms of the contract/agreement made on the basis of self-interest in an original position. As we've seen, the conditions of the original position put everyone in the same situation, and 'self-interest' is therefore non-specific; but given the conditions of ignorance, etc, in the original position, the parties are trying to get the 'best deal' for themselves.

How can they do this, bearing in mind that they knew nothing about themselves? The answer is that they will try to get the highest possible total of primary basic goods. One thing that is removed from the parties is an awareness of their own, particular, plan of life, their conception of what is a 'good life', and what, specifically, they need to live it (time, money, power, responsibility, etc). They do, however, know general facts; one of these general facts is that to fulfil a plan of life everyone wants more and not less of the 'primary basic goods'. These goods 'rights, powers, health, etc' fall into two categories, social and natural; the parties will try to arrange liberties, opportunities, powers, self-respect, income and wealth. Everybody's plan of life will be enhanced by these.

The conditions

What conditions are the parties under?

1. Veil of ignorance: the most obviously necessary condition is one to ensure impartiality, that is, that one's own position and views shouldn't influence the choice. This is a traditional feature of justice theories; a similar device to Rawls' is the impartial spectator.

    Rawls' device is a veil of ignorance, behind which the parties are working. The parties do not know their place in society, their status or class, their fortune, level of natural ability, intelligence and so on. All are in a condition of equality: hence 'justice as fairness', and hence unanimity of result (important, according to Rawls, because it shows a genuine reconciliation of interests). The parties would be rational, free and have knowledge of the general situation but no specific knowledge of the particular. They would know that there is a society; they would know there is intelligence; they would know that there are sexes but they would not know where they as individuals would fit in society. Behind this veil of ignorance any knowledge of all those features which distinguish one person from another will be excluded. Rawls argues that it would be just to impose these conditions and that any decision reached in this condition would become binding. The veil would then be lifted to the extent of the proposition and there would be no possibility of repeal of the principle. Let us see how this works by an example at the end of this section.

2. Non-altruism: the parties must look to their own self-interest and not to the interests of others, or incoherence will result.

3. Non-envy: In any non-equal situation, the problem of envy will arise. If the parties thought they would be envious of anyone who did better than they did, strict equality would be the only choice, and that might mean that increases in wealth for all are missed. To avoid this, Rawls says the parties will not be envious: they will want the best possible result for themselves, but it will not be a factor against an arrangement that someone else might do better.

Great inequalities could be sanctioned in this way: but Rawls' two principles avoid this inequality. The first principle gives liberty to all equally. The second principle does allow the unequal distribution of primary social goods, but within strict limits. In any case, one of these goods being distributed is self-respect, and one's self-respect would clearly be harmed by any massive inequality resulting in a small share of the other goods.

The distribution system favoured by Rawls has been analysed by Shaw (1999) and Cohen (1995). The problem Shaw seeks to address concerns John Rawls' idea that justice demands that primary goods need to be initially distributed equally. To Shaw, and other critics of Rawls, there appears to be a conflict between this idea and the reasons provided for the situation where primary goods are unequally distributed. Rawls argues that a distributional system based on an individual passing an initiative test is unjust because the natural talents of the individual would manifestly produce unequal outcomes. These outcomes cannot be germane to the weal of egalitarianism. To Rawls, natural talents of the individual reflect unequal distribution because talents are arbitrary from the moral point of view. Therefore, both the talented and the untalented should receive equal social primary goods in the initial distribution. The point of contradiction to Cohen and other critics of Rawls is that Rawls' claim that although this initial hypothetical arrangement is the benchmark for judging improvements, if certain inequalities of wealth and organisational powers would make everyone better off than in this hypothetical starting situation, then they accord with the general conception. This point has been emphasised by critics of Rawls who quote this passage to support their contention that Rawls also believes that it is irrational to be dogmatic about equal distribution of primary goods if there is the possibility of bettering the well-being of everyone – both the talented and the untalented – to enjoy more rewards. Cohen interprets the view of Rawls as a Pareto argument for inequality, the idea that a movement from a position of equality to inequality is justified as long as it is beneficial to everyone.

He attributes this to Rawls, and believes that the value judgment appropriate to this argument is the weak Pareto principle, which suggests that if a change is beneficial for everyone then it is a change for the better. The stronger version of the Pareto principle says that if a change is beneficial for at least one person and worse for nobody then it is a change for the better.

The just savings principle/family feeling: the parties are all from the same generation. What is to stop them from deciding as follows: we cannot alter how previous generations have acted? Motivated by self-interest (non-altruism) we care not for future generations. Therefore we will use up as many of the resources of the earth as we wish, and we will not, individually or as a society, be concerned about what investment we make for future generations.

Logical, yes; just, no. To avoid this conclusion, Rawls added a condition that the parties were concerned about their families including other generations thereof. (This, of course, results in the just savings principle in the second principle.)

Risk aversion: the parties will choose the least worst alternative and not the best possible alternative because of their self-interest that dictates that they avert risk of a worst possible scenario.

Let us look at a worked example of how this process is meant to occur. We have entered the original position. The proposition that is put to us is that there should be accorded more rights to men than to women, in other words that there should be discrimination against women in the allocation of benefits in the society. This is one of the questions a society has to address. This is the question. The parties do not know whether they are men or women. Acting in their own self interest (non-altruism) and seeking to avert risk, the parties will apply the maximin principle seeking to maximise benefit while minimising burden. Let us say that the parties opt for sex discrimination; the consequences are as follows.

1. If they are men then that will be the best possible scenario.
2. If they are women then that will be the worst possible scenario.
3. If the the parties act according to the maximin principle they will choose that there should be no sex discrimination in which case whether they are men or women will make no difference. True, they will lose the chance to have all the benefits that accrue to men if there was discrimination, but they will also avert the risk of all the loss were they women.

Thus it seems that the use of this original position together with the conditions stipulated by Rawls will lead to a denial of all arbitrary discrimination in accordance with established liberal thought.

The principles of justice
From the original position, we arrive at the two principles of justice.

1. Each person is to have an equal right to the most extensive total system of equal basic liberties compatible with a similar system for all.

2. Social and economic inequalities are to be arranged so that they are both:
   a) to the greatest benefit of the least advantaged consistent with the just savings principle, and
   b) attached to offices open to all in conditions of fair equality of opportunity.

Generally, the first principle is prior to the second.

We will look at the two principles in three stages. First, the deductive argument for the two principles. Second, the 'main argument', rejecting other conceptions. Third, the argument for priority of the first principle over the second, the priority of liberty.

Deductive argument for the two principles

Assumptions. The conditions of the original position are above, but we should mention at this stage that there are two more assumptions, which shape the form and content of the two principles. The first of these is *social co-operation*. No one can succeed in the plan of life without society, therefore everyone will be willing to enter into social co-operation. Talents are pooled to the benefit of all; the major question is how the results of that pooling should be distributed: what distribution should be decided upon?

It is this assumption that knocks out natural rights theories like those of Nozick's. Is social co-operation a successful argument against the millionaire who argues against re-distributed taxation? Rawls would say that without society that million would not be made or increased. Is the millionaire right to say that he gives more (jobs, investment) than he takes out?

The second assumption is *risk aversion*. The veil of ignorance hides from the parties both the position they will occupy in society and the probabilities relating to the various positions. If there are five million poor people out of 500 million, the odds are one in a hundred that any given individual will be a poor person: but the parties don't know this. In this situation the logicians would suggest the acceptance of an 'insufficient reason' standpoint whereby all possibilities are taken as equally likely. Rawls rejects this, and says the parties would instead choose a maximin position, arranging society so that the position of the least well off class is maximised. The parties are then risk averse: rather than chancing a possibly very poor position by going for an arrangement which produces very good results at the top end, they will choose that situation where the bottom end is as high as possible.

Do you think the parties would be risk averse? Might they decide to gamble?

The argument

The parties set out, then, to derive principles upon which they can agree to arrange society. They wish these principles to result in the best possible arrangement of primary social goods, and they will decide to adopt a maximin outlook.

The starting point is equality: the parties would start by thinking what the principle to be chosen should be, simply that everyone gets equal shares of everything. They would then realise that some inequalities will benefit everyone: incentives to high-flyers, for example, would motivate them to achieve a greater degree of productive enterprise, and thus to produce more for everyone. The yardstick for this is a maximin calculation, looking to see whether the inequalities result in the best possible result for the least advantaged.

This calculation is made for several different areas, as follows.

Liberty. The claims of liberty have, for Rawls, an absolute priority after a certain level of economic well-being has been reached. This priority is a major keynote of the theory. For this reason it is treated separately below.

Above the level of priority, inequality is not allowed: trade-offs for increased economic well-being would not be accepted. Thus, the first principle, the right to the most extensive total system of equal basic liberties compatible with a similar system for all. This is reflected for example in Article 17 of the European Convention on Human Rights and Fundamental Freedoms 1950, which provides that the rights granted in the Convention cannot be used to deprive others of the rights in the convention. This has been the topic of case law, see *The Federal German Communist Party* case (1957) concerning the ban on that party whose objects were held to be incompatible with the freedom of association for others, and more recently the case of *Glimmerveen and Hagenbeck* v *The Netherlands* which concerned the outlawing of the expression of racist sentiments being held to be consistent with the freedom of speech.

It should be noted that Rawls is not here referring to the liberty of the individual but rather to certain liberties.

Fair equality of opportunity. Economic and social advantages are attached to offices and positions open to all in fair equality and opportunity. This is despite the fact that fair equality and opportunity might be contrary to the difference principle (see 'the difference principle' below, the maximin position on social and economic advantages). In some circumstances, one can envisage a 'closed shop' appointment system which might work better than an open system. Rawls argues that those who lost out in a system because fair equality of opportunity was not in operation would feel unjustly treated, and lose self-respect. (In fact that argument seems inconsistent with some other things Rawls says: such feelings and considerations of desert wouldn't convince the self-interested parties. Also, the choice of fair equality of opportunity over available alternatives is not convincing, since criticisms against those alternatives, particularly that they are morally arbitrary, also apply.)

Just savings principle. We have seen the original position presumption that leads to this: the parties are taken to have inter-generational family ties. They are therefore concerned to save for future generations. This is the clearest example of a condition of the original position introduced, as a result of our considered judgments, in the reflective equilibrium process.

The difference principle. With the qualifications in the previous two paragraphs the parties will accept such economic and social inequalities as benefit the position of the least advantaged. In contrast with average utility, the least well-off do not sacrifice themselves for the better off; rather, they are put in the best position available. The difference principle, of course, follows logically from the adoption of a maximin strategy.

The main argument: why prefer the two principles to other possibilities?

It would here be necessary to outline briefly his reasons for rejecting various other conceptions, only some of which appear in his list. *Egoism,* as we have seen, is knocked out by formal constraints (requiring a choice of general principles).

Non-tolerant conceptions are knocked out by the veil of ignorance, because it hides the person's own conception of the good. By a non-tolerant conception, I mean one that would not be prepared to allow (certain) other conceptions to be pursued. For example, an extreme religious fanatic might have a conception of the good life that included a prohibition of other forms of worship: his conception of justice would include this provision. In the original position no one would choose that conception of justice, because there is a chance that they would be the holders of a prohibited religious viewpoint, an intolerable situation.

Non-tolerance will sometimes be linked with *perfectionism,* a conception under which society is organised in such a way that it furthers a particular ideal state of affairs. An extreme religious viewpoint might again provide an example. Such a conception would not be chosen, and this is another argument against non-tolerant conceptions being chosen, because the parties (not knowing their own conception of the good) have no reason to choose principles according with only one theory of the good. Instead they will choose one which allows freedom to differing conceptions in order that they, whatever their own 'good life' turns out to be, can pursue their own chosen course.

Rawls explicitly places *intuitionism* as a last resort. If any acceptable principles can be found by which society's affairs can be arranged, the intuitionist's suggestion that at each point the decision maker should follow his discretion can be rejected. Only if no such principles exist does the intuitionist win.

On the list of other conceptions, there are some *mixed conceptions.* These include the first principle with a different second principle. A particularly important alternative second principle is average utility plus a social minimum condition. Such a condition could resolve the problems average utility has in relation to sacrificing the least well-off. The two principles are to be preferred to this mixed conception, because of the difficulties of deciding the social minimum and the fact that it could be the two principles in disguise! The two principles would match its results, and should be chosen for their greater clarity and precision.

Apart from these various points aimed at showing why the parties would choose the two principles and not any other possibility, Rawls gives at this stage the considerations working in favour of the two principles. The first is that they do not involve sacrificing oneself for the sake of others, and therefore there are not the strains of commitment imposed by other theories. This is true of the least well-off, who are at their best possible position, unless of course they are envious (perhaps they will prefer to be poorer but equal?). High-level producers might not be so enthusiastic about a system which takes away their hard-earned profit to improve the position of the less well-off. Isn't the high-flyer being sacrificed for the bottom rung?

Second, the two principles have the advantage of psychological stability. Since no one is being sacrificed for others, and everyone's self-respect is enhanced, the two principles will receive public recognition and lead to a sense of justice. This 'advantage' is akin to the first; it is subject to the same sort of criticism.

The priority of liberty
The first principle is generally 'lexicographically prior' to the second; this means that its demands must be met in full before the considerations of the second principle are taken into account. (The exception is when the society has not yet reached a sufficiently developed economic position: this point is not explicitly decided by Rawls.) Liberty can only be sacrificed for liberty's sake in two circumstances.

1. Less extensive liberty must strengthen the whole system shared by all; an example is the rules of order in a debate.
2. Unequal liberty must be acceptable to those with less. For example, equality of opportunity might be sacrificed to lead to greater political liberty.

Rawls is not discussing all possible liberties, but a set list, political liberty, freedom of thought and conscience, freedom of the person and the right to hold personal property, and freedom from arbitrary arrest and seizure. The parties would not allow these freedoms to be limited for the sake of an improvement in economic or social well-being. Why not?

Rawls principally used the example of freedom of religious belief. Such belief is so central and important that the parties would realise that its sacrifice would be intolerable, and therefore is prohibited. This can be seen as a maximin point, that a poor economic situation and freedom to worship as you choose is always better than no freedom of worship.

A further argument utilises the fact that a certain level of well-being is required before the priority is absolute. Once that point is reached, survival and economic goods become less important, and cultural and intellectual pursuits (and therefore the freedom to pursue them) become increasingly so. Remember here the Aristotelian principle, that people desire to engage in more complex activities if possible.

Does Rawls establish the priority of liberty? First, he does not discuss sexual freedom (although at one point he says he has proved his point re 'religious and sexual freedom'); nor is it totally clear why the liberties on his list are chosen. Second, he only argues from religious freedom. It seems intuitively possible to distinguish between this and the other liberties. Religious liberty is central to the existence of most people (even if it is the liberty to have no religion) in a unique and most important way; the same is not true of the other liberties. Is owning a house as important as faith? And haven't people often given up their personal freedom for religion? The conclusion here might be that while priority is logical for parties to choose religious liberty, it is not necessarily so with the other liberties.

For these other liberties, the absolute priority of liberty over economic and social development is hard to accept, even given the fact that civilisation must have reached a level where economic needs are not desperate. Assume that by sacrificing five years' political liberty to a totalitarian regime, massive increases in wealth would result, including a great boost to the maximin position. Is it logical for the POP to rule out choosing this sacrifice? Wouldn't the resultant economic gain in fact greatly enhance the value of the restored liberty? In fact, Rawls does not find a proper place for the idea of the value of liberty: but what is the use of freedom of thought if the economic necessity to work proves too exhausting to allow it? And what use the freedom to attend plays/concerts if they cannot be afforded?

Finally, giving liberty this priority seems to me to be allowing into the theory Rawls' own conception of the good life. This point will be discussed more fully in the next section.

21.2 Evaluation of Rawls

There are many criticisms of Rawls' work. I shall consider some of the main ones that appear in the literature.

One criticism is that, through many avenues, his own conception of a proper plan for life, the proper way for someone to live, encroaches on the theory. The parties are denied knowledge of their own plan of life, their own conception of the good: as a result, society will inevitably be tolerant, even though the majority of people within it are in fact non-tolerant. The parties are motivated by a desire to maximise achievement on an Aristotelian scale of complexity, but it is not true for all. A monk, for example, would want no income, wealth, etc; many of the primary social goods would be useless for him. Rawls' original position fits only a certain category of person.

Further, an element is missed in the original position. The parties would logically be interested not only in how many primary social goods they got, but also how many everybody else got. This is not envy but a directly personal concern relating to quality of life. For example, imagine the parties deciding whether they should have cars. They would put into account not only the convenience of an individual having a car, but also the inconvenience and discomfort of living in a society where everyone had a car. This consideration is not mentioned by Rawls: surely it would affect the parties' determination to achieve maximum primary social good level?

Rawls is perceived as adjusting the conditions in the original position to ensure the principles that he wants are arrived at; behind a supposed veil of objectivity his subjectivity emerges. This is regarded as an intellectual sleight of hand trick, as he started from the two principles and their arrangement in lexicographical order and worked backwards. Simmonds takes a less cynical approach to this. He maintains that perhaps Rawls is 'attempting to elucidate the deep philosophical presuppositions that underlie his two principles'.

One of the most important criticisms of Rawls comes from one of his former students, Robert Nozick. Much of the following Chapter is devoted to an elucidation of Nozick's theory of justice, so it will suffice, I imagine, to demonstrate here some of his main criticisms of Rawls which will be further elaborated upon in the following Chapter. Nozick maintains that if one is interested in justice then one cannot deny the importance of Rawls' theory. One has either to work with Rawls' theory or explain why one is not working with it.

Nozick continues by attacking the notion of what he calls 'the patterned distribution of social good'. Any patterned distribution would really require us to consider the following problems.

1. If one is prepared to allow for the coercive redistribution of wealth then why not also allow the coercive redistribution of bodily organs? For example, if one has two healthy kidneys then why not give one healthy one to a person without any healthy kidneys, the point being that to regard ability or organs as common resources appears to give persons rights in other persons, so that the least advantaged have got a right to the best advantaged, raising the standard of living of the least advantaged. The example of taxation can be cited here. Where one person has to pay tax so that the money can be redistributed to the least advantaged then this is in effect a form of forced labour or slavery, because that proportion of one's time is spent working solely for others and not for oneself. It should be noted that Nozick is not talking about the need to raise tax in order to fund roads, hospitals or missiles, but about the tax that is used to pay for the poor such as supplementary benefits.

2. Nozick also rejects the difference principle as being unjust. He cites examples. Let us assume that everyone starts off with the same, an equal distribution. People will then freely enter into contracts and be prepared to pay in order to get what they want. In his Wilt Chamberlain example, to which we will return later, Nozick shows that the spectators will become materially worse off while the player will become much better off. According to Rawls, that distribution is unjust because the least well off become poorer. Of course, this concentrates on the financial position of the parties and that may not be the entire picture. As we shall see, Nozick replaces this patterned distribution with his 'historical entitlement theory'.

Hart questions whether the parties would opt for the two principles and necessarily prefer liberty to equality of opportunity. Why not prefer equality to liberty? According to Hart, Rawls also underestimated the difficulty of balancing conflicting interests. It is the ideal that underlies his treatment of the allocation of resources. Rawls is interpreted by Hart as saying that a public-spirited person imbued with the notion of service to the community will decide never to give up any political freedom for material gain. Essentially this is because Rawls does not have any concept of the state in his theory. He pays too little attention to the institutional arrangements by means of which the distribution is to be carried out, in that those who in effect carry out the distribution will be the most powerful group in society. Can we really expect those people to act in a public-spirited way?

21.3 Political liberalism

Rawls (1993) produced a series of essays in which he replied to some of his critics and modified his earlier position. He makes it clear that his intention was to produce a practical rather than a metaphysical product. That his ideas might assist those who have different viewpoints to co-exist. Riddall (1999) provides a readable account of these ideas:

> 'One approach, Rawls says, might be "to look at the various comprehensive doctrines actually found in society and specify an index of [primary] goods so as to be near to those doctrines' center of gravity, so to speak; that is to find a kind of average of what those who affirmed those views would need by way of ... protection ... [ie, of their own values]." This approach Rawls rejects. Instead he proposes that what a "political conception of justice" (ie, "justice as fairness" wearing its political hat) requires is an "overlapping consensus" between the divergent elements within a pluralistic society: a sufficient area of common ground on which to establish a political structure that has room for the multifarious views that a pluralistic society contains.
>
> "An overlapping consensus ... is not," he explains, "merely a consensus on accepting certain authorities, or on complying with certain institutional arrangements, founded on convergence of self or group interests. All those who affirm the political conception start from within their own comprehensive view and draw on the religious, philosophical, and moral grounds it provides. The fact that people affirm the same political conception on those grounds does not make their affirming it any less religious, philosophical, or moral, as the case may be, since the grounds sincerely held determine the nature of their affirmation." It follows that "those who affirm the various views supporting the political conception will not withdraw their support of it should the relative strength of their view in society increase and eventually become dominant ..." Thus "... the political conception will still be supported regardless of shifts in the distribution of political power. Each view supports the political conception for its own sake, or on its own merits." ' (at p215)

22

Robert Nozick

22.1 *Anarchy, State and Utopia*

Robert Nozick's *Anarchy, State and Utopia* is an important book, containing a new natural rights theory as well as criticisms of utilitarianism and Rawls, a plea for vegetarianism, and much more. It is recommended as a stimulating 'read' on justice and some related topics, though only if you have time and the inclination.

In brief, Nozick's theory is as follows. Man has certain natural rights, including the right to acquire property. These rights must not be violated by anyone, without the consent of the right-holder. They act as moral 'side-constraints' on action. To be justified, a state must be such that it would arise from a no-state position (the state of nature) without infringing the rights of anyone who did not consent; only a minimal state offering protection against violence, theft and breach of agreement would emerge in this way. Any further state is not justified; particularly, a state redistributing wealth is not justified, and taxation to bring this about is the equivalent of forced labour. The only legitimate way of coming to hold property is by just acquisition, just transfer, or rectification of a past injustice.

Nozick extols the virtues of eighteenth century individualism and nineteenth century *laissez-faire* capitalism. It has certainly represented a profound shock to legal theory. The book is a provocative essay and one which in my view has had a very considerable impact on political reality. After reading Nozick one may ascertain where many of the ideas of Thatcherism have derived their origin, although they have undergone some modification in the process. Nozick's views, to the extent that classification is at all legitimate, may be referred to as libertarian. He questions whether liberty and equality are compatible and concludes that they are not. His central thesis rests on the proposition that the individual is inviolable. This point is crucial to an understanding of his theory.

Let us look at his theory in more detail. In his critique of Rawls, as we have seen, Nozick rejects any 'patterned' conception of justice. A patterned conception is one that views justice as a matter of the pattern of distribution of benefits and burdens that is achieved, for example, the Marxist idea of distribution according to need. As stated he prefers his 'historical entitlement theory', the content of which it would be appropriate to outline as follows.

Natural rights

Rather than examine the pattern of distribution, Nozick seeks to concentrate on the question of how the distribution came about in the first place. If that distribution is brought about entirely as a result of freely entered into transactions then it is just. He put it thus, 'If each person's holdings are just then the total set of holdings is just'.

The individual has certain natural rights, including the freedom from violence against his person, the freedom to hold property, and the freedom to enforce his other rights. Concentrating on the right to hold individual property, a person can legitimately acquire property in three ways.

By just initial acquisition
This details the circumstances under which a person may acquire ownership of formerly unowned resources. This right of appropriation follows Locke. Locke had the proviso that 'as much and as good be left for others'. Nozick has a more limited proviso, merely that the remainder be left for others, and not necessarily as much/as good. In any case, MacPherson says that the Lockean proviso ceases to be relevant once money is invented, since there is always some of that property available.

By legitimate transfer
This details the means by which ownership of resources may be transferred from one to another. If I choose to give you some of my property, or we agree to swap bits of our property, then you receive my property legitimately by transfer.

By rectification of past injustice
This details the action to be taken to rectify a distribution which is unjust in terms of the first two principles. If I acquire property in an unjust manner, it can be taken from me and restored to its proper owner. This principle in fact justifies a less limited state, in some circumstances, to remedy a series of past injustices. (Could it justify our present Welfare State?)

These rights cannot be violated without a person's consent; this is his meaning of the distinctness of persons. A person's separateness and individuality must be respected; he must not be treated as a means to an end. Each person has exclusive rights in himself and no rights in others. What is important is that in the pursuit of our own aims we do not violate the rights of others. As we have seen and stated above, Nozick's theory originated in a critical evaluation of Rawls. He has criticised Rawls on the grounds that individual abilities are not common assets to be exploited for the benefit of the least advantaged. For this reason, Nozick rejects goal-based principles of justice. These are principles which judge a society by reference to whether or not it matches a particular goal, a particular end-state. Such principles will require the right of the individual to be sacrificed for the goal or desired end-state, the person being treated as a means to that end. The Wilt Chamberlain example, below, is a graphic illustration of Nozick's point.

Rather than such an end-state, goal-based principle, Nozick insists that a 'historical entitlement' principle be chosen. This means that a situation is judged not with reference to whether or not it matches a given end-state, but rather with reference to whether or not it came about justly, with no infringement of anyone's rights (hence the three just processes by which property may be acquired).

Under this entitlement principle, people's rights are respected: they become moral 'side-constraints' which forbid decisions and actions which violate them. Natural rights can only be infringed with the consent of the right-holder. For example, a road can only be built across someone's property if he consents to it: if he does not, his rights may not be infringed however much some particular goal (average utility, the best position for the least advantage, or whatever) may be enhanced by such an infringement.

These rights are the right to liberty and the right to property. Their inter-relationship is interesting. The right to liberty is defined by reference to the right to property and the right to property is the result of the exercise of rights in one's own labour. The right to property is then an expression of the right to liberty. Nozick believes that private property increases freedom, an idea that has considerably influenced Conservative politicians.

The idea of Nozick that, when one mixes one's labour with an object that is not owned, one acquires a right to that object which can then be transferred, does not address the question as to whether the exercise of one's labour gives a right to the whole value of the object with which it is mixed. What of natural talents and abilities? These are not possessed as a result of any labour but as a result of natural and, therefore, morally arbitrary distributions.

The minimal state

Nozick envisages a state of nature, and asks whether any state would emerge without harming people's rights. In fact, a state will emerge, through an 'invisible hand' process, that is, one which occurs without anyone intending it or aiming for it by morally permissible means and without anyone's rights (in Nozick's sense of the word) being violated. In brief, the process is as follows.

1. To protect themselves, people form protective agencies, pooling their protective resources and leaving themselves free from fear of attack.
2. In each region, one protective agency becomes dominant, but there are still independents.

3. The dominant agency will prohibit independents from enforcing their own rights, since they will distrust the independents' procedure for determining violations. This prohibition involves infringing the independents' rights (to enforce their other rights), and demanding compensation; this compensation is 'paid' by protecting the would-be independents as well.

The dominant agency develops into a 'night-watchman' state, carrying out a minimal range of duties, protection from theft, violence, fraud, and breach of contract. This state claims a monopoly of force. If the state engaged in a patterned distribution then it would be exercising excessive powers as it would entail constant interference with liberty. Nozick does, however, recognise the need for some state, otherwise there would be anarchy. Hence his minimal state can be seen as the way to Utopia where individuals are inviolate.

Distributive justice

Any state other than the minimal state is rejected by Nozick. He would clearly see the present UK set-up as unjust. Through social security and other aspects of the Welfare State, money is taken through taxation from the wealthier people, and given to the poor. This taxation is forced labour in disguise: such proportion of one's working time as is reflected in the national insurance and income tax contributions that are used for redistribution to the least advantaged is spent working for others. The redistribution involves violating rights to property. Unless it involves setting right past injustices (many would argue that it does) it does not fit into any of the three methods of just acquisition. Thus redistribution where resources are justly obtained would not rectify an inequality but would rather produce one.

Nozick rejects the difference principle. Social co-operation is a good thing, since it probably produces better results for everyone, but especially for the weak and poor who would have nothing if they had to act on their own. The difference principle, that economic and social disadvantages should be so arranged as to benefit the least well-off, gives all the benefit of their co-operation to the poor, which is asymmetrical and unjust. (This does not mean that Rawls' argument from the OP is wrong: it might be rational for the POP to choose it.)

The difference between Rawls and Nozick is in their starting points: Rawls starts from a standpoint of equality, and asks for reasons why we should accept inequality; Nozick starts from the idea of rights, with a consequence that a man owns the property he has worked for and created. For Rawls, the rich man must show why his wealth should not be taken; for Nozick, it cannot be taken without his consent. Wealth is created by individuals and they that create it have rights over it. Hence Nozick maintains that one is not entitled to regard society's total wealth as a cake to be divided up.

That this question of distributive justice is linked with that of goal-based versus entitlement principles is illustrated by Nozick's Wilt Chamberlain (a basketball star) example. Assume, says Nozick, that at the start of a season your favourite end–state principle is satisfied in society: let us say, the difference principle. Chamberlain fixes a contract, giving him $1 of every spectator's entrance fee. At the end of the year, the million spectators who have watched him are each $1 worse off, and Wilt is a millionaire. Each $1 has been willingly given, a just transfer. Why should Wilt have to pay back some of his million to satisfy the difference principle again? Where is the justification for redistribution?

22.2 Libertarianism: Nozick's theory of rights

The opening argument of Nozick's *Anarchy, State and Utopia* consists of the following assertion:

> 'Individuals have rights, and there are things no person or group may do to them [without violating these rights] ... Our main conclusions about the state are that a minimal state limited only to the narrow functions of protection against force, theft, fraud, enforcement of contracts, and so on, is justified; that any more extensive state will violate persons rights ... and is unjustified.'

Consequently, the state may not coerce individuals to help others and may not protect an individual from himself. Such a view would seem to be diametrically opposed to that of the utilitarian. Rawls, who criticises utilitarianism because it does not give sufficient priority to rights, is criticised by Nozick for advocating that a priority in state considerations should be the minimisation of violations of rights. This is because, on the basis of Rawls' argument, an innocent man might still be punished in order that a rampage of vengeful citizens might be prevented from violating the rights of still more people. Nozick views the trading off of the rights of the individual in the interests of the rights of the many as a utilitarianism of rights.

Nozick's position is immovable. People cannot be treated as anything other than ends in themselves. The state and law must not violate the individual's rights, even if it is to avert the violation of the rights of others. The side-constraint of all state action is that the state's duty is primarily not to violate an individual's rights. Nozick's argument is that the individual cannot be forced into sacrificing his rights for the community, even if as a free agent he might sacrifice himself for another.

However, Nozick's consideration of utilitarianism is on the basis of the automatic assumption that it is not worth considering. Thus, his critique occasionally becomes absurd in the extreme. He says, for example, that maximising the average utility allows a person to kill everyone else if that would make him ecstatic, and so happier than average.

His attention to social, rather than individual concerns, is evasive:

> 'The question of whether [never violating the individuals rights is an] ... absolute, or whether [this principle] ... may be violated in order to avoid catastrophic moral horror, and if the latter, what the resulting structure might look like, is one I hope largely to avoid.'

Nozick's rejection of utilitarianism is thus on the basis that individuals have rights. What are these rights and how do they come about? The answer is that people (1) have a right to liberty, (2) have a right to the fruits of their labour. One person cannot have rights in another person. The function of the state is to protect the legitimate distribution of assets.

Liberty

Nozick cites Locke's idealist state of nature, where every individual acts as he sees fit, without leave or dependency upon the will of another man. Such individuals subscribe to the law of nature that no one ought to harm another in his life, health, liberty, or possessions. The function of the minimal state is thus to guarantee the laws of nature with minimal interference with individual liberty.

Nozick does not explain why people have the right to liberty. If a person is free to do as he chooses, then the question of rights has no real meaning. In a social situation, a claim of right is to assert that:

1. what the right-holder claims is his right;
2. it is to be preferred against the counter-claim of another.

Nozick is therefore asserting that the right of freedom is a right that prefers the individual's claim of freedom of action, against another's claim that he might restrict that freedom. Yet is this not to contradict the freedom of another to act? If my freedom to act in the way I choose is to be preferred to your freedom to choose to restrict my action, do I not therefore assert that there are limitations on your freedom of action? This would contradict the assertion that all people have the right to act freely. This Nozick explicitly accepts by postulating that natural law states that we cannot use our freedom of action to endanger the life, health or possessions of another. The law is justified to compel obedience to these conditions.

This would seem to solve the problem. However, if I have access to food and you do not, yet I refuse it to you, do I not do as much harm as I would have done had I stolen your food from you? Freedom in a social context depends on the absence of monopoly. We have seen that Nozick criticises the utilitarian on the grounds that he would allow one man to kill everyone for the maximisation of his pleasure. Yet Nozick would allow by default one man, in the name of his individual liberty, to allow all others to starve!

The individual in society, or even in competition, is dependent on either the compromise or weakness of his fellows for his own survival. Since Nozick rules out physical violence as in violation of the rights of others, man is thrown back on the distributive justice of his fellow men.

A further point to note is that a man may become comparatively freer in his opportunities, if he sacrifices his complete autonomy and co-operates with another. In modern society, the benefit of communal action is manifest. One man cannot in his lifetime build all the things that he consumes or uses in his everyday life.

However, neither can I enter into a voluntary transaction with all those from whom I might benefit. Nozick seems to deny non-consensual, co-operative action. If the value of a man's contribution to a particular goal is greater than the benefit that he, as an individual, gets from the common pursuit of that goal, it would be wrong to force him to engage in it. Yet people are unable to gauge the benefits that they get from society in any direct way, and are not always the judge of their own best interests. Nozick simply views people's interests at their own concern. However, in a society people's interests are interdependent. My well-being is not only my own concern, but my family's, my employer's, and those people I am philanthropic towards. I am an individual only because I have a discrete and valuable place in society.

Property

The cry of anarchists such as Proudhon and Kropotkin is that 'property is theft!'. The basis of this is that, by asserting that I may have a sole right to an object or commodity, I may be denying another what he needs. The true libertarian must presuppose that no man has the right to deny another his liberty. A fundamental precondition to liberty is that a person must be alive. Thus, a precondition of liberty is the satisfaction of the basic needs of life. Basic commodities and means of survival must be distributed not according to the means of acquisition, as Nozick suggests, but on the basis of the needs. Most libertarians therefore assert that the right to liberty determines that the individual has the right to the necessities of life, by which he may obtain liberty. Nozick believes that the free market naturally will tend to the satisfaction of needs. He presupposes that minimum needs are satisfied, so that law should not interfere to ensure it.

Conclusion

Lukes says that Nozick fails to appreciate the nature of the individual as a social being. In terms of supplying us an answer to the problem of the nature of the legislators' duty, his theory simply endorses the rights of those who have already got rights. He endorses the inequalities in society on the weak assertion that to interfere would be to damage the rights of some in order to benefit those that have no rights.

22.3 Evaluation of Nozick's theory

Nozick's theory is interesting and a strong challenge to Rawls. It is not, however, without its defects. What becomes clear from an evaluation of this topic is the close relationship that the authors bear to current political agenda. A major evaluative point in favour of Nozick is that many of his ideas are now the topic of intense political debate both in this country and in the United States. In that light perhaps we ought now to examine some of the main criticisms that have been made of his theory.

He takes rights as his starting point. The rights he takes are of uncertain pedigree: how are they derived, where do they come from? There is a strong body of opinion that denies the possibility of any objective rights, such as those Nozick must contemplate. He sees his rights as inherent, as natural. The idea of such rights should be established (if it can be), not assumed. Further, the choice of rights to assume is a value-laden process; why not include a right to welfare and help from others? Or, to put it another way, why limit the 'moral landscape' to just rights? Why not have duties as well, to assist others in need?

The argument from rights to a minimal state is not without its problems either. Particularly, at one stage, the dominant protective association prohibits the use by independents of their own rights-enforcement procedures, at least unless those procedures have been vetted and found acceptable. Surely this involves a strong violation of the independent's rights to protect himself, which is not properly compensated for even by membership of the dominant agency? And wouldn't this compensation be free, resulting in only some people paying for the services?

In any case, it is not clear that the dominant agency idea would work out as Nozick thinks. Might not the strong people in a community think that the only opposition or problem will be from other strong people, and therefore form an organisation with them? It would be cheaper for all concerned if weak people were not allowed to join, and prohibiting their own enforcement would not be necessary, because it is not to be feared (since they are weak). Doesn't the state idea therefore include some element of compassion for the weak?

On the other hand, assuming that we get to a minimal state, does not practical sense require even the right and strong to accept a greater state? Assume you are rich and strong now, and tomorrow you are robbed, or lose all your money on a business deal, or are knocked down and paralysed. And don't most people grow old and infirm? Isn't it practically minded to accept and agree to pay for a state which will provide a safety net in case such things happen to you, or your family and friends?

Lukes argues that Nozick has an unreal conception of the relationship between the individual and the society, to the extent that he has excluded what for Lukes is the ever growing role of the state. Lukes further maintains that the central flaw in Nozick's arguments is 'the abstractness of the individualism they presuppose'. Lukes maintains that it is not possible to divorce an individual from his society.

Hart, not surprisingly, takes issue with Nozick's theory. He maintains that Nozick's assault on utilitarianism is paradoxical as it shows that he is unwilling to disturb the exisiting pattern of distribution. Hart further takes exception to Nozick's likening of taxation for the sake of redistribution of wealth to slavery, which is so rooted in Nozick's belief in the absolutely inviolable character of property rights. Hart maintains that one is talking of two different types of burden. Man is free to decide whether to work, what work and how much work to do; a slave is not so free. Hart would speculate whether rights which are derived from human interests and needs could outweigh property rights.

Lloyd and Freeman are unsure as to how Nozick's minimal state would emerge from the state of nature without infringing individual rights. They say that Nozick does not adequately explain this. Furthermore they maintain that Nozick leaves many questions unanswered and makes a number of assumptions which do not stand up to examination, not least the point of where do people get their rights from? Is this historical, some initial act of appropriation which then confers unlimited rights of use and disposition?

Nozick's rejection of welfare rights neglects the interests of the weak. Nozick's view of the assistance to the weak is privatisation of philanthropy. The matter is essentially one of private charity, a view echoed by one British government minister following the recent cutting of the upper tax levels, when it was suggested that some of the money handed back to those taxpayers ought to go to private charity. Human dignity and the receipt of charity are not clearly compatible.

23

Ronald Dworkin's Theory of Justice

23.1 Liberalism's foundations

In Chapter 7 we have considered in detail Dworkin's scheme of equality of resources. We have seen that it is guided by the important foundational – humanistic – principle that people should be treated as equals. But we have also seen that there is a need for a fully worked out division between the public and private responsibilities of people. We have seen that distinction worked out by Dworkin in a number of different contexts. It is inherent in his rejection, in the ideal world, of utilitarianism, even of the egalitarian sort. Dworkin develops the idea of the division in an attack on the contractarian account of liberalism in his Tanner lectures of 1990. But it is necessary, first, to understand what is the substance of recent debates on the justifications for liberalism, and second, to understand the nature and significance of the contractarian approach.

Dworkin's own liberal theory is best understood by considering his distinction between what he calls 'discontinuity' and 'continuity' theories of the foundations of liberalism. The contractarian theory just described is a discontinuity theory. The discontinuity is between a person's personal ethics – what Dworkin describes as 'first person' ethics, or 'well-being' – and 'third person' ethics, or 'morality'. Thus, contractarian theories allow for first person ethics to provide the justification for the existence of the contract, and for third person ethics to be justified only by reference to the contract itself.

Dworkin says that the paradigm for a social contract theory is an ordinary commercial contract. There are different personal reasons why we might enter into such a contract but the rights and duties are established not by those reasons but by the contract itself. It means that the contract acts as an artificial social construct from which rights and duties flow.

Dworkin cites Rawls as having the most sophisticated version of the continuity strategy. Rawls' view is that the basis of liberalism must be sought in an 'overlapping consensus' among different comprehensive ethical views. In other words, at the basis of liberal political principles could only be a shared assumption that these were required in order to provide for co-operation in society where there were different ethical views. Such liberal principles are not, as Rawls has said, to be thought of as a mere modus vivendi, that is, as necessary to ensure self-interest, but as a moral basis for liberalism. People should come to see that the liberal principles connect to each person's different moral interest.

But the rights and obligations that people have, under Rawls' scheme, derive from a perspective that is not personal, because it is founded in the idea that people of different convictions about personal ethics should endorse liberal perspectives for reasons other than those to be found in their personal ethics. That, at least, Rawls is clear about: that the political principles of liberalism are not to be drawn from any comprehensive theory.

23.2 Liberalism and personal ethics

Dworkin's project, on the other hand, is to make a bridge between personal and political ethics, so that ethics is part of liberalism's foundations. He agrees that the personal perspective is everything the liberal political perspective is not. We are not neutral and impartial, as liberalism claims the state should be, but committed and attached.

The distinction between the continuity and discontinuity strategies is helpful. It serves to distinguish the theories I mentioned earlier. What is the status of the confused argument for liberalism from the basis of the supposed subjectivity of moral judgments? It purported to derive neutral principles from the nature of moral argument itself. Put at its best, buried in its premises is a proposition about mutual respect: since I can no more prove my moral assertions to be true than you can, our moral assertions shall have equal weight. If this is so, then it is a continuity theory.

But another interpretation might find tolerance to rest upon self-interest. We could say that because of the non-provability of moral propositions, we should deal with others at arm's length to ensure that they keep at arm's length from us. That interpretation makes out the connection between one's personal ethics and the political perspective to be discontinuous.

What about the hippy liberalism to which I referred? That clearly is a continuous theory because it requires you to adopt as part of your personal ethics the personal ethics of everyone. That is why it is confused. Nevertheless, its strategy is to encourage everyone to extreme tolerance through the development of each person's personal ethics.

Raz's theory is a continuity theory, too. The political perspective is defined by a personal ethics which places very great weight upon the principle of personal autonomy. That principle must be endorsed by the state in the form of tolerance of a plurality of different exercises of personal autonomy. In other words, state tolerance follows from a personal ethics placing great importance on personal autonomy.

The appeal of liberalism

Let us now examine Dworkin's continuity version of liberalism which, for the political sphere, he calls 'political equality'. Dworkin says that there are three major problems which any theory of liberalism will have to face, those of the visionary appeal such theories should have, the promise they have of attracting a consensus about them and, in particular, what he calls their 'categorical force'.

These problems arise from the difficult problem in liberalism of drawing a line between the personal and political perspectives. In the first place, since it is *premised* on the idea of people having different views in their personal ethics, on what constitutes the good life and personal well-being, how can any such theory hope to have either visionary appeal or consensual promise?

At first sight, the premise of difference seems to deny the possibility of people being equally struck by an equality vision of the future. What appeals to one person's personal convictions will not appeal to another. Further, if that is the case, what is the hope for being able to attract a consensus about the idea? Dworkin goes so far as to say that it is unrealistic to suppose that political liberalism can gain a consensus yet.

There is a particular problem in the idea of the categorical force of political liberalism. From what basis can we claim justification for the moral strength of the principles? If people have different ethical views, views which may be partial and committed to different forms of life, how can independent moral force be accorded to the neutral and impartial liberal principles?

These three questions, concerning visionary appeal, consensus and categorical force, usefully throw into relief the difference between the continuity and discontinuity strategies. Take, for example, the visionary appeal of a discontinuity theory. Since it assumes different ethical views, it is difficult to see what visionary force it can have. Its appeal is not supposed to lie in any person's particular personal ethical perspective. In what, then? The best will be in some idea, such as Rawls', of 'mutual respect and co-operation' but, as I have already pointed out, that idea is only hopefully something beyond self-interest (and self-interest, we assume, is not the same as personal ethics).

A similar problem arises with categorical force. From what moral perspective does this come? The short of it is that no one is going to accept as binding upon him a proposition which is not part of his personal ethical perspective. The discontinuity strategy assumes different ethical perspectives, so that the categorical force can only arise from the contract. Here we can return to the paradigm of the ordinary commercial contract, in which the rights and duties flow from the contract and not the personal perspectives of the parties.

Dworkin claims that it is an 'insane' theory that there was ever actually a contract between citizens to form a state. No obligations of the commercial contract sort arise in advance of the contract coming into existence, not even where such a contract is clearly about to be made. The categorical force, then, of discontinuity theories cannot be located within the structure from which the rights and duties are supposed to flow. The discontinuity theory fails, because it cannot account adequately for the three features which he, reasonably, says are necessary for a successful liberal political theory. But what about the continuity theory? This fares much better on visionary appeal and categorical force. Both are derived from the personal ethical perspective, so that a person can be called upon to endorse from his own perspective the political structure proposed. There is no need to pray aid from an intermediate stage similar to the commercial contract.

Of course, many will have difficulty with this idea in Dworkin, because of the supposed problem of objectivity. What hope is there, ever, that the categorical force for liberal principles can arise from personal ethical perspectives? Perhaps moral views are too radically different for the continuity project to be successful.

There are two ways in which we might take this objection. First, it could merely express the simple view that moral argument, say, about the categorical force of political principles of liberalism, will always be controversial. But, for Dworkin, lack of demonstration of truth is not an obstacle to moral argument (see Chapter 25, on the 'one right answer' thesis).

But second, it could express a more complex view that the controversy is such that *argument* is not possible, that the incompatibility is of a nature that not even modes of argument are shared. This view may be that of people who talk of the presence of irreconcilable conflicts (a 'contradiction' of principles, as opposed to 'competition') in society. They mean that conflicts exist which are simply not resolvable. This view is more sophisticated than the 'subjectivist' view, because it can allow for moral controversy, but asserts that, in some societies, the controversy can be irresolvably deep, where arguments necessarily pass one another.

So, the situation remains, for Dworkin, one where there *is* the possibility of argument, and the categorical force of the political liberal principles will spring directly from the (right) personal ethical perspective. It is not an argument against *this* view that people might disagree, therefore. To point to that fact *that people will disagree* is merely, in his view, to make a statement of the sociology of moral argument.

The categorical force of liberalism

But how can categorical force derive from the personal ethical perspective really? After all, our personal perspective is coloured, as Dworkin points out, by ideas of partiality and attachment, not the ideas of impartiality and detachment required in political liberal principles. It was, in fact, this apparent contradiction which, in his view, sent the contractarians to formulate their discontinuity strategy.

It is instructive to look at two ways of answering this question, each of which Dworkin believes to be unsatisfactory. One is that we could, using the idea common in political philosophy, say that in matters of state, the 'right' takes priority over the 'good'. In other words, perhaps in politics where, as Dworkin says, 'the stakes are higher', morality should be given exclusive force over personal well-being.

But he does not think this argument is sufficient. It is no more than an assertion because it offers no independent reason why morality should have sovereign force in the political sphere. Particularly, he says, the ideas of personal well-being and morality are not independent. The idea of fairness, for example, allows partiality towards friends and family, so that within the idea of fairness, as it were, is the idea that friends and family are important.

So there may be a bridge between the sorts of principles he wishes to endorse at the political level, and the personal ethical perspective. The connection requires a deeper analysis of the relationship between fairness, justice and impartiality, on the one hand, and the personal perspective, which Dworkin later gives. But it is not enough, he thinks, simply to insist that, in the political sphere, the right takes priority.

23.3 Our personal ethics

Dworkin claims that a person should be free to use his resources as he wishes. In other words, a genuine understanding of treating people as equals (the 'principle of abstraction' operating through the 'bridge principle') means that invasions of liberty are invasions of equality as well. Of course, invasions of liberty will be justified where that is necessary to protect an egalitarian distribution of resources and will include, for example, the protection of personal security. Invasion of personal liberty on other grounds, such as intervention to influence private sexual behaviour, will not be justified, however.

The political equality implied by equality of resources means that only equality of 'outcome' is justified, not equality of 'impact'. It follows, says Dworkin, that democracy is defined by outcome as well as by other things flowing from the worthwhile life. He sees political activity as flowing naturally from personal moral experience and this idea is his answer to the charge that his theory lacks the dimension of community. Democracy means more than just the formal opportunity to vote. It requires the much richer idea of politics as a theatre of moral commitment and debate.

The idea of our 'critical' well-being

Dworkin claims that what is important about one's life is constituted not by what one *wants*, what he calls 'volitional well-being', but by one's 'critical well-being'. The difference is this. 'Critical well-being' is what you should want as opposed to what you actually want, which is 'volitional well-being'. The idea of the satisfaction of wants, such as pleasure, is too unstructured and insufficiently complex to explain the judgments we make about what is good in life.

Dworkin's analysis here is obvious. We do not think that what is worthwhile is *constituted* by simple want satisfactions of whatever kind. As he says, your life is not better because certain of your wants, such as being able to sail better, are satisfied, or your life is not worse because you suffered in the dentist's chair. There are some wants, however, which do matter for your life in the relevant way. Dworkin suggests one such as *wanting* to have a better relationship with your family. And the only way to distinguish between those wants that are important and those that are not is by abandoning the simple idea of want satisfaction, or 'volitional well-being', as constituting what is important.

Dworkin does not think that this distinction commits him to a distinction between 'subjective' and 'objective' wants. Clearly, it does not, even granted the general unease his methodology has about the meaning of that distinction. But, to employ the terminology, 'subjectively' I can distinguish between those wants I have that express volitional interests and those that express critical interests. Dworkin's distinction is only a graphic way of distinguishing between what I consider important and what I do not.

The good life constituted by performance

We can be agreed, then, that what is important to a person's life is what is important as judged from the perspective of that person. Dworkin goes on to draw some very useful distinctions. First, he distinguishes between the 'product' value of a life, measured by what that life produces, and a life's 'performance' value, measured by how a life is lived. A life of good product value would be something like Mozart's life, because he produced great works of music, or Alexander Fleming's life, because he discovered penicillin.

A life of good performance value, on the other hand, would be one where a person responds to his circumstances in, as Dworkin says, an 'appropriate' way. We can see what he means. A composer might live a life both of performance and product value. We might say that his life, lived as a performance, achieves value from the *way he lives it*, quite apart from a judgment that *what he produced* is of value.

Employing the idea of critical well-being, Dworkin now says that idea makes most sense only on a judgment about the performance value of a life. If we only judged lives according to their product value, as he says, most of our lives would be 'puny' compared, say, to that of Mozart or Fleming. Under the performance model, however, the response to life is parametered by each person's particular capacities. The goodness of a life is not judged in the shade of that life's 'product' but in terms of how it has been lived. Under this account of critical well-being, the brilliant person produces something better than I do, but the value in his life is measured against his response to his circumstances. You can see that here Dworkin is drawing upon the same sort of argument that led him to devise a tax on talents. At root, it strikes at rewarding people for what is merely a matter of luck. It is true, of course, to the liberal tradition of regarding this sort of *desert* as having no place in the distribution of resources.

The parameters of the good life

What is the role of endorsement of what is of value in your life? Dworkin suggests that the important idea for critical well-being is that the good life is one that you endorse. Further, it does not make terribly good sense to say that your life has value without endorsement, because the good life is one that is constituted by your doing what you critically believe you ought to be doing. In other words, endorsement is 'constitutive' of leading a good life.

What would be an alternative? Dworkin suggests that endorsement could have value in its being 'additive' to whatever else is of value in a critical life. But, as you can see from my previous argument, that idea is going to have very little value on the performance model if, indeed, it has any meaning at all. Dworkin says the additive view fits the product model much better. A person who values what he has produced has additional value in his life, thereby, than someone who does not.

The idea appears bizarre for the product model. Dworkin drops it, by reason of his preference for the performance model. Let us say that Mozart's life is better for his having endorsed his products, as it were, than if he had merely produced the works for money and not thought of them as otherwise worth doing. Does that make much sense? Does it really make any difference to the value we place on Mozart's life whether he valued what he produced?

Perhaps it is another way of saying that the 'added' value could only come from judging a life by its own internal convictions, which is to confirm Dworkin's analysis of the performance model. He gives the example of Alexander Fleming's janitor who disobeys his instructions and omits to throw away the mouldy culture dish from which Fleming later discovered penicillin. Fleming's janitor's life had product value. Would it make the slightest bit of difference that he had endorsed his breach of duty?

23.4 Justice and personal ethics

Now we come to the conclusion of Dworkin's lengthy discussion of philosophical ethics. Do we say that a person's life is critically good measured against the resources he actually has? No. We can say that a person's life was not a good one *just because he had too few resources*. Here is the nub of the argument. It is now clear where Dworkin is going:

> '... the best life for a particular person, we might say, is the best life he can lead with the resources that ought to be at his disposal according to the best theory of distributive justice.'

This is an arresting conclusion. It means that justice enters ethics by limiting the amount of resources a person can have to live a good life because, you will remember, the measure of equality of resources is its true cost to other people. Dworkin claims here that there is in this idea a shadow of Plato's claim that justice is always in a person's interests.

What is congenial about Dworkin's conclusion is that the answer to the question of whether I have lived a good life ties the question of the ideal performance of my life to that of justice. For example, I cannot regret not having done well at politics if it is clear that I could only have done so had I had an unjust amount of resources. Or, says Dworkin, I cannot be (rightly) pleased by having lived well despite my having had only a pauper's share of resources.

23.5 Evaluation

We are now in a position to see the connection between personal ethics and the claims of liberal equality. Justice enters the personal sphere because it sets the parameters of that sphere. Our own ethical life is coloured by the justice of the distribution of freedoms, particularly in the area of resources. Crudely, I cannot escape the effect justice has on my own ethical life, measured as a matter of critical performance and from my own point of view. Justice and my personal ethics cannot be separated. That means that a proper concern for my own personal ethical life must lead me to a proper concern for the just distribution of freedoms in the community. The continuous link between personal ethics and the political structure is, in Dworkin's view, thereby established.

It may be instructive to see how far this conclusion departs from the contractarian line which Dworkin sees himself attacking. Let us go back to what he sees as the paradigm of the contractarian argument, which is the ordinary commercial contract. The contractarian line says that the rights and duties arising under the contract are independent of the personal ethics of each party. That is how the contractarian justifies the neutrality of political liberalism without any inconsistency with personal ethics.

But, if we are to employ the metaphor of a contract, and it is no more than a metaphor, then we can see that it only makes sense to talk of contracts if we endorse the institution of contract-making and contract-enforcement. We see the *ethical* sense of them. (We *need* not. We *can* claim that contracts are merely institutions which in the long run fulfil our non-ethical self-interest.) In other words, it is not too difficult to give personal ethical justification to the contract's neutral way of distributing rights and duties.

These remarks are not critical of Dworkin's project. His attack is against a line of specific contractarian thinking that really does regard the line between personal ethics and political liberalism as genuinely discontinuous. Despite his generous efforts to make the best sense of Rawls' idea of an 'overlapping consensus', in looking for an interpretive account of justice 'deeply embedded' in a pluralistic community,

Dworkin does not succeed in rescuing him. Simply, the way Dworkin denies the contractarian line is to say that the contract can only make sense seen as a striking way of showing that the sense of justice which sets the limits to our personal ethical convictions is the same sense which orders the principles of liberal equality. Dworkin's theory appears to be the only one at present touching these deep issues.

Judicial Reasoning

24

The Common Law Tradition

24.1 Introduction to precedent

The judge has two tasks. He must resolve the dispute before him and he must reach his decision by reference to some impartial rule of law. One of the most obvious aspects of formal justice is that all cases should be treated alike; one of the commonest and most noteworthy features of many human institutions (clubs, societies, companies, etc, as well as states) is the tendency to repeat earlier practice and follow earlier patterns. For these and other reasons, most legal systems have developed a system of precedent, including the use of past decisions as a guide to present decision. A moment's thought by any student of English law should bring scores of decisions based on precedents to mind.

As we shall see, though, the English system – the common law system – in fact uses precedent in a slightly different way from civil law systems. In England, precedents of an appropriate authority not only guide decisions in later cases, but bind the judges in those later cases: within the given hierarchical structure, a judge in an inferior court may obey the decision of a higher court on the same point. This is the doctrine of *stare decisis.*

Any system using precedents will require a method of keeping them in an acceptable and accessible form; this need for law reports is obviously greater where precedents are law (since they bind later decisions, they are actual law, and not just guides to what the law is). In the *stare decisis* based system there will also need to be a defined hierarchy, and an established way of working out what part of an earlier case is binding: we call this the *ratio decidendi* (reason for deciding).

In the following sections, we look at the doctrine of *stare decisis* and how, if at all, it differs from the civil law use of precedent; the flexibility introduced into *stare decisis* in various ways (including an analysis of the problems involved in identifying the meaning of *ratio decidendi*); and the present English rules on precedent and *stare decisis*.

24.2 Stare decisis in theory

From the Latin *stare decisis et non quieta marere*: the doctrine of *stare decisis* lays down that decisions of superior courts bind the lower courts in later cases. The exact details will be discussed in paragraph 24.4. The courts fall into a hierarchy, House of Lords (HL), Court of Appeal (CA), Divisional Court (DC), judges of the High Court (HC) and so on, with the European Court of Justice (ECJ) thrown in for good measure.

This doctrine is the result of a combination of historical factors, really beyond our scope. One necessary factor, as was noted in the introduction, is a satisfactory system of law reporting. From the Year Books onwards, law reporting in England has been a developing and now integral part of our court system. The private collections of law reports (for example, Cokes) gave way in the nineteenth century to the reports of the Incorporated Council of Law Reporting whose reports remain the most authoritative (since they are checked by the judges), although still unofficial. There are many other series: reports in *The Times* each day, the weekly *All England Law Reports* and the *Weekly Law Reports* (published by the council in addition to their main series), and many others. The computer revolution has made possible the storage of details of many more cases; the HL has recently disapproved some of the consequences in terms of increasing citations of cases from computer records.

Past cases – once the *ratio* is determined above – bind. This distinguishes the English doctrine of *stare decisis* from the treatment of precedent in civil law countries, and even in some common law countries. In civil law countries, past decisions are not binding, but merely persuasive, with the strength of persuasion depending on the authority of court and judge; in some common law countries, for example, the United States, the *stare decisis* doctrine is not applied as rigidly as in England. Several factors play a part in this distinction. In both the United States and France, for instance, the court structure is not as strictly hierarchical as in England, with many, particularly state and district courts, of concurrent jurisdiction with no authority over one another. Further, the basis of French and other civil law is a code: past decisions must always be justified on the basis of the code, and its wording can always provide a justification for not following past cases. Similarly, with US Supreme Court decisions on the Constitution; the Supreme Court's role as the arbiter of that document mitigates against strict *stare decisis*, and many of its landmark decisions (for example, *Brown v Board of Education* (1954) outlawing segregation in schools) are in fact reversals of earlier rulings.

The mode of reporting and of giving judgments in France also works against the English model. Judgments tend to be pithy statements, frequently only on the facts; they are often accompanied in the reports by influential commentary on the case and its effects by jurists. This tends to decrease the role of the judgments, and increase the importance of the learned writings, in discovering what the law is.

In any case, the differences between France, for example, and England in this respect can be over-estimated. While the code is the last word, it is – just as English statutes are – often uncertain or vague, and it is the decisions of the courts which make the detailed law. A set of decisions pointing the way will, in France, be quite settled; in England, one decision on a particular point may be binding on lower courts, but certainly not on upper courts. Also, the authority of the French Cour de Cassation is such that its decisions are almost always final.

In marginal cases, there is a difference: even a long series of cases does not fully bind a French judge, and particular precedents considered incorrect or out of date or unjust can be overruled or not followed without fear of criticism by higher courts, and without some of the devices (such as distinguishing) we discuss in relation to our own system in paragraph 24.3 below.

Does the doctrine of *stare decisis* have a value over and above the ordinary precedent system? The advantages held by the latter are certainty (to enable people's affairs to be arranged and conducted within a known legal framework), uniformity (like cases treated alike) and logic (fields of law developing harmoniously), mixed with a degree of flexibility to prevent injustice. The ordinary system sacrifices a degree of the certainty, uniformity and logic of the *stare decisis* system for the benefit of slightly increased flexibility and, hopefully, decreased injustice.

Think about the two options, bearing in mind the various tones of flexibility introduced into the *stare decisis* system. Is either option clearly the better one?

24.3 *Stare decisis* in practice: flexibility

The bald statement of the *stare decisis* doctrine makes it appear rigid and inflexible. In fact, in practice, judges do have a wide measure of flexibility and movement. If a judge does not want to follow a particular precedent, there are several techniques or devices he can use to avoid it: such avoidance is not always possible, but it frequently is.

One factor a judge always has to weigh up is the authority of the report itself and of the court. Present sets of reports are generally considered accurate (although the council's reports are the most acceptable, as they have been checked by the judge), but earlier private sets of reports were not complete, and are of varying quality: Coke's, for example, are thought to be of high quality. Since the hierarchy is so important, a judge must always decide if he is bound by the cited decision or if it is just persuasive. If it is just persuasive (Privy Council, lower courts, other judges of the High Court perhaps, foreign judgments), the judge must weigh how much persuasive authority it has (Privy Council judgments, for instance, since they are normally given by House of Lords members, are very persuasive).

A judge must then decide which parts of the earlier case actually bind him. He must distinguish the *ratio decidendi* of the earlier case from the *obiter dicta* in it (which do not bind him); and this distinction is one of the major sources of flexibility. While any student will quite happily expound on the *ratio* of a past case, and be prepared to inform a judge of exactly the extent to which he is bound, in fact the actual definition of a *ratio decidendi* is uncertain: and frequently it is difficult for a judge to identify the correct *ratio*. Is there any definition of ratio decidendi that adequately captures judicial practice?

Definition of ratio decidendi

The traditional view of *ratio* is that it is the rule of law enunciated by the judge to the extent that it is necessary for the decision of the case. Even if we do think that the judge's expressions of relevant law are the *ratio*, this definition is not practically very useful: the important question is, what part of the judgment is relevant? In *Donoghue* v *Stevenson* (1932) was Lord Atkin's neighbour principle relevant and necessary, or just the narrower principle relating to manufacturers liability? Also, what if the judge does not state the law, but just decides the case before him? In any case, the statements of the judge are not always considered to be correct statements of the *ratio* when considered in later cases: it is not thought doctrinally incorrect to say the case really decided X, even if the judge said Y.

If we reject the traditional view, we find no shortage of suggested alternatives to take its place. Wallbaugh proposes a reversal test: if the reverse of the proposition would have led to a different decision in the case, that is the *ratio*. However, that does not help us distinguish between the two statements of principle in *Donoghue* (since it is not clear for which of them the Wallbaugh test is true), nor between them and general statements such as, there is a tort of negligence, manufacturers can be liable for negligence, and so on. The reversal test can tell us what is *not* the *ratio*, but cannot help us work out what *is*.

Others will argue that one should try to find the underlying principles. At what level of generality? Also, it is acceptable to reject the underlying principle of a case like *Donoghue* (the neighbour principle, perhaps?) while considering the case to be correct on a narrower ground (the manufacturers' liability). The underlying principles test is too vague. Two other tests, which we can quickly reject as being contrary to our experience of how judges work, are those of Lord Halsbury in *Quinn* v *Leatham* (1901), that a case is only authority for the order made on those facts (this seems far too narrow to capture the width given to the *rationes* of past cases), and of Lord Devlin, that the *ratio* is the reason for the decision which the judge wishes to be the source of precedent. (Is it then incorrect to say that a case is a precedent and binding in a way the judge never intended?)

A definition which has carried much persuasive weight is that of Professor Goodhart, for whom the *ratio* is the decision based on the facts treated as material by the judge (he was particularly concerned to move away from treatment of the *ratio* as the judge's statements of law). A judge views certain facts, explicitly and implicitly, as material: his decision on those facts is the binding *ratio*. This view is interesting, and expounded at length by Goodhart (see Lloyd and Freeman's *Introduction to Jurisprudence*); but some problems do arise. It is often difficult to tell which facts the judge implicitly takes into account, and *ex post facto* any interpretations thereof may well be wrong; while there is always the problem of being tied to the facts the judge found as material.

The approach of Professor Stone is illuminating. He maintains that there is not a unique *ratio* of a case, but rather a choice of *rationes* available for later judges to choose from. Stone identifies two possible *rationes*, the descriptive and the prescriptive. This, it is submitted, is a good explanation of the nature of the common law system. The descriptive *ratio* is ascertainable from the decision once given, but the prescriptive *ratio* is how a subsequent court treats the earlier decision. In *Evans* v *Triplex Safety Glass Co Ltd* (1936) where a windscreen smashed and caused injury to the driver of the vehicle, the court – bound by *Donoghue* – held that the *ratio* of *Donoghue* was that a duty of care arose only when there was no possibility of interference with the product between the time it left the manufacturer and the time the loss was caused. The court held that there was such a possibility in *Evans* and so the plaintiff would not recover. The view of *Donoghue* stated in *Evans* was the prescriptive *ratio* of *Donoghue*. Dias goes slightly further, and suggests that the *ratio* should be viewed in a continuing time framework, as the interpretation of the case given by later judges. These views help us to understand a central feature of the *stare decisis* precedent system, that it is important to see how cases are treated in later cases to discover for what they are taken as authority: in *Donoghue*, the example we have been citing, it is clear that it is authority in 1988 for the neighbour principle.

However, the Stone, or Dias, view does not provide us with a definition which explains how the judge decides what the *ratio* of a previous case is: in the case of negligence immediately following *Donoghue* a judge had to decide what its *ratio* was. Knowing that there were several for him to pick from (Stone) and that the full import of the case would not be known until after the series of decisions (Dias) doesn't make it easier for us to understand the use of *Donoghue* made by that next case judge.

Montrose has stated that the argument is essentially one of a terminological nature. His purpose was to reassert the strength of the common law tradition. He seeks the meaning of the *ratio* and identifies three possibilities:

1. the rule of law to be found in the actual opinion of the judge forming the basis of his decision – this is the meaning that Montrose preferred;
2. the rule of law for which the case is binding authority;
3. any reason which ultimately brings about the decision – essentially this relates to the reasons for the ratio.

Does this really take us much further?

No definition of ratio decidendi

We must in fact admit failure: no one has yet adequately defined *ratio decidendi*. A judge looks for the principle of law as applied to facts that appears to him to be appropriate, and takes that as the *ratio*, and we can be no more precise than that. We can close our discussion of *ratio* by looking briefly at why it might be difficult to identify that principle in particular cases; several obvious reasons spring to mind. Judges do not always explain themselves properly; they often give several different reasons for a decision. Sometimes the actual decision may follow as an exception to a field or rule expressly considered in detail (for example, *Hedley Byrne* v *Heller* (1964), where the House of Lords laid down a new rule on negligent mis-statements but decided the case on an exception to the rule, viz the bank's disclaimer), and even sometimes the decision may not seem to follow from the reasoning. In cases with more than one judge, all saying different things, working out the *ratio* can be impossible. In a case from the US Supreme Court, *University of California Medical School* v *Bakke*, the *ratio* is said to be the decision of one of nine judges. This justice, Powell, agreed with four justices on one point, and the other four justices on another. The accepted *ratio* is thus one with which eight of the nine justices would not agree. When you add to these uncertainties the problems of later decisions, choosing one possible *ratio* (as per Stone), and later courts having to decide on a series of cases in this way, the complexities of discovering *ratio decidendi* become apparent!

It is possible that a case will have no ascertainable *ratio* at all. This, according to de Smith, *Constitutional Law*, is the case with *Nissan* v *Attorney-General* (1970) concerning a claim for damages caused by British troops billeted in a Cyprus hotel where the judges in the House of Lords all gave separate reasons for their decision. The case of *Harper* v *National Coal Board* (1974) shows a further difficulty. This was a decision of the House of Lords in which by a majority the decision went one way and the reasons went the other way!

Those parts of a judgment which are not the *ratio* are called *obiter dicta*. These parts – of however high a court or respected a judge – are like the decisions of lower courts, Privy Council (PC), foreign courts, etc: merely persuasive. Some, especially House of Lords, *dicta* are treated as near binding – the statement of principle in *Hedley Byrne* for example, and the CA discussion of precedent rules in *Young* v *Bristol Aeroplane* (1944). Many *dicta* are ignored or expressly contradicted (just as many non-binding cases are not followed).

Flexibility, so far, has entered the *stare decisis* doctrine via authority of court or report, via choice of what is the *ratio* – because it is much in doubt, of course, it almost goes without saying that later judges have flexibility in choosing what it is – and in disregarding or accepting *dicta*. Judges can even avoid a case that is binding on them by a device known as distinguishing; that is, taking it as not covering the facts of the present case. Obviously the choice of *ratio* is important to this process: choosing the relevant facts for the *ratio* at a different level of generality, or suggesting that facts in the previous case which do not appear in the present case were material to the decision. All law students can remember instances of this, and also instances of cases where earlier decisions have been treated as authority only on their own particular facts. In these ways, judges can distinguish past cases, and limit their precedent effect.

The doctrine of *stare decisis* appears fixed and settled; in practice it is a flexible weapon in the hands of a judge. A core area of fixed law is surrounded by a fringe area in which judges, by distinguishing, approving and following past cases, steadily develop the law.

24.4 The rules of precedent

It would be appropriate for general background information to include here a summary of the rules of precedent as they apply in each of the main courts in this jurisdiction.

The House of Lords

The *Practice Statement* adopted by the House in 1966 changed the previous practice of the House of Lords, laid down in *London Tramways Co* v *London County Council* (1898). The previous rule was that the House of Lords would not depart from its previous decisions under any circumstances; the 1966 *Practice Statement* stated that they would do in future if it was right to do so. Their Lordships remained aware of the importance of certainty in the law (particularly in relation to contractual etc arrangements and criminal law), but strict obedience to past decisions could cause injustice and restrict development of the law.

Some surprise has been voiced that this change was made in a Practice Direction. However, rules of precedent do not form part of the *ratio* (nor do rules of statutory interpretation, see below) of cases, and are just judicial practice.

A more interesting question is whether the House of Lords should have changed the rules. It seems to me that the *Practice Statement* was a good thing, allowing the House of Lords to be honest in their treatment of past authorities now felt to be unsatisfactory. Rather than distinguishing, they can now overrule. Certainty is a virtue, but one that can be over-indulged in.

The *Practice Statement* has been directly used less than a dozen times in the last twenty-two years: *Miliangos* v *Frank* (1976), overruling *Re United Railways of Havana and Regla Warehouses* (1961); and *ex parte Khera and Khawaja* (1984), overruling *ex parte Zamir* (1980), are two of the examples.

Is the Court of Appeal bound by the House of Lords?

Fairly recently the Court of Appeal has attempted to free itself of House of Lords' dominance in relation to House of Lords' cases it finds unacceptable. In *Cassell* v *Broome* (1972), the Court of Appeal said that the House of Lords' decision in *Rookes* v *Barnard* (1964) was arrived at *per incuriam* (that is, without citation of relevant binding authority, in this case two previous House of Lords' decisions). The decision was inspired by Lord Denning and was the subject of almost unjudicial condemnation in the House of Lords when the matter went on appeal.

In *Schorsch-Meier* v *Hennin* (1975) the Court of Appeal refused to follow the House of Lords' decision in *Havana Railways* that currency judgments must be expressed in sterling, on the basis that the reason for the rule had gone: *cessante ratione legis: cessat ipsa lex* (if the reason for the rule ceases, so does the law). In *Miliangos* v *Frank* the House of Lords deplored the Court of Appeal action in *Schorsch*. Strict adherence to the hierarchy was required for the precedent system to work.

The Court of Appeal is bound, then, to follow the House of Lords loyally. The problems when it does not, as in *Schorsch*, can be seen from the dilemma of the first instance judge, Bristow J, in *Miliangos*. Should he follow the House of Lords' decision, or the later (but heretical) Court of Appeal? In fact he followed the House of Lords (the Court of Appeal followed itself in *Schorsch*). Opinion is divided on whether Bristow took the right side, but is united on the difficulty of his position!

Is the Court of Appeal bound by its own past decisions?

In *Young* v *Bristol Aeroplane Co Ltd* (1944), Lord Greene MR laid down the still applicable position for the Court of Appeal. It is bound by a past Court of Appeal decision, unless:

1. there are two conflicting decisions – one must be overruled;
2. while not expressly overruled by, it is nonetheless inconsistent with, a subsequent House of Lords' decision;
3. it was arrived at *per incuriam* (relevant binding authority not cited).

We should note two other exceptions: the Court of Appeal is free to follow a later Privy Council decision inconsistent with a previous Court of Appeal decision: and in a criminal case, the Court of Appeal is not bound if it would cause injustice in the instant case. (Remember Court of Appeal (Criminal Division) cases do not bind Court of Appeal (Civil Division) and vice versa.)

In recent years, the Court of Appeal led by Lord Denning has shown an anxiety to throw off these shackles. Lord Denning has said that the Court of Appeal is not bound by previous decisions (*Barrington* v *Lee* (1972) for instance) and that the Court of Appeal could issue a Practice Statement similar to the House of Lords (*Gallie* v *Lee* (1971)). He did not always carry the Court of Appeal with him, but he did lead a five-man Court of Appeal in *Davis* v *Johnson* (1979) which purported to overrule two Court of Appeal cases (*B* v *B* (1978) and *Cantliff* v *Jenkins* (1978)) on the Domestic Violence and Matrimonial Proceedings Act 1976.

In *Davis* Lord Denning said the Court of Appeal should either follow the direction of the House of Lords *Practice Statement*, or add exceptions to *Young* where appropriate. Both come to the same thing: he was claiming that the Court of Appeal could overrule its own previous rulings. The other two in the majority, Baker and Shaw LJ, drew up new exceptions to add to *Young*. The House of Lords roundly condemned the Court of Appeal, reaffirming *Young*. (They did however overrule *B* v *B* and *Cantliff*.)

Should the Court of Appeal be bound by its previous decisions? Bearing in mind that the House of Lords changed the no overruling ourselves rule by a Practice Direction, and that the Court of Appeal can arrange its own procedure, can it issue a Practice Statement on the same lines as Lord Gardiner's in 1966?

An alternative: prospective overruling

The main argument for *stare decisis* is certainty. Certainty is a value in a legal system because it allows people to arrange their affairs in accordance with the law, both not breaking it (crime) and taking advantage of its facilities (contract, wills, etc). If judges departed from their decisions at will, these arrangements would be upset; further, the individual case would be in effect a retrospective law, changing the law as it was and applying the new law to the present case.

In the case of *Great Northern Railway Co* v *Sunburst Oil* (1932), a decision of the United States courts, Cardozo J stated that in order to avoid this problem the court could adopt prospective overruling. This is a method of treating the present case on the old law, but announcing the new law for future cases. This only, of course, avoids the retrospective argument; could it be so arranged (for example, by applying the new law to future arrangements only?) to avoid affecting settled arrangements? Also, would it not be extremely unfair to the losing litigant, who would have persuaded the judge(s) to accept his legal argument but still have lost the case?

The question that is really being asked is whether certainty and development of the law go together?

24.5 An introduction to statutory construction

A subjective approach

More perhaps than is the case in most of the Chapters in this textbook, the selection of topics and contents for this Chapter, and the arrangement of them, is a very subjective one. A quick glance through any of the major textbooks on either Jurisprudence or English Legal System will show that each approaches this area differently, emphasising different points and using different case illustrations. Most of these textbooks would agree, though, in recommending Professor Cross' *Statutory Interpretation* (1976) to any student of the subject.

Interpretation

As our law becomes increasingly statutory, with upwards of 60 public Acts of Parliament each year (as well as innumerable statutory instruments), the interpretation of those statutes becomes increasingly the judges' central role. There will always be a need for such interpretation and construction. Words are ambiguous, phrases and paragraphs are more so; and no legislator can cover every possible future case clearly. Since under our constitution matters of law are decided by the judges, the task of working out the meaning of the unclear statutory provision, and seeing if it applies to the (frequently unforeseen) case before them, falls to the judges.

Ambiguity

Various sorts of problems can arise. A distinction is often attempted between interpretation (deciding the meaning of the words) and construction (seeing if the words apply to a particular case): the definitions in brackets are only one variant. I will not use this distinction, but will instead bear in mind that, apart from those cases where the meaning is obvious and straightforward (enabling both the judge and the layman organising his affairs to see what the statute means immediately), there are cases where a particular word or phrase is ambiguous, cases where it is unclear whether a particular fact-situation was meant to be included, cases where the particular punishment intended is not clear, cases where the legislature appears to have left out an obvious case, and cases where the result on the straightforward meaning of the words is absurd.

Intention

Note how often I have used the word meant. Judges often say that they seek the intention of Parliament: the great debate between the literal meaning and the mischief-purpose approach is said to hinge on whether Parliament's intention is to be gleaned merely from its exact words (he meant what he said) or also from a consideration of why the statute was passed (its purpose) and what Parliament would have done if it had had the particular case in mind. Any search for intention, purpose, etc, is to an extent a fiction. A body like Parliament is made up of many people, who may not vote at all on a measure, or may vote for the measure for tactical reasons without considering its consequences, or may vote for it for tactical reasons apart from the actual content. Often votes are on general principles, and yet the matters that come before the courts will be detailed and perhaps highly technical.

To that extent, then, one cannot say what Parliament intended. However, the judges are looking at Parliament's words and must (under the Parliamentary supremacy doctrine) follow and attempt to apply those words. While guidance may not be available on a particular matter, it is clearly the case that, on general principles at least, it does not seem so absurd to search for a Parliamentary intention. Surely the Sex Discrimination Act was *intended* to remedy some aspects of discrimination against women, the Unfair Contract Terms Act was *intended* to control exemption clauses and the Supplementary Benefits Acts are *intended* to set up a scheme providing those with no income with a state safety-net? And more specific provisions can be seen to be *intended* – a provision repealing an earlier provision or overturning an earlier case; a provision following a Law Commission recommendation where no one in Parliament argued with the Commission's reasons. Whether it be intention of the draftsman, or intention of the proposer, or intention of the majority, there is some sense in the concept of Parliament's intention.

Having said that, again I emphasise that most often in difficult cases Parliament's intention is not clear. On a disputed provision, did Parliament intend to protect from that specific type of exemption clause? It is precisely because the words do not make clear what the intention is that the problem arises in that case, and in general, if the words are not clear, how are the courts to decide what Parliament's intention was? To put it another way, what do the words as enacted by Parliament legally mean?

What Parliament is committed to

Guest (1997a) takes the view that a much better idea than intention, in the context of the interpretation of the intention of Parliament, is that of what Parliament is committed to. The criticisms of the idea that there really is such a thing as parliamentary intention are presented. There is no one intention, since some members of Parliament voted against the Bill that eventually became law; members voted with different intentions, some to please the whips, some for other reasons such as private financial gain. Clearly not all of them voted for it because they thought that it was aimed at a particular problem. Even then some could well have voted when either ignorant of what the Bill contained, or with quite a misguided understanding of what the Bill meant. In any case, if intention means the actual existing psychological intention at the historical time of the voting for the Bill, for old statutes, where most or all of the members are now dead, the intentions are only what those members could have known. So, for example, the prohibition against the repair of carriages in the Metropolitan Police District to be found in the Metropolitan Police Act 1837 would have no application today to cars, since they weren't invented then, and so the members could not possibly have intended their words to apply to them. The difficulties multiply when you consider the hard cases, because then you have to make a fairly wild guess – matched only by those on the other side – of what the members' intentions on the matter (say, roller-skates in the park) would have been had they been apprised of the matter. And, when you consider how you would imagine they would have to be apprised of the matter – by being shown different possible drafts of the statute, or perhaps by confronting them with the facts of the particular case – you can see that the idea of actual existing psychological intentions makes almost no sense at all.

Guest develops an idea from Dworkin, which Dworkin in turn had derived from an American philosopher, Quine. Intention is an opaque concept, meaning that its use is subject dependent. If A intends to reward B but instead, by mistake, rewards C, we say he didn't intend to reward C. (Incidentally, this shows that – contrary to what most people believe – the doctrine of transferred malice is not required by logic, but by policy. If A shoots at C, intending to kill C, but by mistake, shoots and kills D, A can rightly say 'I did not intend to kill D, and so I can't have murdered D, because I lack the mens rea'. It is rather that the law imposes, by policy, a requirement that an intention to kill a particular person must always be read as an intention to kill no particular person – just a person.) Consequently, we find ourselves in the position where we have to say that if Parliament intended to ban the repair of carriages, and it did not have – because it could not have – cars in mind, then Parliament didn't prohibit the repair of cars. Guest says we can alleviate this problem (as we would want to, since clearly the interpretation of statutes has always allowed us a much less restrictive form of interpretation than is implied by the actual historical-psychological intention idea) by using the idea of commitment. Contrast, instead, 'A intends to shoot the first person who comes through the gap' with 'A is committed to shooting the first person who comes through the gap.' In each case, unbeknownst to A, A's wife is the first person. In the case of intention, we cannot conclude that A intended to shoot his wife. The intention does not transfer since, subjectively, A never could have had such an intention. But in the second case, it is easy to say A was – we might say regrettably – committed to killing his wife.

If we use this idea of commitment, we can without much difficulty take the line that, whatever Parliament intended by way of actual psychological states at the time it passed the Metropolitan Police Act 1837, it was committed to a ban on cars since the repair of vehicles in the street is what it was aimed at.

Statutory interpretation

The final introductory part concerns the status of decisions on the question of statutory interpretation. Assume that the House of Lords has to deal with statutory provision X1; the plaintiff claims it means X2 and the defendant X3. The House uses the literal method, and finds for the plaintiff. What is binding on lower courts? Clearly, it would seem, not the literal approach; the rules of statutory construction do not appear to be part of the *ratio* of any case; surely it is only the decision that, in this statute, X1 = X2. If the same words occur in a different statute, the different context and purpose might justify a different result; but on the same statute, lower courts would be bound to follow the House of Lords.

24.6 Canons and presumptions

Apart from the major rules considered here, in cases where statutory words are obscure or unclear judges may use one or other of the following canons of construction and presumptions.

Canons

The statute must be read as a whole
The words of the particular sub-section in question must not be read in isolation, but must be read with the other sections (particularly any interpretation section) and with the schedules. As we shall see below, this canon is now subsumed by Professor Cross' reformulation of the major rules, where he emphasises that the context of the words is in account.

Eiusdem generis
If a general word follows two or more specific words, the general word must be restricted in meaning to a meaning of the same kind (*eiusdem generis*). For example, *Powell* v *Kempton Park Racecourse Co* (1899) turned on whether in relation to places of betting the words house, office, room or other place included the racecourse itself: No, said the House of Lords, since the general words other place were restricted to a meaning of the same kind as the specific words, that is, an indoor place of betting.

Narrow construction of penal provisions
The individual gets the benefit of any doubt if a criminal or tax liability is imposed by statute, in particular against the imposition of liability without fault.

Interpretation Act 1978
This Act gives presumptive interpretations to common words and phrases in statutes: so men includes women (and vice versa), singular includes the plural, distances are to be measured in a straight line on the horizontal plane, time refers to

Greenwich Mean Time and so on: all subject to contrary intention (which must sometimes be expressly stated, but most often must just appear).

Presumptions

Against alteration of the law
This presumption does not work against a change in the general (common) law which appears clearly from the literal meaning of the words; but if there is a doubt, Parliament will be presumed to have left the law unaltered.

Against imposition of without-fault liability
Mentioned above; to create a strict liability offence, Parliament must use clear words.

Against ousting the jurisdiction of the courts
The courts are very protective of their own jurisdiction; although Parliament may alter the courts' jurisdiction even fundamentally, it must do so clearly. In administrative law, for example, in several cases the courts have evaded statutory attempts to forestall judicial review (*Anisminic* v *FCC* (1969), *Padfield* v *Minister of Agriculture* (1968), *Pyx Granite Ltd* v *MHLG* (1960)).

Against the Crown being bound by a statute
The Crown must be expressly named, or it is not bound by a statute.

Against depriving a person of a vested right
The above are just examples. It may be quite possible to find canons and presumptions to support quite conflicting contentions.

24.7 The three rules of statutory construction

It is often said that there are three rules of statutory interpretation, these being the literal, golden and mischief rules. As we shall see they are to an extent contradictory; all can claim judicial support.

Mischief rule

This rule was prevalent in the sixteenth century. The courts have regard to the purpose of the Act, and interpret it in such a way that the purpose is fulfilled or enhanced. The classic statement of the rule is contained in *Heydon's Case* where the barons laid down four things to be considered when interpreting statutes: the common law before the Act, the mischief that the law did not provide for, the remedy appointed for that mischief, and the true reason of the remedy. Of course, not all statutes are altering the common law today, and the exact formulation therefore needs changing. The approach, while not now as prevalent as it was, still commands judicial support, and has authorities following it in many areas (see the examples given in Dias' *Jurisprudence*).

An example can be taken from the law against racial discrimination. Although there is a requirement in the mischief rule that the express words of the statute must reasonably bear the purposive meaning given to them, in *Mandla* v *Dowell Lee* (1983) the House of Lords interpreted the Race Relations Act, where it is stated that it is an offence to discriminate in certain matters against a person on grounds of his race, colour, ethnic or national origin, in quite a different manner. The facts of the case were that a young Sikh male wanted to join a public (fee paying) school. He was granted admission but was required to conform to uniform regulations and remove his turban and cut his hair. For reasons of faith he was unwilling to do this. There were other Sikhs in the school who had conformed to the uniform requirement and there was no suggestion that Dowell Lee (the headmaster) had any inclination to discriminate against Sikhs. The Court of Appeal carefully considered the history of the Sikh people and concluded that they were a group identifiable only by their common religion and that as the statute makes no mention of religion then the actions of the school were reasonable and not illegally discriminatory. The House of Lords, relying on a New Zealand case concerning the position of the Jews (*King Ansell* v *The Police* (1974)), held that the purpose of the section was to cover situations such as the present and that by a stretch the Sikhs could be regarded as a group identifiable by a common ethnic origin. The reason for so holding was to extend the protection afforded by the Act to Sikh people.

Had the court been minded to find otherwise then it might have followed the case of *RRB* v *London Borough of Ealing* (1972) which held to the literal approach (see below) in holding that discrimination against a Polish citizen in the granting of public housing was lawful because it was not on grounds of his national origin but on grounds of his citizenship or nationality. Perhaps this comparison between these two cases reinforces the view that in their choice of which rule of statutory construction to apply the judges in effect determine the outcome of the case. Bishop Hoadley put it thus centuries ago: 'Whoever hath an absolute authority to interpret any written or spoken laws, it is he who is truly the lawgiver to all intents and purposes, and not the person who wrote or spoke them.' Lord Devlin perhaps has it better and in more modern language when in his *Samples of Lawmaking* he states that 'the law is what the judges say it is'.

The mischief or purposive rule is the one favoured by Fuller as elaborated upon in his 'The Case of the Speluncean Explorers' which I discussed in the third Chapter of this book. Perhaps the reader would return to that article at the end of our course and extract more from it. Before you do that let us now examine the other rules.

Literal rule

Various factors, including the declining influence of the judges on legislation and the development of Parliamentary supremacy, led to a retreat from the mischief type approach to the literal approach. Here, the intention of Parliament is considered as contained in the words passed: the literal meaning of those words must be taken, even if the result appears to be one which Parliament did not intend. Lord Esher in *R* v *City of London Court Judge* (1892) stated that 'the court has nothing to do with the question whether the legislature has committed an absurdity'. This follows on the constitutional provision that it is the role of the legislature to make law and the role of the judiciary to interpret the law the legislature so makes.

Many cases support this rule of applying the clear and unambiguous words of Parliament. For example, in *Inland Revenue* v *Hinchy* (1960) the House of Lords was construing a provision which visited upon people incorrectly completing tax returns a penalty of treble the tax that ought to be charged under this Act. Presumably Parliament intended the punishment to be three times the excess owed: but those words meant three times the whole tax bill for the year, which cost poor Mr Hinchy £418 instead of £42!

Note at this stage two things. First, words are often not clear and unambiguous; two equally usual meanings of a word might exist, or the application of words to particular cases might be in doubt, and so on. Second, it is not unknown for judges to consider the literal meaning of the words and end up with different results (for example, *Liversidge* v *Anderson* (1942)).

Golden rule

Judges have often mitigated the strict literal approach by calling into play the golden rule, that is that if the usual interpretation results in consequences so absurd that Parliament could not possibly have intended them, any secondary meaning may be taken. In the case of *R* v *Allen* (1872) which concerned the definition given to the offence of bigamy in the Offences Against the Person Act 1861 as 'whoever being married, marries another' where it was observed that such a definition if applied literally would lead to the absurd conclusion that the offence could never be committed. A person cannot legally marry he is are already married. There the court held that, as Parliament could not have intended to legislate nonsense, the words should be changed to read 'whoever being married goes through a marriage ceremony with the intention to marry etc'. Then the definition has meaning which would probably be consistent with the intention of the legislature.

Obviously, the three rules above cannot really be taken as strict rules: they contradict each other (taking the literal meaning often obscures the purpose of the statute, it might be said). At most they are approaches, with the judges choosing the most appropriate in the circumstances, generally plumping for the literal rule and taking the obvious plain meaning unless some good reason to the contrary appears.

Even this does not seem to be a good explanation of what happens if we accept that the judges generally follow the approach of looking at the literal meaning. What of those cases where two meanings are equally usual and neither of the other two approaches is relevant or helpful? What of technical words?

A rather more successful attempt at formulating the courts' approach overcoming the lack of judges giving reasons has been made by Professor Cross in *Statutory Interpretation*. He suggests that the literal and mischief rules have been mixed, and the vital element of context added: the judges look to see what the ordinary (or, if appropriate, technical) meaning of the words used is in the general context (including the objects) of the statute. It is that ordinary meaning that may be displaced by a secondary meaning if the result would otherwise be absurd: and furthermore, in cases where what seem like simple mistakes make a statute unintelligible, absurd or totally unworkable, a judge may add or delete words, to change nonsense into sense (Cross cites *Adler* v *George* (1964) and Lord Denning in *Eddis* v *Chief Constable* (1969)).

The whole problem stems from the Blackstonian fiction that statutes are intended to govern all eventualities in detail and do not merely lay down guidelines. Taken with the imprecision of words – a problem Hart has dwelt upon when he referred to the core of settled meanings and the penumbral area of doubt that surrounds words – the problem of statutory construction is manifest. This is clearly stated by Lord MacDermott thus: 'the difficulty of finding unequivocal language by which to convey the will of Parliament [lies at the heart of the problem of statutory construction]'.

The Swiss are perhaps more realistic. Their Civil Code in Article 1 states that a judge may decide a case on the basis of a rule which he would lay down if he himself has to act as legislator. The only limitation in this regard is contained in Article 4, to the effect that in exercising his discretion the judge must base his decision on principles of justice and equity. Lloyd and Freeman observe that although this article was initially widely used it is now subject to restrictive interpretation itself. Does this tell us something about the nature of the judicial creature?

Hypothetical examples

Much of what judges do is obvious, even when they construe difficult or ambiguous sentences or phrases: although we must consider the pros and cons of judges following a purposive as against the traditional literal approach, we must also emphasise that in fact it is in comparatively few cases that a straightforward literal v purposive clash occurs. The following fact situations might help to make the point.

1. A particular word or phrase has a straightforward obvious usual meaning, for example driving a motor-car at over 70 mph is an offence. A driver knows that once the speedometer tops 70 he is committing an offence, the judge when he is deciding applies the obvious meaning of motor-car, driving and 70 mph and

convicts. This is straightforward literal approach: in relation to this case, the words have only one meaning.

2. A particular word or phrase has several meanings: for example, the verb wants (wishes or lacks?) the noun will, (volition or the document by which a deceased person leaves his property?).

The context of the phrase in the statute makes it clear which sense is meant: for example, a reference to providing what a lunatic wants will refer to what he lacks; a reference to the will of the testator in a statute on probate will generally mean the document (but could in context mean the volition, as, 'the will of the testator was overborne by force').

The judge applies that obvious meaning. Not quite the literal approach, since there were two usual meanings (and in the case of wants, the one chosen was, if anything, the less obvious or usual of the two). But can this really be called a purposive approach? We are looking at the in-context meaning, and purpose is relevant only as part of the context.

3. As situation (1) except that this meaning either produces an absurd result, for example, (ignoring the Interpretation Act) it is an offence to steal horses, and the defendant steals just one (so he is not guilty under literal meaning), or produces a result clearly against the intention of the Act, for example, if the Race Relations Act defined racial group in a technical way which excluded negroes.

As to the absurd result, holding that the statute meant something else, this clearly involves the judge in rectification, which Cross allows as his third rule; not the golden rule, as there is only one meaning the words can bear (and therefore no secondary one to fall back on).

As to the result clearly against the intention of the Act, any suggestion that the judge acts in accordance with that intention and not the words of the Act does lead to a purpose v intention conflict. Note, however, that in general the courts have not invoked the mischief rule in this sort of case: an attempt by Lord Denning to fill the gap left in a statute in the case of *Asher v Seaford Court Estates* (1949) was slapped down by the House of Lords, Viscount Simmonds rejecting this naked usurpation of the legislative role *(Magor & St Mellons RDC v Newport Corporation* (1951)). If the result is not absurd, the courts will follow the wording of a statute if it only allows of one construction, even if that construction does not follow the general purpose of the statute.

4. As situation (3) except that one meaning is clearly the more usual, but that result leads to either absurd consequences or is totally against the intention of the statute. An example of absurd consequences could be the facts of the tax case *Inland Revenue v Hinchy*. An example of being against the intention of the statute can be seen in the United States controversy over whether reverse or positive discrimination is against the constitutional provision; forbidding laws which deny equal protection of the laws: does that mean that any discrimination is unlawful or could 'equal protection' be taken to include the effect of reverse discrimination in redressing the balance and hence making more equal?

If the judge takes a secondary meaning to avoid absurdity, that is the golden rule in operation; if he takes it to accord with the intention of the statute, that could be taken as using the context of the statute, if not (and in our example, the context doesn't help: the question is, how far did the constitution go?) he is using purpose to displace the literal rule.

5. As situation (2) except that the context does not assist, the purpose of the statute does not assist, and the consequences would not be (more) absurd either way. The judge uses his discretion – but none of our stated approaches/rules!

Literal words v *purpose*

In (3) and (4) then, there are possibilities for a clash between words and purpose: should the judge follow the obvious or only meaning of a phrase or sentence if that goes against the purpose of the statute? Briefly, the arguments for the literal approach are: certainty; avoidance of judicial legislation; due deference shown to Parliament; it is often difficult to identify purpose; and it encourages more careful drafting. For the purposive approach: it is often not possible to work out what the literal meaning is; it is not really deferent to Parliament to refuse to fulfil its purpose; and judicial legislation is common, particularly in the common law.

Which of these sets of arguments convince you? Are there any other points to be made?

24.8 Aids to construction

Where a statute's construction is ambiguous or uncertain, various aids may be used by the judge to help him come to his decision (to minimise tedium, case references are omitted).

The rest of the statute

A statute must be read as a whole, as we have said above; the judge must therefore decide in the light of the rest of the enactment (including the long title). In cases of uncertainty, those parts of the statute which are not integral parts of it (preamble, marginal notes, punctuation) may be called in aid.

Other statutes in pari materia

If construction is uncertain, a statute on the same subject may be called in aid, if it is unambiguous.

International treaties

If an Act is stated to be intended to give effect to an international treaty, uncertainties may be decided by reference to the treaty.

Statutory materials: The landmark case of **Pepper** *v* **Hart**

Pepper (Inspector of Taxes) v *Hart* (1993) is an important case on statutory interpretation. It settles, for the time being, the question of the extent to which 'extrinsic' materials may be used in ascertaining the extent of that well-known personification of the *point* of legislation, parliamentary intention. The House of Lords, in which seven judges appeared, came down in favour of a relaxed rule (although the Lord Chancellor, Lord Mackay, dissented). It was thought that the use of 'parliamentary materials' would be permitted in legal argument regarding the discovering of the purpose of legislation in the following cases:

1. where the legislation was ambiguous or obscure, or the literal meaning led to an absurdity;
2. where the material relied on consisted of statements by a minister or other promoter of the Bill which led to the enactment of the legislation together, if necessary, with such other parliamentary material as was necessary to understand such statements and their effect; and
3. the statements relied on were clear.

Furthermore, the use of parliamentary material as a guide to the construction of ambiguous legislation would not infringe s1, article 9 of the Bill of Rights since it would not amount to a 'questioning' of the freedom of speech, or parliamentary debate. This was provided counsel and the judge refrained from impugning or criticising the minister's statements or his reasoning, since the purpose of the courts in referring to parliamentary material would be to give effect to, rather than thwart through ignorance, the intentions of Parliament. Furthermore, the use of parliamentary material in this way would not question the processes by which such legislation was enacted or criticise anything said by anyone in Parliament in the course of enacting it.

Pepper v *Hart*, in effect, follows the recommendation of the *Renton Committee on the Preparation of Legislation* (1975) that the courts should accept constructions promoting the general underlying purpose.

24.9 Effect on the draftsmen

Past and present practice of the courts on statutory interpretation clearly affects how draftsmen work on future legislation. An example from the Wills Act 1837, cited by Cross *(Statutory Interpretation*, p12), shows how ridiculous were the lengths to which draftsmen then were driven to avoid the rigours of the full-blown literal approach. The courts are not quite as exacting any more, and do take at least the context into account with the words, but the enduring pre-eminence of the literal approach and the eagle eyes of eager lawyers intent on taking every possible point for their clients do still affect the form and structure of present legislation.

Procedure

Generally, the procedure for drafting is a careful one, especially if the statute is lawyers' law, rather than that dictated by party policy. For example, the Law Commission will issue a working paper, followed by a report with draft Bill, or the government will issue draft proposals (in Green or White Paper form) for consultation. As much time as possible is given to allow lawyers and others to look for, *inter alia*, drafting mistakes.

Detail

Often statutes go into great detail to avoid unwanted interstitial interpretation: for example, Employment Act 1980, in its sections defining the outlawed secondary action and secondary picketing.

Examples

Many statutes give examples of the instances intended to be covered as the factors to be taken into account: for example, 1973 Matrimonial Causes Act, ss23–25, detailing the factors to be taken into account by a judge in deciding the financial provision on divorce as examples (because all the circumstances are in account).

Discretion

When judges are intended to have discretion on a particular matter to decide in accordance with the statute's purposes, this is sometimes expressly stated in terms. Section 23 Matrimonial Causes Act is again a good example; the judge must do what is just and equitable in all the circumstances in an attempt to put the parties in the position they would have been in if the marriage had not broken down.

Interpretation

Many statutes contain their own interpretation sections.

24.10 The common law and the Constitution

An exciting, radical approach to judicial decision-making was advocated by Laws J in *Public Law* (1995). His thesis sent shock waves amongst public lawyers and will clearly have an effect on the future direction of the increasingly significant use of the procedure of judicial review. It is most convincing and its chief significance lies in its public avowal by one of the most talented judges in the United Kingdom that judges, by virtue of their inherent jurisdiction to declare whether something is required or permitted by law, could declare purported statutes to be legally invalid. This, of course, cuts through an (unanalysed) general assumption that Crown-in-Parliament may make any laws that it pleases and that it would be wrong for a judge to 'usurp the function of the legislature'. The reasoning of Laws J is as follows. Inherent in the idea of the legitimacy of Parliament is the idea of democracy; that idea, whatever else it means, stands for each individual's stake in the legal system. 'One man, one vote' must mean at least that. What would it mean to give each person a vote and yet at the same time deny that each person had any right to expect a certain minimal level of treatment? Or, abstractly, the idea of democracy entails that people, by virtue of being people, are entitled to a certain level of respect. We do not deny that Parliament has the right to make laws for us by virtue of the fact, amongst others, that it is elected by us. If that is so, if Parliament does something *contrary to the principles that give it meaning* as a legislative body, it is acting *ultra vires*.

This idea is most attractive idea because it gives weight to our intuition that (*contra* Austin) there is more to the idea of legislation than brute power – the mere ability to enforce a command. The form of argument used here is a 'transcendental' one; you look to the nature of Crown-in-Parliament and then you deduce from that nature some other principle which transcends the idea and then acts as a constraint upon it. (Remember the 'transcendental epistemological deduction' of the Grundnorm in Kelsen – see Chapter 9, above) This sounds more difficult than it really is but becomes clearer by using a fairly unlikely – but nevertheless still realistic – example. What if Parliament decided to abolish the vote for unemployed people (perhaps out of a misguided sense that since such people did not work, they did not contribute to society and thus had no 'stake' in our community)? Wouldn't that be contrary to the very principles (of democracy) that lie at the heart of our legal system? What obvious and compelling reasons would there be for denying a judge the right to declare this legislation invalid because ultra vires?

It is useful to array the arguments on either side.

For

1. It makes sense using the transcendental argument referred to above; from what other principles could Crown-in-Parliament gain its validity?
2. It is clear that in other jurisdictions there is no problem in the idea *at all*; the

United States, example. To the reply that there is a written constitution there but not here we could add;

3. There is no significance in the distinction between a written and unwritten constitution in the same way that there is no significance in the distinction between the telling of a story and the writing down of a story, as far as the story itself is concerned. To the reply that writing it down makes the story more certain we could add;

4. There are just as many problems with the interpretation of the written word as there are with the spoken word (witness the enormous litigation in the United States which is still created by the famous phrase 'equal protection of the laws' in the constitution).

Against

1. Very few people in the United Kingdom would accept the idea; in particular, one of the most influential textbooks, *Wade on Administrative Law*, is firmly of the view that Crown-in-Parliament can enact whatever it wants (and this is, of course, an idea as old, even older, than Austin).

2. If Laws J is right, it means that Parliament could never repeal, for example, the relevant parts of the 1832 Reform Act, which greatly extended the franchise.

3. We could pay attention to Bentham's idea of a 'limited disposition to obey'. Bentham, unlike Austin, did not think that the sovereign was legally limitless, and he explained his belief by saying that the sovereign depended upon the ability to command by the willingness to obey displayed by the population at large. To take an extreme example: if Parliament passed a law, similar to the one passed in ancient Sparta, which declared that all male babies were to be kept outside unclothed all night so that only the fittest would survive, *no one* would obey it. It followed for Bentham that it would not be a law, despite the fact that the sovereign had 'commanded' it (in reality it is a failed command, because the threat is not real given the command's content), and so Bentham can preserve his distinction between the 'is' and the 'ought' of law by burying away the idea of the legitimacy of reasons for obeying the law inside the idea of a command.

4. Judges should not make 'political' decisions. But, as Laws J points out, it all depends upon what is meant by 'political'. Judges are political in the sense that their decisions have political consequences; the legislature, true, has certain sorts of competence carved out for it (a judge could not make fundamental decisions about the direction of the economy, for instance). Nevertheless, the legislature cannot be immune from legal criticism for acting outside the principles of democracy fundamental to its legal legitimacy (it could not further economic policy by killing off the unemployed, for instance). Thus Laws J says:

'... the *subject-matter* of a case offers no inhibition to legal adjudication on grounds of its political content.'

This article will have far-reaching effects since it strikes at the heart of commonly accepted (but confused) propositions about the immutability of the principles of statutory interpretation in the light of 'the intention of Parliament'.

25

Dworkin's Law as Integrity

25.1 Introduction

Dworkin's theory is fascinating and highly practical. He is difficult to get into because his writing output is enormous and many articles are difficult to obtain. He is the most important contemporary in legal philosophy. One of the difficulties is that, although he is in the rigorous intellectual mould of Bentham, Kelsen, Hart and so on, he is *not* a positivist. The best start is to read Chapter 2 of his *Taking Rights Seriously* (1978). Students should then go on to read Chapter 4 and then read his *Law's Empire* (1986) especially Chapters 2, 4, 5, 6 and 7. The important point with Dworkin is not to underestimate his subtlety and intellectual power.

25.2 Hercules, the model judge to whom we should aspire

Let us get clear about Hercules. Many people, in particular lawyers, who are introduced to Hercules in Dworkin's article 'Hard Cases' simply dismiss him by saying that no such judge ever existed. This is too glib. Hercules is a model against which, like any other ideal, legal arguments are to judged. Take, for example, the idea of the ideal market. It would be off the point to say that the ideal market does not exist (or that the model of the atom, or that of the DNA molecule, does not exist). To *say* that, is to recognise the idea of the ideal, in any case. The point of the ideal market, about which economists and practical minded politicians argue vociferously, is to show how, in the real world, there are imperfections. Against the model of the ideal market, we see that monopolies and other restrictive practices are 'bad', that transaction costs and imperfect knowledge 'distort' the real market, and so on.

Why not, then, imagine the existence of an ideal judge, against which we can measure bad or distorted legal arguments? There is no reason to suppose that we cannot. But it is worth trying to explore the reasons why people make the mistake of saying, in effect, that there cannot be ideal arguments in the law. The problem is one of superficiality, no more. People like to think of law as historic fact. They do not like to think of legal argument as something as shifting and as controversial as moral argument.

It is necessary for Dworkin to posit an ideal judge because his theory is about law as an argumentative attitude (see Chapter 3). He has to provide a scheme of argument which, among other things, is sufficiently abstract to allow for controversial argument. He cannot provide a set of premises from which conclusions may be drawn by, say, the use of syllogisms. His is not that sort of theory. In fact, he is critical of that sort of theory. He thinks it paints a simple-minded picture of legal reasoning. In order for him to describe the inherently controversial nature of hard cases, he can only provide the general scheme of argument.

Dworkin's device of Hercules is used to characterise correct legal argument. It is not that there is a method which will come up with the right answer, there, uncontroversially for all of us to see. If a problem is raised about whether there *could* be such a right answer, it is one about the objectivity of legal argument, not a criticism of the ideal model of Hercules.

Students should note that a new collection of essays by Ronald Dworkin will be published in this country shortly, by Oxford University Press. It is already published in the US as *Freedom's Law: the Moral Reading of the American Constitution* (1996). It is divided into three sections entitled Life, Death and Race; Speech, Conscience and Sex; and Judges. Many of the articles have appeared over the last ten years in the *New York Review of Books*. Students should read his Introduction: the Moral Reading of the Constitution, as it is particularly helpful for obtaining yet another angle on how he thinks judges should decide cases.

25.3 Hercules and 'hard cases'

The key to understanding how Dworkin thinks a hard case should be decided is in the following idea:

> 'If a judge accepts the settled practice of his legal system – if he accepts, that is, the autonomy provided by its distinct constitutive and regulative rules – then he must,

according to the doctrine of political responsibility, accept some general political theory that justifies these practices.'

Look at the position of the judge. He has convictions about his role, his duties as defined by his judicial oath and by other sources. If he did not, it would certainly be surprising. He has an idea about legislative purpose and principles of the common law.

In this, United States and United Kingdom judges differ. In the United States, judges are more aware of their role as public 'protectors' of the Constitution and they are more explicit (both to themselves and the public) about their position within the separation of powers doctrine and their duties to protect the rights of the individual. United Kingdom judges are, for cultural reasons to do with background and education, more diffident about such matters.

What does Hercules do when constructing the arguments in all the hard cases put before him? We can assume, says Dworkin, that he accepts most of the settled rules of his jurisdiction, rules which lay out for us what are the familiar characteristics of the law. For example, the constitutive and regulative rules that grant the legislature the powers of legislation give judges the powers of adjudication and the duties to follow previous cases, as well as all the settled rules of the various areas of law, such as tort, contract and so on.

We can examine all the possibilities just mentioned in the law reports and academic writings. And these are not exhaustive. We can develop our own theories or, if we prefer, our own arguments. Dworkin's use of Hercules is intended to show the general form – the scheme – of the types of arguments that may be used. We can imagine Hercules producing all the theories, with their attendant sub-theories, for all areas of the law. In each topic, he will have to justify the particular settled rules with the substantive theories he has devised.

He will also have to do more. The division by topic will itself be a matter for justification, which will proceed by way of looking to the settled rules for topic demarcation (say, the division between tortious and contractual liability) and devising a theory which explains that division. He might decide that, for some special cases, the importance of the division may be outweighed, as Lord Atkin, but not Lord Buckmaster, thought it was in *Donoghue* v *Stevenson*.

25.4 The chain novel: 'fit' and 'substance'

Legal argument, for Dworkin, in most hard cases, will develop as the result of a tension between two dimensions of argument, one that argues towards a 'fit' with what is accepted as 'settled' law, the other that argues towards substantive issues of political morality. While the twin abstract injunctions in Dworkin 'to make the best sense' of law, and 'to treat people as equals' propels his legal and political philosophy, it is the distinction between 'substance' and 'fit' that forms the cutting edge, for him, of legal argument.

As a preliminary to getting into the idea, we may employ Dworkin's idea of the chain novel. A number of novelists agree to write a Chapter each of a proposed novel. The first Chapter is written by one, the second by another, the third by another, and so on. We can see that there will be certain constraints of 'fit' upon the author of the second Chapter, and even more on the author of the third Chapter, and so on. Many more lines of fit could be proposed. Is there fit with style, descriptiveness, thematic material, dialect and so on? The important point is that if certain things are accepted as settled within the text of the first Chapter, later creativity is constrained by that acceptance, in order for the other Chapters to be properly part of the novel.

There are familiar responses to this description of 'fit'. It is a matter of argument (or 'opinion'), people say, as to what constitutes 'fit'. It is too 'wooden' to assert that novels cannot allow for the change of name, sex, century, and geography. But what follows from this? That everything and, therefore, nothing, counts as 'fit'? Of course not. We just do hold some framework assumptions, or constraints, constant while we allow others to vary.

Nevertheless, in Dworkin's terminology, the question of 'fit' is itself an interpretive question. For example, the acceptance of the genre of 'novel' for the chain novel is itself open to interpretation. A second Chapter novelist might, for example, decide that the first Chapter is a political tract about conservatism and best seen as the first Chapter of a political manifesto. This interpretive judgment might constrain the way he continued to write the second Chapter. If he did so, perhaps if the chain novel writing project was a commercial one to produce a radio serial, his contract as a chain novelist would be terminated. But there is no reason holding back the *possibility* of making that interpretive judgment, although, of course, his judgment that the first Chapter was the first Chapter of a political manifesto might be difficult to justify.

25.5 Principles and policies

Dworkin is well known for the distinction he drew between arguments of principle, which are arguments about a person's rights, and arguments of policy, which are arguments about community goals. The distinction is important to Dworkin for a number of reasons. First, it is intended to be largely descriptive of distinctions that in fact are drawn by lawyers. Secondly, it represents for him the line to be drawn between the legitimate jurisdictional activities of judges as required by a properly understood democratic separation of legislative and judicial powers. Thirdly, and most importantly for him, it represents his main assault on the most popularly understood version of the moral theory known as utilitarianism.

It is most important to understand the role of the language in the terms he uses. 'Principle' and 'policy' are terms of art for him. Technically, that means he has stipulated meanings for them. He gives definitions for them as follows in Chapters 2 and 4 of *Taking Rights Seriously* and in *Law's Empire* he accepts these definitions without modification:

> 'I call a "principle" a standard that is to be observed, not because it will advance or secure an economic, political, or social situation deemed desirable, but because it is a requirement of justice or fairness or some other dimension of morality.
>
> I call a "policy" that kind of standard that sets out a goal to be reached, generally an improvement in some economic, political, or social feature of the community.
>
> Principles are propositions that describe rights; policies are propositions that describe goals.
>
> A political right is an individuated political aim. An individual has a right to some opportunity or resource or liberty if it counts in favor of a political decision that the decision is likely to advance or protect the state of affairs in which he enjoys the right, even when no other political aim is served and some political aim is disserved thereby, and counts against that decision that it will retard or endanger that state of affairs, even when some other political aim is thereby served.'

Policy causes difficulties for two different reasons, neither of which strikes at Dworkin's thesis.

1. The distinction is not one of content, but of form. This means that for one person a political state of affairs could be a matter of principle and for another it could be a matter of policy. In this way, the distinction stands clear of differences of political opinion. But it is a distinction of substance, too, in the sense that it requires a strong, separate sense in which principles are not reducible to policies. This is borne out by Dworkin's well-known statement that rights 'trump' utilitarian goals.
2. Critics often point to the fact that it is easy to imagine circumstances in which only goals seem to be important, and where rights are of no consequence. Most people, for example, accept the situation in wartime when civilian rights are suspended. Martial law is accepted as a possible option whenever its imposition warrants the pursuit of the desirable goal of winning a war. The problem is thought to be that if there can be situations where there are justifiably no rights, or principles, because of the importance of the goal, what criteria could there possibly be for defining principles independently of goals?

   A special category of emergency is well-described in our moral, political and legal thinking. Martial law is 'martial' law. Its imposition is only justified in wartime, when war is 'raging'. Our concern about the suspension of civilian rights under martial law is characteristically about whether there is a situation which justifies its imposition. Many people, for example, felt that the situation in Romania in 1989, although bad, was not bad enough to justify the Romanian government in imposing martial law. Many felt that it was being imposed, not because it was necessary to preserve the existence of civilian rights, but to protect a particular political system from change, perceived as undesirable.

Some judges are either innovative (in the United States, 'activist') in the chain novel sense to which reference has already been made. Sometimes, rather self-consciously, they will refer to their decisions as decisions of 'policy'. A good example is Lord Denning in the *Spartan Steel* case, referred to by Dworkin in *Taking Rights Seriously*:

> 'At bottom I think the question of recovering economic loss is one of policy. Whenever the courts draw a line to mark out the bounds of duty, they do it as a matter of policy so as to limit the responsibility of the defendant. Whenever the courts set bounds to the *damages* recoverable ... they do it a matter of policy so as to limit the liability of the defendant.'

But it is clear from other remarks that he makes that at least some of his reasons for his judgment attach to the particular parties and do not look to future general impact. He thought the matter should be decided on the basis of relationship of the parties. If other relevantly similar bodies were excused liability (in this case by statute), in Lord Denning's view, this was a strong argument for excusing the defendant. The argument was not helped, in other words, by appealing to *a novel way of arguing*.

And yet other judges (Lord Denning fits into all the categories, representing different stages of his career) are blatant. They *do* decide policy, in Dworkin's sense, but disguise it. A good example is *DPP* v *Majewski* (1976), in which the House of Lords interpreted the following words of the Criminal Justice Act 1967 as excluding evidence offered by a defendant as to whether he intended or foresaw a particular result in a criminal case relating to drink or drugs:

> 'A court or jury, in determining whether a person has committed an offence ... shall decide whether he did intend or foresee that result by reference to *all* the evidence ...'

One of the arguments used was that Parliament could not have intended to overturn a clear rule of exclusion in the common law. But this was a *criminal* case and there is an equally clear common rule that criminal statutes should be construed in favour of the defendant. It was argued that s8 was 'only' a rule of evidence, but this was evasive and unconvincing. The sense of the decision was that the judges knew the havoc that would be created by allowing defendants to plead drunkenness as an excuse rather than as only a mitigating circumstance.

25.6 *McLoughlin* v *O'Brian*

We should look at Dworkin's analysis of the case decided in the House of Lords, that of *McLoughlin* v *O'Brian* (1983). This should be instructive as to how he views legal argument. Remember that, in his view, substantial arguments (relating to the right people have to be treated as equals) have to be matched to fit (the already existing case law).

The plaintiff in this case learned that her husband and children were involved in a car accident. She set out for the hospital some miles away, and when she got there she was told her daughter was dead and she saw that her husband and other children were seriously injured. She suffered severe shock and she sued, among others, the driver of the vehicle, whose negligence caused the accident.

How should the case have been decided? It was a hard case, because in all the previous cases, the facts involved people suffering nervous shock almost immediately upon the accident occurring and more or less at its scene. In these cases, the people suffering shock were allowed to recover.

Dworkin suggests how Hercules might decide this case. He says that Hercules might begin by considering the following six possible interpretations of the case law.

1. *Success (for the victim) only where there is physical injury.* But we can rule this out immediately because it does not fit the law of tort. It is clear that damages may be obtained for *nervous* shock.
2. *Success only where the emotional injury occurs at the accident, not later.* But, says Dworkin, this would just draw a morally arbitrary line.
3. *Success only where a practice of awarding someone like Mrs McLoughlin would be economically efficient.* If this were simply a matter of economic *policy*, Dworkin rejects it because it does not respect 'the ambition integrity assumes, the ambition to be a community of principle'. The argument is, in other words, to be rejected because it is one of naked policy, ignoring Mrs McLoughlin's right to be treated as an equal.

    There is, however, an ambiguity which Dworkin says is inherent in the idea that a community should aim at efficiency. It may be that people have a *right* to a certain amount of redistribution under some system which aims at economic efficiency. Dworkin leaves a developed discussion of the idea, (which first appears in a very obscure fashion in his article 'Hard Cases') to Chapter 8 of *Law's Empire*, in a highly compressed and difficult Chapter. But for present purposes, it is true to say that Dworkin rejects the economic pursuit of economic efficiency in this sort of case where it consisted solely of the pursuit of overall (undifferentiated) communal wealth.

4. *Success only where the injury, whether physical or emotional, is the* direct *consequence of the accident.* But this interpretation has to be ruled out because it is contrary to fit: it contradicts the clear case law, where there is a test of foreseeability which limits the liability of the person who causes the accident.
5. *Success only where the injury is foreseeable.*
6. *Success for foreseeable injury, except where an unfair financial burden is placed on the person who causes the accident.* ('Unfair' meaning 'disproportionate to the moral blame for causing the accident').

According to Dworkin, (5) and (6) are the best contenders. (1) and (4) are ruled out because they contradict 'fit'. They simply cannot be made to cohere with the previous legal decisions. (2) is ruled out because it is an interpretation that relies on an arbitrary assertion that people at the scene can recover, those who are not, cannot. (3) is ruled out because it relies on policy, not principle.

Let us now examine interpretations (5) and (6). 'Which story,' he asks, 'shows the community in a better light, all things considered, from the standpoint of political morality?' Suppose that interpretations (5) and (6) equally 'fit' the precedents. Dworkin says that Hercules should construct two abstract principles. First, that community sympathy towards individuals who are suddenly required to pay large amounts for accidents they cause is an argument in support of public insurance schemes, safety regulations and so on. This is a principle of 'collective sympathy', he says. Second, that it is right that people who are at fault should pay for the consequences of their fault and so costs should be apportioned between private individuals.

These are two principles of exactly the sort that a lawyer could produce in court. If the 'private apportioning' principle should prevail of these two, then interpretation (5) is the correct one. Mrs McLoughlin wins just because Mr O'Brian was at fault. If, on the other hand, the 'collective sympathy' principle prevails, Mrs McLoughlin loses. Why? Because Mrs McLoughlin's injury, while foreseeable, was so remote as to place an unfair burden upon Mr O'Brian in proportion to his fault.

Which interpretation should be preferred? Dworkin thinks that Mrs McLoughlin should have won, favouring interpretation (5), at least in automobile accident cases when there is a widely available and sensible liability insurance obtainable privately.

25.7 The 'one right answer' thesis

Dworkin's point has always been, in line with his theory of interpretation (see Chapter 2, section 2.6), that it makes 'best sense' of our legal practices to suppose that we are all – judges, students, lawyers – striving to argue for, decide, or discover the best answer. That means that there is a 'best' of the matter, and this is supported by the fact that we can clearly have different opinions about what the best answer is without having to fall back into a position of the hopeless relativity of 'your answer is as good as mine' (which is an idea which runs quite contrarily to our adversarial system). There are two major recent papers on this topic. The longest and most difficult is 'Objectivity and Truth: You'd Better Believe It' in *Philosophy and Public Affairs* (1996). A somewhat shortened and simplified version is to be found in S Guest (ed), *Positivism Today* (1996) and it is entitled 'Indeterminacy and Law'.

The basic idea, put first in philosophical terms, is that a theory of truth in a particular domain of thought, such as law, or morality (or art), is a first-order, as opposed to a second-order, theory. That is not as difficult an idea as it might sound. It means simply that you don't have to suppose anything other than a straightforward argument of law to see what counts as law, as a *true proposition* of law. You don't have to jump to a higher plane – a 'second-order' – to 'look down' at ordinary legal argument to see whether it is producing a true conclusion. You don't, for example, say that because you can't prove many legal arguments to be right, they *can't* be right. All you have to do (I use this phrase advisedly) is to show again what these legal arguments are. Another way of putting it is to say that, to attempt to persuade a judge of the truth, cogency, etc, of your arguments there is no need to do anything other than put those arguments to him.

A second-order justification, however, would say something like the following: the fact that there is no independent standpoint from which the objectivity and certainty of the law, or morality, can be assessed as true or false, means there can be no such thing as a right or wrong answer. Dworkin calls this imagined independent standpoint 'the Archimedean point' after the Greek philosopher who said he could lift the world provided he had an independent and sufficiently distanced fulcrum point. Dworkin points out, as he has so many times in the past, that the required Archimedean point doesn't exist to provide objectivity *to itself*, but he is much more concerned to say that, really, it is a waste of time to think that arguments about the 'objectivity' add anything to the actual arguments themselves. So, in 'Indeterminacy and Law' he says:

> '... when lawyers disagree, and there is no knock-down argument available to reconcile them, it follows that the case for neither side is better than the case for the other. There are an unlimited number of reasons why some but not all lawyers might think that one side had the better of a particular legal argument. Someone defending the view that no such reason can in fact tip the balance either way in any controversial case faces an enormously difficult task, much more difficult than that faced by someone who wants to argue for one decision rather than another in a particular case. How can he avoid appealing to some very general and abstract theory, like legal positivism? Someone defending a ... claim ... that there is never a right answer to any question about what we ought to do or how we ought to live ... has an even greater problem ... These are truly heroic claims, of vast theoretic pretension, and trying to dress them in the modest clothes of common sense or raw intuition is more comic than persuasive.'

25.8 The 'universality' of Dworkin's thesis

There has been criticism of Dworkin's thesis in relation to the issue of its 'universality'. It is said that in comparing Hart and Dworkin's respective theories of law, Hart's theory was 'descriptive-universal' but Dworkin's theory was 'normative' and not descriptive. It was partly for this reason that Dworkin devised his theory of interpretation. If Dworkin's theory was descriptive, then because it can 'make sense' only of those legal systems, such as the Anglo-American ones, where there clearly exists a legal discourse of rights, then it had no application to, in fact, most legal systems in the world. Therefore, Dworkin's theory was defective in a way that Hart's theory is not.

The rejoinder to this criticism is that it is true that Dworkin denies the quality of law to wicked legal systems. These are those legal systems such as the Nazi system in which there is no respect, even in the form of lip service, to his fundamental 'right to equal concern and respect'. That Dworkin does so is clear from *Law's Empire* where he denies that there could be a 'full-blooded' theory of law where the 'grounds of law' were discernible but not its 'moral force'. So, for example, if you take the Nazi legal system, it is possible to make an argument for a particular legal case (conducted, let's say, by Siegfried J) by applying Nazi norms. But the resultant arguments would lack moral justification and, because Dworkin thinks that, ultimately, the law's point is morally to 'license the coercive powers of the State', Nazi 'law' is not really law. Such a criticism of a lack of universalism in Dworkin can be viewed as being misconceived for one important reason. Dworkin's theory is clearly normative in character and that means it universally acts as critic to existing systems. So an interpretation of the Nazi law, according to him, is that it is 'defective' law, not 'really' law at all.

These points are developed by Berry (1998). He argues that Dworkin's theory can shed light on the demands made by the creeping internationalisation or globalisation of human rights discourse and the growing procedures for the settlement of international disputes. He thinks that it is reference to the 'ideals' that fosters rights talk in this universal and trans-cultural way, saying '… rights have an aspirational content; they are like shorthand expressions of the complex ideas we have about the meaning of human dignity.' It is precisely the aspirational quality of Dworkin's theory that makes his theory universal. Thinking that it is provincial rather than cosmopolitan just mistakes this quality for one of 'universal-description' only. Thus, Berry says:

> 'Not only does Dworkin's theory offer a more nuanced way of understanding how the aspirational content behind rights can affect their practical meanings but also, and more importantly, it provides us with a way of interpreting competing practices – such as human rights and traditional cultures – so as to reconcile or adjudicate between their different demands.' (at p9)

25.9 Guest's defence of Dworkin

Guest (1997b) takes the line that most of Dworkin's major theses are frequently misunderstood and therefore have attracted unfair criticisms. He explored nine of the criticisms and offered a reply to them.

1. Dworkin is an American and so cannot say anything about our system. But there is no reason why Americans cannot comment on the political and legal system.
2. Dworkin is a liberal. Well, which of the hundreds of forms of liberalism do you have in mind? In any case, is liberalism necessarily wrong?
3. Dworkin is arrogant. Rather that he has convictions and expresses them forcefully which may be mistaken for arrogance. Dworkin is a remarkably clear and forceful writer who has many original ideas of which he has an extraordinary grasp, being able to see all the possible ramifications. It is an enviable intelligence he has. Guest thinks that people are not on the whole used to a philosopher who expresses views as forcefully as a politician does, and that this forcefulness

polarises people. He is not a politician but an academic who expects argument not, like the politician, political support. It is just reneging on the business of engaging in intellectual debate merely to say Dworkin is arrogant.

4. Dworkin says there are provable right answers to everything. Dworkin not only doesn't think this but he has argued against this for well over 25 years. He thinks there is no good argument in saying that there are no true propositions in law and morality which can't be proved.

5. Dworkin thinks that individuals don't have any duty to the community. This is just false. He believes that individual members of a community have duties to other individuals by virtue of their right to equal concern and respect and therefore a duty to work towards a community structured so as to recognise that right. This entails extensive duties to the community.

6. Dworkin is anti-feminist. The claim is made because Dworkin has a belief in rights and feminists say that this means that Dworkin has a selfish male view of justice. But Dworkin's view of equality is so very abstract and it says no more than that people have rights to equal concern and respect, and that must include women. What is peculiarly male about that? Again this is a caricature of Dworkin's thought, because Dworkin has strong views about positive discrimination which he doesn't think violate the idea of equality; he has what he calls the bridge principle, which means that any social structure can be examined from the point of view of the fundamental requirement that people be treated with respect.

7. Dworkin is too narrow because he sees everything from the perspective of a judge. Firstly, the perspective of the judge is wider than people generally understand it to be. All law students, all administrators, all lawyers, all academic lawyers, and many other people, guide their lives according to law as it is predicted judges will interpret it. Note how the way a judge makes a decision about a case is markedly different from anyone else's: the judge's decision stands, and not anyone else's, and so that is why it is important for us to fix our interpretation on what judges do. Secondly, true Dworkin is not a sociologist, but neither are most sociologist lawyers; true Dworkin is not an historian, but neither are ... etc.

8. Dworkin's view of interpretation in law requires judges to paint a rosy picture of the law when in fact it isn't really a good picture. Guest says that this shows a lack of misunderstanding of what making the best sense of something is. It doesn't mean lying or distorting. If a moralist tried to make sense of Hitler as a person, he will not have made best sense of him if he simply says he was a German politician who was a vegetarian who loved dogs and children. He has painted a rosy picture of him. Similarly, the moralist also doesn't make best sense of him to say he was a German politician who instituted the death camps and was indirectly responsible for the torture and death of 40 to 50 million people. Making the best sense will only come from a more complete picture.

9. Dworkin is naive to think that judges don't decide on policy grounds. This is a very common view. Of course, Dworkin is aware that judges occasionally – although not as often as people think – decide on policy grounds. But he says that they are wrong, and he cites all the academic opinion, lawyers, judges and so on, who criticise judges who decide in this way. This is simply a descriptive account of why it is wrong to decide on policy grounds and doesn't require reference to Dworkin's theory at all. (In the same way as we would, as lawyers, say that is wrong to steal, we don't think that we have been naive when it is pointed out to us that, in fact, some people do steal!) In any case, Guest gives his own eye-witness account of ten Court of Appeal and High Court judges at a seminar telling him – unanimously – that they thought it would be quite wrong for a judge to put the case law to one side and judge solely on the criterion of what was good for the community.

Legal Concepts

26

The Analysis of Rights

26.1 Introduction: the place of law

Rights claimed in modern society have a contradictory quality about them. We can easily place strongly affirmed rights in direct conflict. For example, people claim the right to life yet there are others who claim a right to abortion; people claim the right not to be killed by another, yet there are also claims to a right to die; and people claim the right to free information, yet there is also a claim to privacy.

These are but a few examples. The claim to right is thus ultimately a claim to self-determination, which can produce logical contradictions and is itself in contradiction to the aspect of social control by law. However, the contradiction is one of degree. Thus, the issue of rights in the social context is one of balancing conflicting claims and determining which claims have priority.

The law has a special function within this framework. Law presupposes free choice at least to the extent that by implying that you ought to obey, you might otherwise choose to do something else. However, law restricts the way in which you may act in certain circumstances, even to the extent of physically restraining you. Thus, the law itself claims that the citizen ought to do as the law chooses, regardless of whether there are other non-legal reasons for doing otherwise. The origin of the right or authority to make law has been intermittently discussed, since this is the question of the authority to make law and of the obligation to obey it. However, it begs the question, does law extinguish individuals' claims to rights? The question may be broken down further.

1. Are there strong normative reasons for law to prefer an individual's choice to the prescriptions of legal norms? This must be considered the normative jurisprudential question of rights.

2. When a legal system concedes the existence of rights, what does this mean and what does a legal right do? This is a question of analytical jurisprudence.

26.2 Some contrasting views on rights

The legislators' duty, in ethical terms, is to society as a whole. Yet society is made up of interest groups and individuals. The immediate need of society may be seen as being in irreconcilable conflict with that of the individual. When should an individual or class claim of right be upheld in spite of the interests of the whole of society?

Marxism

The orthodox Marxist perspective on morality and rights stems from two premises.

1. Morality is an ideology that derives from the particular stage of development of productive forces of a society. Thus, Marxism cannot criticise the infringement of rights of workers in capitalist societies in moral terms. The critique of capitalism is a scientific one.
2. Man in socialist society requires no such ideology because he will naturally orient himself to social usefulness.

As a result, Marx views morality as relative to the particular stage of societal development and human rights as an ideology that alienates one man from another. As we have observed, rights presuppose restraint and conflict, mediating between them. Such alienation and mediation are seen by Marx and Engels as delaying revolutionary change to a society where conflict no longer exists. To adhere to a concept of rights, is to adhere to a maintenance of the status quo and unequal distribution. Marx denies therefore that there are strong normative reasons for rights that can be accepted by law, since law merely shields the interests of the dominant class.

Jeremy Bentham

Bentham, as has been observed in the Chapters on imperative theory and utilitarianism, completely rejects the concept of rights as anything other than fantasies of the mind. To Bentham rights derive entirely from the law and are legal constructs. However, it must be remembered that Bentham is sceptical about the concept of morality as a whole. Human beings act on the principles of pleasure and pain. It would seem to be vastly illogical that the interests of the rest of society should be subverted for the pleasure of an individual or class of individuals. The crude utilitarian perspective sees the legislators' duty as being solely the maximisation of pleasure in society, potentially at the expense of the rights of the minority.

However, this does not mean that all utilitarians follow this rather simplistic view. It is possible to demonstrate that a presupposition of weak rights is compatible with the utilitarian perspective. We shall investigate the rights versus utility debate a little later on.

Bentham himself subscribes to the view that an individual should be granted the maximum independence that is conducive to the good of his fellows in society, but he still reserves the right of the state to intervene on behalf of the collective good.

Natural law

In Chapter 11 we discussed the views of natural lawyers, who tend to view natural law duties as ones that transcend legal duties. By appeal to natural law, we might have rights that exist independently of law that we would expect law to fulfil. However, it has been observed that natural law proofs tend to be open to empirical attack. In order to assert the existence of natural rights one needs to believe in natural law. Faith, either secular or religious, is a strong normative reason for an individual to expect rights, but not for an agnostic society to accept those rights. A further problem with natural law is that, historically, the distribution of rights has been uneven and thus a recipe for the denial of rights to some in favour of the privilege of others.

The facts of the 'human condition'

Both Hume and Hart suggest that there are certain empirical facts about the nature of the human condition that one would normally expect to see responded to in legal or moral systems. These amount to their respective theories of natural law. Inevitably, if we look at history, we can see that certain legalised actions have been ultimately detrimental to societal interests. Thus, genocide, torture and certain other extremes of state action in the name of society have served no particular benefit to society. In these terms, it is common sense for a historically informed legislator to avoid such excesses. Moreover, this is linked to a weak moral argument that law, while necessary to mediate between conflicting wills, should leave a certain amount of moral autonomy to the subject.

The rather common sense approach does, however, rely on practical reasoning and experience. This means that pragmatism can trump this conception of rights. The torture of a terrorist may save the lives of hundreds of potential victims of a bomb that he has planted. The argument against doing so is largely a moral one.

We shall explore interest theories, the chief modern theorist being Neil MacCormick, and Hart's will theory in greater depth later on, since they are concerned chiefly with the nature of rights actually found in law, rather than the reason why law should have a concept of rights.

It must be remembered from Chapters 20 to 23, however, that normative theories of rights, those of Rawls, Nozick and Dworkin, are to be found as part of their theories of justice.

26.3 Hohfeld's scheme of rights

Within the area of the analytical jurisprudence of rights the starting point for any study must be, according to Lloyd and Freeman, the work of Wesley N Hohfeld. Hohfeld's writing on the subject of rights was undertaken in the early years of the twentieth century and it could indeed be said with some justification that he has made a considerable though hardly acknowledged contribution to our understanding of law. In his work *Fundamental Legal Conceptions as Applied in Judicial Reasoning*, Hohfeld stated that the aim of his theory was to clarify different kinds of legal relations and the different uses to which certain words that are employed in legal reasoning are made. He sought to expose the ambiguities and to eliminate the confusion that surrounds these words. He was concerned to give meaning to the phrase 'X has a right to R' and to explain the set of jural relations that such a statement gives rise to. That objective can be achieved by the concept of right (which he also referred to as a claim); of privilege (liberty); of power and of immunity. These he saw as the lowest common denominators in which legal problems about rights could be stated. That proposition is one that is not without criticism. Indeed the contention of his critics is that while his scheme works for some propositions in which the phrase 'X has a right to R' could be fitted, it does not always work because his scheme could not take account of paternalistic criminal law. It is proposed to deal with this criticism in more depth below.

For Hohfeld these words (claim; privilege; power; and immunity) are to be explained in terms of correlatives and opposites, as each of these concepts has both a jural opposite and a jural correlative. These contain eight fundamental conceptions and all legal problems could be stated in their terms. They thus represented a sort of lowest common denominator in terms of which legal problems could be stated. This he did by method of the following:

Jural opposites – right/no right; privilege/duty; power/disability; immunity/liability.
Jural correlatives – right/duty; privilege/no right; power/liability; immunity/disability.
These terms can be defined as follows.

1. By a right (claim) he meant that everyone is under a duty to allow X to do R and that X would have a claim against anyone from everyone to enforce that right.
2. By a privilege/liberty he meant that X is free to do or refrain from doing that which is the subject of R. Y has no claim against X if X either exercises or refrains from exercising that liberty.
3. By a power he meant that X is free to do an act whether or not he has a claim or a privilege and that this act would have the effect of altering the legal rights and duties of others.
4. By an immunity he meant that X is not subject to anyone's power to change his legal position.
5. By a duty he meant that Y must respect X's right.

6. By no claim he meant that where X has a liberty Y has no claim that X should not exercise that liberty.

7. By disability he meant that the party has an inability to change another person's legal position.

It is important to emphasise that Hohfeld was examining legal rights and that the meanings attributed to his terms are technical and do not necessarily accord with their common usage.

Dias utilises a model developed by Glanville Williams which can be set out as follows:

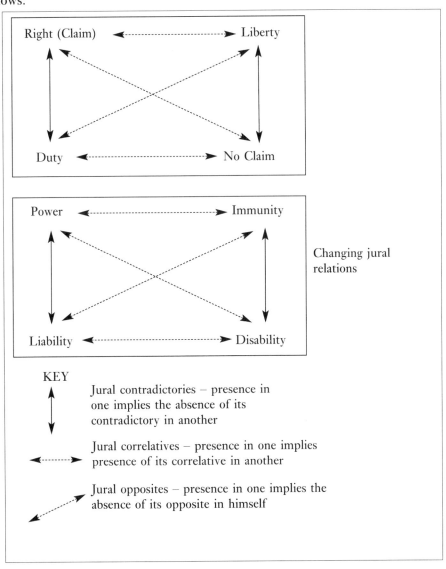

The problem with this diagram is that while it appears to work on its face it does not use the same terminology as Hohfeld himself used and has therefore perhaps added to the confusion. On examination of the Glanville Williams diagram the arrows for jural correlatives are inverted with the arrows for jural contradictories. On the definitions offered by Hohfeld for his own terminology it would appear that a claim could not be regarded as the correlative of a liberty in the sense that the presence of a claim in one implies the presence of a liberty in another. It is submitted that the relation between a claim and a liberty is better described in Hohfeldian terms as a jural contradictory in that the presence of a claim in one implies the absence of its contradictory (a liberty) in another. This point is not however settled.

The aim of Hohfeld was to provide a model for the correct solution of legal problems and to make that solution easier and more certain. He urged that the judge and the legal theorist employ the above scheme in order to ensure greater understanding of these legal concepts. He wrote of the need to use the term right in a very strict sense and not indiscriminately to cover a privilege, power and immunity. Nonetheless, it would not be necessary to Hohfeld that the legal practitioner actually employ the terms claim, power, etc, so long as he thinks in terms of Hohfeld's scheme. It is thus possible to think Hohfeld without talking Hohfeld. This adequately deals with the criticism of Hohfeld that he has adopted an unusual terminology which it would be naive to expect the legal profession to adopt overnight. Indeed Hohfeld's scheme was developed seventy years ago and still nothing much has happened by way of the legal profession adopting his terminology in the effort to clarify legal problems. Nonetheless, his contribution has been quite substantial, although underrated to date. Hohfeld's scheme does, too, provide an excellent starting point for any theoretical discussion of rights.

Dias suggests that it is useful to view the relationship between the jural relations at rest and the changing jural relations in a *temporal* perspective. He argues that a change in the power/liability relation will have a knock-on effect on the claim/duty relation. The power/liability relationship would be anterior to the claim/duty relationship since the claim/duty relationship would be created or amended by the power/liability relationship and would reflect any change therein. An example would be in the adverse possession of land. Here a change in power/liability where formerly the tenant could exclude the squatter has now changed and the squatter gains title to the exclusion of the tenant. Thus T previously had power, that is, the facility to alter another's (S) legal status. On the running of time S now acquires power and T is under a liability. This would then lead to a change in the claim and duty relation.

26.4 Evaluation of Hohfeld's scheme

While Hohfeld's scheme of jural relations is useful not only for illustrating the different forms which the word right can take, it also illustrates the inter-relationships between these words. It is thus useful for distinguishing between claims, liberties, powers and immunities but it is argued that it would also be both necessary and desirable to retain a general concept of right to denote institutions such as ownership or possession. As Cook, who was the editor of Hohfeld's work and generally sympathetic to his task, observes, Hohfeld mistakenly considers all rights as sets of any number of his four elementary rights, namely: claim, privilege, power and immunity. Rights are not sets of these. Their possession entails the possession of other rights or of powers and duties. For example, the concept of ownership includes rights of possession, transfer, sale, hire, use and enjoyment. Thus ownership creates a set of claims and powers. The concept of ownership can be seen as a set of rights. It does not denote the relationship between the owner and the tangible object.

His contribution has been useful although the difficulty is that it is not as widely used as he would have advocated. Nonetheless, as Lloyd and Freeman observe, it is the point to which all lawyers return. They perceive the value of his analysis in enabling the reduction of any legal transaction to relative simplicity and precision and in the enabling of the recognition of its universality.

Harris identifies three important advantages to his approach. First, that it enables real normative choices to be disentangled from verbal confusions. Secondly, that if lawyers and judges were to employ his terminology that was not too far removed from that already employed, then clarity would reign. The third advantage lies in their use. Hohfeld believed that juristic problems concerning the nature of compound concepts could be dissolved.

Although he has been criticised for insisting on correlativity in situations where correlativity is hardly present as, for example, in the criminal law, the implicit answer that Harris finds in his defence of Hohfeld is that all litigation cases involve two opposing parties and as such viewing these concepts as correlatives is in that frame quite meaningful. It does however make an explanation of rights *in rem* impossible. Nonetheless, there are important criticisms of Hohfeld's scheme. In that he purports to analyse fundamental legal concepts he does so without taking account of any concept of law. He fails to provide an explanation of the process by which those conceptions are given their legal character. He further assumes that there is only one concept of duty. It is said that this is because his examples are drawn from civil and private law.

In criminal law his scheme hardly works. This, it is submitted, is because of the nature of the duty under criminal law. While, as Harris observes in defence of Hohfeld, Hohfeld was concerned with the lowest common denominator in litigation, this would not in my view be applicable in a prosecution. The duty is not owed to the prosecution but to the society as a whole. That duty does not give rise to a right in anyone. Hohfeld's scheme is designed to cover one to one relations and not the relations between an individual and the society. Furthermore, it is suggested that with respect to paternalistic criminal law such as the laws that govern the wearing of seat belts in cars and the law of murder which forbids the defence of consent of the victim, the nature of the duty is one that the individual owes both to the society and to himself. As such, when an individual has both a claim and a duty with regard to the same thing, the scheme would be without application.

Roscoe Pound in *Legal Rights* noted that some of Hohfeld's conceptions are without what he called juridical significance yet in a generally appreciative work Pound suggested that had Hohfeld lived he would have dealt with this point.

In spite of these criticisms, viewed in a chronological frame his contribution has been substantial. However, since the publication of his work there have been further developments and elucidations such as the works of Hart and MacCormick on rights. They benefited from having available to them Hohfeld's analysis.

26.5 The choice theory versus the interest theory

In this context the debate between Hart and MacCormick over the role and nature of legal rights is particularly informative. The essence of the debate should be viewed within its political perspective.

Hart's will theory

Hart views rights as legally protected choices. He emphasises the power or option of one person to waive someone elses duty. Thus having a right is to do with the legal or moral recognition of some individual's choice as being pre-eminent over the will of others as to a given subject matter in a given relationship. This is applicable in the civil law area in matters such as contract. The essence of the holding of a right is that the holder has the choice whether to waive the duty owed to him. The connection with Hohfeld's scheme of jural relations is apparent in that such a view assumes a correlativity of rights and duties. In this theory the choice could be expressed in Hohfeldian terms as the choice of whether or not to exercise that right or power or privilege or immunity. A problem with this approach is that it makes the enforcement of a duty conditional on the exercise of a choice or will of a person other than the person who is under the duty. Y will only be under a duty if X who has a right in respect of that duty decides to exercise that right. A difficulty that Hart readily admits with this approach is that it fails to take account of the fundamental rights of the individual as against the legislature. For this right Hart invokes the immunity as defined by Hohfeld.

MacCormick's interest theory

MacCormick criticises Hart's theory on the grounds that there are some rights which do not seem to involve the exercise of a choice at all. He argues that, particularly in the area of paternalistic criminal law, the law limits the power of waiver without destroying a substantive right. An example would be in respect of assault or of murder. The law will not admit the consent of the victim in defence to a prosecution. MacCormick argues that if one cannot consent to assault it follows that one is not exercising a choice on the right to freedom of the person. MacCormick maintains that the nature of rights can be viewed as protecting the interests of the right holder.

Looking at the difficult example of the rights of a child MacCormick draws a distinction between the substantive right and the right to enforce the substantive right. He shows that the child possesses the substantive right to have its interest protected but lacks the right to enforce that right – the right to enforce is exercisable by the child's guardian on behalf of the child. Further the child cannot in fact or in morals or in law relieve his or her parents of their duty towards it. MacCormick then prefers the view of rights as protecting certain interests in the sense that either moral or legal normative constraints are imposed on the acts and activities of other people with respect to the objects of one's interest.

Hart admits that if rights are all about choice then a young child would not possess any rights in that sense. As to the question of the protection of the child, Hart maintains that rights are not the only moral basis for protection and that other factors such as humanity, love and compassion also provide the basis for protection. If that is so then there would be no need for a formal assignment of rights to the child on its attaining the age of choice. Until that assignment of rights the parent would act as the child could have acted had it possessed the power to choose.

Hart rejects the view that rights are legally protected interests because he maintains that the interest analysis does not explain rights independently of duties. If a right is merely a protected interest then rights can always be expressed as a reflex of duties. MacCormick gives an example of the right of succession in intestacy. He shows that such a right cannot be rephrased in terms of the rights of the personal representatives because the right vests at death, prior to these duties. MacCormick maintains that the idea of correlativity obscures the fact that duties are imposed in order to protect rights.

Nigel Simmonds in 'The Analytical Foundations of Justice', *Cambridge Law Journal* (1995) sympathetically (but also critically) discusses Hillel Steiner's book *An Essay on Rights* (1994). Particularly useful to Jurisprudence students in Simmonds' review is his admirably clear discussion of Steiner's equally useful discussion of the distinction between the choice and interest theories. Steiner's basic idea is that human rights are fundamental to all theories of justice, which is a view that has been going out of fashion in recent years with the growth of communitarian theories of justice in which communities, or groups, or families are the 'building blocks' of a just and good society. The attraction of the communitarian view is that, whereas rights-centred type theories do not, at first sight anyway, easily accommodate the idea of individual duties to the community (albeit to other individuals to respect mutual rights), communitarian type theories do. Raz, for example, thinks that people do not have rights to certain public goods such as the public culture displayed in art galleries etc (or, more mundanely, to the air) but nevertheless have *interests* in them which the community has a collective duty to maintain. Steiner, instead, claims:

> 'Rights are the items which are created and parcelled out by the justice principle. We learn something about justice by examining the formal or characteristic features of rights.'

Simmonds does not agree fully with this view since there are logical problems. He believes in the reductionism involved being able to re-describe all propositions in terms of rights accruing to individuals. Examples such as Raz's proposition that individuals do not have rights to public goods is a compelling one; nevertheless there is also difficulty in understanding what the purpose of public goods is (why they are 'goods') unless they are good *for someone*. The fact that a very large number of people benefit from public goods is a reason for denying them wholesale direct interest, eg in the form of granting them a formal right, and is an explanation of why we think that no one has a right to a public good. But it would not follow from this that there was no right of a more abstract kind. In a very basic sense, it is true that one has a right to be respected in decisions involving participation in public goods without having the right to a portion of a public right to be delivered. Simmonds points approvingly to Steiner's revival of the analytical method employed by Hart and the linguistic school of philosophy of the 1950s (and implicit in English analytical jurisprudence since the time of Austin). A close examination of the 'meaning' of 'right', Steiner thinks, will lead to insights about the nature of justice in general, in contradistinction to the avowedly evaluative approaches to enquiry about law engaged in by Finnis and Dworkin.

There may, however, be a problem with identifying the beneficiaries of a duty. In his book *Central Issues in Jurisprudence*, Simmonds uses the example of the crash helmet law whereby all people riding on a motor bike are under a legal duty to wear a crash helmet. Who is the beneficiary? Surely not the manufacturers of crash helmets? MacCormick may not be entirely correct in his contention that the power to waive a right is not a necessary part of a right but is just something that a right often includes. In support of that contention he demonstrates that in certain circumstances it is necessary to override freedoms – for example, in contract the freedom to contract the terms is overridden by the recent consumer protection legislation. Simmonds sums it up thus:

> 'Even if MacCormick has provided a convincing case against the correlativity of rights and duties, it is by no means clear that he has provided a convincing alternative.'

MacCormick does admit the importance of the will theory in the explanation of rights. He put it thus:

> '... it cannot be denied that the central point of the theory is that apart from children and incapacitated persons the holder of a legal right is empowered in law to choose whether he should avail himself of his right on a specific occasion by insisting on performance of the correlative duty.'

If that is so it might be assumed (albeit wrongly, it is submitted) that Hart's and

MacCormick's theories are compatible, but that would be to fall into the linguistic trap which was so much the concern of Hohfeld. For MacCormick the difficulty is in the absence of choice with regard to children's rights, the argument going that those rights are among those referred to in a footnote by Hart in his notion of immunity rights dependent upon individual benefit. In the Hohfeldian sense the rights of children as envisaged by MacCormick are claim rights whereas Hart's are immunity rights. Hence while both rights are fundamental and important they have different lowest common denominators.

27

Legal Personality

27.1 Introduction

27.2 Different types of legal personality

27.3 Is legal personality a useful concept?

27.4 The theories: what theories are used to explain legal personality?

27.5 Do the theories obscure?

27.1 Introduction

A right is not the only legal concept to have attracted much jurisprudential discussion. Another such concept is that of legal and especially corporate personality. Why are certain bodies treated in law as persons and some bodies (trade unions, partnerships, unincorporated associations) generally not? What, if anything, does it mean to say that a company is a person?

27.2 Different types of legal personality

There are three types of personality recognised in English law; in relation to any question, you should ask yourself if it is about one or all three.

Human beings

No distinction is drawn in law between legal and natural persons. Hohfeld sees human beings as merely a multitude of claims, liberties, powers, etc. But it should be noted that the notion of a human being is more flexible than might be thought. We shall examine some of these.

A foetus

What is the legal status of an unborn child (re pre-natal deformity? child destruction?) The example of the legal personality of a foetus has raised interesting and emotive questions recently. In the case of *C* v *S* (1987) one such question arose for consideration. Briefly, in that case a man who claimed to be the father of a foetus attempted to prevent the mother of the foetus from proceeding with an abortion after their relationship broke down. His grounds were to invoke the criminal law against the destruction of a child capable of being born alive (s1 Infant Life Preservation Act 1929). The rather controversial interpretation given to that phrase by the House of Lords need not detain this text. What is of importance is the observation that it was the father (as an interested person) who brought the action and not the foetus, yet if the foetus had been deemed to be a legal person it could have brought the action itself. Practical problems of instructing solicitors, etc, from the womb can in this legal system be overcome – there are procedures to enable the incompetent to be party to actions. The implication though is wide. The foetus would have a separate legal personality from the mother carrying it. The mother would merely be a walking incubator for another legal person. The mother would owe that person a duty of care that would give rise to that person having a cause of action where, for example through smoking cigarettes, the mother caused the foetus damage. If the foetus were a legal person then it would be party to an action to prevent an abortion, etc. I would imagine that other factors will be considered in seminars – enough for present purposes to raise the questions. By way of anecdote for those interested, I understand that although the House of Lords held that the foetus could be aborted as at the stage of gestation it had reached, it was not capable of sustaining life if born, the mother continued with the pregnancy and the child is being brought up by the father. (A happy ending?)

A dead person

Legal personality extends to those humans who are alive and of an existence independent of their mother. What is the position with regard to the dead? They have legal interests, such as that their wishes as expressed in their wills are carried out, for example. The law has studiously avoided any definition of death – see *R* v *Malcherek and Steel* (1981) – probably for the very sound reason that advances in medical science and technology would outstrip the capacity of the law to keep pace and we would arrive at a situation, as we have for example in criminal law, where the definition of insanity became fossilised in 1843 (*McNaghten's Case*) in spite of very considerable advances since then. So what constitutes legal death is not clear. I think the proposition stated at the start of this sub-section to the effect that so far as natural persons are concerned a prerequisite of legal personality is independent live existence is true. The dead may have certain rights, such as to have their property disposed of according to their legal wishes, but that is as far as it goes.

A married couple

The example that used to be used was that a husband and wife were treated as one person for certain tax matters, for example, mortgage interest relief and the filling of tax return forms that required a wife to disclose to her husband all the sources of her taxable income, because the husband was under the legal duty to declare that income of his wife to the Inland Revenue. That position has been changed in the

Finance Act 1988 although aspects of it have not at the date of writing entered into force. I do not envisage this rather antiquated rule that regarded a wife as an appendage of her husband being revived.

Status

Another flexible aspect is that there are different relationships to think about – status (parent, slave, consumer) and capacity (the same person can have two or more in some factual situation; trustee and beneficiary, shareholder and employee and company director, for instance).

Corporations sole

A corporation sole is a person with a perpetual existence, that is, an office, the personification of an official capacity. Examples are parsons, bishops, the Crown (the Queen has a different personality for each country where she is the monarch). The main rationale behind the corporation sole is that the continuity of jural relations, such as the holding of property, is made possible. This need hardly detain us further.

Corporations aggregate

These are companies or other corporations created by charter, statute or under the Companies Acts. They are treated as persons in law unless the contrary is stated (statutes use individuals if they mean humans and unincorporated associations but not corporations). Some unincorporated associations are given some of the incidental benefits of corporations but they are still not persons. Partnerships, for example, can issue writs in their own name and can make contracts, but the individual partners remain fully liable as individuals.

27.3 Is legal personality a useful concept?

The flexibility of treatment given to the notion of a human being is useful and corporations sole have their limited effectiveness allowing in the continuation of property ownership and contractual relations. This question as to the usefulness of the concept of legal personality is, though, most relevantly considered with regard to the corporations aggregate.

The uses of corporations aggregate

These have been stated as follows.

Convenience

The convenience offered by conferring powers and liabilities on a unit rather than on each individual shareholder involved (imagine suing British Telecom if it were otherwise!).

Limited liability

Shareholders do not attract liability except to the extent of their respective shareholdings, and directors and employees are only liable for their personal negligence; this is subject to the frequent requirement of personal guarantees, from participants in small companies.

Perpetuity of succession

This applies on death, retirement, sale of shares.

Ability to sue

Can sue or be sued, can own property (this is really an aspect of Chapter 26).

Separate ownership

Ownership and control can be separated, allowing investors to risk their money but under the control of expert management. In many public quoted companies, ownership and control are totally divorced in this way.

Other advantages

Generally, an individual trader can escape personal liability (subject to personal guarantees) and it is easier for a company to raise capital than for a sole trader. Note though that the courts do sometimes lift the corporate veil (there is a list of instances of this in Dias). Note also that some of the advantages can be achieved without a separate personality being used. For example, writs can be served on partnerships, and property is often held by only some of the partners. This allows ownership to be passed more easily. Also, a big partnership will often separate its management from the bulk of the owning partners. Think also of the special treatment of trades unions and employers associations in English law.

Problems with corporations aggregate

Corporations aggregate also raise the following problems.

Groups

English law has difficulties in dealing with the idea of a group of companies. For most purposes, they are treated as separate units rather than as a collective entity, which is most unrealistic. Some inroads have however been made into this problem; group companies now submit consolidated accounts and are taxed as a unit, for example.

Inflexibility
Even small companies have to fulfil statutory requirements suitable for much larger outfits. The present government is committed to relaxing some of these requirements and it is already the case that small companies have to submit less complete accounts, for instance.

Unfairness
Small creditors never have security and so can lose heavily in an insolvency. There are some restrictions in the Insolvency Act 1986 on directors involved just setting up another, similarly named company in such cases (only time will tell if they are effective) and there are various possibilities of penalties or civil remedies (including disqualification) against directors involved in an insolvency – see the Companies Directors Disqualification Act 1986. But these generally will not benefit small unsecured creditors, who can't afford to rely on them. It is a myth that a customer or supplier is safer dealing with a limited company than an individual trader or partnership – often the reverse is the case.

Inconsistency
It is not at all clear why some legal rules and regulations apply to all companies but not to other (often larger) organisations which organise themselves as partnerships. Often the choice of business medium is based on taxation considerations rather than on which medium is more suitable in terms of its inherent characterstics.

27.4 The theories: what theories are used to explain legal personality?

There are four main theories for us to consider, albeit in each case rather briefly. We will try to analyse for each theory which elements of the law it can, and cannot, account for.

Fiction theory

First, we will look at the fiction theory, supported by von Savigny and in England by Coke, Blackstone and especially Salmond. Juristic or artificial persons are only treated as if they are persons, under this view. They are fictitious, not known as persons apart from the law. The law gives them proprietary rights, grants them legal powers and so on, but they have no personality and no will (except to the extent a will is implied by the law). This is an obviously flexible viewpoint, since it can account for any apparent inconsistency in legal treatment by simply saying that they are only treated as persons to that extent. The doctrine of *ultra vires*, under which a company cannot do anything not authorised by its memorandum of association might be thought to support the fiction theory, on the basis that the law only gives personality to the limit of the memorandum, and so might the doctrine that a company is separate from its members, epitomised in the leading case of *Salomon*. This case shows that the law treats the company as a separate unit, even though in fact it is not, especially in the one-man company cases like *Salomon*.

Further support for this theory could be claimed from the criminal law, which originally accepted that a company could not commit a criminal offence which depends on mental intention. The fiction view explains this on the basis of the will of the person only being that given by law, and therefore presumably being limited to lawful intention. Recent developments show a more pragmatic and sensible approach to the question of corporate liability, with companies being subject to more criminal liability (and also subject to liability for the torts of their servants). Also, the cases where the law allows the corporate veil to be lifted aside can be explained as limitations on the grant of the fictitious personality.

Acceptable explanations, then, are provided by the fiction theory for many aspects of company law (although many of them can be explained acceptably by other theories, see below).

However, no explanation is given of why the law uses the idea of personality; is there an essential similarity to real persons or not? Hart has emphasised some of the faults identified in relation to this theory, particularly the illogicality involved in denying that a company can commit certain crimes because it has no mind.

Some other theories are similar to and bound up with the fiction theory, notably the concession theory (that legal personality flows from the state) and the symbolist theory of Ihering.

Hohfeld's theory

This theory is not mirrored in English writing on the subject. Since only human beings have juristic relations, one must, according to Hohfeld, explain companies in a complex way by looking at the capacities, rights, powers and liabilities of the individuals involved. This view is clearly related to Hohfeld's analysis of rights. However, it again fails to give us an explanation of why the notion of a company is used, the notion of a separate personality.

Realist

This view sees an artificial person as a real personality, having a real mind, will and power of action. It is associated with Gierke, Dicey, Pollock and (though Hart doubts it) Maitland.

If independent power of action was the only requirement of our definition of a person and personality, perhaps an artificial person would qualify (but has a company really got a power of action independent of its members and officials?); surely though there is something more. To say a corporation is a real person implies an individuality, and that implies some consciousness, experience, inner unity. Some groups may seem to have such a unity and consciousness. Perhaps one could talk of such a feeling over the reaction to the Somalian famine crisis, for instance, a corporation sole (consisting of successive holders of one office) hasn't a consciousness, nor has a multi-national company, nor even a small company? Perhaps a university might be thought to fit?

In any case, even if the legal personalities could be counted as real persons, a further problem arises. If a two-man company is a person in reality, why not a two-man partnership? If a one-man company, why not a one-man business? If a university, why not a private law college, one that is unincorporated? The realist theory fails to explain why the legal definition of personality does not match the extended realist definition.

Returning to some of the aspects of English law already considered, realist theory can account for the *ultra vires* doctrine (the real personality constituted by the company as set up by its documents), albeit rather weakly (isn't it a weakness to have to refer to legal documents to establish the limits of reality?); but it can't successfully accommodate the tearing aside of the corporate veil. If the company is a real entity distinct from its members, surely it should always be viewed as such and not sometimes viewed as a collection of its members?

Finally, realism can account for those instances where criminal law applies to a company: can it account for those when it doesn't (if a board meeting orders an execution, the company isn't guilty of murder: why not)? The reason why it would not be guilty of murder in the likelihood of a board resolution so ordering is that it is incapable of forming the necessary *mens rea* for murder. Obviously, considerations as to suitable penalty will also be relevant (it is impractical to imprison a company!). The recent suggestions of possible prosecution whether public or private against a ferry operating company for corporate manslaughter, as a result of suggestions in the inquiry into the events at Zeebrugge, demonstrate an actual example of the criminal law responsibility of a corporation.

Hart has raised some additional points. The theory (as with the fiction theory) has illogical barriers; for example, it has been suggested that a company cannot be bound by an agreement with another company because that would be degrading, and the realist view has difficulties with a one-man technical company – isn't such a company not a real entity but just a convenient device for the individual proprietor?

Linked to this theory is the organic theory, the name of which is quite accurate and suggests that a company acts through the various organs that constitute it. In this theory the board of directors will take decisions concerning the day to day running of the company whereas the general meeting will take decisions concerning the constitution of the company. So long as the proper decision is taken in the proper way by the proper body it will be considered at law as the act or decision of the company.

Purpose

The final view is the purpose theory developed by Brinz and, in England, by Barker. On this view, only human beings are persons, but the law protects certain purposes other than human beings. The creation of artificial persons just gives effect to a purpose (for example, a charitable corporation is created to give effect to various devices by which the law aids the charitable cause). So company property is held not by a person, but for a purpose.

This view has a fundamental flaw. It does not answer the question. It is obviously true that companies and other artificial legal persons are given their status for a purpose (or various purposes). The question remains, why call them persons? What aspect of these entities makes them so akin to real people that the law uses the same name and to a great extent applies the same rules?

A purpose view can explain the *ultra vires* doctrine (a company is limited to its express purposes, as mentioned in the memorandum), and even the tearing aside of the veil (the countering weight of other legal purposes), cannot explain the concept of an artificial person.

Our conclusion at this point is that none of the various explanations given of the nature of corporate personality is satisfactory.

27.5 Do the theories obscure?

Both Paton in *Jurisprudence* and Hart in his inaugural lecture at Oxford, *Definition and Theory in Jurisprudence,* think that the answer to the question is yes, because the theorists, in trying to ascertain what is the nature of corporate personality, are asking the wrong question. Paton writes that seeking the essence of, the connecting factor between, the various different types of legal persons, natural and artificial, is the wrong approach because there is no connecting factor except the similarity and treatment meted out by the law to the different persons.

Hart's views are somewhat different. The slim booklet containing his inaugural lecture (which is also included in his *Essays in Jurisprudence and Philosophy*) is well worth reading. Briefly he considers that the question 'What is corporate personality?' is seeking the wrong type of definition.

Just as with other concepts found in law, such as a right or a duty, corporate personality has no straightforward connection with the world of fact, nothing to which it corresponds. It should not, therefore, be defined in the same way as the concept of the table or chair you are sitting at or on, since these concepts do have an object to which they correspond in nature – they exist and can be touched in the real world of scientific cause and effect. Hart goes on to say that the theories which we have looked at above are often in the clouds and do not deal with practical realities.

What then is Hart's alternative? Well, he says, picking up an idea that he attributes to, among others, Bentham, corporate personality and the other legal concepts should be defined not by looking just at the words themselves but rather by considering a characteristic sentence in which they appear and then explaining the conditions under which the words are used – under what conditions does the law ascribe liabilities to corporations? By this method we can avoid questions such as those relating to a corporation's supposed will.

Hart in *Definition and Theory* imagines an innocent lawyer from Arcadia to whom the notion of a legal or corporate personality is introduced for the first time. He would learn what types of legal personality there were and the forms of statement in general use by which rights were ascribed to Smith & Co Ltd, in circumstances in some ways similar to and in some ways different from those in which they were ascribed to Smith as an individual. He would see that the analogy was sometimes thin but that given the circumstances set out in the Companies Acts and in the general law the statement Smith & Co Ltd owes White £10 applied as directly to the facts after its own fashion as Smith owes White £10.

On his return to Arcadia he would tell of the extension to corporate bodies of rules worked out for individuals and of the analogies followed and the adjustments of ordinary words involved. He would, in short, have explained corporate personality without any need to get into the confusing and obscure theories which I have set out above. In Hart's words we could make the simple Arcadian feel the theorist's agonies only by inducing him to ask what is Smith & Co Ltd and not to admit in answer a description of how, and under what conditions, the names of corporate bodies are used in practice, but instead to start the search for what it is that the name taken solely describes, for what it stands, for what it means.

Bibliography

Ackerman, B
    (1984) *Reconstructing American Law*
Adler, M
    (1922) *Die Staatsauffassung des Marxismus*
Aquinas, T
    (1948) *Selected Political Writings*
Austin, J
    (1873) *Lectures on Jurisprudence*
    (1995) *The Province of Jurisprudence Determined*

Barkun, M
    (1968) *Law Without Sanctions*
Bentham, J
    (1970) *Of Laws in General*
    (1987) *An Introduction to the Principles of Morals and Legislation*
Berlin, I
    (1962) *Does Political Theory Still Exist?*
    (1969) *Four Essays on Liberty*
Berry, D
    (1998) Interpreting Rights and Culture: Extending Law's Empire, *Res Publica, 1*
Bix, B
    (1999) *Jurisprudence*
Black, D
    (1972) Boundaries of Legal Sociology, *Yale Law Journal* 1086
Bohannan, P
    (1967) The Differing Realms of Law in *Law and Warfare*
Bork, J
    (1971) Neutral Principles and Some First Amendment Problems, 47 *Indiana Law Journal*
    (1990) *The Tempting of America*
Brudney, D
    (1993) Two Links of Law and Morality, 103 *Ethics* 280
Burke, E
    (1790) *Reflections on the Revolution in France*

Capps, P
    (2000) Being Positive about Positivism, *Modern Law Review* 774
Cardozo, B
    (1921) *Nature of the Judicial Process*
Chodorow, N
    (1978) *The Reproduction of Mothering*
Coase, R
    (1960) The Problem of Social Cost, *Journal of Law and Economics* 1–44
Cohen, G
    (1995) The Pareto Argument for Inequality, *Social Philosophy and Policy* 160

Cohen, M (ed)
   (1984) *Ronald Dworkin and Contemporary Jusirprudence*
Comte, A
   (1974) *The Positive Philosophy*
Cross, R
   (1976) *Statutory Interpretation*

D'Entrèves
   (1970) *Natural Law*
Dahl, T
   (1987) *Women's Law*
Daniels, N
   (1990) *Reading Rawls*
Detmold, M J
   (1984) *The Unity of Morality and Law*
   (1989) *Courts and Administrators; A Study in Jurisprudence*
Devlin, P
   (1962) *Samples of Law Making*
   (1965) *The Enforcement of Morals*
   (1979) *The Judge*
Dias, R
   (1968) Legal Politics Behind the Grundnorm, *Cambridge Law Journal*
   (1985) *Jurisprudence*
Durkheim, E
   (1893) *The Division of Labour in Society*
Dworkin, R
   (1976) *Philosophy of Law* (ed)
   (1978) *Taking Rights Seriously*
   (1980) Is Wealth A Value?, *Journal of Legal Studies* 191
   (1981) A Trump Over Utility, *Oxford Journal of Legal Studies*
   (1981) What is Equality? Equality of Resources, *Philosophy and Public Affairs* 283
   (1985) *A Matter of Principle*
   (1986) *Law's Empire*
   (1990) *A Bill of Rights for Britain*
   (1993) *Life's Dominion*
   (1996) Objectivity and Truth: You'd Better Believe It, *Philosophy and Public Affairs* 87
   (1996) Indeterminacy and Law, *Positivism Today*
   (1996) *Freedom's Law: the Moral Reading of the American Constitution*
No Right Answer?, *Law, Morality and Society; Essays in Honour of H L A Hart*, Hacker and Raz (eds)
Dyzenhaus, D
   (1991) *Hard Cases in Wicked Legal Systems*
   (2000) Positivism's Stagnant Research Programme, *Oxford Journal of Legal Studies* 703

Ebstein, B
   (1945) *The Pure Theory of Law*
Eeklaar, J M
   (1967) Splitting the Grundnorm, *Modern Law Review*
Ehrlich, E
   (1936) *Fundamental Principles of the Sociology of Law*
Eisenstein, Z R
   The Sexual Politics of the New Right

Engels, F
(1935) Letter to Conrad Schmidt, *Marx and Engels Selected Correspondence*
(1973) *The Origins of the Family*
Evans-Pritchard, E
(1951) *Social Anthropology*

Felsteiner
Influences of Social Organisation and Dispute Processing
Finnis, J
(1980) *Natural Law and Natural Rights*
Finnis, J and Grisez, G
(1981) The Basic Principles of Natural Law, *American Journal of Jurisprudence* 21, 28
Fish, S
(1975) *History and Reason in Rawls' Moral Theory*
(1989) *Doing What Comes Naturally*
Fletcher, G
(1996) *Basic Concept in Human Thought*
Frank, J
(1930) *Law and the Modern Mind*
(1949) *The Courts on Trial: Myth and Reality in American Justice*
Fromm, E
(1961) *Marx's Concept of Man*
Fuller, L
(1949) The Case of the Speluncian Explorers, *Harvard Law Review* 616
(1958) Positivism and Fidelity to Law – A Reply to Professor Hart, *Harvard Law Review* 593
(1969) *The Morality of Law*

Gallie, W B
Essentially Contested Concepts, *Proceedings of the Aristotelian Society* 167
George, P
(1992) *Natural Law*
Gerwith, A
(1983) The Epistemology of Human Rights, *Social Philosophy and Policy* 1
Gilligan, C
(1982) *In a Different Voice*
Glover, J
(1977) *Causing Death and Saving Lives*
Gluckman, M
(1967) *The Judicial Process Among the Barotse of Northern Rhodesia*
Goodhart, A
(1930) The Ratio Decidendi of a Case, *Yale Law Journal* 161
Gottlieb, G
(1968) *The Logic of Choice*
Gramsci, A
(1957) *The Modern Prince and Other Writings*
Gray, J C
(1909) *The Nature and Sources of the Law*
Griffith, J A G
(1984) H L A Hart: Jurisprudence and Linguistic Philosophy, *Modern Law Review*
(1985) *The Politics of The Judiciary*
Gross and Harrison (eds)
(1993) *Jurisprudence: Cambridge Essays*

Grotius, H
 De Jure Belli ac Pacis
Guest, S
 (1996) *Positivism Today* (ed)
 (1997) *Ronald Dworkin*
 (1997a) Interpretation and Commitment in Legal Reasoning, *Legislation and the Courts*, Freeman
  (ed)
 (1997b) *Ronald Dworkin*
Gutmann
 (1985) Communitarian Critics of Liberalism, *Philosophy and Public Affairs* 308

Hacker, P and Raz, J (eds)
 (1978) *Law, Morality and Society*
Hagerstrom, A
 (1953) *Inquiries into the Nature of Law and Morals*
Hall, S and Scraton, P
 Law, Class and Control, *Crime and Society*
Harris, J W
 (1971) When and Why Does the Grundnorm Change?, *Cambridge Law Journal* 103
 (1977) Kelsen's Concept of Authority, *Cambridge Law Journal*
 (1979) *Law and Legal Science*
 (1980) *Legal Philosophies*
Hart, H L A
 (1952) Signs and Words, *Philosophical Quarterly* 59
 (1954) Definition and Theory in Jurisprudence, *Law Quarterly Review* 37
 (1958) Positivism and the Separation of Law and Morality, *Harvard Law Review* 593
 (1959) Scandinavian Realism, *Cambridge Law Journal* 233
 (1961) *The Concept of Law*
 (1963) *Law, Liberty and Morality*
 (1976) Law in the Perspective of Philosophy, *New York University Law Review* 51
 (1977) American Jurisprudence Through English Eyes: The Nightmare and the Noble Dream,
  Georgia Law Review 11
 (1982) *Essays on Bentham*
 (1983) *Essays in Jurisprudence and Philosophy*
Hay, W
 (1975) Albion's Fatal Tree, *Crime and Society*
Hobbes, T
 (1996) *Leviathan*
Hoebel, E
 (1954) *The Law of Primitive Man*
Hohfeld, W
 (1917) Fundamental Legal Conceptions as Applied in Judicial Reasoning, *Yale Law Journal* 710
Holmes, O W
 (1881) *The Common Law*
 (1897) The Path of the Law, *Harvard Law Review*
Horkenheimer, M
 (1936) *Studien über Authorität und Familie*
Howarth
 (1993) Making Sense out of Nonsense, *Jurisprudence: Cambridge Essays* 29, Gross and Harrison
  (eds)
Hume, D
 (1977) *A Treatise of Human Nature*

Hunt, A
   (1978) *The Sociological Movement in Law*
   (1981) Dichotomy and Contradiction in the Sociology of Law, *British Journal of Law and Society* 47
Hutchinson, A
   (1998) The Reasoning Game: Some Pragmatic Suggestions, *Modern Law Review* 263

Jackson, B
   Law, Fact and Narrative Coherence
Jagger, A
   (1983) *Feminist Politics and Human Nature*
Jhering, R Von
   (1924) *Law as Means to an End*

Kelsen, H
   (1920) *Sozialismus und Staat*
   (1934) The Pure Theory of Law, *Law Quarterly Review* 474 and 517
   (1945) *General Theory of Law and State*
   (1965) What is Justice?, *Stanford Law Review* 1141
   (1967) *The Pure Theory of Law*
   Professor Stone and the Pure Theory of Law, *Stanford Law Review* 1139
Kennedy, D
   (1982) *The Ideological Content of Legal Education*
King
   (1959) *The Norm in a Bottle*
   (1966) *The Concept, the Idea and the Morality of Law*
Kohlberg, L
   (1976) *Moral Development and Behaviour*
Kolakowski, L
   (1978) *Main Currents in Marxism*
Kozinski, J *et al*
   (1999) The Case of the Speluncean Explorers Revisited, *Harvard Law Review* 1876
Kramer, M
   (1998) Scrupulousness Without Scruples: A Critique of Lon Fuller and His Defenders, *Oxford Journal of Legal Studies* 235
   (1999) *In Defence of Legal Positivism*

Lauterpacht, H
   (1933) Kelsen's Pure Theory of Law, *Modern Theories of Law*
Lenin, V I
   (1960–70) *Collected Works*
   Materials Relating to the Revision of the Party Programme
   The Victory of the Cadets and the Tasks of the Workers' Party
Levinas, R
   The Ideology of the New Right
Llewellyn, K
   (1940) *The Normative, The Legal and the Law Jobs: The Problem of Juristic Method*
   (1941) *My Philosophy of Law*
   (1960) *The Common Law Tradition*
Llewellyn, K and Hoebel, E
   (1941) *Cheyenne Way*
Lloyd and Freeman
   (1994) *Introduction to Jurisprudence*
Locke, J
   (1967) *Two Treatises on Government*
   (1993) *Essay Concerning Human Understanding*

Loevinger, L
    (1949) Jurimetrics: the Next Step Forward, *Minnesota Law Review* 455
Lukes, S
    (1977) State of Nature, *Essays in Social Theory*
Lundstedt, V
    (1956) *Legal Thinking Revised*

MacCormick, N
    (1978) *Legal Reasoning and Legal Theory*
    (1981) *H L A Hart*
    (1983) Contemporary Legal Philosophy: The Rediscovery of Practical Reason, *Journal of Law and Society* 1
Mackie, J
    (1977) *Ethics*
MacKinnon
    (1983) *Feminism, Marxism, Method and the State*
McCoubrey, H and White, N
    (1999) *Jurisprudence*
Maine, H
    (1986) *Ancient Law*
Malinowski, B
    (1926) *Crime and Custom in Savage Society*
Marmor, A
    (1992) *Interpretation and Legal Theory*
Marx, K
    Capital Vol 1
Marx, K and Engels, F
    (1956) *Selected Writings in Sociology and Social Philosophy*
Milgram, S
    (1974) *Obedience to Authority*
Miliband, R
    (1983) *State Power and Class Interests*
Mill, J S
    (1937) *On the Constitution of Church and State*
    (1950) *Mill on Bentham and Coleridge*
    (1974) *On the Subjection of Women*
    (1993) *On Liberty*
Montrose, J
    (1968) *Precedent in English Law and Other Essays*
Morris, C
    (1996) Well-Being, Reasons and the Politics of Law, *Ethics* 817

Nader, L
    (1964) An Analysis of Zapotec Law Cases, *Ethnology* 404
    (1965) Choices in Legal Procedure, *American Anthropologist* 394
Nonet, P
    (1976) For Jurisprudential Sociology, *Law and Society Review*
Nozick, R
    (1974) *Anarchy, State and Utopia*

Okin, S
    (1998) Feminism and Multiculturalism: Some Tensions, *Ethics* 661
Olivecrona, K
    (1971) *Law as Fact*

Packer, H
(1969) *The Limits of the Criminal Sanction*
Pappe, H
(1960) On the Validity of Judicial Decision in the Nazi Era, *Modern Law Review* 260
Parsons, T
(1966) Social Dimensions of Law and Justice, *Israel Law Review* 173
Pashukanis, E
(1978) *Law and Marxism*
Pateman, C
(1987) Feminist Critiques v the Public/Private Dichotomy, *Feminism and Equality*, Phillips (ed)
Paton, G
(1972) *Jurisprudence*
Patterson
(1953) *Jurisprudence: Men and Ideas of the Law*
Phang, A B L
The Hart-Dworkin Debate Revisited
Phillips
(1987) *Feminism and Equality*
Pollock, F
Jurisprudence and Legal Essays, Goodhart (ed)
Popper, K
(1945) *The Open Society and its Enemies*
Posner, R
(1973) A Theory of Negligence, *Journal of Legal Studies* 323
(1983) *The Economics of Justice*
(1995) *Overcoming Law*
Pospisil
(1971) *Anthropology of Law*
Postema, G
(1986) *Bentham and the Common Law Tradition*
Poulantzas, N
(1973) *Political Power and Social Classes*
Pound, R
(1943) *Outline Lectures on Jurisprudence*
(1954) *Philosophy of Law*

Quinney, R
(1970) *The Social Reality of Crime*
(1974) *Critique of Legal Order*

Radbruch, G
(1947) *Introduction to Legal Philosophy*
Rawls, J
(1972) *A Theory of Justice*
(1993) *Political Liberalism*
Raz, J
(1975) The Institutional Nature of Law, *Modern Law Review*
(1979) *The Authority of Law*
(1979) *Identity of Legal Systems*
(1982) *The Problem About the Nature of Law*
(1986) *The Morality of Freedom*
(1986) *The Concept of a Legal System*
(1990) *Practical Reason and Norms*

(1993) H L A Hart (1907–1992), *Utilitas* 146
(1994) *Ethics in the Public Domain*
(1998) Two views of the nature of the theory of law: a partial comparison, *Legal Theory*
Rees, W J
(1950) *The Theory of Sovereignty Re-stated*
Renner, K
(1949) *The Institutions of Private Law and their Social Functions*
Rhode, D
(1989) *Justice and Gender*
Richards
(1986) Separate Spheres, *Applied Ethics*
Riddall, J
(1999) *Jurisprudence*
Roberts, D
(1992) Review of Ronald Dworkin, *Modern Law Review* 225
Roberts, S
(1979) *Order and Dispute*
Rosen, F
(1998) Individual Sacrifice and the Greatest Happiness: Bentham on Utility and Rights, *Utilitas* 129
Ross, A
(1946) *Towards a Realistic Jurisprudence*
(1958) *On Law and Justice*
(1968) *Directives and Norms*
Rousseau, J
(1973) *The Social Contract*

Safiotti
Women and Class Society
Sartorius, R
(1975) *Individual Conduct and Social Norms*
Schofield, P
(1991) Jeremy Bentham and Nineteenth Century Jurisprudence, *Journal of Legal History* 58
Selznick, P
(1959) *The Sociology of Law*
Shaw, S
(1999) The Pareto Argument and Inequality, *The Philosophical Quarterly* 353
Sheleff, L
(1973) *From Restitutive Law to Repressive Law – Durkheim's Division of Labour in Society Revisited*
Simmonds, N E
(1986) *Central Issues in Jurisprudence*
(1990) Why Conventionalism Does Not Lapse Into Pragmatism, *Cambridge Law Review*
Law, Justice and Rights
Simpson, A W B
(1973) Common Law and Legal Theory, *Oxford Essays in Jurisprudence*
Singer, P
(1973) *Democracy and Disobedience*
Smart, C
(1989) *Feminism and the Power of Law*
Smart, J J C and Williams, B (eds)
(1973) *Utilitarianism: For and Against*
Smith
De Republica Anglorum

Soper, P
   (1984) *A Theory of Law*
Stalin, J
   (1946) *Works*
Stavropoulos, N
   (1996) *Objectivity in Law*
Stephen, J
   (1873) *Liberty, Equality and Fraternity*
Stewart, I
   (1987) Closure and the Legal Norm, *Modern Law Review*
Steyn (Lord)
   (1996) Does Legal Formalism Hold Sway in England?, *Current Legal Problems* 43
Stone, J
   (1963) Mystery and Mystique in the Basic Norm, *Modern Law Review*
   (1965) *Human Law and Human Justice*
   (1966) *Law and the Social Sciences*
Stuchka, P
   (1968) *Essays in Legal Philosophy*
Sunstein, C
   (1996) *Legal Reasoning and Political Conflict*

Taylor, I, Walton, P and Young, J
   (1973) *The New Criminology*
Twining, W
   (1985) *Karl Llewellyn and the Realist Movement*
   (1994) *Blackstone's Tower: the English Law School*

Von Savigny, F
   (1814) *Vom Beruf unserer Zut fGr Gezetzgebung und Rechtswissenshaft*

Wacks, R
   (1984) Judges and Injustice, *South African Law Journal* 266
Waldron, J
   (1987) *The Law*
   (1992) The Irrelevance of Moral Objectivity, *Natural Law*, George (ed)
   (1993) *Liberal Rights*
Waluchow, W
   (1994) *Inclusive Legal Positivism*
Walzer, M
   (1982) *Spheres of Justice*
Weber, M
   (1978) *Economy and Society*
Wilson, A
   (1980) Material and Formal Authorisation in Kelsen's Pure Theory, *Cambridge Law Journal*
   (1981) The Imperative Fallacy in Kelsen's Theory, *Modern Law Review*
Williams, G
   (1945) Language and the Law, *Law Quarterly Review* 71
Wittgenstein, L
   (1953) *Philosophical Investigations*
Wolff, J
   (1996) *An Introduction to Political Philosophy*
Woozley, A
   (1968) *Mind*

Young, I
(1991) *Justice and the Politics of Difference*

Zaretsky, E
(1976) *Capitalism, the Family and Social Life*

Index

Suggested Solutions to Past Examination Questions 1998–1999

The Suggested Solutions series provides examples of full answers to the questions regularly set by examiners. Each suggested solution has been broken down into three stages: general comment, skeleton solution and suggested solution. The examination questions included within the text are taken from past examination papers set by the London University. The full opinion answers will undoubtedly assist you with your research and further your understanding and appreciation of the subject in question.

Only £6.95 Published January 2001

Constitutional Law
ISBN: 1 85836 389 6

Contract Law
ISBN: 1 85836 390 X

Criminal Law
ISBN: 1 85836 391 8

English Legal System
ISBN: 1 85836 392 6

Jurisprudence and Legal Theory
ISBN: 1 85836 393 4

Land Law
ISBN: 1 85836 394 2

Law of Tort
ISBN: 1 85836 395 0

Law of Trusts
ISBN: 1 85836 396 9

Forthcoming titles of Suggested Solutions 1999–2000 due early December 2001

Company Law
ISBN: 1 85836 442 6

European Union Law
ISBN: 1 85836 443 4

Evidence
ISBN: 1 85836 444 2

Family Law
ISBN: 1 85836 445 0

Public International Law
ISBN: 1 85836 446 9

For further information on contents or to place an order, please contact:
Mail Order
Old Bailey Press
200 Greyhound Road
London
W14 9RY

Telephone No: 020 7381 7407
Fax No: 020 7386 0952
Website: www.oldbaileypress.co.uk

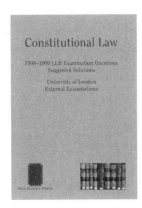

Law Update 2001

Law Update 2002 edition – due February 2002

An annual review of the most recent developments in specific legal subject areas, useful for law students at degree and professional levels, others with law elements in their courses and also practitioners seeking a quick update.

Published around February every year, the Law Update summarises the major legal developments during the course of the previous year. In conjunction with Old Bailey Press textbooks it gives the student a significant advantage when revising for examinations.

Contents

Administrative Law • Civil and Criminal Procedure • Company Law • Conflict of Laws • Constitutional Law • Contract Law • Conveyancing • Criminal Law • Criminology • English Legal System • Equity and Trusts • European Union Law • Evidence • Family Law • Jurisprudence • Land Law • Law of International Trade • Public International Law • Revenue Law • Succession • Tort

For further information on contents or to place an order, please contact:

Mail Order
Old Bailey Press
200 Greyhound Road
London
W14 9RY

Telephone No: 020 7381 7407
Fax No: 020 7386 0952
Website: www.oldbaileypress.co.uk

ISBN 1 85836 385 3
Soft cover 246 x 175 mm
408 pages £9.95
Published March 2001

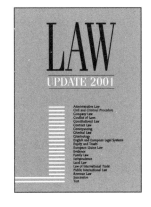

Old Bailey Press

The Old Bailey Press integrated student law library is tailor-made to help you at every stage of your studies from the preliminaries of each subject through to the final examination. The series of Textbooks, Revision WorkBooks, 150 Leading Cases/Casebooks and Cracknell's Statutes are interrelated to provide you with a comprehensive set of study materials.

You can buy Old Bailey Press books from your University Bookshop, your local Bookshop, direct using this form, or you can order a free catalogue of our titles from the address shown overleaf.

The following subjects each have a Textbook, 150 Leading Cases/Casebook, Revision WorkBook and Cracknell's Statutes unless otherwise stated.

Administrative Law
Commercial Law
Company Law
Conflict of Laws
Constitutional Law
Conveyancing (Textbook and Casebook)
Criminal Law
Criminology (Textbook and Sourcebook)
English and European Legal Systems
Equity and Trusts
Evidence
Family Law
Jurisprudence: The Philosophy of Law (Textbook, Sourcebook and
    Revision WorkBook)
Land: The Law of Real Property
Law of International Trade
Law of the European Union
Legal Skills and System
Obligations: Contract Law
Obligations: The Law of Tort
Public International Law
Revenue Law (Textbook,
    Sourcebook and Revision
    WorkBook)
Succession

Mail order prices:	
Textbook	£14.95
150 Leading Cases/Casebook	£9.95
Revision WorkBook	£7.95
Cracknell's Statutes	£9.95
Suggested Solutions 1998–1999	£6.95
Law Update 2001	£9.95
The Practitioner's Handbook 2001/2002	£45.95

To complete your order, please fill in the form below:

Module	Books required	Quantity	Price	Cost
		Postage		
		TOTAL		

For Europe, add 15% postage and packing (£20 maximum).
For the rest of the world, add 40% for airmail.

ORDERING

By telephone to Mail Order at 020 7381 7407, with your credit card to hand.

By fax to 020 7386 0952 (giving your credit card details).

Website: www.oldbaileypress.co.uk

By post to: Mail Order, Old Bailey Press, 200 Greyhound Road, London W14 9RY.

When ordering by post, please enclose full payment by cheque or banker's draft, or complete the credit card details below. You may also order a free catalogue of our complete range of titles from this address.

We aim to despatch your books within 3 working days of receiving your order.

Name

Address

Postcode   Telephone

Total value of order, including postage: £

I enclose a cheque/banker's draft for the above sum, or

charge my   ☐ Access/Mastercard   ☐ Visa   ☐ American Express
Card number

☐☐☐☐ ☐☐☐☐ ☐☐☐☐ ☐☐☐☐

Expiry date   ☐☐☐☐

Signature: ....Date: ....